STRUCTURES OF THE CHURCH

HANS KÜNG

STRUCTURES OF THE CHURCH

With a Preface to the New Paperback Edition
"TWENTY YEARS LATER"

CROSSROAD · NEW YORK

1982

The Crossroad Publishing Company
575 Lexington Avenue, New York, N.Y. 10022

Originally published as *Strukturen der Kirche*
© 1962 by Verlag Herder, Freiburg im Breisgau
English translation © 1964 by Thomas Nelson and Sons, New York
"Twenty Years Later" © 1982 by Hans Küng

Printed in the United States of America

Library of Congress Cataloging in Publication Data

Küng, Hans, 1928–   Structures of the Church.
Translation of: Strukturen der Kirche.
Includes index.
1. Church. 2. Councils and synods, Ecumenical.
3. Catholic Church—Doctrinal and controversial works
—Catholic authors. I. Title.
BX1746.K8713 1982   262   82-4706
ISBN 0-8245-0508-5 (pbk.)

Nihil Obstat: Rev. Daniel J. O'Hanlon, S.J.
Diocesan Censor Deputatus
Imprimatur: Richard Cardinal Cushing
Archbishop of Boston
November 27, 1963

The Nihil obstat *and* Imprimatur *are a declaration that a
book or pamphlet is considered to be free from doctrinal or moral error.
It is not implied that those who have granted the* Nihil obstat *and* Imprimatur
agree with the contents, opinions or statements expressed.

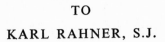

TO
KARL RAHNER, S.J.

TWENTY YEARS LATER

PREFACE TO THE NEW PAPERBACK EDITION

This book has had its history and it will, I hope, now have a future. It was the first of my books that the Roman inquisitional authorities subjected to formal proceedings, which then, thanks to the help of Augustin Cardinal Bea, ended with an acquittal. The book was written at a time when theology and Church were moved by the outbreak of conciliar renewal. The announcement of an ecumenical council by John XXIII made the recovery of largely forgotten structures of the Church into an exciting undertaking. For this announcement of a council was doubtless the greatest surprise experienced by the Catholic Church from within during this century.

In earlier centuries, the announcement of a council would never have occasioned such surprise. In the past, calls for a council for the purpose of "reform of the Church in head and members" were frequently heard. Many calls for reform had been raised in the Church of the past decades, yet nobody had ever seriously called for the convocation of an ecumenical council. Outside the Catholic Church, there was widespread acceptance of the view that the centralization process of the Catholic Church had reached its peak in Vatican I and that this council would be the last Catholic council. Even within the Catholic Church, nobody really believed in ecumenical councils any more, or in any case one no longer reckoned with them in a concrete way. In the manuals of Catholic dogmatic theology, the treatises on the pope became increasingly longer and those on the council correspondingly shorter, sometimes disappearing altogether—precisely in the thickest ecclesiological tomes. Both in the life and theology of the Church, councils were no longer wanted.

Wasn't this all a sign that certain necessary structures of the Catholic Church in theology and in life had been not only insufficiently perceived but even overlooked? In fact this conciliar announcement shook us theologians up and made us—after Vatican I—think again about the Church and its structures.

vii

This study does not bear the pretentious title "*The* Structure of
the Church": it does not pretend to give a *comprehensive* description of the essential nature of the Catholic Church; I attempted this
later in my book *The Church* (1968) and reached the logical
conclusion of my train of thought in *Infallible? An Inquiry* (1971).
The present study deals with "Structures of the Church": my
intention is to offer a carefully aimed description of certain
essential characteristics of the Catholic Church. I wish to illuminate the structure, the living fabric of the Church, in order to
rediscover once again certain central elements and connections
within its organization. This was not an easy procedure. The
dogmatic theologian was forced to include the results of his
colleagues' investigations in exegesis, church history, and canon
law, without any possibility of rechecking them all individually.

Not all questions can or should be treated with the same
exhaustiveness. In an ecclesiological work, written in a German-
speaking country, one could assume it was self-evident, given the
then state of the ecumenical conversation, that the work would
deal especially with Protestant theology; out of this grew a particular concentration on the structure of the relationship between
church and office, council and pope. It follows from this that the
central concerns of the Eastern Church and its theology are also
considered, although there is no direct confrontation with Eastern
theology here.

The writer would be happy if that which is sketched theologically and ecclesiologically in his book had also come to pass in the
practical ecclesiological realm. Alas, this is not the situation. Although there has been much progress in the *oikoumene,* we have
not moved any further in the decisive ecumenical questions of the
constitution of the Church, and this despite—or precisely because
of—the Constitution on the Church of Vatican II, which to a large
extent has either screened out the questions treated in this book, or
else determined them in traditional fashion. On the contrary, the
Roman Curia and the episcopacy, which is largely controlled by it
in a state of preconciliar dependency, are doing everything at the
moment to hinder the realization of these ecumenical desiderata
everywhere. The questions that this book raised exactly twenty
years ago must be fearlessly discussed in Catholic theology once
again during the period of restoration we now seem to have
entered:

1. In a time of new papal absolutism and triumphalism, we seem to have forgotten that *conciliarity* is a fundamental structure of the reality of the Church. How else can we explain the attempt of the new Code of Canon Law to minimalize as much as possible, contrary to the great Catholic tradition, the ecumenical council and its ecclesiological and practical significance? How else can we explain the fact that the collegiality so ceremoniously urged by Vatican II is still not taken seriously by pope and bishops (not to mention priests and laity), and that the bishops' synods merely serve as an alibi for Roman centralism?

2. It has been confirmed meanwhile by numerous official ecumenical commissions, in which the Catholic Church was also represented, that the question of *apostolic succession* cannot be answered by the chain of the laying on of hands alone. It has been confirmed that the question of succession of ecclesiastical office need no longer divide the Church. It is precisely here that the hopes of this book for an ecumenical consensus have been best fulfilled. But if this is the case, why then does the Catholic Church still not recognize the validity of Protestant and Anglican offices and celebrations of the Eucharist and still consider all Protestant and Anglican ministers and bishops—from the Archbishop of Canterbury to the last curate—as pious but unfortunately invalidly functioning laypersons?

3. Even a pope like Paul VI has meanwhile publicly admitted that the *primacy and infallibility of the pope* are the greatest obstacles on the path to ecumenical understanding. The writer of this book could not suspect in 1962 what price he would have to pay seventeen years later for forging ahead, in an ecumenical spirit, on precisely this question. With that stroke, a critic who continues to regard himself, with the approval of a major part of the Catholic ecclesial and theological community, as a Catholic theologian was disavowed, but the questions and the solutions offered here remain. Even those in Rome, if they are honest, will have no illusions about the fact that without the solution to the question of primacy and infallibility, all the ecumenical embraces of Orthodox, Protestant, and Anglican church leaders remain ineffectual gestures that perpetuate the split in the Church by concealing it. What is the use of setting up ever new ecumenical commissions when they are not ready to put the results of commissions that have been active for years into practice, instead of

hiding them in a drawer in the Vatican?

The logical conclusion: Finally, finally, let *deeds* follow the many lovely ecumenical words, gestures, and trips of popes, cardinals, and bishops! The unification document of this year between Rome and Canterbury is and remains a test case. In Rome, without any reason and without any ecumenical tact, it has been disavowed—in order to preserve the power of the Roman apparatus and to the detriment of the *oikumene* and of the Catholic Church! There exists perhaps no better confirmation of the line already taken in this book than this truly ecumenical Catholic-Anglican document. This book has had its history and it will, I hope, now have a future.

HANS KÜNG

Tübingen
Feast of the Apostles Peter and Paul, 1982

FOREWORD

ONE of the chief tasks of the bishops assembled for the Second Session of the present Vatican Council was the study of the Church—the nature, the mission, the structure of the Church of Jesus Christ. Indeed, one can say that the chief *theological* concern of the Council, yes, of all the Christian communities today, is ecclesiology. As I sat with my brother bishops in the Basilica of St. Peter during those initial weeks of the Second Session, I frequently heard from the council floor the voices of many appeal to the present pastoral needs and modern ecumenical urgency for a deep and long study of the Church.

Several years ago in a pastoral letter to my people I wrote that one of the hopes and aims of the then forthcoming Council was that the Church take a searching look at herself, and this in the renewing spirit of the Gospels. Good Pope John had proclaimed this as one of the purposes of the Council he had called; this his great successor Pope Paul VI has repeated; this the Council is fulfilling.

Because the implications of ecclesiology involve each member of the Church, each member has the responsibility to share in this study. And because the study of the Church, with its structure given to it by Christ and its structures conditioned by history, is so intimately related to unity and ecumenism, I say that every Christian has a responsibility to take part in this study. The Church of Christ is not a static entity, it is a dynamic organism: it is the Body of Christ and the People of God—as Vatican II so repeatedly asserts. The "building up of the Church," the *edificatio Corporis Christi*, which St. Paul proclaims (Col. 2:7; Eph. 4:16) is the vocation and the duty and the mission of all the members.

For this reason the study of Father Küng on the structures of the Church, theological and historical, is a laudable one. It can assist us in appraising and re-appraising ourselves—the people of God and Spouse of Christ. It can give us insights into the historic dynamic of the Church's self-consciousness; it can provide us with serious matter for reflection and meditation on the wondrous Mystery which is the Church; it can help us fulfil our responsibility to study the Church. I do not necessarily agree with every conclusion and proposal that this priest-scholar makes; I do not doubt for a moment, however, his scholarly integrity or priestly dedication. My meetings and conversations with him in Boston and in Rome have convinced me of these.

Christians in America are familiar with his former works on the Council. Indeed, in the American mind the name Hans Küng has been linked as few others have been with the Council and Catholic theological renewal. He has done us a great service in this country— by his writings, by his visit, by his lectures. He has not always met with unanimous approval and agreement; but he has always won overwhelming admiration for his scholarship and humility—the true mark of the Christian scholar. This book, which has been so well received in Europe, is a great contribution to scholarship in America. To the English-speaking Christians of the world it should prove a valuable help in their study of the Church, a study to which the Council calls us.

RICHARD CARDINAL CUSHING
Archbishop of Boston

LIST OF ABBREVIATIONS

CC   *Corpus Christianorum seu nova Patrum collectio*, Turnhout, Paris, 1953ff.

CIC   *Codex Iuris Canonici* (Code of Canon Law)

CR   *Corpus Reformatorum*, Brunswick, Berlin, 1834ff, Leipzig, 1906ff.

CSEL   *Corpus scriptorum ecclesiasticorum latinorum*, Vienna, 1866ff.

Denz   H. Denzinger, *Enchiridion Symbolorum, Definitionum et Declarationum de rebus fidei et morum*, Freiburg i. Br., 1960.

Mansi   J. D. Mansi, *Sacrorum conciliorum nova et amplissima collectio*, 31 vols., Florence and Venice, 1757–98: new printing and continuation published by L. Petit and J. B. Martin in 60 vols., Paris, 1899–1927.

PG   *Patrologia Graeca*, edited by J. P. Migne, 161 vols, Paris, 1857–66.

PL   *Patrologia Latina*, edited by J. P. Migne, 217 vols, Paris, 1878–90.

WA   M. Luther, *Werke. Kritische Gesamtausgabe* (Weimar Edition), 1883ff.

CONTENTS

I

A THEOLOGY OF
ECUMENICAL COUNCILS?

FOR ecclesiology an ecumenical council is like a prism. Filtered through a triangular glass prism, white, visible-invisible sunlight discloses its rich, multicoloured spectrum, its inner nature and mode of being. In an ecumenical council, the pure, visible-invisible Church reveals the image of her mysterious, manifold nature to the eye of the believer. As though projected against a screen, the tension-charged structures and the dynamic components of the Church become optically perceptible, presenting themselves with particular clarity for theological analysis. Whoever reflects upon ecumenical councils reflects, expressly or not, upon the Church herself. Reflection upon ecumenical councils in this essay aims expressly to be a reflection upon the Church and her structures: a theology of ecumenical councils seen as a task pertaining to ecclesiology, and the converse. Whoever reflects upon ecumenical councils reflects upon the Church —but this statement is not automatically reversible. One can reflect upon the Church, deeply and fundamentally, and take no account at all of ecumenical councils. There is an historically valid reason for this: The concept of ecumenical councils faded very much into the background of the life and theology of the Church after the First Vatican Council. But there is also a fundamental theological reason for the irreversibility of this statement, one that concerns the basic relationship existing between the Church and councils.

However, we must first cope with the fundamental obstacle that lies in the path of every theological consideration of the nature of an ecumenical council, namely: Is a theological consideration of the nature of an ecumenical council, hence a theology of ecumenical councils, at all possible? Does theology really have something binding to say about ecumenical councils?

True, canon law does make binding statements about them; Canons 222–229 of the *Codex Iuris Canonici* deal with ecumenical councils.[1] Church history also undoubtedly does make binding state-

---

[1] Cf. in addition the commentaries on the *Codex Iuris Canonici*: A. Toso, *Commentaria minora* (Rome 1923) II, 16–25; M. Conte a Coronata, *Institutiones Iuris Canonici* (Turin 1928) I, 368–372; F. X. Wernz and P. Vidal, *Ius Canonicum* (Rome ³1943) II, 522–540; E. Eichmann and K. Mörsdorf, *Lehrbuch des Kirchen-*

1

ments on ecumenical councils. Hefele's history of the councils is a nine-volume work, and Mansi's *Amplissima Collectio*, the standard reference work on the history of the councils, in one edition numbers thirty-one volumes and in a revised edition numbers sixty volumes.[2] But does *theology* have anything binding to say about ecumenical councils? By theology here we do not mean a non-biblical theology, which discusses everything possible and impossible, without imposing any binding conclusions, and which obviously also is able to discuss

rechts (Paderborn [6]1949) I, 328–330; A. Vermeersch and J. Creusen, *Epitome Iuris Canonici* (Paris [7]1949) I, 292–294; E. F. Regatillo, *Institutiones Iuris Canonici* (Santander [4]1951) I, 280–282; C. Holböck, *Handbuch des Kirchenrechts* (Innsbruck–Vienna 1951) I, 294–297; S. Sipos and L. Gálos, *Enchiridion Iuris Canonici* (Rome [6]1954) 156–159; J. A. Abbo and J. D. Hannan, *The Sacred Canons* (St. Louis [2]1957) I, 288–291. Cf. also N. Jung, art. "Concile," in *Dictionnaire de Droit Canonique* (Paris 1942) III, 1268–1301.

[2] On the history of the councils see, in addition to the works on the individual councils: C. J. v. Hefele, *Conciliengeschichte*, vols. I–IX (VIII and IX by Hergenröther) (Freiburg i. Br. 1855ff; [2]1873ff); newly revised by H. Leclercq, *Histoire des conciles d'après les documents originaux*, vols. I–IX (Paris 1907ff); *Le concile et les conciles. Contribution à la vie conciliare de l'Église* (Paris 1960); *Die ökumenischen Konzile der Christenheit*, edited by H. J. Margull (Stuttgart 1961). For a summary objective orientation see H. Jedin, *Kleine Konziliengeschichte* (Freiburg i. Br. 1959; [3]1961); for valuable observations on the history of the councils see H. Fuhrmann, "Das Ökumenische Konzil und seine historischen Grundlagen," in *Geschichte in Wissenschaft und Unterricht*, the organ of the Association of German History Teachers, 12 (1961) 672–695. Likewise the corresponding articles on councils in general in: *Kirchenlexikon* III, 779–810 by M.-J. Scheeben (Freiburg i. Br. 1884); *Dictionnaire de Théologie Catholique* III, 636–676 by J. Forget (Paris 1923); *Lexikon für Theologie und Kirche* VI, 182–188 by L. Mohler and E. Schneider (Freiburg i. Br. 1934); *Lexikon für Theologie und Kirche*, 2nd ed., VI, 525–532 by H. Jedin and H. Lais (Freiburg i. Br. 1961); *Catholicisme* II, 1439–1444 by Y. Congar and G. Marsot (Paris 1950); *Realenzyklopädie für protestantische Theologie und Kirche* XIX, 262–277 by A. Hauck (Leipzig 1907); *Religion in Geschichte und Gegenwart*, 3rd ed. III, 1800–1806 by H. D. Altendorf and H. Barion (Tübingen 1959); *Evangelisches Kirchenlexikon* II, 934–942 by G. Kretschmar and G. Dickel (Göttingen 1958). Also see J. D. Mansi, S*acrorum conciliorum nova et amplissima collectio*, vols. I–XXXI (Florence–Venice 1747–98; new printing and continuation, edited by L. Petit and J.-B. Martin in 60 vols. (Paris 1895–1927). See also the somewhat fuller collections of the proceedings of individual councils (especially those of Ephesus, Chalcedon, Constantinople II, Constance, Basle, Ferrara-Florence, Trent, and the First Vatican Council). The older council collections are listed in *Lexikon für Theologie und Kirche*, 2nd ed., VI, 534–536 and *Catholicisme* II, 1444f. Among manuals on general Church history see especially: J. Lortz, *History of the Church* (Milwaukee, Wis. 1939); Bihlmeyer and Tüchle, *Kirchengeschichte*, vols. I–III (Paderborn [13]1952); Fliche and Martin, *Histoire de l'Église*, vols. I–XXIV (Paris 1946ff). Finally, on the history of the popes, which is closely linked with the history of the councils, see: L. v. Pastor, *Geschichte der Päpste seit dem Ausgang des Mittelalters*, vols. I–XVI (Freiburg i. Br. 1885ff); J. Schmidlin, *Papstgeschichte der neuesten Zeit*, vols. I–IV (Munich [2]1933); F. X. Seppelt, *Geschichte der Päpste*, vols. I–VI (Munich [2]1954).

ecumenical councils. By it we mean Christian theology, which is conscious of the fact that it is bound to the revelation of God in Jesus Christ and *hence* has something binding to proclaim. Is it possible, then, to make *theologically* binding *strict dogmatic* statements on ecumenical councils?

It would be all too easy, though in the last analysis not strictly theological, simply to map out a "theology of ecumenical councils" on the basis of the present regulations of the *Codex Iuris Canonici* or to deduce a "theology of ecumenical councils" from the proceedings of such a council as that of Trent or of the First Vatican Council. The fact that this procedure has been followed in almost all textbooks does not make the procedure itself better. A theology of ecumenical councils cannot concern itself only with describing a past, or even a present, form of an ecumenical council. Rather, a theology of ecumenical councils—without becoming unhistorical—should penetrate to the very nature of an ecumenical council.

In order to scrutinize the problem area exactly let us first presuppose something that certainly does not exist, namely, a canonist who thinks *only* in terms of present-day canon law and a Church historian who thinks *only* in terms of ecclesiastical history. A theologian should find food for thought in the fact that a canonist who thinks *only* in terms of the present *Codex Iuris Canonici* and a Church historian who thinks *only* in terms of conciliar history could scarcely agree on how an ecumenical council essentially should look. There is hardly a canon of the *Codex* dealing with ecumenical councils against which the Church historian could not raise the objection that this or that particular ecumenical council simply had *not* proceeded in this way but that, nevertheless, it had been a genuine ecumenical council. What has not changed in the course of the history of councils? Not only the meeting places and the whole setting of councils but also the person and the official status of the one convoking councils and of the one presiding over them, the participants, the agenda, the order of procedure, and the necessity of an express approbation.[3] Thus the Church historian may then quote the first,

[3] On the position of councils in the history of canon law and of the constitution of the Church see: P. Hinschius, *System des katholischen Kirchenrechts* = "Kirchenrecht III," 325–666 (Berlin 1883); U. Stutz, *Geschichte des Kirchenrechts* = "Kirchenrecht I," in *Enzyklopädie der Rechtswissenschaft*, ed. by Holtzendorff and Kobler (Munich–Leipzig 1914) V, 293–294, 340–343; A M. Koeniger, *Grundriss einer Geschichte des katholischen Kirchenrechts* (Cologne 1919 44–47); B. Kurtscheid, *Historia Iuris Canonici. Historia institutorum ab Ecclesiae fundatione usque ad Gratianum* (Rome 1941. ²1951) 44–46, 150–154; I. Zeiger, *Historia Iuris Canonici* vol. II: *De historia institutorum canonicorum* (Rome 1947) 50–52, 111–118; H. E. Feine, *Kirchliche Rechtsgeschichte* (Weimar 1950) I, 46–48,

fundamental and perhaps most pregnant canon of the *Codex Iuris Canonici* pertaining to ecumenical councils: "Can. 222—§1. There cannot be an ecumenical council which is not convoked by the Roman Pontiff.—§2. The Roman Pontiff presides over an ecumenical council in person or through his delegates; he establishes and designates the matter to be handled and the order to be followed; he transfers, suspends, and dissolves the council and confirms its decrees."

The Church historian will not dispute that this corresponds with present-day Church discipline, but he will calmly add that this was precisely *not* the case with the first ecumenical councils of early Christianity, which are of fundamental importance and are recognized as ecumenical by all Christian denominations of East and West. It simply was *not* the pope who convoked these councils, who determined the agenda, and who established the order of procedure, who transferred, adjourned, or closed the councils. Furthermore, neither he nor his legates always presided over them. Finally, the fact of express papal approbation is questioned. And as a historical reverberation in regard to Canon 222, he perhaps would cite several sentences from the article "Council" in the *Lexikon für Theologie und Kirche*, stating the following about the first ecumenical councils: "Owing to the close relations between State and Church they were matters directly affecting the State and the Empire (imperial synods). They were convoked, adjourned, or postponed by the Emperor. Their overall organization lay in the hands of the Emperor or in those of his commissaries; their decrees acquired legal force through imperial confirmation just as their enforcement was ensured by the State. The synods themselves, as well as the popes, recognized these rights."[4]

93–95, 271–293, 380–407; W. M. Plöchl, *Geschichte des Kirchenrechts* (Vienna 1953–59) I, 55–56, 134–136, 297; II, 102–111.

[4] L. Mohler, "Konzil," in *Lexikon für Theologie und Kirche* (Freiburg i. Br. 1934) VI, 183. Cf. also Y. Congar, "Concile," in *Catholicisme* (Paris 1949) II, 1439; P. M. Goemans, *Het algemeen concilie in de vierde eeuw* (Nijmegen 1945); P.-Th. Camelot, "Les Conciles oecumeniques des IVᵉ et Vᵉ siècles," in *Le concile et les conciles* (Paris 1960) 45–73. For the legal position of popes at councils, cf. specifically F. X. Funk, "Der römische Stuhl und die allgemeinen Synoden des christlichen Altertums," in *Tübinger Theologische Quartalschrift* 64 (1882) 561–602; "The convocation of ecumenical synods in antiquity. The papal confirmation of the first eight general synods," in Funk, *Kirchengeschichtliche Abhandlungen und Untersuchungen* (Paderborn 1897) I, 39–121; "Concerning the Question of Convocation of General Synods in Antiquity," in Funk, *Kirchengeschichtliche Abhandlungen und Untersuchungen* (Paderborn 1907) III, 143–149, 406–439; J. Forget, "Le rôle des papes dans la convocation des huit premiers conciles," in *Mélanges Moeller* (Louvain 1914) I, 179–191; E. Schwartz, "Über die Reichskonzilien von Theodosius bis Justinian," in *Zeitschrift der Savigny-Stiftung für*

Naturally, the canonist can meet this objection and point out distinctions. As regards the functions of the pope and emperor at the councils he will perhaps counter with a sharp differentiation between *formaliter—materialiter* or *implicite—explicite* and thereby dispose of all the difficulties of the first thousand years in a dogmatic fashion.[5] But presumably the Church historian will not be quite satisfied with such *a priori* distinctions. It is a matter of historical fact that the emperor, and he alone, as the ruler of the empire, actually convoked the first ecumenical Council of Nicaea, and the seven subsequent councils as well: "Therefore I make known to you, beloved brothers, that it is my will that all of you assemble without delay in the city mentioned (that is, in Nicaea)."[6] Later in Constantine's address to the synod we read: "As soon as I heard that intelligence which I had least expected to receive, I mean the news of your dissension, I judged it to be of no secondary importance, but with the earnest desire that a remedy for this evil be found through my means, I sent to require your presence."[7] Nothing has been handed down to us relating to explicit approbation or even tacit authorization on the part of the pope. No one had asked for papal approbation, nor even expected it. Like all the other patriarchs and bishops, the pope simply had to accept the convocation as an imperial order.[8] The

---

Rechtsgeschichte, Kanonist. part 11 (1921) 208–253; V. Grumel, "Le Siège de Rome et le concile de Nicée: convocation et présidence," in *Échos d'Orient* (1925) 411–423; F. Dvornik, "De auctoritate civili in conciliis oecumenicis," in *Acta conventus VI Velehradensis* (Olomucii 1933) 156–167; "Emperors, Popes and General Councils," in *Dumbarton Oaks Papers* 6 (Cambridge, Massachusetts 1951) 1–23; J. A. Eisele, *Die Rechtsstellung des Papstes im Verhältnis zu den allgemeinen Konzilien* (Emsdetten, 1938); A. Michel, "Die Kaisermacht in der Ostkirche (843–1204)," in *Ostkirchliche Studien* 2 (1953) 1–35, 89–109; 3 (1954) 1–28, 133–163; 4 (1955) 1–42, 221–260; (1956) 1–32.

[5] Compare also the previously made distinctions between *per se–per alios; potestate propria–potestate delegata;* coactive–exhortative; *auctoritative–opitulative* (which one avoids using today in this context because of doubts regarding their historical accuracy).

[6] The original of the written convocation has not been preserved. What has been preserved is the announcement of the transfer of the meeting place of the synod from Ankara to Nicaea. It has been retranslated by E. Schwartz from the Syrian into Greek. Quoted after F. X. Funk, *Kirchengeschichtliche Abhandlungen und Untersuchungen* (Paderborn 1907) III, 149.

[7] Eusebius, *Vita Constantini* III, 12; *PG* 20, 1068.

[8] H.• Jedin, *Ecumenical Councils of the Catholic Church—An Historical Outline* (London and Edinburgh 1960), p. 14: "The question whether the early councils were convened by the emperors with the previous assent of the Bishop of Rome, or even by commission, has been the subject of controversy from the time of the Reformation. More recently the question was once more vehemently debated between Scheeben, the theologian, and Funk, the Church historian. As far as the facts go, the question may be answered in the negative."

bishops also were fully aware of the fact that this was a matter concerning an authoritative legal imperial act of the emperor and of the
emperor alone. They themselves attested to and recognized this
fact: "The great and holy synod met in Nicaea by the grace of God
and of our Emperor Constantine, beloved by God, who had summoned us all thereto."[9] Likewise, there was no need for an express
subsequent approbation of the council decrees (which is something
fundamentally different from acceptance or non-repudiation).[10]
The Church historian's summary reply to all *a priori* distinctions
will therefore be that the solid and heavy granite blocks of historical
facts cannot be budged a single inch by such statements, profound
as they are in themselves. It almost seems as though that which is
not permissible also cannot have been.[11]

For the theologian this dispute between law and history causes no
little consternation. Seemingly, the early history of the councils and
the modern conciliar law mutually disavow each other. Where
should one turn, then, in the search for a possible theology of
ecumenical councils? But the theologian need not think that he is
a Hercules at the crossroads who must choose between virtue and
vice. Conciliar law and conciliar history would equally and rightly
resent a bad classification. The theologian will have to dig more
deeply in order to reach solid ground. He will have learned from the
dispute and will, first of all, soberly and objectively establish something of great importance; namely, that *on this plane of the discussion
one can discern factual and practical legal maxims, but that no binding
theologico-dogmatic statements can be made.* Actually there is a great
variety in the historical forms of ecumenical councils. Some authors
introduce essential differences between the ecumenical councils of
antiquity or of modern times and the Roman "general synods" of
the twelfth century (1123, 1139, 1179) which were not regarded as
ecumenical councils, either by their sponsors or by their contemporaries, and which even in the late Middle Ages, along with the First
Council of Lyons in 1245, were not reckoned among the ecumenical
councils. And actually there is no official list of recognized ecumenical councils so that therefore (that is mostly according to one's
theological leanings) one counts 22, 21, 20, 19, or even fewer ecumenical councils. It is certainly not necessary to point out here that
Denzinger's *Enchiridion* has no particular historical authority.

[9] Synodal letters to the Egyptians in Athanasius, *De Decretis Nic. Syn.:*
Socrates, *Historia Eccl.* 1, 9: *PG* 67, 77.
[10] Cf. footnotes 4 and 8.
[11] These questions will be treated in greater detail later. Cf. Chap. VII, 6.

Above all this, the view generally held by Catholic theologians today is that the Catholic Church could do without ecumenical councils altogether (that is, that ecumenical councils are not an essential part of the Catholic Church). "Although the convenience and the ability of councils cannot be denied, there is neither a command of Christ nor an apostolic regulation which could prove their necessity: hence councils must be described as of *ecclesiastical law*."[12] Thus, if not only the concrete historical forms of ecumenical councils but also the very necessity of their existence within the Church is called into question, there can then be no binding theology of ecumenical councils on *this* plane. This does not mean that the regulations of the *Codex Iuris Canonici* pertaining to ecumenical councils *could* not contain a binding theology. This will have to be examined. At any rate it cannot be presumed. Hence a binding theology of ecumenical councils cannot simply be deduced from the present *Codex*.[13]

[12] B. Kurtscheid, *Historia Iuris Canonici* (Rome 1941; [2]1951) 44; also cf. F. X. Wernz and P. Vidal, *Ius Canonicum* (Rome [3]1943) II, 524, 529f; S. Sipos and L. Gálos, *Enchiridion Iuris Canonici* (Rome [6]1954) 157; W. M. Plöchl, *Geschichte des Kirchenrechts* (Vienna 1953) I, 55; N. Jung, art. "Concile," in *Dictionnaire de Droit Canonique* (Paris 1942) III, 1209 *passim.* —For the ecumenical councils, cf. further the various ecclesiological treatises: M.-J. Scheeben, *Handbuch der katholischen Dogmatik. Gesammelte Schriften* (Freiburg i. Br. 1948) III 242–261; art. "Concil," in *Kirchenlexikon* (Freiburg i. Br. [2]1884) III. 779–810; J. Heinrich, *Dogmatische Theologie* (Mainz [2]1882) II, 459–526; Ch. Pesch, *Institutiones Propaedeuticae ad sacram Theologiam* (Freiburg i. Br. [5]1915) I, 310–326; B. Bartmann, *Lehrbuch der Dogmatik* (Freiburg [8]1932) II, 157–159; L. Billot, *De Ecclesia Christi* (Rome [5]1927) 718–723; F. Diekamp, *Katholische Dogmatik* (Münster [13]1958) I, 69–71; H. Felder, *Apologetica* (Paderborn [2]1923) II, 256–260; T. Zapelena, *De Ecclesia Christi* (Rome 1954) II, 175–184; J. Salaverri, *Sacrae Theologiae Summa* (Madrid 1955) I, 682–685; C. Journet, *Church of the Word Incarnate* (London and New York 1955).

[13] Cf. Y. Congar, "Concile," in *Catholicisme* (Paris 1950) II, 1439f: "The accounts that are found in the manuals and in the treatises *De Ecclesia* propose a theology of councils that exactly follows the actual regulations of canon law. In particular, it has been asserted that a council is not ecumenical unless it has been convoked, presided over, and approved by the pope. This is perfectly legitimate and even necessary if it is a matter of stating what a council must be in order to be ecumenical in the actual state of discipline. But history shows that the norms thus posed cannot be exactly applied to a number of ancient councils, especially to the first ecumenical councils. None of these councils was convoked by the pope. Certain of them were not presided over either by him or by his legates (this, seemingly, is the case with Nicaea), and papal approbation of them did not seem to be viewed as necessary, at least before the fifth century, and in the form of a pontifical act (again Nicaea). . . . There is nothing surprising or disconcerting about this. The councils, in fact, do not constitute a part of the *essential structure* of the Church, as do the Sacraments or the primacy of Peter, for example. They are of ecclesiastical institution, at most of apostolic institution, and depend upon the canonical power of the Church, not strictly on 'divine law.' " Cf. also

Thus, if we do not wish to limit ourselves merely to a treatise on ecumenical councils in terms of canon law or Church history and renounce the idea of a specific theology of ecumenical councils, we must find an authentic theological point of departure in order to be able to develop a theology of ecumenical councils. Ecclesiology must provide this point of departure, which can be decisive in connection with many matters. We shall elaborate this point in the next chapter with the appropriate brevity. At the same time it will prove to be the authentic theological point of departure for bringing into focus the decisive structures of the Church herself.

R. Aubert, "Qu'est-ce qu'un concile?" in *Qu'attendons-nous du concile?* (Études pastorales I. Brussels-Paris 1960) 21: "It was only gradually that the modern type of ecumenical council, as it materialized in the Vatican Council of 1870 and became fixed in 1917 in the Code of canon law, was fixed along precise lines. Nothing suggests that this actual formation is the last and that other procedures may not come into being in the future."

II

THE CHURCH AS AN ECUMENICAL COUNCIL BY DIVINE CONVOCATION

WHEREAS the expression σύνοδος was used later as a technical term in Greek church language (at the time of Dionysius of Alexandria it was reported by Eusebius in his *Church History*[1]), the Latin *concilium* had already been used for the first time about 200 by Tertullian, the great artificer of Latin church language.[2]

In our context it is striking to notice that linguistically *concilium* and *ekklesia* have the same root. This is not a mere superficial resemblance. The word *con-cilium* is derived from *con-kal-ium*, or from *con-calare*.[3] *Calare* is employed as a religious technical term for "to announce," "to summon." Thus *concilium* (or "council") means "assembly." Etymological dictionaries trace *concilium* expressly to σύγκλητος or ἐκκλησία. The Latin *calo* corresponds to the Greek καλῶ which in the Gospels sometimes simply means "to call." Simultaneously, however, the Synoptics and, above all, Paul use it in the specific theological sense of calling, that is, of *vocation*.[4] If we simply survey the New Testament vocabulary of καλῶ, the following is disclosed: God Himself is the καλῶν, it is He who calls and summons on the ground of an eternal election bestowed by grace (Rom. 8:30; 9:12, 24; I Cor. 1:9; 7:15, 17; Gal. 1:6, 15; 5:8;

[1] Eusebius, *Hist. eccl.*, VII, 7, 5; *PG* 20, 651.

[2] Tertillian, *De ieiunio* 13, 6–7; *CC* 2, 1272; cf. *De pudicitia* 10, 12; *CC* 2, 1301; and later on Cyrpian, *Ep.* 75, 4; *PL* 3, 1205f.

[3] Cf. Ernout and Meillet, *Dictionnaire Étymologique de la langue Latine* (Paris [4]1959); Walde and Hofman, *Lateinisches etymologisches Wörterbuch* (Heidelberg [3]1938).

[4] In addition to the dictionaries of the New Testament (F. Zorell, W. Bauer) and the bible theologies of the New Testament (M. Meinertz, J. Bonsirven, F. Prat, A. Wikenhauser, R. Bultmann, E. Stauffer) the following lexicographic articles are of special importance: K. L. Schmidt, "καλέω," etc., in: *Theologisches Wörtebuch zum NT* (Stuttgart 1938) III, 488–505; E. Neuhäusler, "Berufung," in *Lexikon für Theologie und Kirche* (Freiburg i. Br. [3]1958) II. 280–283; G. Molin, "Berufung," in *Bibeltheologisches Wörterbuch*, ed. by J. B. Bauer (Graz 1959) 66–72 Cf. further E. Egel *Die Berufungstheologie des Apostels Paulus* (Diss. Heidelberg 1939); H. H. Rowley, *The Biblical Doctrine of Election* (London 1950); P. J. Daumoser, *Berufung und Erwählung bei den Synoptikern* (Munich 1954); H. Schlier, "Der Ruf Gottes," in *Geist und Leben* 28 (1955) 241–247; S.-J. d'Arc, "Le mystère de la vocation," in *La Vie Spirituelle* 38 (1956) 167–186; W. Bieder, *Die Berufung im Neuen Testament* (Zurich 1961).

9

I Thess. 2:12; 4:7; 5:24; II Thess. 2:14; II Tim. 1:9; Heb. 5:4; I Pet. 1:15; 2:9; 5:10; II Pet. 1:3). He calls and summons to *salvation*, which lies in sanctification through the Spirit and in faith in the truth (II Thess. 2:14), to suffering (I Pet. 2:21), to peace (I Cor. 7:15), to the peace of Christ (Col. 3:15), to freedom (Gal. 5:13), to sanctification (I Thess. 4:7), to hope for a calling (Eph. 4:4), to the inheritance of a blessing (I Pet. 3:9), to the promise of eternal life (Heb. 9:15), to eternal life (I Tim. 6:12), to God's marvellous light (I Pet. 2:9), to God's eternal glory in Christ (I Pet. 5:10), to fellowship with His Son Jesus Christ (I Cor. 1:9), to the marriage feast of the Lamb (Apoc. 19:9). God calls and summons then through grace; He, the God of all grace (I Pet. 5:10), calls and summons in Christ: not on the ground of the deeds of men, but on the ground of His calling (Rom. 9:12), by virtue of His glory and perfection through His grace (II Pet. 1:3; Gal. 1:15), through the grace of Jesus Christ (Gal. 1:6) in a holy calling not according to our works but according to His own previously conceived purpose, and the grace that was granted to us in Christ Jesus before all time, which now, however, has been made known by the advent of our Saviour Jesus Christ (II Tim. 1:9; cf. Heb. 9:15; I Pet. 5:10). Therefore the calling of God, which is revealed to us in the gospel of the death and resurrection of Jesus Christ, is not only a word reporting our salvation in Jesus Christ, nor is it only a word of announcement but a word that activates and actualizes. Jesus Christ, the exalted Lord Himself, through the power of the Spirit in His word that calls and summons, effects the salvation of all those who believe in Him.

What can be said about the verb "to call" can be confirmed by the noun κλῆσις, which likewise is used in a specific theological sense.[5] Here, too, it concerns the calling through God in Christ, the "heavenly call in Christ Jesus" (Phil. 3:14; cf. Rom. 11:29; I Cor. 1:26; 7:20; Eph. 1:18, 4:1, 4; II Thess. 1:11; II Tim. 1:9; Heb. 3:1; II Pet. 1:10). Thus Christians are simply the "called" (cf. Rom 1:6, 7; 8:28; I Cor. 1:2, 24; Jude 1; Apoc. 17:14). Everyone is called, not as an individual, however, but as a member of the one people, of the one body: called in one body (Col. 3:15), *one* body and *one* spirit (Eph. 4:4). Thus all Christians constitute "a chosen race, a royal priesthood, a holy nation, a purchased people; that you may proclaim the perfections of him who has called you out of darkness into his marvellous light. You who in times past were not a people, but are now the people of God" (I Pet. 2:9f). Thereby all Christians in the Church share in the royal, priestly, and prophetic office of Christ.

[5] Cf. footnote 4.

It is in this sense that the word ἐκ-κλησία must be understood. As is well known in the New Testament the word, even apart from its profane use, encompasses a manifold and complex content of religious meaning. It can designate both the whole community of the people of the New Covenant redeemed through Christ and the local Christian community, the Christian household community, and especially the community assembled for worship.[6] In all these different ways, however, *ek-klesia* means the community of the new people of God called out and called together. One was hardly aware any longer of the etymology, the ἐξ, in that context. After all, one thought primarily in terms of the Old Testament. In the Septuagint ἐκκλησία was used for the translation of the Old Testament key word קהל or קהל יהוה. After the Jews, however, in their unbelief had rejected the cornerstone, the youthful, primitive community had to regard itself as the true people of God of the last days, as the true people of the Covenant that God had gathered together in Israel. The Old Testament people of God were now legitimately succeeded by the people of the Covenant, summoned and gathered together through the word of the gospel of Jesus Christ. Thus, according to the testimony of the Acts of the Apostles, the original community in Jerusalem was first called *ekklesia*: there the individual community and the whole community, the individual Church and the whole Church coincided. But soon there was also mention of the *ekklesia* in Judea, in Galilee, and in Samaria. Finally people spoke of *ekklesiai*, in the plural. Each individual *ekklesia* was a copy of the original community, each represented the whole *ekklesia*. Paul uses *ekklesia* above all for the individual community (especially for the community gathered for worship) and he often uses the word in the plural. His captivity epistles, above all, speak in an entirely new and profound way of the *ekklesia* as the universal Church.[7]

[6] In addition to the dictionaries and theologies of the New Testament listed in footnote 4, cf. A. Médebielle, "Église," in *Dictionnaire de la Bible*, Supplément (Paris 1934) II, 487–691; K. L. Schmidt, "ἐκκλησία" in *Theologisches Wörterbuch zum NT* (Stuttgart 1938) III, 502–539; H. Haag, "Kirche," in *Bibellexikon* (Einsiedeln 1951) 920–929; V. Warnach, "Kirche," in *Bibeltheologisches Wörterbuch* (Graz 1959) 432–459, as well as the bibliographies given in these works.

[7] For the biblical theology of the Church, cf. the following recent Catholic publications: A. Wikenhauser, *Die Kirche als der mystische Leib Christi nach dem Apostel Paulus* (Münster 1937. ²1940); L. Cerfaux, *The Church in the Theology of Saint Paul* (London and Edinburgh 1959); H. Schlier and V. Warnach, *Die Kirche im Epheserbrief* (Münster 1949); Th. Soiron, *Die Kirche als der Leib Christi* (Düsseldorf 1951); E. Sauras, *El cuerpo místico de Cristo* (Madrid 1952); M. Villain and J. de Baciocchi, *La vocation de l'Église* (Paris 1954); F. Mussner, *Christus, das All und die Kirche* (Trier 1955); H. Schlier, *Die Zeit der Kirche* (Freiburg i. Br. 1956. ³1962); J. Bonsirven, *Le Règne de Dieu* (Paris 1957); R. Schnackenburg, *God's Rule and Kingdom* (London 1963).

The universal community and the universal Church is the individual community and the individual church writ large: the assembled community of the New Testament people of God summoned and gathered together out of the world by God for the sake of Christ and in Christ through the Gospel. It is the universal Church which in St. Paul's letters from prison is simultaneously the exalted mystery of God's saving work for man, the mystery of Christ and the pleroma of Christ, his body to be built up gradually through Baptism and the Eucharist, through faith, love, and suffering; His bride, still waiting and yet already bestowed, and the Temple of the Holy Spirit. *Thus the universal Church is the mysterious assembly of those who believe in Christ.* Otherwise expressed, *the Church is the great concilium of the faithful, convoked in the Spirit by God Himself through Christ. Both* are constitutive elements of this council, the summons of the God calling from above and the community of summoned *people* from below, the foundation of the assembly by God (*institutio Dei*), taking effect through Scripture, sacrament, and ecclesiastical office, *and* the community of the assembled people (*communio fidelium*) living wholly from God's grace in faith and love. This *concilium*, therefore, has at one and the same time the character of personal event and of institutional being. It is not only an atomistic total of believing individuals; nor is it only a supernatural bureaucratic apparatus dispensing "graces" and ruling the people. This *concilium*, is the community of grace of the chosen people of the covenant with God through Christ in the Holy Spirit ever newly gathered together and kept together, through the propagation of the word, the celebration of the sacraments, and the service of the apostolic office.[8]

[8] In the history of theology the Church as assembled community of the faithful has been too often neglected in favour of the Church as institution. But it was never quite forgotten, either in the Patristic period, in Scholasticism, or in the modern era of the Counter-Reformation. To mention but a few characteristic examples: (1) The Patristic period: The mere etymological exposition of the word *ecclesia* could not but lead the Fathers towards this concept of the Church: "The name 'ecclesia' is to be explained through the fact that the Church has convoked and united all men" (Cyril of Jerusalem, *Catecheses for those to be baptized*, XVIII, 24; *PG* 33, 1044). The Apostolic Fathers already spoke of the Church as "the number of the elect," "the chosen saints," "the new people," "the fourth race" (after the Barbarians, Hellenes, and Jews), etc. This view was expressed even more strongly by the later Fathers, as for example by Hippolytus: "The holy assembly of those who live in justice" (in *Dan. comment.* I, 17, 6 ed. Bonwetsch 1, 28); Clement of Alexandria: "the assembly of the elect" (*Stromata* VII, 5; *PG* 9, 437); Origen: "coetus populi christiani" (in *Ez. hom.* I, II; *PG* 13, 677), "credentium plebs" (in *Ex. hom.* IX, 3; *PG* 12, 365), "coetus omnium sanctorum" (in *Cant. lib.* I, 1; *PG* 13, 84); Augustine: "congregatio societasque hominum . . . in qua fraterna caritas operatur" (*de fide et symb.* 9, 21; *PL* 40, 193),

All the peoples of the earth are summoned to this council through God's gracious will, which excludes no one but wills that all men be saved. All the peoples of the earth are summoned to this council in order to accept God's gracious choice in the decision of faith, and in order to be gathered in one Spirit, joined together through the bond of Charity, the power of the Word and the Sacraments under apostolic guidance: "all" as "one in Christ Jesus" (Gal. 3:28). God's gracious call to this council is universal, it is ecumenical; it

"universa societas sanctorum atque fidelium" (*ep.* 98, 5; *PL* 33, 362), "christiana societas" (*contra litteras Petiliani* II, 39, 94; *PL* 43, 293), "societas credentium" (*de bapt.* VII, 53, 102; *PL* 43, 243), "societas sanctorum" (in *Jo-tract.* 26, 17; *PL* 35, 1614), "catholicae Ecclesiae communio" (*ep* 93, 1, 3; *PL* 33, 323; cf. *ep.* 112, 3; *PL* 33, 428), "christianae fidei communio nostra" (*ep.* 87, 1; *PL* 33, 297).

(2) *Middle Ages:* From the "Definition" of Isidore of Seville, "Ecclesia vocatur proprie, propter quod omnes ad se vocet, et in unum congreget" (*de ecclesiasticis officiis* I, 1; *PL* 83, 739f; cf. *Etymol.* VIII, 1, 7f; *PL* 82, 295), the tradition leads to Rhabanus Maurus, Remigius of Auxerre, Placidius monachus, Bonaventure, Durandus of Mende (cf. de Lubac, *Catholicism* (London, 1950). The roots of the word *ecclesia* (= *convocatio*) are a constant subject of reflection. The customary medieval theological and canonistic definition of the Church was *congregatio fidelium* or *societas fidelium* or else *adunatio, collectio, collegium, coetus, corpus, communio, populas, unitas, universitas . . . fidelium, christianorum, catholicorum.* Cf. B. Tierney, *Foundations of the Conciliar Theory* (Cambridge 1955); Y. Congar, *Lay People in the Church* (London 1957). Special mention in this context should be made of Thomas Aquinas who frequently speaks of the Church as *congregatio fidelium.* In his commentary on the article of the creed, "Sanctam Ecclesiam catholicam," he writes the following: "Circa quod sciendum est quod Ecclesia est idem quod congregatio. Unde Ecclesia sancta est idem quod congregatio fidelium et quilibet christianus est sicut membrum ipsius Ecclesiae" (*Expos. in Symb.* art. 9; cf. *c. Gent.* IV, 78; *S. th.* I, q. 117, a 2, obj. 1; III, q. 8, a. 4, ad 2; *De Ver.* q. 29, a. 4, obj. 8; *Comp. theol.* I, 147; in 1 *Cor.* c. 12, lect. 3; in *Heb.* c. 3 lect. 1).

(3) *Counter-Reformation:* Even when the designation *congregatio fidelium* was discredited through heretical interpretations, this most important traditional definition of the Church was never abandoned in the Catholic Church. The evidence of the *Catechism of the Council of Trent* suffices to prove this. There the term *ecclesia* is expressly derived from *evocatio* and stress is laid on the equation *ecclesia-concilium*, "And because the word *ecclesia* was taken by the Latins from the Greeks and they applied it to sacred things after the gospel had been spread it must be shown what significance this word has. *Ecclesia* means 'calling forth'; later writers used it for 'council' and 'meeting.' " Further, the Church according to Holy Scripture is described in the following manner: "Later on this word was commonly used in sacred writings to refer to Christianity and the congregations of the faithful, those who are called to the light of truth and the cognition of God through faith, so that they might, after having rejected the darkness of ignorance and error, piously and devoutly venerate the true and living God and serve Him with all their heart. And to conclude all this with one word: *ecclesia*, as St. Augustine says, 'is the faithful spread over the whole earth' " (*Catech.*, c. 10, 2).

And so the title of the second chapter of the *Schema constitutionis secundae de ecclesia Christi secundum reverendissimorum patrum animadversiones reformatum* (Mansi 53, 308–317) of the First Vatican Council is: "Ecclesiam a Christo institutam esse coetum fidelium."

is directed towards the *oikumene*. This council bridges over what seemed to Jewish eyes the fundamental *religious* opposition between the chosen people and the sinful Gentiles. For God "has called not only from among the Jews but also from among the Gentiles" (Rom. 9:24; cf. I Cor. 7:18). Also overcome is what seemed to the Gentiles the fundamental *social* opposition between free men and slaves (I Cor. 7:20–24). The Holy Spirit is to be poured forth over *all* (Acts 2). The gospel is to be preached to the whole world, to the whole *oikumene*, as a testimony to all nations (Mt. 24:14) and the word of the Good Tidings has penetrated to the furthermost borders of the *oikumene* (Rom. 10:18). Thus we may say that *the Church is truly the ecumenical council convoked by God Himself:* ἡ μεγάλη καὶ ἁγία σύνοδος οἰκουμενική.

What, then, is the truly theological point of departure for a theology of ecumenical councils? It is the statement just formulated, in terms of which all the structures of the Church must be understood: the Church is an ecumenical council by divine convocation. This statement must now be explained and related to the concept of ecumenical councils as it is commonly understood, that is, to ecumenical councils by *human* convocation. What is the relationship between an ecumenical council by *human* convocation and an ecumenical council by *divine* convocation, that is, the Church? The answer to that can be formulated as the second principle of a theology of ecumenical councils.

III

THE ECUMENICAL COUNCIL BY HUMAN CONVOCATION AS A REPRESENTATION OF THE ECUMENICAL COUNCIL BY DIVINE CONVOCATION

A N ecumenical council by human convocation is a representation of the ecumenical council by divine convocation. This statement has a function that is negative and critical, and one which is positive and constructive: the ecumenical council by human convocation is *only*, but at the same time *really*, the representation of the ecumenical council by divine convocation.

1. A REPRESENTATION ONLY

An ecumenical council by human convocation is *not simply the Church* but only the representation, presentation, and actualization of the Church. This has a twofold meaning.

(*a*) The Church is *in essence* the ecumenical council by divine convocation. The Church presents and constantly renews herself as the council of believers in Christ convoked by God through Christ in the Spirit: in the proclamation of the Word as appointed by Christ through the apostolic office and in the celebration of the sacraments; in the profession of the common faith; in the exercise of an all-uniting love, in the hopeful expectation of the Second Coming of the Lord. The Church manifests herself most intensively during the act of worship, in the common listening to the word of God, and in the common participation in the Sacrament of the Eucharist. The word of the Lord binds the Church to *this* self-representation. In accordance with her nature as an ecumenical council by divine convocation, however, the Church is not bound to another representation of her nature, namely to an ecumenical council by human convocation for common consultations and decisions, for the ordering and shaping of the universal Church. No word of Christ or of the apostles imposes such an obligation upon the Church. Thus the Church can exist even without ecumenical councils by human convocation,[1] a fact confirmed by the very history of the Church. During the first three decisive centuries, as well as during later centuries, the Church actually managed without ecumenical councils. The first ecumenical council in the history of the Church can be traced back, not to an initiative of the Church's government, but to the government of a pagan state in the person of a still-pagan emperor who wielded the influence and kept the title and office of the *Pontifex Maximus.*

(*b*) The *existence* of an ecumenical council by human convocation does not derive from the intrinsic property of the Church as an ecumenical council by divine convocation. Still less is a particular outward form of the ecumenical council by human convocation indicated, even if we assume that a representation of the Church in her permanent nature is truly implied. The concrete significance of this argument will require a close scrutiny. An ecumenical council by human convocation can manifest and represent the Church in a great variety of historical forms. According to the evidence of church history the mutability above all concerns the person and the office of the individual convoking a council and presiding over it, the participants, the agenda, the order of business, and the necessity of an express papal approbation.[2] Hence it is precisely with respect to the reunion of separated Christians and eventual negotiations for union at a later council that questions concerning existing laws and ceremonial should in no case be turned into questions of dogma.[3] Rather, existing laws should be tested in order to determine to what extent they could be revoked and to what extent they are *really* irrevocable *on the basis of the gospel of Jesus Christ.* The distinction between *ius divinum* and *ius humanum* that can be discerned in the gospel of Jesus Christ should have an absolutely fundamental meaning precisely with respect to councils and reunion. Yet it is not given sufficient attention, either with respect to ecumenical councils or to the life of the Church in general. While it seems to us Catholics that the Protestant churches have dangerously weakened the framework of their church constitutions, or even have abandoned it, the Catholic Church has strengthened the constitutional framework for reasons of safety. The Catholic Church has tried to hold this frame together by methods that are frequently irritating and distorting. They

---

[1] Cf. Chap. I.   [2] Cf. Chap. I.

[3] Thus it is important to note today, for example, that at a Union Council such as the one of Florence the participating schismatic Orientals enjoyed equal privileges. Cf. J. Gill, "L'accord gréco-latin au Concile de Florence," in *Le concile et les conciles* (Paris 1960) 190f; for sources, cf. J. Gill, *The Council of Florence* (Cambridge 1959).

tend to offend the eye of the non-Catholic observer more often than the picture as a whole tends to charm him into a mood of reflective consideration.

2. REALLY A REPRESENTATION

The ecumenical council by human convocation *is really* a representation of the ecumenical council by divine convocation. The first account of church councils in Christian literature already testifies with extraordinary clarity to this concept of a council. Tertullian writes: "Aguntur praeterea per Graecisa illa certis in locis concilia ex universis ecclesiis, per quae et altiora quaeque in commune tractantur, et ipsa repraesentatio totius nominis Christiani magna veneratione celebratur. Et hoc quam dignum fide auspicante congregari undique ad Christum! Vide, quam bonum et quam iucundum habitare fratres in unum!— . . . In fact those councils of all the churches are held in Greece in certain places, at which matters of common concern, including the loftiest things, are discussed, and the representation of the whole of Christendom is celebrated with great veneration. And how fitting, to be gathered together unto Christ under the sign of faith! Behold, how good and joyful it is when brethren dwell together!"[4]

The principle of representation plays a great role in Holy Scripture itself. The whole history of salvation develops according to the principle of representation. In creation man already appears as representative of all creation, then the people of Israel as representative of the whole of mankind; further the remnant of Israel appears as representative of the whole people of Israel; and finally Christ appears as representative of the remnant. Thus in the Old Testament representation develops in the form of a progressive reduction towards Christ, from the manifold to the One. Conversely, in the New Testament representation broadens progressively from the One to the manifold. By virtue of the fact that Christ as the One suffers death for the many, and that He arose from the dead, the many are now to represent the One: the apostles are to represent Christ for the Church; the Church is to represent Christ for mankind in the eschatological perspective of a redeemed mankind of the future kingdom of God and a redeemed creation of the new heaven and the new earth.[5] At this point we must investigate how in our interim

---

[4] Tertullian, *De paenitentia* 13, 6–7; *CC* II, 1272.

[5] Cf. O. Cullmann, *Königsherrschaft Christi und Kirche im Neuen Testament* (Zollikon–Zürich 1941) 35f; *Christus und die Zeit. Die urchristliche Zeit- und Geschichtsauffassung* (Zollikon–Zürich 1946. ²1948) 99–103 (English trans. *Christ and Time*, London 1950).

period a specific gathering of faithful, in turn, can represent the Church: the ecumenical council by human convocation as the representation of the ecumenical council by divine convocation.

If but two or three are gathered in the name of the Lord, He Himself is among them through His Spirit. Even in such a small gathering the communion with Christ in the Spirit is realized, the Church becomes existent, the Church herself is present, the Church exhibits herself. This small gathering, of course, is not *the* Church pure and simple; the Church is *the whole*, the whole of the people of God, of the Body of Christ, of the Temple of the Holy Spirit. But this small gathering already presents the Church, realizes, actualizes and *represents* the Church because the whole Christ is present in it. If this is true of a small gathering, how much more is it of a large gathering, which consists of not just a few individuals but behind which stands expressly—and this is not only a quantitative but also a qualitative distinction—the whole, the *oikumene*, the people of God of the entire inhabited world. For Athanasius, the great champion of orthodoxy at the first ecumenical council, the Council of Nicaea is superior to all other synods: "For if one compares number with number, then those gathered at Nicaea are so much more than those gathered at a particular synod (τῶν κατὰ μέρος), just as the whole is more than the part."[6]

This council—convoked by man out of the whole *oikumene* for common deliberation and decisions, for the regulation, order and organization of the Church—does not represent the *concilium* of the Church convoked by God Himself in the most intensive form of common worship. Nor, on the other hand, does it represent this merely in the most general form of a meeting of individual Christians. Rather the character of representation is markedly apparent: The representation of the Church occurs not only in an *isolated and particularistic* way—that too being a great thing in itself; it takes place—and the whole is not simply "greater" than its parts—in an overall and all-inclusive way, precisely in *ecumenical* fashion.

If an ecumenical council by human convocation is understood here as the markedly apparent ecumenical representation of the Church, the term "representation" is used in its general sense of "re-presenting" and not in its special sense of "deputising". This latter concept of an ecumenical council is presupposed in an understanding of the

---

[6] Athanasius, *Ep. contra Arianos, ad honoratissimos in Africa episcopos* 2; *PG* 26, 1032. The same line of thought can be also found in Augustine. Cf. F. Hofmann, "Die Bedeutung der Konzilien für die kirchliche Lehrentwicklung nach dem heiligen Augustinus," in *Kirche und Überlieferung*, edited by J. Betz and H. Fries (Freiburg–Basle–Vienna 1960) 85f.

term "representation" as it was first elaborated in the Middle Ages under the influence of theories of natural law and which became established in the conciliar period. To "represent" the Church at ecumenical councils by human convocation it is not necessary that the participants *represent* their Church as plenipotentiaries. What is required is that the participants (in what form, is a matter to be examined more closely later) represent their Church in some degree by personifying it. True, the participants at ecumenical councils by human convocation are able to represent the Church in this sense only through the power of our Lord present in the Holy Spirit. This applies in equal degree to an ecumenical council or to a council of the local Church, or to a *concilium* of two or three. Nevertheless, it is only when the participants in a council have the Church of the whole *oikumene* behind them, in the sense previously defined, that they are capable through the power of the Lord of projecting the Church not only in a particularist way, but in a truly *ecumenical*, overall, and all-inclusive way.

From this it is also evident that ecumenical councils by human convocation, too, cannot materialize without the aid of God. On the other hand one must add that the ecumenical council by divine convocation, which is the Church, in turn cannot materialize without the aid of man. But in the case of the Church, in the strict sense, the summoner is God alone. In the ecumenical councils by human convocation the summoner is man, but not without God. It can be expressed in Scholastic terminology as follows: In the case of the calling of the Church the *causa principalis* is God; man can be only a *causa instrumentalis* therein. In the case of a summoning of an ecumenical council by human convocation the *causa principalis*—under divine providence as *causa prima*—is man as *causa secunda*.

In his exhaustive historical investigation of ecumenical councils in the fourth century, Goemans has shown convincingly that the representation of the universal Church is their decisive feature.[7] This is the reason given again and again in the early Church for their special authority. This is mostly done by bringing into relief the limited importance of particular synods. The linguistic designations are already significant. The title itself is revealing in this respect. It is only with reference to general councils that we find expressions such as "the great, holy and ecumenical,"[8] "the Catholic synod,"[9]

[7] M. Goemans, *Het algemeen Concilie in de vierde eeuw* (Nijmegen–Utrecht 1945); Y. Congar reviewed the work favourably in "Bulletin d'Ecclésiologie," *Revue des Sciences philosophiques et théologiques* 31 (1947) 287–291.

[8] Cf. J. B. Pitra, *Analecta Sacra Spicilegio Solesmensi* (Paris 1883) IV, 224, 451.

[9] Athanasius, *Apologia contra Arianos* 25; *PG* 25, 289.

and generally a solemnity about the Bible, which we look for in
vain in connection with particular councils.[10]

Just as there was no established theory of the Church in the
first millennium, so was there no established theoιy of ecumenical
councils. One lived the Church, one lived the ecumenical council;
the heresies of the first centuries aimed less at the Church than at
the doctrine of the Trinity and Christology. At that time people were
not yet so conscious of the earthly juridical form of the Church.
Nevertheless, just as the Fathers referred time and again to the essential features of the Church. so also they pointed out those of an
ecumenical council which in its participants represented the whole
Church. There is abundant evidence of this, especially in connection
with the first ecumenical council. Athanasius expressly emphasizes
the distinction between particular and ecumenical representation:
"Therefore, namely, the ecumenical council took place in Nicaea,
where 318 bishops came together for the sake of the faith on account
of the Arian heresy, so that *particular* (synods) could no longer take
place under the pretence of faith. . . . This one (in Nicaea) has fulfilled the whole *oikumene*."[11] In the same letter he speaks of the Council Fathers as of those "who came together in Nicaea from our whole
oikumene."[12] Further Phoebadius Aginnensis writes: "What did you
do, O men of blessed memory, who gathered in Nicaea from all
parts of the world?"[13] And Hilary: "They hastened from all parts of
the world to one place and gathered in Nicaea."[14] And Sulpicius
Severus: "The synod of Nicaea gathered from all over the world."[15]
And Marius Victorinus: "When in Nicaea, a city confirmed in the
faith by the presence of more than 300 bishops, excluding the followers
of Arius, in which synod of these men were the luminaries of the
Church of the whole world."[16] For Augustine also an ecumenical
council stands above a provincial council not because of ecclesiastical
and constitutional law, but for the reason that the provincial council
represents a province only, whereas an ecumenical council represents
the whole Catholic world. Ecumenical councils "represent the authority of the whole world ('universi orbis auctoritas'; *De bapt.* 2, 4, 5)

[10] M. Goemans, *Het algemeen Concilie in de vierde eeuw* (Nijmegen–Utrecht
1945) 44.
[11] Athanasius, *Ep. contra Arianos, ad honoratissimos in Africa episcopos* 2;
PG 26, 1032.
[12] Athanasius, *Ep. contra Arianos, ad honoratissimos in Africa episcopos* 1;
PG 26, 1029.
[13] Phoebadius Aginnensis, *Liber contra Arianos* 6; *PL* 20, 17.
[14] Hilary, *Fragmenta Historica* 2, 26; *CSEL* 65, 149.
[15] Sulphicius Severus, *Chronicorum* 2, 35; *PL* 20, 149.
[16] Marius Victorinus, *Adversus Arium* 1, 28; *PL* 8, 1061.

and their decrees are the expression of the consensus of the universal Church ('universalis ecclesiae consensio'; *De bapt.* 7, 53, 102). Hence they are a proclamation of the universal Church (*Contra Cresc.* 1, 33, 39) which as an inspiration of God are almost equivalent to a revelation (*De bapt.* 6, 39, 76)."[17]

In the Middle Ages, however, in the West, emphasis was placed on the legal structure of the Church. That and the corporate way of thinking produced a major reinterpretation of the idea of representation, which we shall have to examine more closely later. At this point we are primarily interested in the fact that even the medieval general synods, to the extent that they claimed an ecumenical character at all, were regarded as a representation of the Church. In any case this perforce applies to the Fourth Lateran Council, which represented the Church in a new way. This was not simply a bishops' synod, but a representative assembly of the clerical and secular estates of Christendom. Although the decretalists did not at that time analyse more closely the concept of representation, this greatest council of the Middle Ages as a conciliar model has exerted a great influence on the development of the "conciliar theory" and its idea of representation. Thus in the fourteenth century representation was no longer understood in the sense of pure personification solely but also in the sense of delegation.[18] It is now that the concept of the representation of the universal Church becomes even expressly recorded in council decrees. The councils of Constance and Basle frequently make use of the formula "*universalem Ecclesiam repraesentans*," which later became famous. It goes without saying that this formula contains some implications that are not necessarily germane to the concept of the representation of the Church. Yet there is no doubt that every Catholic is strictly bound by what the Council at that time required the followers of Huss and Wyclif to affirm: "Likewise, whether he believes, holds and declares, that every general Council, including that of Constance, represents the universal Church."[19] At the Council of Trent violent discussions raged, not about the reality, but around the formula "*universalem Ecclesiam repraesentans*," which H. Jedin has very accurately described.[20] When Bishop Braccio Martelli of

---

[17] F. Hoffmann, "Die Bedeutung der Konzilien für die kirchliche Lehrentwicklung nach dem heiligen Augustinus," in *Kirche und Überlieferung*, edited by J. Betz and H. Fries (Freiburg–Basle–Vienna 1960) 86.

[18] Cf. B. Tierney, *The Foundations of the Conciliar Theory* (Cambridge 1955) 46f.

[19] Denz. 657 (cf. Denz. 658).

[20] H. Jedin, *A History of the Council of Trent;* vol. II: *The First Sessions at Trent 1545–47* (tr. by Dom Ernest Graf, O.S.B.; Edinburgh 1961).

Fiesole at one of the first sessions demanded that the Council designate itself as a representation of the universal Church and that the
formula *"universalem Ecclesiam repraesentans"* be inserted in the
decree, almost all the bishops following him agreed. The papal legates
did not dispute the justification of the formula, but questioned its
opportuneness. Cardinal del Monte declared: "He too did not deny
that it [the present gathering] represented the universal Church,
but was it advisable, in view of its actual composition, when less than
three dozen bishops were present, to use so pretentious a formula,
which could only call forth hostility and derision of their opponents?"[21] It was also remarked that the concept "ecumenical"
already implied the concept of the representation of the universal
Church. Almost a third of the bishops entitled to vote insisted upon
inserting the representation formula as soon as the Council had a
greater number of participants.[22] The insertion of the formula was
demanded over and over again on different grounds.[23] The legates
were obviously worried over the fact that the conciliar spirit of Basle
might rise again. Nevertheless, even they never dared to question the
claim that an ecumenical council represents the universal Church.
In fact, the Council president, Cardinal del Monte, even declared his
readiness to present the following canon before the Council: "If
anyone says that a legitimately convened General Council does not
represent the universal Church, let him be anathema." Actually he
could hardly have acted otherwise without infringing the authority
of the very Council over which he was presiding. The unwillingness to
embody the formula of Constance in the Tridentine decrees was
prompted solely by the fear of conciliar theory which we have long
ago come to know as an obstacle to the timely convocation of the
Council and as a continual hindrance of its direction by the legates."[24]

The main issue discussed at the First Vatican Council above all
concerned the office of the pope, and not ecumenical councils. But
even here there was some marginal discussion on ecumenical councils
as the representation of the universal Church. Thus at that time
they still often spoke of an ecumenical council as the *Ecclesia
coadunata*. Thirty Neapolitan bishops had declared through Cardinal
Riario Sforza that it was necessary to speak of the teaching office
of the Church dispersed throughout the world as well as that of the
Church united in the Council: ". . . videri necessarium esse ut etiam

---

[21] H. Jedin, *op cit.* II, 23.
[22] H. Jedin, *op cit.* II, 24.
[23] H. Jedin, *op cit.* II, 26, 39f, 92, 265f, 307, 346, 394.
[24] H. Jedin, *op cit.* II, 347.

agatur de magisterio ecclesiae tum dispersae tum in concilium congregatae."[25] And when the reporter of the Deputation on Faith, Bishop Zinelli, had to make an authoritative statement in regard to the supreme power of jurisdiction in the Church held by an ecumenical council, he used the formula of representation: "We willingly grant that we, in an ecumenical council or in the bishops together with their head, have supreme and full ecclesiastical authority over all the faithful: which is certainly most fitting for the Church, joined with her head. Therefore the bishops congregated in an ecumenical council, in which case *they represent the entire Church,* or dispersed but in union with her head—in this case they are the Church herself—truly have full authority."[26] And Pope John XXIII spoke of the Second Vatican Council, as a representation of the Christian people: "la grande riunione del popolo cristiano."[27]

Thus there is no doubt that, seen against the background of the history of the councils, an ecumenical council by human convocation is the representation of the ecumenical council by divine convocation, whether it is designated through a formula or whether it is explicitly stated in one way or another. The ecumenical council by human convocation represents the one, holy, catholic and apostolic Church, and precisely thereby reflects the essential structure of the Church. What this means in connection with ecclesiastical office will be discussed later. Here we shall make only a general statement: All the individual Churches, so different from one another, scattered throughout the *oikumene* in all countries and continents, made up of all races, languages, and cultures, belonging to societies with different political and social structures, and having different rites, liturgies, theologies, and forms of piety and law, by virtue of their assemblage constitute and realize the visible-invisible *unity* of the whole Church as a special, concrete event: the representation of the *one* Church!

Precisely because this gathering of peoples, coming from the most varied countries and continents, the most varied races, languages, cultures, the most varied social and political structures, the most varied rites, theologies, and forms of piety and law, has been summoned and convoked; precisely because this assemblage is a concrete actualization of the unity of the different, heterogeneous, independent,

[25] Mansi 51, 823.

[26] Mansi 52, 1109; Bishop de la Tour d'Auvergne suggested to add to the chapter on the infallibility a chapter on the ecumenical council "*Ecclesiam universalem repraesentans*" [as representing the universal Church] (Mansi 51, 816).

[27] *L'Osservatore Romano*, April 8, 1959.

individual Churches with their own problems and difficulties, needs, concerns, and demands, it clearly follows that the realization of this unity through the council simultaneously makes present in fact world-wide *catholicity* in its liturgical, theological, legal, and cultural pluralism: the representation of the *Catholic* Church!

Thus we have the ecumenical council by human convocation as a representation of the one and Catholic Church! But is it also a representation of the holy Church? This is not so obvious. The history of councils protects us from the illusionary speculation that at an ecumenical council we can, from the outset, count upon an assembly of especially holy men (possibly candidates for canonization), in short, upon a council of saints. Rather an ecumenical council by human convocation is even in this instance the true reflection of the ecumenical council by divine convocation: in both instances it is a convocation of men. Consequently we always deal with councils in which the human, the all-too-human, and sinful element cannot be excluded. Everything in the Church that involves failure and weariness, mediocrity and malice, unintentional and intentional distortion can also be found at a council by human convocation.[28] And according to the evidence of history it has been found at such councils again and again. Yet in accordance with the tradition of the Church not only the council by divine convocation but also those by human convocation have been called ἅγιον, indeed even sacrosanct.

We must, however, remember that in the early period the attribute "holy" was used extremely seldom in reference to the Church and that its original meaning in no way referred to the moral holiness of her members but to the relation of the Church to God (holy in terms of "heavenly"), and above all to the Holy Spirit (holy as "spiritual") Further, we must remember that the original question asked in Baptism, in conformity with apostolic tradition, was not merely formulated: "Do you believe in the Holy Church?" but asked

---

[28] For a theological evaluation of the human nature and the sinfulness of the Church composed of men and sinners, cf. H. Küng, *Justification. The Doctrine of Karl Barth and a Catholic Reflection* (New York 1964) 250–253; *The Council and Reunion* (London 1961) 34–50; as well as F. Pilgram, *Physiologie der Kirche* (Mainz 1860. ²1931); Ch. Journet, *L'Église du Verbe incarné*. 2 vols. (Bruges 1941. 1951) I, XIIIf; 395f, esp. II, 893–934; K. Rahner, *Die Kirche der Sünder* (Freiburg 1948 esp. 14f; Y. Congar, *Vraie et fausse réforme dans l'Église* (Paris 1950) 63–132 (cf. also E. Mersch, Dom Vonier, K. Adam, Pinard de la Boullaye, J. Bernhart, P. Courturier, H. Rahner quoted by Congar). The sharp and daring commentaries of the Fathers on the human nature and sinfulness of the Church is shown by H. de Lubac, *Catholicism*, (London 1950), and with great brilliance and innumerable examples by H. U. von Balthasar, "Casta meretrix," in *Sponsa Verbi. Skizzen zur Theologie* II (Einsiedeln 1961) 203–305.

precisely: "Do you believe in the Holy Spirit *within* the Holy Church for the resurrection of the body?"[29] Because of the Holy Spirit the Church of men and sinners may be called holy.

Thus if an ecumenical council convoked by man represents the holiness of the ecumenical council by divine convocation it can do so only by virtue of that sanctifying Spirit who, as the Spirit of Jesus Christ, is alive and at work in the Church; the Spirit who in accordance with the promise of Jesus will remain for ever in the Church (Jn. 14:16f), teaching and reminding her of all that Jesus has said (Jn. 14:26), testifying to a new truth not on His own authority but in witness to the truth of Christ, and thus lead us to all truth (Jn. 16:13f.)

In this way the Holy Spirit is active in the Church in accordance with Jesus' promise and thereby also on the occasion of her special representation: in the ecumenical council by human convocation. As the particularly outstanding, precisely ecumenical, representation of the Church, the ecumenical council by human convocation also stands under the special protection of the Holy Spirit promised to the Church. The ecumenical council by human convocation as the special representation of the ecumenical council by divine convocation also derives its special ecumenical *authority* from this assistance from the Holy Spirit. From this as a point of departure the usage of the *and* —though it does not follow as a matter of course—may be ventured. According to Acts (15:28) it was daringly used in the decree of the Council of the Apostles and continued to illumine the later ecumenical councils and their decrees: "For the Holy Spirit and we have decided to . . ." As an assembly gathered *in the Holy Spirit*, an ecumenical council by human convocation is a representation of the *holy* Church. But is it also a representation of the apostolic Church? We must inquire into this more closely later. Before doing that we must first turn our attention to another decisive matter.

[29] P. Nautin, *Je crois a l'Esprit Saint dans la Sainte Église pour la résurrection de la chair. Étude sur l'histoire et la théologie du symbole* (Paris 1947).

IV

CREDIBLE OR NON-CREDIBLE* REPRESENTATION?

FOR an ecumenical council by human convocation the representation of the one, holy, Catholic Church is not only a spiritual gift, but also a task, and indeed a difficult one. Ecumenical councils were never merely innocuous, periodic ecclesiastical general assemblies held in times of peace and tranquillity. They were always gatherings of the Church held in times of unrest and of danger from without and within. In each case the hour of the ecumenical council struck whenever the conscience of the Church was alarmed by heresies or by still-unmastered historical tasks challenging the whole Church to a decision. In such times of unrest, of gathering storm and of new decisions, much will depend upon whether the representation of the one, holy, Catholic Church is an event hastily contrived in some way or other, or a good, that is, a truly convincing event for people in and outside this Church.

The following applies even to the ecumenical council by divine convocation: Faced with doubting, questioning people in search of concrete assurances it is not enough to demonstrate *abstractly* that the Church with her structural elements is a *"signum levatum in nationes."*[1] It does not suffice to point out abstractly the marks (*notae*) of the Church, her unity, holiness, catholicity, and apostolicity, first of all as the necessary attributes of the true Church of Christ, and then as actually given in the present-day Catholic Church. "Abstract" here means, to disregard all that which in the concrete reality of the Church's life, or even of the defects in that life, hides the *signum levatum* and obscures and distorts the unity, holiness, catholicity, and apostolicity. It means, therefore, to disregard all that can make her unity, holiness, catholicity, and apostolicity unconvincing, so that the required *obsequium rationi consentaneum*[2] the concrete case of the concrete individual, is not concretely possible or is made very difficult. Cardinal Newman pointed out very clearly

---

*The word "credible" is used here to render the author's word "glaubwurdig." But the German adjective also conveys the meaning "authentic" in the sense that the event it describes is seen to be genuinely convincing—or not.

[1] *Concilium Vaticanum*, Const. de fide catholica, chap. 3. Denz. 1794.

[2] *Ibid.* Denz. 1790.

the Church's status of not being *of* the world as a being *in* the world has a dark, worldly side and that this dark, worldly side is turned outwards:

"Now, the true account of this is, that the Church so far from being literally, and in fact, separate from the wicked world, is within it. The Church is a body, gathered together in the world, and in a process of separation from it. The world's power, alas! is over the Church, because the Church has gone forth into the world to save the world. All Christians are in the world, and of the world, so far as sin has dominion over them; and not even the best of us is clean every whit from sin. Though then, in our idea of the two, and in their principles, and in their future prospects, the Church is one thing, and the world is another, yet in present matter of fact, the Church is of the world, not separate from it; for the grace of God has but possession even of religious men, and the best that can be said of us is that we have two sides, a light side and a dark, and that the dark happens to be outermost. Thus we form part of the world to each other, though we be 'not of the world.' "[3]

"That the world may believe" (Jn. 17:21) depends entirely upon whether the Church presents her unity, holiness, catholicity, and apostolicity *credibly* in accordance with this prayer of our Lord. Credible here does not mean without any shadows; this is impossible in the Church composed of human beings and indeed sinful human beings. Credible does mean, however, that the light must be so bright and strong that darkness appears as something secondary, inessential, not as the authentic nature but as the dark flecks on the luminous essence of the Church during this time of pilgrimage. "Unity, holiness, catholicity, and apostolicity are definitive, essential features of the Church. But all four of them are only imperfectly realized here on earth. They are gifts bequeathed to the Church, but in her eschatological orientation they are also *tasks* to be carried out."[4]

At ecumenical councils by human convocation, too, "that the world may believe" depends entirely upon whether or not the unity, holiness, catholicity, and apostolicity of the ecumenical council by divine convocation is *credibly* depicted and represented to people inside and outside the Church. The bitter words of Gregory of Nazianzus, bishop and doctor of the Church, quoted by Martin Luther in his tract "On the Councils and the Churches,"[5] should still be a warning to us: "To tell the truth, I am in favour of avoiding any

[3] J. H. Newman, *Parochial and Plain Sermons*, London, 1875, Vol. 7, 3, pp. 35–6.

[4] J. L. Witte, "Die Katholizität der Kirche," in *Gregorianum* 47 (1961) 235.

[5] M. Luther, "On the Councils and the Churches": *WA* 50, 604.

council of bishops since I have never yet experienced a felicitous conclusion to any of them, nor even the abolition of abuses, on the contrary, always ambition or wrangles over procedure. . . ."[6]

1. THE ONE CHURCH

The *one* Church would be represented *non-credibly* if the ecumenical council by human convocation were only an external (perhaps very magnificent and impressive) manifestation of unity, after the manner, say, of a well-organized congress of a totalitarian political party, where the congress leadership from the very outset is able, by a variety of methods and devices, to reduce free initiative to the minimum and to manipulate the agenda and the executive leadership, and where the uncritical, enthusiastic *placet* to the plans of the leader is the sign of loyalty. The one Church is *credibly* represented when the unity at an ecumenical council is a true inner unity of faith and charity, namely a unity in a unifying Holy Spirit at work in the unanimity of the free decision of all. Thus the true tradition of the universal Church, the *sensus Ecclesiae*, is expressed and the council bequeaths to the Church, not disputes and divisions, but peace in freedom.

The unity of the Church is not a natural dimension; it is naturalistically misunderstood if it is switched wholly to externals (Church language, canon law, administration, etc.).[7] The unity of the Church is primarily a *spiritual* dimension: "The unity of the *Spirit* in the bond of peace: one body and one Spirit, even as you were called in one hope of your calling; one Lord, one faith, one Baptism; one God and Father of all, who is above all, and throughout all, and in us all" (Eph. 4:3–6). Or as Heinrich Schlier has comprehensively described the unity of the Church according to St. Paul: "This unity is the effect and hence also the reflection of the unifying unity of God in Jesus Christ by virtue of the Holy Spirit. It rests upon the redemptive nature and will of God. But it develops out of the means and gifts of salvation which God utilizes in Jesus Christ through the Holy Spirit which are likewise of an essential unity; out of the one Word and Sacrament effecting unity, the one office protecting and fostering unity, the one charism animating and nourishing it. This is how the

---

[6] Gregory of Nazianzus, *Ep. 130 ad Procopium; PG* 37, 225.

[7] For problems concerning the unity of the Church, cf. recently: H. Volk, "Einheit als theologisches Problem," in *Münchener theologische Zeitschrift 12* (1961) 1–13, esp. 11–13; H. Volk, *Die Einheit der Kirche und die Spaltung der Christenheit* (Münster i. W. 1961); both articles are reprinted in Volk's symposium, *Gott alles in allem* (Mainz 1961).

unity of the Church proves to be a unity that is concrete and histo-rical and not merely an ideal, a current not a future unity: a given unity of the one people of God which is the one Body of Christ and the Temple of the Holy Spirit, and not a unity that is yet to be estab-lished. This unity is perceived and preserved in the experience of faith in and our knowledge of this, in the experience of hope and charity, and first and last of humility. As experienced, it is a unity of the heart."[8]

It is fitting that the inner spiritual unity of the Church should be manifested outwardly. A manifestation of this kind is not sheer externalization: "The justified tendency to make the supernaturally grounded unity of the Church visible should not lead to ranking the importance of uniformity in the natural sphere alongside the spiritual principles of the unity of the Church. The sign of unity could then become the principle of unity. There is even the danger of a type of naturalism, if there is no reliance on the strength of spiritual principles to effect unification, and stress is laid upon too many external signs of unity, as though the unity of the Church depended upon them. Here some re-examinations may be necessary, as we do not wish to pass off or consider as a principle of unity something that is but a variable phenomenon of unity."[9]

The great and difficult task facing an ecumenical council by human convocation is the representation—the credible representation—of this not merely external but deeply grounded inner-spiritual unity, this unity of the Church in Spirit. The consensus of the Church should be expressed at a council, that is, the common feeling, the common thinking, and the common agreement of the whole Church. This common feeling, thought, and agreement is expressed at an ecumenical council by human convocation through concord and through striving for the greatest possible *unanimity*[10] in conciliar decisions. An ecumenical council is not a democratic parliament in which it is merely a matter of producing a majority, even a slim one, for or against a decision. Rather, an ecumenical council is the repre-sentation of the Church and of her unity, which can be credibly

[8] H. Schlier, "Die Einheit der Kirche nach dem Apostel Paulus," in: M. Roesle and O. Cullmann, *Begegnung der Christen* (Stuttgart–Frankfurt a. M. 1959) 112f.

[9] H. Volk. *Die Einheit der Kirche und die Spaltung der Christenheit* (Münster i. W. 1961) 25.

[10] We use the term "greatest possible" because a council would otherwise be condemned to the indecision of a former Polish Sejm or achieve the kind of coercive unanimity characteristic of totalitarian parliaments. The latter is death to unity within responsible freedom and would indeed undermine the credibility of the council.

expressed only in the unanimity of decisions effected by the Spirit. It is not in the large "fraction" that the Holy Spirit of unity manifests His presence but in the concord of all.

The early Church was quite aware of the importance of the unanimity of conciliar decision. No feature is mentioned so consistently and in so many ways in the records of the synods as unanimity. The records always point out that the decision was adopted by all those present: *omnes uno consenu, de consensu communi, quid decrevimus communi consilio, de communi conlatione, universi iudicavimus.*[11] This was not an empty formula; this frequently attested fact was also expressly raised as a demand: "For this is the true doctrine as the Fathers have transmitted it, and this is in truth the sign of teachers: to agree with one another and not to quarrel either with each other or with the Fathers."[12]

Unfortunately, this was obviously not the case. The history of synods show that there were many attempts, either on the part of secular authorities or on the part of one of the parties present, to force a decision by political or other dubious means. For the Fathers, however, such an enforced unanimity was not considered genuine and such synods were not true synods. The synodal letter quoted by Athanasius of the synod of Alexandria in 338 repudiates the synod held at Tyros in 335 for the following reasons: "What kind of an episcopal synod was that then? Was it an assembly that was based upon truth? Were not most of them hostile towards us? ... How did such persons want to hold a synod against us? How did they really dare to call such a thing a synod when a state official was in charge of it, an overseer was present, and a secretary ushered us in instead of deacons of the Church? The former began to shout, but those present were silent, or rather they submitted to the state officials."[13] In contradistinction to this, the right to the free expression of opinion frequently guaranteed: ". . . Superest ut de hac ipsa re singuli quid sentiamus proferamus neminem iudicantes aut a iure communicationis aliquem si diversum senserit amoventes."[14] Unanimity is demanded, but a unanimity that emerges as a result of free discussion:

---

[11] M. Goemans, *Het algemeen concile in de vierde eeuw* (Nijmegen–Utrecht) 23, 157–158, 181, 238. In Greek the following expressions are used: ὁμολογεῖν, ὁμονοεῖν, ὁμοφωνεῖν, συμφωνεῖν; ἡ συμφωνία; ἡ σύνοδος ὁμοφωνοῦσα; κοινῇ γνώμῃ; ἐκ κοινῆς γνώμης; μιᾷ γνώμῃ; παμψήφει; πάσαις ψήφοις, κοινὴ ψῆφος; διὰ ὁμοψύχου καὶ ὁμόφρονος συνέσεως; πάντων συνθεμένων; σύμφωνον ψῆφον ἐξενεγκόντες; συναινούντων πάντων καὶ εἰς ταὐτὸν συνιόντων.

[12] Athanasius, *Epistola de decretis Nicaenae synodi* 4; *PG* 25, 429.

[13] Athanasius, *Apologia contra Arianos* 8; *PG* 25, 261–264.

[14] Cyprian, "Sententiae episcoporum de haereticis baptizandis," *CSEL* III/1, 435–436.

"May this be said with regard to the statement of faith with which indeed we all agree, but not without testing it. Rather, only after we had compared our opinions on the matter."[15]

Constantine doubtless expressed this view of the Council of Nicaea when he wrote that the judgment of God, the Holy Spirit, is operative in the unanimous decision of a council: "More than three hundred bishops, highly estimable for their wisdom and acumen, affirmed the one and same faith which alone is in accord with the perfect truth of the divine law. Let us, then, accept the verdict that the Almighty ruler of the universe bestows. . . . That which the three hundred bishops have deemed to be correct is not different from the judgment of God, for the very reason that the Holy Spirit dwells in the mind of such great men and brings the divine will to light. Therefore let there be no doubt. . . ."[16] This was also the meaning expressed by the customary acclamations at the early councils, mentioned sparingly at the Council of Ephesus, but with great frequency at the Council of Chalcedon and later councils.[17]

Thus Y. Congar is backed by the old tradition of the Catholic Church when he asserts: "It is not the law of the majority but unanimity which counts at a council. Naturally voting takes place at councils, too, because no other means of expression have yet been discovered, just as the only way we can test a pupil's knowledge is to let him take an examination. But this voting at a council is only a means for achieving unanimity; by means of a majority the true mind and directive of the Church as such is determined so that perhaps those few who had not yet perceived it could now—after it had been interpreted and determined—recognize it as a law binding upon all. *Hence a council is not the sum total of the individual votes, but the totality of the consciousness of the Church.* As in the first days, its ideal is *in unum convenire* (St. Cyprian, *epist.* 55, 6, 1), namely, unanimity. When the bishops affixed their signatures to the decisions with *Consensi et subscripsi*, they did not so much mean to say, 'I

[15] Eusebius, *Epistola ad Caesarienses* 8; *PG* 20, 1541.

[16] Socrates, *Hist. Eccl.* I, 9; *PG* 67, 85.

[17] P.-Th. Camelot, "Les Conciles oecuméniques des IVᵉ et Vᵉ siécles," in *Le concile et les conciles* (Paris 1960) 65f: "This presence, indeed this inspiration of the Holy Spirit, to the Council was manifested in the loud and repeated acclamations with which the bishops proclaimed their faith, acclaiming Celestine, Cyril or Leo, Theodore or Martin. They appeared like a manifestation of the Holy Spirit who is in them. The louder and the more unanimous the acclamations, the more does one believe in the presence and in the action of the Holy Spirit." Cf. Th. Klauser, "Akklamation," in *Reallexikon für Antike und Christentum* (Stuttgart 1950) I, 216–233, esp. 225–227; Y. Congar, "Conclusion," in *Le concile et les conciles* (Paris 1960) 313.

am in agreement' as 'I share in the consensus, that is, I enter into the unanimity.' "[18]

Seldom will conciliar unanimity be reached without great effort. In most cases it must be laboriously achieved: in many discussions and talks, in earnest negotiations, and often in lively, exasperating arguments which take place prior to, during, and sometimes even after a council. This is not solely because the human—all-too-human—factor of *quot capita tot sensus* can make it difficult to reach a *consensus ecclesiae* in a council by human convocation. Apart from all individual peculiarities, individual attitudes, and individual actions, the antagonisms of theological schools, of national traditions, and of the different interests pursued by ecclesiastical offices—all play a part at councils by human as well as by divine convocation. How much theological, philosophical, geographical, cultural, political, and temperamental dissension there has been in the long history of councils! The dissension between the Alexandrians and Antiochians, Easterners and Westerners, between Rome and Byzantium, between partisans of the popes and of the emperors, curialists and bishops, Italians and Germans, Dominicans and Franciscans, Thomists and Scotists, Gallicans and Ultramontanists! Only the universally persistent *sentire* in *Ecclesia* (thus reads the famous phrase of Ignatius Loyola which is much more profound and correct than *sentire* cum *Ecclesia*) in each case, and against all opposition, led to an harmonious con-sensus of the Church. This *sentire* in *Ecclesia* is not reconcilable with either a non-ecclesiastical *sentire* contra *Ecclesiam*, or an heretical *sentire* extra *Ecclesiam*, still less with an absolutist-totalitarian *sentire* supra *Ecclesiam*.

The harmonious consensus of the Church was not always achieved as perfectly and as purely, and hence as convincingly as one might have wished. Naturally no one who reckons with a council by human convocation will expect mathematical unanimity; two bishops refused to affix their signatures even at the first ecumenical council. But even the moral unanimity which was striven for was often seriously called into question by the stubborn and arbitrary party intrigues in which dissenting groups were forced to give way, to the impairment of unanimity, thus conjuring up the danger of a schism. "Truth is reached in any community by means of an exchange of

[18] Y. Congar, "Die Konzilien im Leben der Kirche," in *Una Sancta* 14 (1959) 161f; on the meaning of the term "unanimity" at the pre-Nicene councils, cf. H. Marot, "Conciles anténicéens et conciles oecuméniques," in *Le concile et les conciles* (Paris 1960) 38–43; P.-Th. Camelot, "Les Conciles oecuméniques des IVe et Ve siécles," *loc. cit.* 54, 65; H. S. Alivisatos, "Les Conciles oecuméniques V, VIe, VIIe et VIIIe siècles, *loc. cit.* 115.

opinions, by arguments for and against, that is, by means of an intellectual struggle. At the councils, as in any other place where men contend with one another for the truth, fallen human nature exacts its toll: the former, that is the struggle, is ordained by God, the latter He permits. Opinions may differ about the methods used by St. Cyril at Ephesus or by Innocent IV at the Second Council of Lyons, without the legality of these two councils being called in question. The toll paid by human nature in the councils is the price which the visible Church has to pay for being in the midst of the human race."[19]

The dangers to unanimity here referred to must not be minimized. For harmony had been sought through moral unanimity not only at the ancient councils but also at the general synods of the Middle Ages. To forestall the formation of an Italian majority at the ecumenical Council of Constance, voting was done not only by nations, instead of by heads, but there was a simultaneous fostering of the unanimity of the nations themselves.[20] At the Council of Trent, Pius IV stressed that in the handling of important questions of dogma "he wished to define only that which had been decided by the unanimous consensus of the Church Fathers." This regulation was cited at the First Vatican Council by the many bishops (among them Hefele, the highly competent conciliar historian) who protested vigorously against using a simple majority vote for changing the agenda.[21] They considered this point of such importance that they declared that if this regulation was not observed "their conscience would be weighed down with an intolerable burden, and that they must fear that the character of the Council would be called into question and its authority undermined, as though it were lacking in

---

[19] H. Jedin, *Ecumenical Councils of the Catholic Church* (New York, 1960) 234–235.

[20] C. J. von Hefele, *Konziliengeschichte* (Freiburg i. Br. ²1874) VII, 83: "On the same day, i.e. February 7th, a much more important question was raised, namely whether one was to vote singly or by nations. Half of the votes were those of Italian prelates and doctors; to curb their predominance it was decided to vote by nations contrary to the will of the Pope and contrary to previous usage. All present were divided into four nations: the Italian, the German (including the Poles), the French and the English. To each nation a specific number of deputies —clerics and laymen—were assigned together with the procurators and notaries. Each nation was headed by a president, changed each month. Each nation met separately to discuss those matters that were to be brought before the council. The decisions arrived at were communicated to the other nations in order to forestall possible remonstrations. If the nations agreed on a specific issue a general congregation of the four nations was held. If the point at issue passed that instance also, it was brought before the next general session, for confirmation by the council."

[21] Butler, *Vatican Council 1869–1870* (Westminster, Md. 1962).

freedom." Characteristically, the matter was also never settled up to the premature break-up of the Council. There is obviously now no question of assailing the legitimacy of the decisions of the First Vatican Council. Moral unanimity, which in emergencies can also be achieved through abstention and subsequent agreement,[22] was nevertheless reached—albeit belatedly—on the question of papal infallibility.[23] As little as calm, objective judgment can approve all Cyril's methods at the Council of Ephesus, likewise a calm, objective judgment cannot approve of all the methods employed by the partisans of infallibility against the minority faction: restriction of the right of proposal to the pope, the complete exclusion of minority factions from the Deputation on Faith, the abnormal Italian over-representation,[24] the extreme partisanship of Pius IX in contrast to his initially confirmed non-partisanship, etc.[25]

Obviously moral unanimity by its very nature (as is likewise the case with *certitudo moralis*, for instance, a concept which is indispensable in moral theology) is not an *exact*, that is, a *mathematically* ascertainable and applicable *positive* norm. It cannot be mathematically proved in each case, since with a single nay-vote moral unanimity ceases. Nevertheless, it is at least a highly important *negative* criterion. It cannot be claimed, at least in the present-day constitutional set-up of the Church, that the opposition of a minority, perhaps even a considerable one, can call the *legal* authority of

[22] It is not meant to imply that the decisions did so precisely *because* they regarded them as binding. What is implied is that the voters have a moral duty, an opportunity to serve in all seriousness the cause of moral unity.

[23] R. Aubert, *Le pontificat de Pie IX* (*Histoire de l'Église*, compiled by Fliche and Martin, vol. 21 (Paris 1952)) 361: "Even if the procedure followed by the Council had been illegal, as some believe, it must at least be recognized that the assertion of papal infallibility had been ratified in Rome itself by a notable fraction of the episcopate and that, by the addition of individual expressions of support which followed later, rapid progress was made towards moral unanimity."

[24] R. Aubert, *Le pontificat de Pie IX* (*Histoire de l'Église*, compiled by Fliche and Martin, vol. 21 (Paris 1952)) 324: "Despite the undeniably ecumenical character of the assembly, the place held by the Italians constituted an anomaly that was often pointed out. This was the result of historical circumstances that had increased the dioceses in southern and central Italy and had given the Italians a preponderant place in the Curia. Not only did the Italian prelates by themselves constitute 40 per cent of the European episcopate, but two-thirds of the consultants and all the secretaries were Italians, as were all the presidents of the commissions. Of the forty-eight persons who performed official functions at the Council, only five were foreigners. Aware of this difficulty, the pope had invited the learned Austrian canonist and historian, Fessler, to be secretary and Cardinal von Reisach to be the first president of the Council. Unfortunately, the latter died a few days after the opening of the Council and thereafter the presidencies all continued to be exercised by Italians. . . ."

[25] Cf. Butler, *op cit.*

council decisions into question. But the entire question is not yet resolved by this indirect juridical consideration. An answer must be given to the question: What are the *moral* obligations of the Council Fathers in this respect? This is why the principle of moral unanimity is important. Through this principle at any rate it can be established that in a particular case it is certainly *not* possible any longer to speak in a *true* sense of unanimity.[26] Under certain circumstances this may be of crucial importance. It is after all also a question of whether the unity and unanimity of the Church is *credibly* expressed by a council. Such is not the case when the numerical majority overruns an essential minority of individual Churches (which is something decisively different from an heretical or schismatic sect which is practically written off before a council and which in any case must be excluded from it) against their express will, thereby calling the genuine *consensus Ecclesiae* into question. In cases of this kind it would be fitting that the majority—in accordance with Pius IV's rule, which was often successfully applied at the Council of Trent—refrain from overpowering the minority for the sake of the unity and unanimity of the Church.[27] Only thus can the danger of schism be avoided. We owe it entirely to the loyal and utter devotion to the Church of the minority bishops at the First Vatican Council that the regrettable schisms that followed from the definition of infallibility did not spread further. One could indeed ask oneself whether a less partisan and more understanding and harmonious procedure might not have prevented any schismatic development.

". . . Unanimity must come sooner or later. Should it not be

[26] To illustrate it with a simple example: It is not possible to compute with mathematical exactness the loss of which particular hair constitutes the beginning of baldness. One can, however, ascertain negatively when it is no longer possible to speak of "a shock of hair," and when one must rather apply the term "baldness."

[27] R. Aubert says of the "minority" at the First Vatican Council that, from the beginning, took a stand against a conciliar discussion of infallibility and was in favour of the status quo: "The five documents were signed by 136 persons and those who had sparked the opposition were very satisfied with the result. Obviously they were only a minority, no one doubted this, but one that represented 20 per cent of the Council and that drew attention to itself because of the scholarly fame of many of its members and because of the importance of the dioceses represented: practically all of Austria-Hungary, whose influence was still quite considerable in Rome, a notable part of the French episcopate, all the great sees of Germany, many important archbishops of America and Italy, and three Eastern Patriarchs. Given these conditions, could not one hope that Pius IX would follow the example of Pius IV, who had instructed his legates at Trent to withdraw proposals that would engender frictions in the discussions?" (*Le pontificat de Pie IX* (Paris 1952) 332f.).

achieved, it would then be a sign that the council does not represent the ecumenical Church in her fullness. Unanimity and fellowship are the work of the Holy Spirit (see II Cor. 13:13, *koinonia*). In order to grasp the deeper meaning of councils we must take into consideration the Holy Spirit as the person deciding. Councils always call themselves assemblies in the Holy Spirit at which Christ invisibly presides (sometimes this presence of Christ is concretely represented by a picture of Christ, or better still by Holy Scripture, which lies open on an altar). The passage in Matthew (18:20), which holds out the promise of the presence of the Lord wherever the Church is gathered in harmony and brotherhood, is always quoted."[28] Thus time and again what the first Christian testimony states about the councils of the Church must always be realized anew: ". . . the representation of the whole of Christendom is celebrated with great veneration. How worthy of a guiding faith that this council be gathered from all places for Christ! Behold, how good and joyful it is when brethren dwell together!"[29]

2. THE CATHOLIC CHURCH

The *Catholic* Church would not be credibly represented if at the ecumenical council by human convocation all the individual Churches with their specific histories and their traditions, with their problems and needs, their objections and concerns, their wishes and demands, did not really find expression. Or if one particular Church in a totalitarian fashion were to force her special tradition, her special doctrine, her special discipline upon the others. The Catholic Church is credibly represented when, on the one hand, all individual Churches can integrate their particularity in the decisions of a council as a whole. The Church is credibly represented if the unity of a council and of its decisions encompasses gratefully the multiplicity of individual opinions in an authentic biblical *koinonia*, in short, a *koinonia* that does not consist merely of a centralist orientation of everyone towards a visible organization centre, but is above all a brotherly communion with each other in the spirit of the exalted Lord of the Church. On the other hand, the Church is represented credibly if in each and every thing the council does, it takes into consideration not only these represented in it, but also those who do not take part—although they are baptized Christians and their absence is in some sense the fault of the Catholic Church.

[28] Y. Congar, "Die Konzilien im Leben der Kirche," in *Una Sancta* 14 (1955) 162.
[29] Tertullian, *De paenitentia* 13, 6–7; *CC* II, 1272.

Variety within the Church is not an unavoidable evil. God Himself is not an inflexible monotone unit, but the living Trinity. Further, He did not will to create *one* creature but a wonderful variety of created beings who are held together in Christ (Col. 1:16ff). The multitude of creatures fallen away from the union with God has again been joined together within the same Christ (Eph. 1:10). They were to become fruitful in the Church and to make known the manifold Wisdom of God (Eph. 3:10) until the end when God will be all in all (I Cor. 15:28). In the Church there is *one* Spirit, but many gifts, *one* word of God, but many languages, *one* body, but many members, *one* people of God, but many nations. Variety in the Church is a gift of God. The Church surrounded, endowed with variety (cf. Ps. 44:10): since the Middle Ages these words have been far too superficially understood as the variety of the virtues, of the Sacraments, of the grades of hierarchy. But the ancient Church gave these words a deeper meaning in terms of the variety of the individual churches, peoples, rites, and languages.[1]

[1] W. de Vries, *Wegbereitung zur Einheit der Christen aus ostkirchlicher Sicht* (Recklinghausen 1961) 5–7: "This may sound like a paradox: the greatest obstacle to reunification is precisely the high degree of homogeneity achieved by the Western Catholic Church; or rather, not the homogeneity in itself—which might be necessary for a Church within an essentially homogeneous culture area—but the ideal of unity for the world Catholic Church which we have created on the basis of the existing conditions of Western Catholicism. The unitary Mass, for example, is hailed as an ideal; if possible, sung to the same choral music. Latin, as a matter of course, is regarded as *the* language of the Catholic Church. If attention is called to the fact that in Catholic Churches of Eastern rites native languages are used, the argument is then limited to include only the whole Latin Church. The very fact that we speak of the 'whole Church' as a matter of course, without taking into account the diversity which is very much part of the real universal Church, indicates that we lack the right breadth of view with regard to catholicity; it indicates that we are not aware of the fact that a worldwide Church must be capable of including the variety and manifoldness of all peoples who are to find a spiritual home in this Church. If we were to impose on all those many Christians who for hundreds of years have followed their own ways—who have developed their own specific forms of worship, their own religious traditions, their own expressions of piety; who within the context of their intellectual tradition have given Christian truth their own linguistic form—if we were to impose upon all of these Christians Western Catholicism as we have developed it—including its choral music, its incense, and the form and colour of its liturgical garb—as the only true Catholicism, we would then bar the way to the true Church of God, necessary for salvation. In such a case we might convert individuals to the Catholic Church; but we would have to renounce the unification of separated communities. We should therefore rather ask what is essential for the unity of the Church; what is it that all who belong to the Church of Christ *must* agree upon; and what are the matters of secondary or purely ornamental importance." With regard to the catholicity of the Church, cf.: H. de Lubac, *Catholicism* (London and New York 1958); Y. de Montcheuil, *Aspects de l'Église* (Paris 1949) 55–64; Y. Congar, *Esquisses du mystère de l'Église* (Paris

This catholic manifoldness, however, is not only a gift of God, but it is also—and precisely for this reason—*the task of the Church*. This catholic manifoldness should not be neglected, still less throttled (either by legal or illegal means!) but rather preserved and protected. Indeed, it should be *fostered* and *developed* (with all legal means) with all the means available within the framework of catholic unity. "This pluralism is thus not simply a feature which is later supplanted by unity, but is something which is to remain and to which we should aspire. And obviously not only in the sense that the Church is composed of many members numerically distinct from each other. The members are to be qualitatively distinct, and not merely through characteristics not pertinent to their membership as such, but also through those which are important in and for the Church. The Church is to be constituted not simply of many members but of qualitatively different members. The variety is not only an irreducible fact but something to be cherished. . . . This legitimate and necessary pluralism in the Church is not only a pluralism of the individual members, but also of the larger groups, of local Churches, of countries and peoples, especially since these too, as such, have a 'vocation' to the light of the Gospel."[2]

The development of a genuine catholicity has become especially pressing at this fateful historical hour: (1) The national awakening of the peoples of Asia and Africa and the failure of the Christian Mission, jubilantly acclaimed by non-Christians, in China, India, Japan, and also in parts of Africa, especially among the Moslems,[3]

---

[2] 1953) 117–127; H. Fries, "Aspekte der Kirche heute," in *Kirche und Überlieferung*, ed. J. Betz and H. Fries (Freiburg-Basle–Vienna 1960) 288–310, esp. 299–301; J. L. Witte, "Die Katholizität der Kirche. Eine neue Interpretation nach alter Tradition," in: *Gregorianum* 42 (1961) 193–241 (further recent literature on catholicity on page 194f).

[2] K. Rahner and J. Ratzinger, *The Episcopate and the Primacy* (London 1962) 105–106.

[3] This rejoicing can be detected, for example, in the article on missions in the *Great Soviet Encyclopedia* (1958). One should not be too much impressed by the numbers of converts if compared to the pagans their numbers seem ridiculously small. One should calmly take notice of what the Indian K. M. Panikkar has observed in his well-known book *Asia and the Rule of the West* (Zürich 1958): "In the meantime many of the generous supporters of mission funds in Europe and America have become aware of the fact that the results achieved with their money do not correspond to their expectations and that the assault upon the religions of the Far East has failed" (p. 402).—"The greatest efforts were made in the case of China which also seemed to hold the greatest promise. It was in China where the missionary endeavours failed almost completely. There are still Chinese who call themselves Christians, but European missionary activity has ceased to exist. The Christian Church also continues to exist in India as it has since the days of doubting Thomas but, apart from the fields of medicine and educational

makes it unlikely that these peoples will ever be converted to a centrally directed Western, Latin, unified Church. Even the emerging world-civilization (which in any case will not be Western, Latin, or Roman in character) will not simply eradicate racial, cultural, or religious peculiarities, but will in some respects even reinforce them. The closer drawing together of culture areas promotes the awareness of differences and up to now characteristically it has not led to the emergence of a single universal language.[4] (2) The centuries-old development of an autonomous Christianity outside the organized Catholic Church, namely the Orthodox Christianity of the East and the Protestant Christianity of the West, which arose out of the Church schism, with all their many Christian values of a clearly evolved faith, of piety, of theology, and the like, cannot be dismissed as illegitimate (no matter how one may judge the doctrinal or institutional shortcomings of this Christianity). It would not only be unreasonable from the viewpoint of ecclesiastical policy but fundamentally untenable theologically if, in order to bring about a reunion of Orthodox and Protestant Christians, they should be called upon to surrender their own sound Christian values (which frequently derive from a deepened understanding of Scripture and of the oldest traditions) while declaring that the Catholic Church is not open to these additional riches.[5]

"It is now a question of realizing what the manifestation of catholicity means in the world of today, and to have the courage to repent and to admit what is still lacking. With respect to the object

---

missionary work, is of no importance. In Japan, Siam, and Burma the hopes of Christian missionaries have become slim since the rise of nationalism and the Eastern religions" (p. 406).—Cf. H. Küng "Theologische Neu-orientierungen in der Weltmission," in *Priester und Mission* (Aachen 1960) 111–130.

[4] H. Volk, *Die Einheit der Kirche und die Spaltung der Christenheit* (Münster i. W. 1961) 10: "The Church's power to bear witness can at no time be a matter of indifference to us. For the Church's power to bear witness is not overwhelmingly great. Despite great successes in specific missionary areas and despite the devoted work of missionaries, the number of Catholics as compared to the global population has increased only 0·14 per cent between 1880 and 1958."

[5] W. de Vries gives a concrete example: "One might ask whether the rebellion against Rome of the great majority of Germanic peoples was not also ultimately caused by the over strict enforcement of liturgical unity? At any rate, after the break with Rome, these peoples developed their own liturgical forms in their native languages. Will it be possible to disregard all this when a large-scale attempt at reunification of these communities is undertaken? Once it is recognized that liturgical differences are caused by differences in national traditions and the right conclusions are drawn from this, it will be necessary to leave open the question of possibly recognizing something that has developed in the soil and in the particular tradition of these peoples, even though outside the Catholic Church" (12f).

of catholicity (Church and mankind as a concrete community of human beings) the present hour of decision seems to call for the following: (1) The Church must present herself as the truly universal Church which mysteriously encompasses other Christian 'churches' and stands wide open to all people—she should not appear as merely exclusive and withdrawn into the ghetto. (2) The Church must show herself as the Church which respects all languages, traditions, and spiritual experiences in the forms peculiar to each of the different nations. These are indeed the objects of the Church's catholicity-minded mission activity, that is, to seek not 'souls' but communities of concrete human beings, consisting of body and soul."[6]

The great and difficult task of an ecumenical council by human convocation is that of representing (allowing for variety both from within and without) the authentic catholicity of the ecumenical council by divine convocation, which is the Church, and also to represent it credibly. The very name "ecumenical council" lays down the claim and the task of such a council to present credibly the "ecumenicity" of the Catholic Church. Ecumenical (which means the inhabited earth, that which concerns the whole globe) and "catholic" (which means universal, worldwide or universally valid), are closely related words, owing to their original meaning as well as to their Christian usage. In the first millennium especially, "ecumenical" council and "catholic" Church were closely linked concepts. In this context ecumenical means "belonging to the Church as a whole or representing her"; hence it also means "possessing universal eclesiastical validity."[7]

The recognition of a council by the individual churches of the Catholic Church was a matter of great importance ever since the first ecumenical Council of Nicaea. Athanasius, the champion of the Nicene Creed, among others,[8] repeatedly cites this fact of catho-

[6] J. L. Witte, "Die Katholizität der Kirche. Eine neue Interpretation nach alter Tradition," in *Gregorianum* 42 (1961) 239.

[7] For the complex meaning of the term "ecumenical" or "catholic," cf. W. A. Visser t' Hooft, *The Meaning of Ecumenical* (London 1953); by the same author "Ecumenical," in *RGG* IV, 1569f (Tübingen 1960); E. Kinder, "Der Gebrauch des Begriffs 'ökumenisch' im älteren Luthertum," in *Kerygma und Dogma* 1 (1955) 180–207; E. Fascher, "Ökumenisch und katholisch. Zur Geschichte zweier, heute viel gebrauchter Begriffe," in *Theologische Literaturzeitung* 85 (1960) 7–20; J. L. Witte, "Die Katholizität der Kirche," in *Gregorianum* 42 (1961) 224–225; H. van der Linde, *Wat is oecumenisch? Een onderzoek naar de betekenis von de woorden oecumene en oecumenisch* (Roermond-Maaseik 1961).

[8] It applies already to the pre-Nicene councils that: "A first point that our texts dwell upon is the great number of bishops present in the councils. It can be stated that, and for the whole ante-Nicene tradition, a council's authority is in direct proportion to the number of participants." H. Marot, "Conciles anténicéens et conciles oecuméniques," in *Le concile et les conciles* (Paris 1960) 37.

licity against his opponents: "At that time the whole *oikumene* had agreed to it (the Nicene Creed) and now that many synods are meeting, everyone from Dalmatia, Dardanelles, Macedonia, Epirus, from Greece, Crete and the other islands, from all of Egypt and Libya and most of those from Arabia remember and recognize it."[9] "This (the Nicene Creed) was everywhere recognized and proclaimed by the whole Church."[10] "Know, then, Augustus much beloved by God, that this has been proclaimed since eternity, that the Father's who have come together in Nicaea have professed this very faith and all the Churches all over the world have concurred with it: the Churches in Spain, in Britain and Gaul, the Churches of the whole of Italy, of Dalmatia, Dacia, and Mysias, Macedonia, the whole of Greece and Africa, Sardinia, Cyprus, Crete, Pamphylia, Lycia, Isauria, Egypt, Libya, Pontus, and Cappadocia, the Churches in our proximity and those in the East, save for a few which were Arian-minded. . . . The whole *oikumene* holds to the apostolic faith."[11] Pope Liberius also confirmed: "Cum constiterit omnes in expositum fidei quae inter tantos episcopos apud Nicaeam praesente sanctae memoriae patre tuo confirmata est, universos consensisse."[12]

True, this recognition of ecumenical councils by the individual churches is not to be understood as a kind of subsequent plebiscite on conciliar decrees. Nor can the binding character of conciliar decrees be made dependent *de jure*, as it were, on the agreement of all believers and ecumenical councils therefore be denied the right to make binding decisions in matters of faith. Such is the contention of the doctrine of "Sobornost" as espoused by many Slav theologians (especially Sergij Bulgakov, d. 1944), and which goes back to Alexei Chomjakov (d. 1880).[13]

On the other hand it can hardly be denied—especially in connection with the ecumenical councils of the first millennium, recognized by all Christian denominations—that the crucial factor making for the ecumenicity of an ecumenical council was not in fact a legal act (of the person who summoned the councils or gave them his approbation) but the general recognition (in part only much later) of the whole

[9] Athanasius, *Ep. contra Arionos, ad honoratissimos in Africa episcopos* 1; *PG* 26, 1029.

[10] Athanasius, *Ep. ad. Iovianum Imperatorem* 1; *PG* 26, 816.

[11] Athanasius, *Ep. ad Iovianum Imperatorem* 2; *PG* 26, 816f.

[12] Liberius, *Ep. ad Constantium Imperatorem* 6; *PL* 8, 1354.

[13] Cf. P. Johannes Chrysostomus, "Das ökumenische Konzil und die Orthodoxie," in *Una Sancta* 14 (1959) 177–186; P. Leskovec, "Il Concilio Ecumenico nel pensiero teologico degli Ortodossi," in *La Civiltà Cattolica* III (1960) 140–152; B. Schultze, *Die Glaubenswelt der orthodoxen Kirche* (Salzburg 1961) 149–153.

Church. Thus H. Jedin asserts: "For the first millennium, and even beyond it, the ecumenical character of these assemblies is not decided by the intention of those who convened them, even if they wished them to have that character; in fact, during the whole of this period even papal approval of the decisions does not, from the first, bear the character of a formal confirmation, as was the case with regard to the ecumenical councils of a later period. The recognition of the ecumenical character of the twenty assemblies cannot be traced back to one comprehensive legislative act of the Popes. Their ecumenical character was only established by the theological schools and by actual practice."[14] And H. E. Feine: "The Metropolitans above all were officially invited. Whenever possible they brought their suffragan bishops along. All bishops and their representatives had both the right to vote and to cosign the decisions. Nevertheless, the presence of the patriarchs or their representatives was regarded as indispensable, and their votes were of a decisive importance. The bishop of Rome was regularly represented by legates. However, they were able to assume a leading position only at the Council of Chalcedon in 451 (Leo the Great). Yet at that time they refused to affix their signatures to the documents because of opposition against the so-called Canon 28. In antiquity a papal confirmation of conciliar decisions was unheard of. Imperial confirmation gave them the force of law throughout the whole Empire, and their enforcement was executed with the help of the secular arm. Nevertheless, the decision on the ecumenicity of the Church was subsequently accepted or rejected by the consciousness of the Church as a whole."[15]

Councils that were not originally convoked as ecumenical could later be regarded as such. Thus the second ecumenical council (Constantinople 381), which was the first one to be specifically called "ecumenical," was not convoked as an ecumenical council. It took place without any co-operation on the part of the pope as an Eastern general synod and was first reckoned among ecumenical councils in the Western Church at the time of Gregory I, or from the time of the Lateran synod of 649. Likewise, the fifth ecumenical

[14] H. Jedin, *Ecumenical Councils of the Catholic Church* (New York 1960) 3–4. Cf. for the pre-Nicene councils, H. Marot: "Conciles anténicéens et conciles oecuméniques," in *Le concile et les conciles* (Paris 1960) 39: "From this unanimity within a council, or between several councils, in that which concerns their solemnization, one easily passes over to the support given by the rest of the bishops of a region, and even by the whole of Christendom. There is a certain indistinctness between the two notions. This poses the problem of the approbation, at least implicit, of the decisions of a council by other Christian bodies or certain more important Sees."

[15] H. E. Feine, *Kirchliche Rechtsgeschichte* (Weimar 1950) I, 94.

council (Constantinople 553), which had been convoked by Justinian against the will of Pope Vigilius, was first recognized in the West as late as the seventh century. Similarly, the Frankish Empire hesitated a long time before recognizing the seventh ecumenical council, and so on. Thus P.-Th. Chamelot has correctly described the second ecumenical council as "a kind of *consensus* of the Church which bestows this character after the event to a council which was not ecumenical either in intention or in fact."[16] Even the councils of the smaller synods of the East such as those of Ankara 314, Neo-Caesaria (Pontus) *ca.* 320, Antioch 329(?), Gangra (Paphlagonia) 342, and Laodicae (Phrygia) *ca.* 350, acquired importance in the West by their acceptance.

But the reverse is also true: Councils which were convoked as ecumenical councils could not successfully assert their ecumenical character. This applies to the imperial synods of Sardica, Ephesus II (449), and to the second Trullan Synod as well as to the Western general synods of Arles in 314 and Rome in 341.

In the course of time, however, the first seven ecumenical councils —save by some heretical groups—were recognized by the whole Catholic Church, by the whole Christian *oikumene* of the East and West.[17] Thus the ecumenicity of these councils of the first millennium shines forth with an unbroken authority, in terms of credibility up to the present day. This, unfortunately, cannot be said about any one of the ecumenical councils of the second millennium. The councils of the Middle Ages, in part, were not even planned and conducted as ecumenical councils (for example, the Lateran synods of

---

[16] P.-Th. Camelot, "Les conciles oecuméniques des IVᵉ et Vᵉ sicèles," in *Le concile et les conciles* (Paris 1960) 73.

[17] One should not underestimate the difficulties that arise when an explanation of the process of recognition is attempted. H. Jedin. *Ecumenical Councils of the Catholic Church* (New York 1960) 4 notes: "The process that led to this acceptance has not as yet been studied in detail. . . ." To which E. Schlink adds correctly: "Apart from this the problem of recognition is one of the most difficult problems of history, systematics and canon law. If one looks at the whole history of councils, one discovers that the recognition process has undergone as many changes as the councils themselves. Recognition is, after all, a concept correlated to that of conciliar authority. It is certain that at the councils of the early Church the politico-legal concept and the actual ecclesiastical process of recognition did not overlap. The latter led to far-reaching corrections to the legal decisions of the imperial Church, which the emperors had established by the confirmation and promulgation of synodal decrees. On the basis of these imperial acts conciliar decisions became binding in imperial law for all Churches. Actually, though, a number of these decisions did not stand up in the life of the Church and had to be changed and replaced by later conciliar decisions." "Okumenische Konzilien einst und heute," in *Der kommende Christus und die kirchliche Traditionen* (Göttingen 1961) 247f.

1123, 1139, 1179). Today they are again often referred to as papal general synods in contrast to the ecumenical councils of antiquity. In the Middle Ages the adjectives *generalis* and *universalis* were often used interchangeably in connection with the synods.[18] At any rate only the Western Church attributes an ecumenical character to the ecumenical councils of the second millennium. The Unions of Lyons (1274) and Florence (1439 and 1442) remain mere episodes. This state of affairs became even worse in modern times, after the Reformation. The two ecumenical councils of modern times (Trent and Vatican I) were able to achieve only partial recognition, even within Western Christendom. Hence today we face the sad fact that the Second Vatican Council, proclaimed as "ecumenical," actually has only about half of the Christian *oikumene* behind it. The other half maintains that the ecumenicity of Vatican II is merely an alleged ecumenicity, that half an *oikumene* is not the real *oikumene*. In reality, therefore, it is asserted, this council is not an ecumenical council, but a Roman Catholic council. Thus even within the Protestant ecumenical movement the word "catholic" is deliberately avoided in favour of "ecumenical," so as not to give rise to any association with the Roman Catholic Church. This despite the fact that in itself "catholic" (understood not only statically but dynamically, not only as a safeguarding datum but as a binding obligation) overlaps with the present-day meaning of "ecumenical," an expression used to indicate awareness of the unity of Christendom and the yearning for this.

Whatever can be said about the inner ecumenicity and catholicity of these Roman Catholic councils of modern times—a question whose answer is contained within the framework of the answer to the more comprehensive question concerning the one, true Church and the relation between Catholic and non-Catholic Christendom—from the Catholic side one will seriously have to face the sad reality. Whatever the inner ecumenicity of these Roman Catholic councils may be, and no matter how justified may be their claim to ecumenicity, it certainly is not *universally credible* within Christendom. The other half of Christendom disavows it. Ecumenicity is here understood to mean not only the objective possibility (credibility *in se et de iure*) of recognizing the Catholic Church as the true Church of Christ, and the objectively justified claim of the Church and of her council to ecumenicity. It is a question of *de facto* concrete credibility. But this is absent insofar as the ecumenicity of Catholic councils is not believed in by all Christians. Further one can hardly say that

[18] Cf. Y. Congar, "Conclusion," in *Le concile et les conciles* (Paris 1960) 316.

this ecumenicity could only be deliberately misunderstood. It is just this factual ecumenicity, however, that is of the greatest importance for people outside our Church. Therefore, a council must strive with all its power to achieve it.

Given this situation, the full factual ecumenical credibility of a council cannot be established by theoretical arguments, but only by the reunion of separated Christians. This can be achieved only if a future council should again really represent the whole *oikumene* and thus gain the recognition of the whole *oikumene*. It may take a long, an unbearably long time, before this comes to pass. But what is decisive today is that the first step has been taken in this direction. By the epoch-making fact of orienting the Second Vatican Council towards the goal of reunion, John XXIII not only aroused great hopes; he also greatly strengthened the ecumenical credibility of this council. The crucial contribution to the enhancement of ecumenical credibility must be achieved individually by each council itself. It can do this by trying to be representative of the *oikumene* in the best sense of the word, by truly acting in its place, by focusing attention on both the genuine and good theological, as well as the practical, concerns of the whole *oikumene* and by granting them due consideration at the Council: it can do this by a renewal within the Catholic Church to be effected by a successive realization of the justified demands of the Orthodox, Protestant, Anglican, and even of the Free Churches.

Thus the ecumenical credibility of an ecumenical council by human convocation is dependent upon the continuous unfolding of the catholicity of the Church represented at a council. The Catholic Church, whose very name indicates the catholicity that characterizes her, will lose nothing by its further growth. Rather, she will become more credibly catholic by removing the need for the objections that are raised against her in a most illuminating and tangible way through their incorporation in a renewed and extended catholicity.[19]

The Eastern Churches already united with the Catholic Church act at the council as an indicator, as it were, of the willingness of the Catholic Church to broaden her catholicity and to strengthen the

[19] Cf. Y. de Montcheuil, *Aspects de l'Église* (Paris 1949) 56: "By calling herself catholic, the Church proclaims that she does not accept her actual situation as definitive, that she strives to change it, and that each one of her members is duty-bound to work toward this along with her. To say that the Church is catholic is to say that she is universal by her very essence, that the life which she bears tends to a universal diffusion, that the Church has been instituted for the whole of mankind. Consequently, for as long as the Church does not coincide with mankind, she will strive to surpass what she has already achieved in order to gain that which is still alien to her."

credibility of her ecumenical character. Will these Eastern Churches be listened to and—more than at the First Vatican Council—taken seriously? Will they be regarded as a fully legitimate development of Catholicism *or* only as a (provisionally) tolerated marginal phenomenon, an appendage of the "authentic" Latin Church?[20] Will they be regarded as independent and equal member churches of the one Church acting with relative autonomy (with a different theology, liturgy, spirituality, piety, and church constitution) *or* only as forms ("rites") of a different kind and archaic museum pieces?[21] Will they be regarded as the important (often sadly misunderstood by both sides) representatives of their Eastern sister churches separated from the Catholic Church (partly through the fault of the latter!) *or* as a "Fifth Column" of the Latin Church within the Church of the East under the guise of Oriental "rites"?[22] *Salvis privilegiis omnibus et iuribus eorum* (as the Oriental patriarchs were solemnly promised at the Union of Florence[23]), will they be regarded as a model for a future reunion (also with Protestant Christians!) *or* only as a repository of a catholicity heavily overplayed by Latinity and Romanity?[24]

[20] Patriarch Maximos IV of Antioch, "Der katholische Orient und die christliche Einheit. Unsere Berufung als Werkzeug der Einigung," in *Una Sancta* 16 (1961) 3: "In the opinion of many priests the Eastern Catholic Churches or, as they are more frequently referred to, 'the Oriental rites' represent nothing but a concession on the part of the Holy Roman See to the Eastern Church on grounds of old established traditions. It is seen then as a concession, a privilege, an exception. Since the Eastern Church cannot quite be transformed into a Catholic, i.e. Latin-Catholic, Church, one tolerates rather adroitly that while their members remain 'Orientals,' they are also regarded as Catholics, in a word, second-rate Catholics."

[21] Patriarch Maximos IV, *op cit*. 6: "Those who favour Uniatism really show respect only for the rites of the East. Apart from that, they attempt to wrest the very best away from the Eastern Church. In exchange, something of lesser worth from the West is offered or pressed upon the Eastern Church. The Catholic West, as a whole, as yet has failed sufficiently to realize what should be preserved for the good of the whole Church from the traditions of the Eastern Church; this pertains in particular to the liturgical rites and other spiritual, artistic, theological, and institutional treasures. Owing to this the Catholic West has attempted to destroy all that was not like it. One must admit that it has been quite successful in this; nothing indeed looks more Western than this uniated Eastern Church. This is true of most of the Catholic-Eastern communities with the exception of liturgical rites (and even there!). Thus it becomes understandable that the proposed model for unification is hardly suitable to facilitate our mission."

[22] Cf. Maximos IV, *op cit*. 5; II: "What we represent to our orthodox brothers of the East."

[23] J. Gill, *The Council of Florence* (Cambridge 1959) 414–415.

[24] Patriarch Maximos IV, *op cit*. 9: "Despite the fact that the Roman Church has made efforts to maintain the Oriental rites, some of its representatives have diligently worked to deprive the Eastern Churches of their own inheritance, their

Will a future Council succeed in word and deed in representing the Catholic Church in a more credible manner than has been the case heretofore in this second millennium soon drawing to a close? One of the highest dignitaries of the Catholic Church, the Melchite patriarch of Antioch, Maximos IV Saigh, demands the following: "Hence we must be convinced that Christianity will never fulfil its mission in the world unless it is catholic not only in principle but also in fact, that is to say, all-embracing. If to be catholic means to renounce one's liturgy, one's hierarchy, one's patristics, and one's history, one's hymnology, and one's arts, one's language and one's culture, in short one's whole spiritual legacy in order to accept the rites, the philosophy, and the theological thought, the literature, the liturgical language, the culture and spirituality of a given group, were it even the best, then the Church would no longer be God's greatest gift to mankind. Rather, she would represent a community of interests—no matter how large this community may be—a human institution linked to the interests of a definite group. She would then no longer be the Church of Christ. If, therefore, we resist the Latinization of our institutions, by so doing we do not defend the petty interests of parochial politics or an obsolete traditionalism. Rather, we are convinced that we are defending the vital interests of the apostolic Church in order to remain true to her mission, to her calling, which we cannot betray without disowning ourselves and without distorting the message of Christ before our brethren."[25] What Maximos IV stated earlier applies not only with respect to Eastern Christians: "We must therefore begin to convert the Latin West to catholicism, to the universality of the message of Christ . . . a levelling conformity is not reconcilable with catholic universality."[26]

---

own canonical institutions, their own traditional organization and to impose upon them a Latinized form. An example of this is the recent codification of Eastern canon law in Rome: One must regretfully note that despite an impressive critical apparatus, despite a terminology inspired by Eastern sources, despite meritorious and painstaking work, the dominant tone of the codification has retained a 'Latinizing' quality. This was not always the fault of those engaged on the project; rather, it was owing to the spirit prevailing in the milieu in which the work was performed. In this milieu the ultimate ideal remains a most complete approximation to the Latin canon law, both in content and in form. Those institutions peculiar to the East, as for example the Patriarchate, are tolerated as exceptions and reduced to the narrowest possible scope, if their very content is not ingeniously voided or neutralized—all as a consequence of an exaggerated administrative centralization."

[25] Patriarch Maximos IV, *op cit.* 10.

[26] As quoted by W. de Vries, *Wegbereitung zur Einheit der Christen aus ostkirchlicher Sicht* (Recklinghausen 1961) 6.

3. THE HOLY CHURCH

The holy Church is not credibly represented at an ecumenical council by human convocation when party interests and church diplomacy supplant truly spiritual matters, when personal interests instead of revelation, human law instead of the gospel of Jesus Christ, preservation of the *status quo*, and an opportunistic policy instead of a renewal of the Church are placed in the foreground. The holy Church is credibly represented when a council carries out the will of the heavenly Father, when it hearkens to a Jesus Christ who speaks to the Church through Holy Scripture, when it is open to the Holy Scripture, when it is open to the Holy Spirit which bloweth where it listeth, within or without any institution.

In the previous chapter we have seen that the holiness of an ecumenical council by divine convocation, like the holiness of an ecumenical council by human convocation, can be understood only in terms of the Holy Spirit. The Church is not holy by virtue of a morality of sinful men, which they have acquired by and through themselves. The Church is holy through her vocation in the Spirit of Jesus Christ to community with God. The saints of the Church— and *all* her members should be saints—are not self-made saints. They are *called to be saints: κλητοὶ ἅγιοι* (Rom. 1:7; I Cor. 1:2). This assembled community is "holy" and remains "holy" by virtue of the fact that Christ in the Holy Spirit summons them to the Church, gathering and uniting them to her: to the Church which lives in contradiction to the world, and is persecuted by it—but which never-theless serves the world by preaching the gospel and by deeds of love; "a chosen race, a royal priesthood, a holy nation, a purchased people; that [it] may proclaim the perfections of him who has called [them] out of darkness into his marvellous light" (I Pet. 2:9), the Temple wherein dwells the Holy Spirit (I Cor. 3:16f; Eph. 2:21f). Thus the Church is holy by virtue of the sanctifying Spirit who continuously establishes and animates the Church anew, and pre-serves, illuminates, guides, and sanctifies the Church as the ecu-menical council by divine convocation. "But we, brethren beloved of God, are bound to give thanks to God always for you, because God has chosen you as first-fruits unto salvation through the sanctification of the Spirit and belief of the truth. For this purpose he also called you by our preaching to gain the glory of our Lord Jesus Christ" (II Thess. 2:13f).

The spirit who guides the Church can never be merely a human spirit, no matter how clever, or how experienced or versatile. The

Church must always be guided by the Spirit of Jesus Christ. The Spirit of Jesus Christ can indeed be mistaken for the spirit of man. When this happens, human thoughts are held to be inspirations of the Holy Spirit, human ways are held to be His ways. It may occur then—and it does so time and again—that some enraptured "Illumined One" believes himself moved by the Holy Spirit while in reality he is hearing nothing but the vocal manifestations of his own spirit. It is possible that even a Church dignitary—particularly prone to that kind of temptation and danger—may consider his human impulses, thoughts, wishes, and dictates to be those of the Holy Spirit. Here, as everywhere else in the Church, the distribution of spiritual gifts (διάκρισις πνευμάτων) among the members is involved (I Cor. 12:10).

The Holy Spirit is not just any kind of spirit held captive within the Church, in one way or another identical with her and of whom the Church can dispose at will. No, the Spirit "blows where it wills" (Jn. 3:8). Neither is the Holy Spirit some "absolute" free-floating world-spirit which develops His own dialectic. No, He is the spirit of Jesus Christ (Phil. 1:19). The Holy Spirit proclaims nothing new to the Church. He proclaims the word of Christ to her: "But when he, the Spirit of truth, has come, he will teach you all the truth. For he will not speak on his own authority, but whatever he will hear he will speak, and the things that are to come he will declare to you. He will glorify me, because he will receive of what is mine and declare it to you" (Jn. 16:13–15). Thus the Holy Spirit will recall to the Church all that Christ has said to her (Jn. 14:26). He will remind the Church of the gospel of Jesus Christ. The Spirit of truth whom Christ sends from the Father will bear witness of Christ to the Church, so that the Church too may bear witness to Him (Jn. 15:26f). The Church is and proves herself holy by bearing witness to Christ and His gospel in word and deed as a council gathered together in the Holy Spirit.

The great and difficult task of an ecumenical council by human convocation is to represent, and to represent credibly, the holiness of the ecumenical council by divine convocation which is the Church, grounded in the Holy Spirit of Jesus Christ. The discussions and the decisions of an ecumenical council by human convocation— according to the testimony of the Acts in regard to the Council of the Apostles—must not only seem good to those present but also and primarily to the Holy Spirit. "For the Holy Spirit and we have decided . . ." (Acts 15:28).

To view ecumenical councils merely as parliamentary gatherings is to view them externally in purely organizational terms. By doing so one overlooks precisely the fact that ecumenical councils are representations of the holy Church and that their dominant trait is that of being a community of worship. "In the Old Church the synods grew historically out of the meetings of local congregations, that is, out of gatherings held for the purpose of worship. Just as the gathering for worship and the divine services taking place therein became the central impulse for the development of the order of offices, such was also the case with the growth of the synod. The synod came into being when leading members of other congregations took part in the deliberations of the local community. But the character of worship that marked the gathering was preserved even with the increase in the number of members assembled from different local churches. All deliberations were imbedded in the act of worship, emanating from it and subordinated to it. The supplication to the Holy Spirit and the certainty of His guidance determined the synod's discussions and decisions in the same way as prayers, testimonies and doxologies during divine services."[1]

Already the early councils regarded themselves as being gathered together in the Holy Spirit. So much so that the Council of Ephesus forbade any symbol of faith other than "that defined by the holy fathers who with the Holy Spirit came together at Nicaea."[2] Many formulations go even further, permitting the inference that the councils were open to an "inspiration" of the Holy Spirit.[3]

In fact, even before Nicaea, at the Council of Carthage,[4] we read "placuit nobis Spiritu sancto suggerente," and likewise at the Council of Arles in 314,[5] "placuit ergo praesente Spiritu sancto et angelis eius." This applies especially to the Council of Nicaea, according to which, "What has been decided by the three hundred holy bishops is to be regarded exclusively as the pronouncement of the Son of God."[6] Great importance was attached to the inspiration of the Holy Spirit, particularly by Cyril of Alexandria, according to whom at Nicaea "the Fathers formulated the definition of the immaculate Faith under the inspiration of the Holy Spirit; . . . it was the Spirit of God who spoke through them according to the Word of the

[1] E. Schlink, "Ökumenische Konzilien einst und heute," in his collected articles: *Der kommende Christus und die kirchlichen Traditionen* (Göttingen 1961) 244.

[2] Denz. 125.

[3] H. Bacht. "Sind die Lehrentscheidungen der ökumenischen Konzilien göttlich inspiriert?" in *Catholica* 13 (1959) 128–139, contains rich material on this question.

[4] Cyprian, *Epistola synodica ad Cornelium Papam*, ep. 54; *PL* 3, 887.

[5] J. D. Mansi, *Sacrorum conciliorum nova et amplissima collectio*, 2, 469.

[6] Mansi 2, 992.

Saviour."[7] Leo the Great shared the same view: "regulae sanctionum
. . . in synodo Nicaena ad totius ecclesiae regimen spiritu Dei
instruente sunt conditae";[8] ". . . illa Nicaenorum canonum per
spiritum vere sanctum ordinata."[9] The acclamations at councils—
to which reference has already been made—must also be viewed
in this context, as divine inspirations of those present indicating the
presence of the Spirit. This is why the number and the strength
of these acclamations were exactly established in the protocols.
Subsequently the conception of councils as inspired by the Holy
Spirit was supported by the widely held view that the first four
councils were to be ranked on a par with the four Gospels.[10] The
first sign of this tradition is the decree, attributed to Pope Gelasius
I (492–496), entitled "De recipiendis et non recipiendis libris,"
where in the fourth chapter we read: "The Holy, that is the Roman,
Church after having accepted consistently the writings of the Old
and New Testaments does not prohibit accepting these writings, i.e.,
the holy synod of Nicaea . . . Ephesus . . . Chalcedon."[11]

In 519 Pope Hormisdas, in accordance with the Eastern custom,
added the Council of Constantinople, which was held in 381 without
Western participation. Theodosius, as the leader of the Palestinian
monks loyal to Chalcedon, had already proclaimed in 516: "Anyone
who does not accept the four synods as the gospels should be
excommunicated." Justinian not only accepted the canon of the
four councils in his confession of faith, but also included it in his
legislation. Gregory the Great continued an already widespread
tradition when he asserted in various formulations of the same kind:
"Sicut sancti evangelii quattuor libros, sic quattuor concilia susci-
pere et venerari me fateor."[12] This tradition continued in the Middle
Ages primarily by way of Isidore of Seville. It was carried on by different synods as well as by different popes (Leo IX, Gregory VII),
by canonists (already in the Decretum Gratiani) and by theologians
(Abelard, Hugo of St. Victor, Peter Lombard, but not by the great
Scholastics). Even at the time of the Council of Trent the four
councils ranked very high both with the Reformers and Catholic

---

[7] Cyril of Alexandria, *Ad monachos Aegypti*, ep. 1; *PG* 77, 16.

[8] Leo the Great, *Ad Marcianum Augustum*, ep. 104, 3; *PL* 54, 995.

[9] Leo the Great, *Ad Anatolium Episcopum*, ep. 106, 2; *PL* 54, 1003; further
passages in H. Bracht, "Sind die Lehrentscheidungen der ökumenischen Konzilien göttlich inspiriert?" in *Catholica* 13 (1959) 130f.

[10] This tradition has been thoroughly investigated by Y. Congar, "La primauté
des quatre premiers conciles oecuméniques. Origine, destin, sens et portée d'un
thème traditionnel," in *Le concile et les conciles* (Paris 1960) 75–109.

[11] Quoted according to Y. Congar, *op cit*. 75.

[12] Cf. Y. Congar, *op cit*. 76–80; H. Bacht, *op cit*. 132f.

theologians. Only subsequently did this tradition practically die out in Catholic theology—save for the exponents of Gallican theology.

What is the significance of these preceding statements? We cannot go more closely into the tradition of the primacy of the first four councils here. Apart from the "mystic" significance which the ancient as well as the medieval world attributed to quaternity—derived from both biblical and profane sources—the importance of this doctrine lies in the following consideration: Without trying to belittle or disregard the importance of later councils, it remains a fact that the first four ecumenical councils (and especially Nicaea which occupies a unique position among the four) defined the Catholic faith in a fundamental and decisive fashion. Hence they provide a definite norm for all subsequent councils. There is a hierarchy among the councils and they vary in their importance. This is particularly relevant to the question of reunion with the East.[13] But how should we evaluate the character of "inspired" councils? H. Bacht has pointed out, in connection with the research conducted by G. Bardy and J. de Ghellinck, that in the ancient sources "inspiration" is attributed not only to the councils but also to the "Fathers." This attribution is conferred either by the Fathers themselves (from Clement of Rome and Pastor of Hermas up to Gregory the Great) or by one Father to others. (Gregory of Nyssa, for example, attributed it to Basil, Augustine to Jerome, and medieval theologians in turn to Augustine and Gregory the Great, and so on.) Every possible attempt has been made to harmonize the mutually contradictory statements of the Fathers. But inspiration and infallibility were attributed even to emperors. All this merely indicates the ambiguity of the concept of inspiration that plays such a great role in the Graeco-Hellenist philosophy of religion and history of religion. "If in the ancient world and in the early Church *any kind* of divine causation might be included under the notion of 'inspiration,' the progress of theological reflection has taught us to make careful distinctions. In modern theology we speak of inspiration properly so called in cases where the true, primary authorship must be ascribed to God."[14] Nowadays a specific distinction is made between infallibility (which even in connection with statements made by human beings, such as conciliar or papal definitions, is given "with the *assistance* of the Holy Spirit") and inspiration (which is given *only* in the word of God of Holy Scripture "with the *inspiration* of the Holy Spirit").

---

[13] Cf. Y. Congar, *op cit.* 101–109.
[14] H. Bacht, *op cit.* 137.

Hence Holy Scripture alone is the inspired word of God in the authentic sense, God's word effected and realized by the Spirit, attested in and through the word of man. The First Vatican Council exactly circumscribed the basis for the primacy of Scripture: The Church holds the writings of the Old and New Testaments to be holy and canonical: "not on the grounds that they were produced by mere human ingenuity and afterwards approved by her authority; not on the mere score that they contain revelation without error. But they are held to be sacred and canonical because, being written as a result of the prompting of the Holy Spirit, they have God for their author, and as such they were entrusted to the Church."[15] T. Zapelena states: "Holy Scripture, in regard to its coming about is formally the word of God, whereas tradition, in the same respect, is not formally the word of God but contains it."[16] Likewise Franzelin: "There are in addition to Holy Scripture outstanding Church documents containing God's word which are produced with the assistance of the Holy Spirit, infallibly ruling out any error. Yet there are no inspired works save Holy Scripture."[17]

Thus it is clear that ecumenical councils are not "inspired" by the Spirit but are only "assisted" by the Spirit. The definitions also of ecumenical councils are not really the word of God; rather, as human statements they testify indirectly (with assistance from the Spirit) to the revelation of God. Hence ecumenical councils do not stand above Holy Scripture but—precisely as serving to explain and

[15] Denz. 1787.

[16] T. Zapelena, *De Ecclesia Christi* (Rome 1954) II, 274; cf. P. v. Leeuwen, "Regula credendi," in *Genade en Kerk* (Utrecht-Antwerpen 1953) 341f.

[17] J. B. Franzlein, *Tractatus de divina Traditione et Scriptura* (Rome ²1875) 364; cf. A. Deneffe, *Der Traditionsbegriff* (Münster 1931) 161; C. H. Baumgartner, "Tradition et magistére," in *Recherches de Science religieuse*, 41 (1953) 171–185. Cf. "Note by G. de Broglie, S. J., on the Primacy of the Argument from Scriptures in Theology," in L. Bouyer, *The Spirit and Forms of Protestantism* (London, 1955) pp. 230–231: "Consequently, Scripture has always had a place apart in the teaching of the Church. For, if the essential function of a theologian is to transmit the divine message in its entire purity, and if Scripture is in fact the sole *immediate* source at his disposal whence he can derive that message in the very words of the God who sent it, his primary concern must needs be to recur continually to that source to the fullest possible extent, and so to refer in the first place to the testimony of Scripture in preference to any other. So it is that Pope Leo XIII (whom no one will accuse of underestimating the importance of the Magisterium) could well observe that recourse to Scripture should be, as it were, the 'soul' of all theology; and he continued: 'This was, in all periods, the doctrine of all the Fathers and the greatest of the theologians, one which they followed out in their own practice. *They set out to establish and confirm, primarily by the sacred books, all the truths of faith as well as those which follow from them.*' (Encyclical *Providentissimus Deus*)."

interpret it—below Holy Scripture. What, according to the Vatican definition, applies to the pope likewise applies to ecumenical councils: They cannot reveal a new truth but only preserve and faithfully explain revelation as handed down by the Apostles. "The reason for this is that the Holy Spirit was promised to the successors of St. Peter not that they might make known new doctrine by His revelation, but rather, that with His assistance they might religiously guard and faithfully expand the revelation or deposit of faith that was handed down through the apostles."[18] In the Catholic Church it is taken for granted that Holy Scripture—precipitate, effected and realized by the Spirit of the preaching of the primitive Church—may not be interpreted by individual believers in isolated and self-glorifying intellectual certainty, as a book that has fallen from heaven. Rather, it is to be regarded as a book of the Church originating in and for the Church. Obviously, then, Scripture and Church may not be separated. Rather, according to the Council of Trent, Scripture and Church tradition are to be accepted "with the same sense of devotion and reverence."[19] Yet it is also obvious (although unfortunately there has not always been a clear awareness of it and it has not been given its full value) that Holy Scripture is the norma *normans*, whereas the definitions of the councils indeed were also norma but only norma *normanta*, that is, they can only be norms regulated by Holy Scripture. Thus it is clear that the doctrine of a council, as regulated by Scripture, becomes a norm for the individual Christian for the correct understanding of Scripture. Just as the proclamation of the early Church was condensed and crystallized in the testimony of Scripture, effected by the Spirit, so, on the other hand, the whole preaching of the later Church, including its authoritative interpretation by ecumenical councils, revolved around and gravitated towards Holy Scripture, to which the *complete* content of Christian Revelation (at least fundamentally and implicitly) has been entrusted.[20] "Without any doubt, councils, as for that matter the whole ecclesiastical teaching authority, have no autonomy

---

[18] Denz. 1836.   [19] Denz. 783.

[20] Cf. the works of R. Geiselmann, "Das Missverständnis über das Verhältnis von Schrift und Tradition und seine Überwindung in der katholischen Theologie," in *Una Sancta* 11 (1956) 131–150; "Das Konzil von Trient über das Verhältnis der heiligen Schrift und der nicht geschriebenen Traditionen. Sein Missverständnis in der nachtridentinischen Theologie und die Uberwindung dieses Missverständnisses," in *Die mündliche Überlieferung*, ed. by M. Schmaus (München 1957) 125–206; "Die Tradition," in *Fragen der Theologie heute*, ed. by J. Feiner, J. Trütsch and F. Böckle (Einsiedeln 1957) 69–108; "Depositum fidei," in *Lexikon für Theologie und Kirche* (Freiburg 1959) III, 236–238; *Die lebendige Überlieferung als Norm des christlichen Glaubens. Die apostolische Tradition in der Form*

whatsoever in regard to the objective rules of the faith, namely, the divine revelation made by the prophets in Jesus Christ, by the apostles, a revelation of which the Scriptures are the absolutely normative written attestation."[21]

It was precisely the early councils which showed with the most extraordinary clarity that by means of their definitions they simply wanted to proclaim and interpret the gospel of Jesus Christ, His message as recorded and transmitted in Scripture. Indeed, the conscious striving of the first four councils for closeness to Scripture may ultimately account for the fact that they, in an analogous fashion, *sicut sancti evangeli quator libros*, could be considered as "inspired." Their teaching is holy because it is a reflection of the inspired word of God to which they bear witness. Councils can demand reverence and obedience by virtue of the authority of Christ and His word: "Sacerdotium iudicium ita debet haberi, ac si ipse Dominus residens

---

der kirchlichen Verkündigung—das Formalprinzip des Katholizismus dargestellt im Geiste der Traditionslehre von Joh. Ev. Kuhn (Freiburg i. Br. 1959); "Schrift—Tradition—Kirche. Ein ökumenisches Problem," in *Begegnung der Christen,* ed. by M. Roesle and O. Cullmann (Stuttgart-Frankfurt ²1960) 131–159.—Similar conclusions were reached earlier by E. Ortigues, "Écriture et tradition apostolique au concile de Trente," in *Recherces de Science religieuse* 36 (1949) 271–299; also H. Holstein, "La tradition d'après le concile de Trent," in *Recherches de Science religieuse* 47 (1959) 367–390; E. Stakemeier, "Das Konzil von Trient über die Tradition. Zu einer Untersuchung von H. Holstein," in *Catholica* 14 (1960) 34–55; Y. Congar, "Traditions apostoliques non écrites et suffisance de l'Écriture," in *Istina* 6 (1959) 279–306; *La Tradition et les traditions. Essai historique* (Paris 1960) 107–232. For the sufficiency of content of the Holy Scripture, Geiselmann in his treatise, "Schrift–Tradition–Kirche" (154f) quotes for the nineteenth century: Dobmayer-Senestrey, J. A. Möhler, J. H. Newman, Joh. Ev. von Kuhn; for the present time he quotes: A. Deneffe, K. Rahner, O. Karrer, P. A. Liégé, M. Chenu, J. Daniélou, H. St. John, S. Bullough, O. Semmerlroth, J. Ratzinger, A. M. Dubarle. Among others the following authors should be added: H. Jedin, M. Schmaus, J. Ternus, P. Lengsfeld, L. Scheffczyk. Cf. also the important work on this question by G. Biemer, *Überlieferung und Offenbarung. Die Lehre von der Tradition nach J. H. Newman* (Freiburg–Basle–Vienna 1961), and W. Kasper, *Die Lehre von der Tradition in der Römischen Schule* (Diss. Tübingen 1961; Freiburg i. Br. 1962). Geiselmann's interpretation of the decrees of Trent has been criticized by H. Lennerz and J. Bäumer. Geiselmann points to this in the following: "There is no reason to change the opinion expressed in this treatise. Evidence for this must be given elsewhere" (*op cit.* p. 142). An answer from the historical point of view to H. Lennerz was given by Y. Congar, *La tradition et les traditions* (Paris 1960) 215–218; from a systematic point of view the answer was given by K. Rahner, "Virginitas in partu. Ein Beitrag zum Problem der Dogmenentwicklung und Überlieferung," in *Kirche und Überlieferung* (Festschrift J. Geiselmann, Freiburg–Basle–Vienna 1960) 601–605. A further contribution of Geiselmann *Die heilige Schrift und die Tradition*, has appeared in the series "Quaestiones disputatae (No. 18, 1962)."
[21] Y. Congar, "Conclusion," in *Le concile et les conciles* (Paris 1960) 291.

iudicet, nihil enim licet his aliud sentire, vel aliud iudicare, nisi quod Christi magisterio sunt edocti."[22] Hence the holy council and Holy Scripture belong together.

A council must bear witness to Scriptural doctrine: the teaching "which Christ has given, which the apostles have proclaimed, and which the Fathers, who came to Nicaea from the whole *oikumene*, have handed down."[23] The Fathers of Nicaea "wrote so trenchantly that anyone who turns to their writings with an upright mind will perceive therein the reverence before Christ that is commanded by Holy Scripture."[24] "Nevertheless it is clear to all that this is the true and correct faith in the Lord, known and recognized from the Holy Scriptures."[25] The Fathers "breathe Holy Scripture,"[26] they have spoken *secundum scripturas*,[27] and they have set forth the confession of the faith *in sacris voluminibus pertracti*,[28] and hold fast to "quia hoc accepimus a prophetis: hoc nobis Evangelia locuta sunt: hoc apostoli tradiderunt, hoc martyres passione confessi sunt."[29]

There was also at the later councils an awareness of the decisive importance of the word of God with respect to conciliar actions and omissions, discussions and definitions. In any case at many councils the Bible was solemnly displayed on a throne in sight of the whole gathering as an admonition to the council Fathers that their thoughts, words, and deeds had to revolve around this centre. Matters were not to be settled by some kind of scholarly predilections and political tendencies, nor by any kind of fanciful philosophy or fanciful theology, nor by any kind of scholastic theses or scholastic systems, nor by any national, university or monastic traditions, but by the word of God in the holy writings of the Old and New Testaments. Can what Athanasius said about the Fathers of Nicaea "breathing Holy Scripture"[30] be said about the Fathers of *all* councils? We cannot overlook the fact that the closeness to Scripture of individual coun-

---

[22] Constantinus I. Imperator, *PL* 8, 488.

[23] Athanasius, *Epistola contra Arianos, ad honoratissimos in Africa episcopos* 1; *PG* 26, 1029.

[24] Athanasius, *Epistola de synodis Arimini in Italia, et Seleuciae in Isauria, celebratis* 6; *PG* 26, 689.

[25] Athanasius, *Epistola ad Iovianum Imperatorem* 1; *PG* 26, 816.

[26] Athanasius, *Epistola contra Arianos, ad honoratissimos in Africa episcopos* 4; *PG* 26, 1036.

[27] Ambriosius, *De fide ad Gratianum Augustum libri quinque* I, 18; *PL* 16, 555–556.

[28] Phoebadius Aginnensis, *Liber contra Arianos* 6; *PL* 20, 17.

[29] Phoebadius Aginnensis, *Liber contra Arianos* 22; *PL* 20, 30.

[30] Athanasius, *Epistola contra Arianos, ad honoratissimos in Africa episcopos* 4; *PG* 26, 1036.

cils has been very different. There was a great difference between Nicaea, where it was primarily a question of the interpretation of Scripture, and the later post-Chalcedon councils where it was often primarily a question of seeing who could forge the longest chain of proofs for his argument, made up of quotations from the Fathers.[31] In the second millennium, the first period of the sessions of the Council of Trent was marked by the fact that they tried as far as possible to isolate controversial Scholastic opinions, that they restrained Scholastic terminology, and strove for a truly biblical language.[32] The work of the Fathers of Trent was presented as a model to be followed even at the First Vatican Council.[33] In all that the Fathers decide and teach at a council they should be "sacris voluminibus pertracti."

Holy Scripture, however, should be the primary norm not only for doctrinal decisions but also for all the other activities of an ecumenical council. It is not enough merely to display the Bible before the council. What will be decisive is whether the Gospel at the council will play the dignified role of an "honorary presidency," honoured undoubtedly but practically without influence (how often have former active presidents been promoted to the status of honorary presidents because of old age?) or whether it will actively set the tone and effectively guide this assembly even in its details. This because one tries to hearken ever anew to the ancient and not always convenient word of the Gospel—and to give it its full value in the context of a new era: in the preparatory work of the commissions, for example, in the (so important) selection of speakers, in the order and direction of discussions, in the mode and manner of debates,

---

[31] Ch. Moeller indicates two essential traits already present in the theology of the sixth century: "... the usage of collections of patristic poetry, which is matched by the disappearance of arguments based on Scripture. The growing dialectic, which in certain sectors was soon frankly Aristotelian ..." "Le chalcédonisme et le néo-chalcédonisme en Orient de 451 á la fin du VIᵉ siècle," in *Das Konzil von Chalkedon*, ed. by A. Grillmeier and H. Bacht (Würzburg 1959) I, 650.

[32] Cf. in this connection, H. Jedin, *History of the Council of Trent* (Edinburgh 1961) II.

[33] Among many critical voices attacking the first Schema *De fide catholica* was the voice of Archbishop Connolly of Halifax: "His was a most trenchant attack on the whole substance and manner of the schema: unlike all previous Councils, and notably Trent, it discourses 'de omni scibili in re dogmatica,' and raises theological speculations into articles of faith; questions recognized as open in the theological schools are decided in a particular sense; the theologians of Trent will rise from their graves and say, 'Look how we did the thing!' The schema should not be patched up or emended, but decently buried (cum honore sepeliendum): it should be wholly recast by the deputation *de Fide*." Cf. Dom Cuthbert Butler, *The Vatican Council* (London 1940), I. 188f.

in the definitions and decrees. All this should "breathe Holy Scripture"! The council is then truly credible.

Hence, a council will represent the holiness of the Church credibly when it proceeds *evangelically,* when it acts according to the Gospel in major as well as in minor matters. In order to represent the holiness of the Church credibly the external framework, the basic inner attitude, the conciliar decisions at a council, just be determined and permeated by the Gospel. A council will then be credible! The threatening dangers must be clearly perceived. They must be viewed here as tasks that earnest Christians will deliberately set themselves.

(*a*) *External Framework:* A gathering which has the lofty and difficult task of representing the holiness of the Church is always in danger of also representing itself, of mirroring itself, of presenting itself as a "representation" rather than representing in everything the Church and her holiness. An ecumenical council by human convocation, however, should not be its own representation but the representation of the ecumenical council by divine convocation. It is not a brilliant congress of secular "representatives" of imperial princes. It is not a "religious" sensation and not a spectacle for television and picture magazines. It should not seek to impress the world, but to represent the Church in imitating Christ and His apostles by inconspicuousnesses, modesty, and humility. Magnificence, pomp, and splendour make a council, which aims to represent the Church and her holiness, non-credible for those whose thinking is rooted in the Gospel.[34]

(*b*) *Basic inner attitude:* A gathering that has the lofty and difficult task of representing the holiness of the Church is always in danger of representing the Church as a *goal in itself,* her brilliance and glory, her greatness, virtue, organization, and truth, instead of representing in everything the holiness flowing from God and leading to God. But an ecumenical council by human convocation should not repre-

---

[34] "One can be assured that the press, even the Catholic press which today is so mute about the Council, will increase the news photos and coverage. Radio and TV will join in. But what is the good of this interest in the external and folkloristic aspects, if such an expression may be permitted? It will be magnificent, all these mitred and coped bishops . . . and the pope on his *sedia gestatoria* moving forward to open the twenty-first Ecumenical Council! In Jerusalem neither Peter nor Paul wore a mitre or a cope, yet it was there that the Church definitely emerged from Judaism in order to work for the pagans. The important thing will not be seen: what is at stake at the Council is the evangelization of the world and the unity of the Church." *Qu'attendons-nous du concile? Avant-propos* (Brussels–Paris 1960) 7.

sent the Church triumphant but the Church militant, and the latter not as a self-glorifying entity. The council is not a parade of the Church's general staff, nor a demonstration of clerical power. It does not purpose to rule, but to serve; to serve in the humble imitation of the Lord, whose examples it should hold up to men; to serve in a spirit of atonement, without shrinking from openly confessing mistakes where the Church could definitely, and actually did, make mistakes. The Church does not exist for her own self, but in order to serve the world in the Spirit through Christ for the Father. The Church is the way, not the goal. She exists wholly for the kingdom of God, which will come. A council that praises and glorifies the Church instead of the Lord does not represent the holiness of the Church. Demonstration of spiritual power, arrogance, self-righteousness, insistence upon rights and mandates, pharisaical legalism, and an uncharitable and proud sitting in judgment on others makes a council that aims to represent the Church and her holiness noncredible to those whose thinking is rooted in the Gospel.[35]

(*c*) *Conciliar Decisions:* A gathering which has the lofty and difficult task of representing the holiness of the Church is always in danger of representing this holy Church only through words instead of through deeds. It is in danger of discussing, of distinguishing, of hesitant, wavering action. But the ecumenical council by human convocation should represent the ecumenical council by divine convocation through words and deeds, through whole and not by half measures. It is not a party congress at which, above all, proclamations are issued and the leader is hailed. Neither is it a meeting of shareholders in which the owners preserve their rights only form-

---

[35] "Contrary to what certain persons may be temped to think, for the Church a general council is not the occasion for a spectacular show of power, in which she displays her complete general staffs and her massive unity before the world in order to impress it with her achievements. Instead, an ecumenical council is above all else an act of great humility in which, with the single concern of a rigorous fidelity to the commandments of the Lord, the Church periodically asks herself, in the light of the Spirit, to what measure her members, to whatever grade of the hierarchy they may belong, have little by little lost sight of one or other of these. Or, an even more subtle danger, whether they are not running the danger of betraying the spirit by an external respect for the letter. For the Church, in all loyalty, it is a question of asking herself if there is not something that needs to be rectified, certainly not in her profound nature but in her outward bearing, so that she may again appear, without equivocation, as 'a sign among nations' and remove all pretexts for criticism or simply for hesitation from those who reproach the Church so often for being a screen to the radiant power of the Gospel by certain aspects of her outer behaviour.' R. Aubert. "Qu'est-ce qu'un concile?" in *Qu'attendons-nous du concile?* (Brussels–Paris 1960) 12f.

ally in order to leave the actual direction of the business to the board of directors. An ecumenical council should not only represent the Church formally but with a full active responsibility. It must contribute its share in order to make the Holy Church credible before the world. And this task at all times, but particularly in the present conditions of historical upheaval, requires deeds of renewal— opportune or inopportune—daring deeds in the light of the gospel of Jesus Christ. Proclamations and declarations without actions, or administrative measures without underlying reforms, make a council that aims to represent the Church in her holiness non-credible for those whose thinking is rooted in the Gospel.[36]

Here are three examples (chosen wholly arbitrarily) to show concretely in the context of the contemporary situation what is meant, and what is not meant, by action in the light of the Gospel. (1) It is possible in a renewal of the Mass to patch up externals, *or* it is possible to reflect upon the Lord's Supper and during the canon (whispered quietly against the wall) to reflect upon the words: "For as often as you shall eat this bread and drink the cup, you *proclaim*

[36] A long list of reform proposals was advanced for the First Vatican Council (300 folio pages). But not one of the expectations for reform was fulfilled. Forty-six proposals had been made concerning church discipline and monastic orders; four of them were discussed; not one was acted upon! Even though the proposals had been discussed from January 8 to February 22, and the decrees had been revised and discussed again in May! The extensive preparatory work that had been done by the third and fourth Commission on the orders, the Eastern churches and the missions was not discussed at all. The failure of conciliar attempts at reform can obviously not have been due merely to lack of time. It was, among other things, owing to the two following reasons: (1) The preparatory work had been done with great zeal but with considerable one-sidedness: it was not representative of all regions and tendencies within the whole Church, which were then given expression by the bishops. (2) Too much attention was paid to secondary questions of detail rather than to essential demands in the light of the Gospel. As a consequence one became entangled in these details. The archbishop of Paris, Darboy, remarked in a discussion at the Council: "Forty days had now been spent on particular questions brought forward without order or connection. What were the evils to be cured, and what the remedies proposed? They had hoped that a conspectus of the proposed work of the Council would be provided, not in an oratorical and diffuse form of words, but a short synopsis that they might have before their minds what they were aiming at. If the principles were laid down the solution of particular and less important things would follow. But we are confusedly walking through a thicket of particulars and the vain and uncertain 'placita' of the schools. We are gravely discussing questions for canonists and are being set to labour over all kinds of trivialities (puerilia). Many had been fearing that the Vatican Council was going to attempt greater things than a sick society could bear. My fear is, lest having arrested the attention and the expectation of all, the Council be found unequal to the task it took in hand, in the judgment of those who make up that queen of the world, public opinion." Quoted according to Butler, *The Vatican Council* (London 1930), I, 220.

the death of the Lord, until he comes" (I Cor. 11:26), in order to gain *there* the courage to restore to the Church the simply phrased and immediately understandable Eucharistic prayer with the loudly proclaimed rememberance of the Lord's Supper. (2) It is possible to take care of the reform of the Breviary with similar secondary measures, as we often have seen happen before (reform of the rubrics instead of a reform of the priest's prayer), *or* it is possible on this occasion to reflect upon the word of the Lord: "But in praying, do not multiply words, as the Gentiles do; for they think that by saying a great deal, they will be heard." (Mt. 6:7), in order then to have the courage for a *fundamental* reform, which renounces the required completion of a definite number of prayers and gives the parochial clergy a definite amount of time to be devoted each day to prayer, a suitable prayerbook in their native language, as well as the opportunity of a continuous reading of Holy Scripture in its entirety. (3) It is possible in the reform of canon law to increase, decrease, or change paragraphs, *or* it is possible to reflect upon the accusing word of the Lord: "And they bind together heavy and oppressive burdens, and lay them on men's shoulders; but not with one finger of their own do they choose to move them" (Mt. 23:4), in order then from thence to have the courage to ensure a minimum of prescriptions and a maximum of freedom (for bishops, priests, and laymen) in the Church of God.

A credible or non-credible representation of the Church? That is the question that decides upon the inner *success or failure* of an ecumenical council. Let it not be said that an ecumenical council cannot be a failure. True, there have been no ecumenical councils that, in some open or hidden way, directly or indirectly, will not have had some beneficial effects; but so much (or so little) can be said about many a gathering. And even a council that has had some sort of beneficial effects may—viewed as a *whole*, namely with respect to the purpose for which it was convoked—nevertheless be a failure. The assistance of the Holy Spirit, which is promised to the Church, does not necessarily protect a council from failure. There is a difference between an ecumenical council by divine convocation and an ecumenical council by human convocation. The *divine* convocation of the council from the very outset mercifully takes care that the ecumenical council which is the Church, viewed as a whole (and only thus), cannot be a failure. *Human* convocation, however, from the outset cannot ensure that the council composed of human beings will not be a failure. Doctrinal definitions—correct in themselves—that a council can proclaim do not suffice to guarantee the inner

success of a council as a whole. There is a possibility that even
definitions which are correct and true in themselves (which as
definitions are not simply identical with their contents, since the
content has been raised to the level of reflected consciousness by the
act of defining) may not be opportune; that definitions may be issued
which by-pass the crucial requirements of the times and of the Church
(which may perhaps call for other definitions). More important is the
maintenance of this principle: it is a result of the essential *humanity*
of an ecumenical council, which at an ecumenical council of human
convocation is operative quite differently from that of the ecumenical
council by divine convocation, that the inner success of a council is
not assured at the outset through its human convocation; an ecumenical council can be held and yet—despite all its impressive outer
solemnity and all its proclamations and excommunications—it can
pass over the crucial needs of the times and of the Church.

The Fifth Lateran Council (1512–17) shows that this is not a mere
hypothetical case. "Instead of any hesitations and misgivings with
which such a Council might have been regarded—not without good
reason—its announcement was hailed with enthusiasm as the dawn of
a new and better age, as the beginning of the reform of the Church."[37]
Church reform had been put forward as the main task of the council
by the Augustinian general Egidio of Viterbo in his opening address
A voluminous memorandum on reform was submitted by the two
Venetians, Tommaso Giustiniani and Vincenzo Quirini, who shortly
before had entered the order of Camaldolese monks; it was "the most
extensive and most radical of all the reform programmes since the
era of the councils."[38] The ecumenical council was convoked, its
great purpose was proclaimed, it gathered in session and issued proclamations against Averroism,[39] and talked at length about reforms:
Despite all this, it turned out to be an appalling failure: "It is no
exaggeration to say that the reform programme of the two Camaldolese monks preoccupied the Church for more than a century. The
Council of Trent, the liturgical reforms of Pius V, the Bible of Sixtus

---

[37] H. Jedin, *A History of the Council of Trent*, vol. I: *The Struggle for the Council*
(tr. by Dom Ernest Graf, O.S.B.; Edinburgh 1957) 114.
[38] H. Jedin, *op cit.* 129.
[39] K. Rahner, "Zur Theologie des Konzils," in *Stimmen der Zeit* 87 (1962) 336:
"I suspect that not only Luther but Catholic Christians as well have entertained
the thought that the Fifth Lateran Council actually had more important problems
to solve, which it left unsolved, than the formulation of the definition on the
natural immortality of the human soul, important as this definition be. The few
neo-Aristotelians who were thereby rebuked were not the danger that was at that
time threatening the Church. The prelates at that Council should have searched
closer to home for that danger."

V, the foundation of Propaganda, are all in line with these plans. But the vision which the trained and prophetic eye of the high-minded Venetians beheld was too lofty for the Pope to whom they addressed themselves and for the Council assembled before their eyes. Pope and Council disappointed the hopes that had been set on them."[40] The failure of this ecumenical council, which had been in session for many years, was catastrophic for the Church: the Lutheran Reformation broke out six months after its closure.

4. THE APOSTOLIC CHURCH

An ecumenical council by human convocation is the representation of the one and holy catholic Church. But is it also a representation of the apostolic Church? Here we must touch upon a number of problems already present in the background of the issue on the representation of the one, holy, catholic Church. We must discuss how, in general, each mark (*Nota*) of the Church—understood in its whole depth in the sense of the New Testament—fosters and includes the others. Indeed, how could the *one* Church truly be *one*, if at the same time the full range of catholicity, the strengthening source of holiness, and the apostolic origin had not been given to her? How could the *catholic* Church be truly *catholic* if she also were not bequeathed the maintenance of unity, the selflessness of sanctity, and the driving power of apostolicity? Now could the *holy* Church be truly *holy* if at the same time the backbone of unity, the magnanimity of catholicity, and firmly rooted apostolicity were not bequeathed to her? And finally how could the *apostolic* Church be truly *apostolic* if the collegiality of unity, the manifoldness of catholicity and the spirit of holiness were not bestowed upon her?

The attributes of the Church are not static labels. Rather, as different dimensions of one and the same Church they dynacidally penetrate each other at every point (in a *circumincessio* and *circumin-sessio* of a unique kind). Amid all the differentiations her problems are one. And if special difficulties arise in connection with the question of the representation of the apostolic Church—these are the same ones that presented themselves earlier, somewhat more hidden but no less real, on the question of the one, holy, catholic Church. We must now reach back and return to Martin Luther.

[40] H. Jedin, *op cit*. 130.

V

CHURCH, COUNCIL, AND LAITY

1. LUTHER'S DEMANDS

THE whole history of Luther was bound up with the question of ecumenical councils. We shall see this still more clearly in another context.[1] Directly after the formulation of the Theses on Indulgences,[2] Luther in his dispute with the Dominican Prierias in 1518 already had upheld this pointed assertion against the papacy: "I know the Church virtually only in Christ, representatively only

[1] Cf. Chap. VI, parts 1–2. Concerning the view of councils held by Luther and the reformers, cf: J. Kolde, *Luthers Stellung zu Concil und Kirche bis zum Wormser Reichstag* 1521 (Gütersloh 1876); K. G. Steck, "Der 'Locus de Synodis' in der lutherischen Dogmatik," in *Theologische Aufsätze, Karl Barth zum 50. Geburtstag* (Munich 1936) 338–352; H. Jedin, *A History of the Council of Trent*, vol. I, *The Struggle for the Council* (Edinburgh 1957) 166–196; F. Hübner, "Das Konzil als Leitbild für ökumenische Konforenzen," in *Gedenkschrift für D. Werner Elert* (Berlin 1955) 387–399; E. Kinder, "Der Gebrauch des Begriffs 'ökumenisch' im älteren Luthertum," in *Kerygma und Dogma* 1 (1955) 180–207; R. Stupperich, "Kirche und Synode bei Melanchthon," in *Gedenkschift für D. Werner. Elert* (Berlin 1955) 199–210; "Die Reformatoren und das Tridentinum," in *Archiv für Reformationsgeschichte* 47 (1956) 20–63; E. Bizer, "Die Wittenberger Theologen und das Konzil 1537," in *Archiv für Reformationsgeschichte* 47 (1956) 77–101; F. W. Kantzenbach, *Das Ringen um die Einheit der Kirche im Jahrhundert der Reformation* (Stuttgart 1957); P. Meinhold, *Der evangelische Christ und das Konzil* (Freiburg-Basle-Vienna 1961); "Das Konzil im Jahrhundert der Reformation," in *Die ökumenischen Konzile der Christenheit*, ed. by H.-J. Margull (Stuttgart 1961) 201–233; M. Seils, "Das ökumenische Konzil in der lutherischen Theologie," in *Die ökumenischen Konzile der Christehneit*, ed. by H.-J. Margull (Stuttgart 1961) 333–372; J.-L. Leuba, "Das ökumenische Konzil in der reformierten Theologie," in *Die ökumenischen Konzile der Christenheit*, ed. by H. J. Margull (Stuttgart 1961) 373–392; J. Pelikan, "Luthers Stellung zu den Kirchenkonzilien," in K. E. Skydsgaard, *Konzil und Evangelium* (Göttingen 1962) 40–62.

[2] E. Iserloh, "Luthers Thesenanschlag, Tatsache oder Legende?," in *Trierer Theologische Zeitschrift* 70 (1961) 303–312: "Thus up to Luther's death the many sources make no mention of the nailing of the theses. According to these sources, on October 31, the Reformer had sent his theses to Archbishop Albrecht of Mainz and soon thereafter also handed them to colleagues in and outside of Wittenberg. The latter made further distribution of them. Then these theses, both in handwritten and printed form, found such a rapid and widespread circulation as no one, including Luther himself, could have foreseen. Not only is there no mention of a nailing of theses, but facts render such an event improbable, and indeed exclude it. At any rate it played no role in the consciousness of his contemporaries" (pp. 311f). Iserloh's study is based especially on H. Volz, *Martin Luthers Thesenanschlag und dessen Vorgeschichte* (Weimar 1959).

in the Council,"[3] and "And we will await both an explanation and a disposition of this matter from the Church or council."[4] At the trial that had meanwhile been instituted against him, after the Augsburg discussion with Cardinal Cajetan, which he published,[5] on October 16 or 22, 1518, in Augsburg, Luther appealed, "From the poorly informed Pope to the Pope who should be better informed."[6] In order to protect himself, however, on November 28 he certified before a notary and witness an appeal from the Pope to the council in Wittenberg, which against his will was immediately published: "Therefore not having been rightly consulted by the aforementioned Most Holy Leo, our ruler . . . I will freely go, or one appointed by me will go, to a legitimately called future council, and to that place or those places, and I do petition and appeal to that person or those persons to whom by right, privilege, custom, or other ways I am permitted to petition and appeal. . . ."[7] Two years later, threatened with excommunication by the Bull "Exsurge Domine," Luther renewed this appeal.[8]

The idea of the priesthood of the laity had already cropped up in a letter which Luther, inspired by I Peter 2:5–9, had written to Spalatin on December 18, 1519.[9] This fundamental idea of Lutheran ecclesiology was applied to the ecumenical council in the "Address to the Christian Nobility of the German Nation for the Reform of the Christian Social Estate,"[10] which along with "*De captivitate babylonica ecclesiae praeludium*"[11] and "Concerning Christian Freedom"[12] are reckoned among the so-called three main reformatory writings that appeared in 1520. In his address to the German nobility, Luther formulated the serious programme of a reform council; the accusations against the pope, cardinals, and curia,[13] and the very concrete proposals for reform, numbering 28 points. [14] Previous to this, however, he dealt with fundamental theological questions. According to Luther the Romanists had erected three walls in defence against a reform of the Church: in opposition to the will to reform on the part of the secular power, they assert the superordination of the spiritual power over the secular; in opposition to the re-

---

[3] M. Luther, *Werke, Kritische Gesamtausgave* (Weimar 1883ff; in the following footnotes the translated quotations from this complete German edition of Luther's works, known as the "Weimar Ausgabe," will be referred to as *WA*) 1, 656.

[4] *WA* 1, 658. [5] Acta Augustana 1518; *WA* 2, 6–26.
[6] *WA* 2, 28–33. [7] *WA* 2, 39f.
[8] *WA* 7, 75–82. [9] *WA* Briefwechsel [Correspondence] 1, 595.
[10] *WA* 6, 404–469. [11] *WA* 6, 497–573.
[12] *WA* 7, 20–38. [13] *WA* 6, 415–427.
[14] *WA* 6, 427–469.

forming power of Holy Scripture they maintain that Scripture can
be interpreted by the pope alone, and in opposition to a council they
prohibit any council that is not convoked by the pope: "When
threatened with a council, they claim that no one but the pope can
summon a council."[15]

Only the third point is of interest to us in this context. What was
Luther's answer to the question posed by this matter? First of all he
adduced arguments taken from conciliar history: According to
Acts 15:6, even the Council of the Apostles was not called by Peter
but by all the apostles and the presbyters, just as, also, the very
famous Council of Nicaea and the many subsequent councils were
not convoked by the pope. Finally, the councils convoked by the
popes did not produce results of any special character.[16] Of relevance
to the dire state of the Christendom of his day, however, was the
following consideration: "If a fire were to break out in a town,
should everyone stand by and let it burn on and on, simply for the
reason that no one had the mayor's authority, or perhaps because
the fire originated in the mayor's residence? Is it not the duty of each
citizen, in such a circumstance, to stir up the rest and summon them
for help? Ought this not to be the case even more in the spiritual
city of Christ if a fire of scandal were to break out, either in the papal
government of the Church or anywhere else?"[17]

Hence Luther's fundamental theological answer, which was
based on the concept of the universal priesthood of all believers:
"So, when need requires it, and the pope scandalizes Christendom,
let him who is a true member of the whole body take steps as early
as possible to bring about a really free council. No one can do this
as well as the secular arm, especially since they are also fellow
Christians, fellow priests, fellow religious, and sharing authority in
all matters. They should exercise their office and do the work, which
they have received from God above every man, wherever it may be
necessary or useful to do so."[18]

What does Catholic theology have to say in reply to this demand
of Luther's? To the question of the *convocation* of a council we have
already given a partial response in the introductory chapter. Later,
we shall discuss this question in greater detail. At this point we are
interested primarily in the question: What does Catholic theology,
historically and in principle, have to say about the *participation* of the
laity in ecumenical councils?

[15] *WA* 6, 406.   [16] *WA* 6, 413.
[17] *WA* 6, 413.   [18] *WA* 6, 413.

2. THE LAITY IN CONCILIAR HISTORY

(*a*) Conciliar history exhibits a great variability in regard to the participants at councils. Obviously, the "Council of Apostles" did not consist exclusively of the Apostles. Rather, a significant role was assigned to the presbyters and the whole congregation. True, the epistle to the Christians at Antioch mentioned only "apostles and presbyters" (Acts 15:23). Nevertheless, the account gives special prominence to the following features: (1) The community, the apostles and the presbyters welcomed the Antioch envoys and accepted their guidance (Acts 15:22). (2) The apostles, the presbyters, and the whole community formulated the decision to select representatives from among the assembled brethren and to send them with Paul and Barnabas to Antioch (15:22). The same ἔδοκεν (to decide)[19] that in the epistle is employed only by the apostles and by the presbyters is also expressed by the whole community in the crucial account as reported in 15:22.[20] There is no reason to assume that 15:22 in the book of Acts might be a false report. Rather, in the epistle (15:23; cf. 16:4), the community is obviously included under the "apostles and presbyters"; the modern contrast between "clergy" and "laity" must not be read into the text.

The Council of the Apostles, however, can serve even less than the *regional synods of the second and third centuries*, already described by Tertullian, as a model of the first ecumenical council. The origin of these synods can be explained in many ways: either as broadened assemblies of the congregations (R. Sohm); or as assemblies copying the model of the governmental provincial council (E. Friedberg); or as assemblies arising from the need of the Church to hammer out an agreement over thorny questions (K. von Schwartz); or as gatherings born of a spirit of unity and lively contact between the early communities, at which potentiaries of many congregations there assembled for discussion of matters of common concern, and in order to adopt decisions with respect to these (A. Hauck). In the judgment of historians, at any rate, it would be difficult to prove that

[19] Cf. W. Bauer, *Wörterbuch zu den Schriften des Neuen Testaments* (Berlin [5]1958) 366.

[20] A. Wikenhauser, *Die Apostelgeschichte* (Regensburg [3]1956) 142: "James' proposal was raised to the rank of a decision by the leading members with the approbation of the whole community." E. Haenchen, *Die Apostelgeschichte* (Göttingen [12]1959) 392: "ἔδοξε here does not, as in Luke 1:3, designate a private resolve but a public decision which establishes a prevailing—holy—law. Not only does the Church hierarchy (apostles and presbyters) participate in this decision, but also the community named besides which, of course, is not cited again in the introduction of the text."

these gatherings originally consisted exclusively of bishops. An anonymous author in Eusebius testifies to the oldest synods known to us, which were held in the second half of the second century in Asia Minor, and against the Montanists, with a noteworthy formulation: "This brazen spirit taught defamation of the truly catholic Church spread under the whole of heaven, so that the pseudoprophetic spirit grants her neither honour nor access. For this reason believers in Asia often assembled in many Asian localities, examined the new doctrines and condemned the heresy so that it was expelled from the Church and excluded from the community."[21]

In the course of time the bishops emerged almost exclusively into the foreground. Nevertheless, the congregations still played an important role at the African provincial synods in the middle of the third century, which have been described by Bishop Cyprian. Of importance is Cyprian's principle for the guidance of his Church, *nihil sine consilio vestro et sine consensu plebis mea privatim sententia gerere*, "I cannot by myself reply to the communication which our fellow presbyters Donatus, Fortunatus, Novatus, and Gordius have made to me. For, at the very beginning of my episcopal office, I decided to do naught on the basis of my own opinion alone without your counsel and the agreement of the people. When, however, through the grace of God, I again come to visit you we shall then together deal with all that has already happened or must happen, as the exchange of reciprocal viewpoints may require."[22] In this connection Y. Congar has observed that it was required, at any rate, that the whole congregation be involved during the informational and consultive stages, even though the collaboration was not always equally intensive.[23] According to Cyprian a sentence, a judgment of the people is called for especially in connection with reacceptance of lapsed persons into the church community: "acturi et apud nos et apud confessores ipsos et apud plebem universam causam suam," "examinabuntur singula praesentibus et judicantibus vobis," "conlatione consiliorum cum episcopis, presbyteris, diaconis, confessoribus pariter ac stantibus laicis facta."[24]

[21] Eusebius, *Historia Ecclesiastica* V, 16, 9; *PG* 20, 468. In addition, H. Marot, "Conciles anténicéens et conciles oecuméniques," in *Le concile et les conciles* (Paris 1960) 25: "This text reveals that lay persons, conjointly with the bishops, took part in these assemblies."

[22] Cyprian, *Ep. ad presbyteros et diaconos* 5, 4; *PL* 4, 240.

[23] Cf. Cyprian, *Ep. ad presbyteros et diaconos* 28, 3; *PL* 4, 309, "matters to be handled . . . not only with my colleagues, but with all the people."

[24] Quoted according to Y. Congar, *Jalons pour une théologie du laïcat* (Paris 1953) 335; further examples are cited therein.

Thus in North Africa (and probably also in Asia Minor and Syria), under the influence of Cyprian's ecclesiology, the community of bishops arrived at their decisions, made in common, in the presence of presbyters, deacons, and of the whole congregation. All the bishops signed the council letter (written in the plural) as senders. In Rome, however, and in Egypt as well, it was primarily the Bishop of Rome, or of Alexandria, who made the decisions—likewise in the presence of the congregation. The other bishops (who were regarded more as a college of advisers to the one bishop) in general did not sign the council letters (written in the singular) as senders (except, for instance, in order effectively to demonstrate their support of the Bishop of Rome). In Origen's circles, finally, we come upon a third type where —likewise in the presence of the congregation—the central position is not occupied by the bishop but by the professional theologian.[25] Even Eusebius describes different synods in Arabia and probably also in Palestine and Greece at which the learned presbyter Origen took his stand in regard to controversial theological questions. It was only a few years ago, however, that the protocol of a council of this kind was found; the papyrus of Tura.[26] This protocol provides an extraordinarily vivid picture of the discussion before the council in which a solemn struggle was waged over the proper interpretation of Scriptural texts. At this council there was no attempt simply to condemn or exclude others, but to convince them and win them over. "In the presence of different bishops and of the whole community, Origen strove to set aside the theological obscurities of one of those present, presumably the local bishop of this community, which was probably also located in Arabia."[27] Thereby attempts were made to arrive at binding decisions, to which Origen alludes: "Often it is written that decisions should be subscribed to, that the bishop should sign with the inculpated person, so that an end could be put to any dispute and discussion. By the order of God, and of the bishops in the second place, and of the presbyters and of the community in the third place, I shall now once more set forth my views on this matter. . . ."[28] Often the decisions were forwarded to other Churches.

[25] Concerning these three types of councils and the following, cf. G. Kretschmar, "Die Konzile der alten Kirche," in *Die ökumenischen Konzile der Christenheit*, ed. by H.-J. Margull (Stuttgart 1961) 21–25.

[26] *Entretien d'Origène avec Héraclide et les évêques ses collègues sur le Père, le Fils et l'âme*, ed. by J. Scherer (Cairo 1949); in English: *Alexandrian Christianity* ed. by J. E. L. Oulton and H. Chadwick (LCC 2) 1954; G. Kretschmar reports on this find in *op cit.* 25–27; for the interpretation of the text, cf. G. Kretschmar in *Zeitschrift für Theologie und Kirche* 50 (1953) 258–279.

[27] G. Kretschmar, *op cit.* 25.

[28] Quoted according to G. Kretschmar, *op cit.* 26.

Eusebius also describes a similar discussion that took place before
the congregation under Dionysius the Great, the disciple of Origen
and the Bishop of Alexandria.[29] So much for the situation of synods
in the third century.

(*b*) In the great *conciliar* era, which was ushered in with the *fourth
century*, the councils were primarily episcopal synods.[30]

Nevertheless, other Christians were not simply excluded for this
reason. At the Synod of Elvira (305) priests were present and they
affixed their signatures after the bishops. Deacons and lay persons
also were present but they did not sign. At Arles (314) deacons and
lower clergy took part in the proceedings and affixed their signatures,
probably as proxies of absent bishops. The young deacon Athanasius
played a crucial role in the discussion at the first ecumenical Council
of Nicaea. The Arian party utilized the help of pagan philosophers who
were also able to intervene in the discussions. Lay persons, however,
did not take the floor in connection with the actual decision.[31] Here
(as in later councils) careful attention must be paid to the role of the
emperor. Let us once more recall the concrete significance that the
position of Constantine, a layman (and still pagan), had for the first
ecumenical council: He laid down the regulations for this council to
the bishops in every form; he decided on the number and on the
names of the participants, the meeting place, the agenda to be
discussed; he selected the steering committee; he intervened personally in the negotiations: he exerted pressure for the acceptance
of the Nicene Creed; he recognized it as legally binding; he punished
those who refused their signatures; he himself publicized the decree
on the feast of Easter; he imposed its observance as a duty upon the
bishops. Finally, to a great extent, Constantine also bore the costs
of the council.

Emperors also played an important role in the later ecumenical
councils. True, Christian emperors were invested with a sacred
character and performed liturgical functions. Actually, however,
among masses of clerics with their officials, they constituted the
remnant of the universal priesthood of the people of the Church
that had been present at the Council of the Apostles and at the earlier
synods. The emperor's signature is found in a remarkable form on

[29] Cf. G. Kretschmar, *op cit.* 28.

[30] G. Tangl, *Die Tielnehmer an den allgemeinen Konzilien des Mittelalters*
(Weimar 1922) 2–12.

[31] Cf. D. Stone, *The Christian Church* (London ³1915) 333–348 (quoted according to Y. Congar, *op cit.* 336).

the main list of signatures at the sixth ecumenical council (Constantinople 681): "We, Constantine (Poganatus), in Christ, our God, King and Ruler of the Romans, have taken cognizance and concur."[32] At the eighth ecumenical council (Constantinople 869) the signatures of the Emperor Basilius and his sons Constantine and Leo follow directly after the signatures of the papal delegates and of the representatives of the three Eastern partiarchates. "Together with the representatives of the lower clergy, those representing the secular power also often played a role of decisive importance in regard to the proceedings of the councils. Apart from the convocation of the councils by the emperor, as we know them from the different letters convening the councils, his influence, especially on the participants, is shown by the letter of Theodosius II concerning Barsumas. Here he simply forced upon the council an authorized participant from a social estate which at that time had not yet achieved any importance at the council. That the emperor not only could participate but could, under certain circumstances, also meaningfully take a hand in the proceedings is especially proved by the records of the sixth and eighth councils which even preserve the imperial signature on the list of signatories."[33]

The ecumenical Council of Nicaea constituted the model for the subsequent ecumenical councils of early Christianity. Further developments took place, especially in connection with two points: The circle of representatives was extended further (the representatives of bishops were not exclusively bishops but, increasingly, priests, deacons, subdeacons, lectors, and even, on one occasion, a notary). Since the sixth ecumenical council (Constantinople 681), even the monastic Orders came more strongly to the fore. The following observation applies to the seventh ecumenical council (Nicaea 787): "Monks, some of whose names have been preserved, participated in the decision in regard to both the voting on the truth of the propositions contained in Pope Hadrian's letter and the signing of the council's Decree on Faith, which contains the signatures of 131 monks and one presbyter (who probably also belonged to a monastic Order). On the other hand names of monks, with the exception of those who functioned as representatives, are missing from the final list of signatories of the conciliar decrees."[34] Hence it is out of the question to speak of exclusively episcopal synods in connection with the ecu-

---

[32] Mansi 11, 656.

[33] G. Tangl, *Die Teilnehmer an den allgemeinen Konzilien des Mittelalters* (Weimar 1922) 11.

[34] G. Tangl, *op cit.* 6.

menical councils of antiquity. We should also not pass over in silence
the fact that there was an ecumenical council presided over by a
woman: The seventh ecumenical council (Nicaea 787) was convoked
and in part presided over by the Empress Irene (at which Charlemagne took umbrage).

(c) Lay persons also acquired an increased influence at councils
with the formation of *medieval* society, following the great migrations
of peoples and the close link between the Church and secular communities at all levels. The presence of lay persons is attested to by a
Roman synod under Leo the Great as early as 444: "Residentibus
itaque mecum episcopis ac presbyteris ac in eundem consessum
Christianis viris ac nobilibus congregatis. . . ."[35] Two prominent laymen were especially entered on the lists at a Roman synod held in
495.[36] At the beginning of the sixth century the position of lay persons
was especially strong at the Roman synods, in the time of Theodoric
the Great, which the emperor had in part convoked and on which
he exerted a strong influence.[37] Lay persons were also represented at
Spanish and French synods of the sixth and seventh centuries, and
at the Anglo-Saxon synods of the eighth and ninth centuries. The
concrete composition of the individual synods varied greatly. Yet
in connection with all these councils, it cannot be said that lay
persons were on a par with bishops.[38]

The influence exerted by the kings of the early Middle Ages at the
synods deserves special attention. In a wholly different way from the
earlier Theodoric, Charlemagne in 799 energetically convoked a
great Roman synod that also included many Frankish and Roman
lay persons—obviously this too was a representation of all the social
estates in Christendom. He presided over and directed this council,
which sat in judgment on Pope Leo II, who had to take on oath of
purgation in his defence.[39] A similar event took place in 823. The
Frankish influence altogether lasted throughout the first half of the
ninth century without a countervailing force. Emperor Louis II
often intervened imperiously in the discussions, especially at the
Roman synods held between 847 and 855, and also pronounced

[35] Leo M. "Sermo de ieiunio decimi mensis," *PL* 54, 178.
[36] Mansi 8, 179.
[37] G. Tangl, *op cit.* 43–51; the influence of the Roman Senate should be borne
in mind here.
[38] Cf. Y. Congar, *Lay People in the Church* (London and Westminster, Md.
1957).
[39] E. Amann, *L'époque carolingienne* (Fliche and Martin, Histoire de l'Eglise,
vol. 6) (Paris 1947) 153–165.

judgment. A papal reaction can be ascertained first under Pope Nicholas I, based on the pseudo-Isidorian forgeries, which appeared at that time. In the dark century of the papacy, during the time of the emperor and Church reformer Otto the Great, all important synods took place in the presence of the emperor. The position of the laity was much stronger at these synods. At a Roman synod, held in 963 in the Church of St. Peter, Otto with the co-operation of the clergy and the people,[40] had the corrupt John XII deposed and the outstanding layman (!) Leo elected as pope. At a later synod in 964, he effected the deposition of the antipope Benedict.[41] The Roman synods under Otto were of momentous importance for the future: "The unequal representation, which had become a factor of some importance, of the lower clergy, of the Roman nobility and citizenry, of the German potentates, and the beginning of the participation of South Italian princes were of a significance not to be overlooked in connection with the transformation of the old Roman bishops' synods into the general councils of the Middle Ages. Otto I produced a synod very much like the one that Charlemagne had in mind, but he did this more emphatically and effectively.[42] As had the three Ottos, Henry II and Conrad II likewise exerted a decisive influence on the Roman synods, and also on those often meeting in session outside Rome.

After a renewed decline of the papacy under Benedict IX, in 1046 Henry III put an end to the chaos surrounding papal succession at the epoch-making synods of Sutri and Rome. He simply deposed the three rival popes and had the German pope (Clement II) elected, thereby making the rise of a reform-papacy possible. "The sessions of Sutri and Rome in December of 1046 again showed the German monarchy to be at the peak of its ecclesiastical influence and of its power position *vis-à-vis* Rome and the papacy. It was the German king who convoked and presided over these synods and who appointed and removed popes at them, as once Charlemagne had done. In general at that time his vigorous interventions met with approval and approbation even in strictly ecclesiastically minded circles, although there was also no lack of isolated opposition on the part of Bishop Wazo of Liège and the author of the treatise 'De ordinando pontifice,' who viewed the deposition of Gregory VI as wrong. Thus Peter Damian, who at first had welcomed the pontificate of Gregory VI with extravagant joy and high hopes, as early as 1052

[40] G. Tangl, *op cit.* 109f.
[41] Cf. F. X. Seppelt, *Geschichte der Päpste* (Munich ²1955) II, 368–371; C. J. von Hefele, *Conciliengeschichte* (Freiburg i. Br. ²1879) IV, 609–616.
[42] G. Tangl, *op cit.* 114f.

in his 'Liber gratissimus' hailed Henry III a person to be prized, who 'next to God has wrested us from the jaws of the insatiable dragon and with the sword of divine power has chopped off all the heads of the multiheaded hydra, that is, of simonistic heresy.' "[43]

Under the subsequent German popes (especially Leo IX and Victor II) a large number of reform synods were held in and outside of Italy, marked by a strong participation of secular persons. Thus in connection with the Roman synod held in 1050 there is also an account mentioning the laity's approbation of the canonization of Bishop Gerhard of Toul: "Ad quod cuncti tam archiepiscopi quam episcopi, tam abbates quam clerici et laici, quorum utrorumque magna intererat multitudo, quasi uno ore clamaverunt."[44] Lay persons also played an important role at the synods of the subsequent popes, Nicholas II and Alexander II (especially in South Italy). Lay persons also participated in the important synods of Gregory VII. Gregory VII, in 1083, was the first to formulate the idea of a synod at which both the clerical and secular social estates of Christendom were to be represented. The project failed, however, because of the outbreak of the historic struggle between the papacy and the empire in the dispute over investitures.[45] Abbots were also invited formally for the first time, under Gregory.[46]

Gregory's successor, Victor VII, was elected at a synod held in Capua in 1087, at which both the urban Roman and the Norman influence (especially that of the Norman duke Roger) was strong.[47] A new development took place under Victor's successor, the Frenchman Urban II. A strong Norman influence was also perceptible at the synod of Melfi in 1089. But the pope now broadened in all directions the circle of participants, as shown by the synod of Piacenza held in 1095. Even though the chronicler Bernold counts more than 30,000 lay persons in addition to 4,000 clerics, this may be a greatly exaggerated figure. At any rate it was necessary to hold the council in an open field. In addition to Matilda of Tuscany, the Empress Praxedis made her appearance, and here she made accusations against herself and especially against Henry IV. There was also a delegation representing the Byzantine emperor, Alexius.[48] The Council of Clermont, convoked by Urban in 1095, is of even greater importance.

---

[43] F. X. Seppelt, *op cit*. 418; cf. C. J. von Hefele, *op cit*. IV, 706–715.
[44] Mansi 19, 770; cf. C. J. von Hefele, *op cit*. IV, 747.
[45] G. Tangl, *op cit*. 165–169.
[46] G. Tangl, *op cit*. 155f.
[47] C. J. von Hefele, *Conciliengeschichte* (Freiburg i. Br. ²1886) V, 189f; G. Tangl, *op cit*. 169.
[48] C. J. von Hefele, *op cit*. V, 215f; G. Tangl, *op cit*. 172f.

Individual princes, who enjoyed good relations with the pope or who
were accountable to him, had been invited to the earlier synods.
"Here a general participation of the lay world was fostered for the
first time. This broad inclusion of all Christendom was linked to
Urban's plans for a crusade. The organization of crusades was a
matter of general importance for all Christendom. Hence this very
plan warranted the holding of councils on a great scale which, at
least represented the main parts of the Western world."[49]

This Council of Clermont was called a "general council," by the
pope himself.[50] Nevertheless, this council has never been reckoned
among the ecumenical councils. Here, as already was the case with
previous synods in the West, "general council" meant simply a synod
encompassing larger and broader areas. At the same time we see that
there is a continuous line leading to the great papal Lateran synods of
the twelfth century, which today are frequently considered as ecumenical councils. In these councils both the circle of their participants
(clerical and lay), and their tasks had been steadily broadened along
the strict lines of papal synods, which very often were held outside of
Rome because of the political situation. The specific Roman diocesan
synod more and more faded into the background in favour of the
consistory, which attended to current matters affecting the papacy.
After Clermont the important stages on the way to the great Lateran
synods were the three councils under Paschal II: of Guastalla in 1106
(with strong lay participation); of the Lateran Council of 1112
("with abbots and countless multitudes of clerics as well as of lay
persons"[51]); and of 1116 (where for the first time the letter of invitation contains a deliberate reference to the models of the old councils,
although perhaps not to those of the general councils[52]). Finally,
under Calixtus II, there was the strongly attended Council of Reims
in 1119, in which for the first time the French king, Louis VI, took
part.[53]

"It was hardly a further step in this direction when Calixtus II
convoked the Lateran Synod of 1123 as a 'general' synod. For by
this means he purposed, whatever difficulty might arise, to set it
alongside the old ecumenical councils. This indeed did happen later,
although only gradually. Even the Synod of Constance placed only
three new councils with the eight old councils: the Lateran Synod of
1215, the Council of Lyons of 1274, and the Council of Vienna held

---

[49] G. Tangl, *op cit.* 177.
[50] C. J. von Hefele, *op cit.* V, 220.
[51] G. Tangl. *op cit.* 189.
[52] G. Tangl. *op cit.* 191.
[53] C. J. von Hefele, *op cit.* V, 350.

in 1311."[54] Thus with the papal general synods of 1123, 1139, and 1179, convoked by Calixtus II, Innocent II, and Alexander III, no other type of council was aimed at than that of the enlarged synods that had been held around the turn of the century. They especially stand out because the Roman synods had meanwhile wholly died out (in favour of the consistories), and because the synods held outside of Rome gradually ceased meeting on account of the political situation. The lists of participants of the first two papal general synods held in 1123 and 1139 are missing (according to Gerhoh of Reichersberg, who was present, a delegation representing Emperor Henry IV appeared at the First Lateran Council).[55] At the Third Lateran Council, besides the clerical participants, mention is also made of "many representatives of the secular authorities, among which were the still semi-clerical delegations of the Johannites and Order of the Templars who had attended the Council because of their quarrels among themselves and with the Eastern bishops. The *Gesta Henrici II* also report that 'nuntii fere omnium imperatorum, regum, principum totius christianitatis' were also present, and although this is a statement of a somewhat general character we must, nevertheless, conclude from it that there was a strong participation of secular authorities at the Council. It cannot, however, flatly be stated whether or not these knightly orders and princes, as well as the clerical participants, were expressly invited or not. Among the secular participants there was also a delegation of Waldensians, headed by their founder, which expounded its dogmas before the Council."[56]

With the Fourth Lateran Council, held in 1215, Innocent III wanted deliberately and formally to revive the tradition of the early ecumenical councils. Both spiritual and secular Christendom was to be represented at the Council. Thus at this Council we find the ambassadors of Emperor Frederick II, of the kings of France, England, Hungary, Byzantium, Jerusalem, Cyprus, Aragon. In addition there were representatives of cities, especially of the northern Italian city-republics, and a great number of other secular potentates.[57] "This

[54] A. Hauck, "Synoden," in *Realencyklopädie für protestantische Theologie und Kirche* (Leipzig ³1907) XIX, 271; cf. H. Jedin, *Ecumenical Councils of the Catholic Church* (New York 1960) 66–69.

[55] G. Tangl, *op cit.* 205.

[56] G. Tangl, *op cit.* 218f.

[57] In connection with the language used at councils the following note may still be of interest today: In order to be understood by lay persons at the Fourth Lateran Council the archbishop of Toledo, Ximenes, after his speech in Latin, repeated the main arguments in five languages: in French, German, English, Basque, and Spanish. "According to Garzias Loaisa such a miracle of tongues

combination of spiritual and secular elements applied primarily to the first three great public sessions, which in the main were but solemn show-sessions, whereas the actual work of the Council, the discussion and formulation of the conciliar canons, and the settling of the hundreds of disputes brought before the pope, naturally had to be the concern of a smaller but wholly initiated and competent group, especially the cardinals. Nothing of a more exact character has been handed down to us concerning the composition of these intermediate negotiations. The question as to how broad the participation was to be must have been left to the discretion of the pope according to the specific points that had to be dealt with. Here, at any rate, the clerical element must have constituted the main element at the Council."[58]

The three subsequent ecumenical councils continued along the lines set by the Fourth Lateran Council. At the First Council of Lyons, in 1245, under Innocent IV—for political reasons, the Council was held against Frederick II and led to his deposition—the participation was much smaller than that of the last Lateran Council. Yet many lay persons also showed up here: "Prelates or their representatives from almost all of Christendom," says Matthew of Paris, "were present, as well as procurators of the emperors and of many princes."[59] The Second Council of Lyons under Gregory X (a new crusade, union with the Greeks, rules for conclaves): besides King James I of Aragon, also present were "the representatives of both knightly orders, the Templars and the Johannites, together with the ambassadors of the kings of France, Germany, England, Sicily, and the procurators of many other princes, lords, cathedral chapters, and Churches."[60] Third, the ecumenical Council of Vienne in 1311–12, under Clement V (suppression of the Order of the Templars, the dispute over Franciscan poverty, reform decrees): under pressure from Philip the Fair for the first time in the history of the ecumenical councils a selection was made from among the bishops who had been summoned to the council; only a small number of all the French bishops turned up. The ambassadors of the kings of France, England, and Aragon were present among the lay persons.[61]

---

had not been experienced since the time of the apostles" (C. J. von Hefele, *op cit.* 875).

[58] G. Tangl, *op cit.* 232.

[59] C. J. von Hefele, *op cit.* V, 1106.

[60] C. J. von Hefele, *op cit.* VI, 133.

[61] J. Leclercq, "Concile de Vienne," in *Dictionnaire de Théologie catholique* (Paris 1950) 15, 2974.

(*d*) Ecumenical councils, in the form of a medieval papal general synod, were called into question by the Great Schism in the West. Since the position of the pope had been shaken by the papal schism, the council began to be taken seriously in a new way as the legitimate representation of the whole Church. This of itself led to a strengthening of the laity at councils. A council was convoked at Pisa in 1409 by the cardinals in order to heal the schism. Present besides patriarchs, bishops, abbots, and generals of Orders, were the "Grand Master of Rhodes with 16 associate knights, the Prior General of the Knights of the Holy Sepulchre, the Procurator General of the Teutonic Order, the deputies of the Universities of Paris, Toulouse, Orleans, Angres, Montpellier, Bologna, Florence, Cracow, Vienna, Prague, Cologne, Oxford, and Cambridge, plenipotentiaries of more than 100 cathedral chapters, more than 300 doctors of theology and of canon law, and finally the ambassadors of almost all the kings, princes, and republics of the Western world."[62] True, the schism was not healed at Pisa; indeed, instead of two popes, now three wanted to rule the Church.

The *ecumenical Council of Constance* was the first to restore unity to the Church. This Council is the only one in Church history which succeeded in restoring unity to the Church not only piecemeal as the Second Council of Lyons and later that of Florence, but permanently, at least in the West. Hence, this Council is all the more deserving of attention in our context. It was attended by an extraordinary number from both ecclesiastical and secular social estates. "When attendance at the Council was at its height, there were 3 patriarchs, 29 cardinals, 33 archbishops, about 150 bishops, over 100 abbots, about 50 priors, and nearly 300 doctors of theology. The whole clerical representation, including a part of the numerous retinue of servants accompanying them (the Archbishop of Mainz, for example, brought about 500 persons with him) amounted to 18,000 persons. . . . The most prominent among the lay persons, besides Emperor Sigismund, was the Elector Ludwig of the Palatinate (later Protector of the Council), Elector Rudolph of Saxony, Margrave Frederick of Brandenburg, the Dukes of Bavaria, Austria, Saxony, Schleswig, Mecklenburg, Lorraine, Teck (Louis, the last scion of this royal house, was at that time the Patriarch of Aquileia and represented at the synod by an ambassador), further, the ambassadors of the kings of France, England, Scotland, Poland, Sweden, Denmark, Norway, Naples, Sicily, and later also of the Spanish kings and of Emperor Manuel Palaeologos of Constantinople. In addition there was an almost

[62] C. J. von Hefele, *op cit*. VI, 994.

countless number of counts and knights who had come to Constance either on their own or in the retinue of the great princes."[63]

It is of extraordinary importance, however, that at this ecumenical council, which was the only one to succeed in restoring Church unity, full voting rights were had not only by theologians and canonists but also by important lay personages. Pope John XXIII, of the Pisan line, had brought a great number of prelates from Italy with him. Moreover, he had also appointed many more through a kind of wholesale nomination so that he had the majority of the prelates on his side. "Thus when the question of who should have the right to vote at the synod came up for discussion, his followers wanted to grant it only to bishops and abbots, basing themselves on the practice of earlier synods. But their proposal encountered stormy resistance. Cardinal d'Ailly, especially, in a special treatise argued that the early councils had been constituted in a variety of ways and that it would be unjust for a titular bishop who was not responsible for the guidance of a single soul to have the same right to vote as, say, the Archbishop of Mainz. He demanded that even doctors of theology and of canon and civil law should be granted definitive voting rights especially the forum who teach and preach and whose judgment was much more important than that of an unlearned titular prelate. That there were no doctors of theology at the old councils was only because there formerly was no rank of this kind. At the synods of Pisa and Rome (in 1412), however, the doctors had had a decisive vote. Finally, d'Ailly also demanded that the Christian kings and princes and their ambassadors also have a right to vote. A similar memorial, written in even sharper language, was circulated by Cardinal Fillastre, and this view won the day."[64]

[63] C. J. von Hefele, *op cit.* VII, 91.

[64] C. J. von Hefele, *op cit.* 82f. Hence it was not only a matter of a consultative vote but also one of a definitive or decisive (conclusive) vote of theologians and leading lay persons. Cf. Cardinal d'Ailly's proposal: ". . . one cannot exclude from decisive vote the doctors of sacred theology, canon and civil law, especially the theologians, who have received the authority to preach and teach everywhere. This is no small authority over the faithful. It greatly exceeds that of an individual bishop or an ignorant abbot. Since this ancient authority of the doctors was not introduced by way of the *studium generale*, as it is observed by ecclesiastical authority nowadays, there is no mention of them in ancient canon law; but their authority was asserted in the Councils of Pisa and of Rome and they subscribed with a decisive vote. Hence to exclude them in a similar matter by the present Council, which is the continuation of the afore-mentioned Council of Pisa, is not only absurd but in some way a reproach to the Council of Pisa. . . . The same can be said in regard to kings and princes and their ambassadors, as well as the proxies of absent prelates, and chapters, as it is also clear from the bull of our Pope who orders the present Council, and especially from the canonical causes of hindrance

As has already been mentioned,[65] in order to prevent an Italian majority during the voting there was not a counting of heads, but votes were cast by nations. This procedure, which had proved its usefulness at Constance, was overelaborated at the ecumenical Council of Basle. "To an even greater degree than Constance, the Council of Basle was an assembly of proxies and doctors. In a vote taken on December 5, 1436, three cardinals, nineteen bishops, and twenty-nine abbots were faced by three hundred and three other participants at the council; the bishops, therefore, formed much less than a tenth of the participants. Any member of the council had a right to a vote and could be elected to any one of the four committees dealing with general questions, faith, reform and peace."[66] The most important rule of procedure at Basle was the following: "All members, regardless of their rank, are to be divided into four *deputations*, corresponding to the four main tasks of the Council, namely the *Deputatio fidei, pacis, reformationis*, and the *Deputatio communis*. An equal number of persons from each of the four nations (Italy, France, Germany, and Spain) must be on each deputation, as well as persons of all classes, so that each deputation may contain cardinals, bishops, abbots, teachers, doctors, etc. Thereby the lower clergy achieved ascendancy because they were in the majority."[67]

The Council was transferred to Ferrara in 1437 by Eugene IV; there a dispute arose over whether the order of business should be conducted on the basis of national representation or of deputations (commissions). Finally, it was agreed that "all members be divided into three ranks: (*a*) cardinals, archbishops, and bishops; (*b*) abbots and prelates; (*c*) doctors, etc.; and that the agreement of two thirds of its members was required for the formulation of a decision on the part of a rank."[68] The German emperor (although Sigismund died a month before the opening) and the Greek emperor (present in the person of John VIII Palaeologos) had honorary seats next to the pope's throne, which were higher than those of the cardinals, bishops, and prelates. Then, for financial reasons, the Council in 1439 had to shift the scene of its activities to Florence.

---

for those who cannot come to the council personally at this time and place. Furthermore, those who are thus hindered should not postpone sending delegates in their name who are God-fearing and have knowledge and experience in the matter and are endowed with the necessary mandate so that they can take the places of those who sent them in the mentioned council" (Mansi 27, 561).

[65] Cf. Chap. IV, 1.
[66] H. Jedin, *Ecumenical Councils of the Catholic Church* (New York 1960) 129.
[67] C. J. von Hefele, *op cit.* VII, 494.
[68] C. J. von Hefele, *op cit.* VII, 664.

(*e*) The radicalism of the Basle Council, especially in its last phase, the conciliar and political success of the pope and of his cardinals, and finally Cardinal Torquemada's "Summa de Ecclesia" led to an epoch of restoration which found its expression in the *Fifth Lateran Council* (1512–17), convoked by Julius II in defence against the schismatic council of Pisa, held in 1511, which was primarily attended by Frenchmen. This council was deliberately linked to the papal councils of the Middle Ages. It took place under the presidency of the pope and was almost exclusively attended by Italian bishops. But it could not stem the Reformation.

Lay persons also played their role at the *Council of Trent*, although not in the same way as at the Council of Constance. Even Paul III's bull convoking the council at Mantua "Ad Dominici gregis curam" (1536), besides all bishops, abbots and other prelates, also invited the emperor, kings, and other princes to appear personally, or at least to send ambassadors.[69] The same applies to the first convocation to Trent "Initio nostri huius pontificatus" (1542)[70] and likewise to the final convocation "Laetare Jerusalem" (1544).[71] "The ambassadors of the princes still attended the council sessions at the Council of Trent and they could exert influence on the discussions pertaining to questions of dogma and canon law. They did this both by intervention as individuals (especially the ambassador of Venice during the discussion of the canon on marriage) and in a body (after the twenty-second session) in their written protest against the postponement of Church reform. It even came to pass that a lay person, Count L. de Nogarola, preached a sermon to the Council Fathers on Christmas Eve. The secretary of the Council, Angelo Massarelli, a protonotary apostolic, was a layman. He was consecrated as bishop during the Council. One of the presiding officers of the Council, Cardinal Reginald Pole, was not a priest. His colleague in the presidium, Cervini, later Pope Marcellus II, also was not a priest when he was appointed a cardinal."[72]

The right to vote, however, was radically limited as compared to the councils of the fifteenth century: The representatives of ecclesiastical corporations, of universities, and of cathedral chapters received the right to a conclusive vote as little as did lay persons. "Rome was firmly resolved to prevent an extension of the right to

---

[69] *Concilium Tridentinum. Diariorum, Actorum, Epistularum, Tractatuum nova Collectio.* Ed. by Goerresiana (Freiburg i. Br. 1910ff; in the following referred to by the initials *CT*) IV, 2–6.

[70] *CT* IV 226–231.

[71] *CT* IV 385–388.

[72] P. Fransen, "Das Konzil und die Laien," in *Orientierung* 25 (1961) 3.

vote on the model of the reform Councils of the fifteenth century, but the Curia was equally anxious to have the generals of the Orders of mendicants—those papal guardsmen—accepted as full members of the Council while the abbots, who were expressly mentioned in the Bull of Convocation, were not to be completely excluded."[73] The abbots who were present were granted a collective vote as representatives of their congregations. The vote was no longer taken by nations, but by counting heads.

The participants of the *First Vatican Council* were similarly ranked: All bishops present were invited with the right to a conclusive vote, but not doctors of theology and of canon law, and lay persons. On the other hand, purely titular bishops, Generals of Orders, and the presidents of congregations of monks could vote.[74] Originally, the intention had been to invite the ambassadors of Christian states, but the plan was soon dropped for political reasons. Indeed, lay persons were expressly prohibited from attending the proceedings except for the liturgical celebrations. A rigidly enforced "council secrecy," which in fact was not maintained, was also supposed to prevent the clergy and people from following the proceedings even from afar as listeners.[75]

What a difference between the First Vatican Council and the ecumenical Council of Constance! What a difference especially between the First Vatican Council and the first synods, which were held before and with the people! What a difference between the First Vatican Council and the "Council of the Apostles"! What P. Fransen says about Vatican I is essentially correct: *"Never in the whole history of the Church was the participation of the laity so meagre."*[76]

The reasons Fransen adduces for this fact are very sound: "The old religious and social structures, which had made possible the co-operation of lay holders of authority no longer existed. And there were not yet any new institutions which might have allowed the laity to associate itself with the work of the council as an independent social estate within the Church. Further, the question was posed here in this form for the first time. In addition, an all-too-clerical theology of the Church paralysed all attempts in this direction. It was the unfortunate consequence of the controversies with

---

[73] H. Jedin, *A History of the Council of Trent* (Edinburgh 1961) II, 19.

[74] C. Butler and H. Lang, *Das vatikanische Konzil* (Munich ³1933) 78–79.

[75] Concerning the "maladroite tactique de silence" which did great harm to the Council and which in time was in fact given up, cf. R. Aubert, *Le pontificat de Pie IX* (Fliche and Martin, Histoire de l'Église, vol. 21) (Paris 1952) 346.

[76] P. Fransen, "Das Konzil und die Laien," in *Orientierung* 25 (1961) 3.

the Protestants and the laicism of that time. The scandal —completely unjustified—aroused by J. H. Newman's article in *The Rambler* in 1859, "On Consulting the Laity in Matter of Doctrine," gives us an idea of the kind of theological and practical difficulties one faced at that time. The time was not yet ripe."[77]

3. REPRESENTATION OF THE LAITY TODAY

The variability of the findings in Church history is obvious. What can we conclude from these facts of the Church's tradition?

(*a*) Lay persons *can* participate in councils. Or in other words: There is no *ius divinum* that excludes the participation of the laity at ecumenical councils. However this participation is justified and legally regulated, it is certain that conciliar history provides impressive evidence of a manifold participation of the laity at such gatherings. In this respect, a special importance must be attached— in addition to the accounts of the first Church councils in the second and third centuries—to the evidence in the Acts of the function of the whole community at the "Council of the Apostles," which exhibits an organic unity of office and community. It is precisely the model prescribed in the book of Acts which reveals how erroneous it would be to make the First Vatican Council, clearly the furthest removed from this model, into an ideal image of a council developed to the peak of perfection. This example clearly shows how oversimplified and basically wrong it would be to understand historical development in the Church as a steady forward movement to an ideal, to an ever-greater perfection—whether this advance is understood (in the sense of the Enlightenment) as a linear, spiralling movement toward perfection or (in the Hegelian sense) as an ascending dialectical process in a fruitful interplay of opposites. Neither of these two theories of development is sufficiently Christian; neither of them gives sufficient weight to the humanity and the sinfulness in the Church and her history.

After having been often in the position of defensively warding off the idea of development in the Church, nowadays one is often exposed to the danger of justifying *everything* that has developed in the Church, by enlisting the aid of the concept of development: as though there were only periods of flowering and not also of decay, as though there were only enrichment and not also impoverishment, as though there were only fulfilment and not also depletion, as though there were only progress and not also regression. In short, as though there

---

[77] P. Fransen, *op cit*. 3f.

were no marks of the all-too-human and of the sinfulness that clings
to all human development. The διάϰϱισις πνευμάτων (I Cor. 12:10)
applies to all development in the Church, namely the discernment of
spirits by the mature Christian who not only feeds on milk but can
also digest solid food and thus train his faculties to distinguish
between good and evil (Heb. 5:14). It is not a question of holding fast
to everything; rather must everything be shed and the good alone
retained (I Thess. 5:21). The testing standard is not the *status quo*
(itself to be tested) of the Church, but the gospel of Jesus Christ.
Hence it is precisely in connection with the question of lay participation that one should take care not to start out from the *status quo*,
tacitly regarded as the optimal peak of development up to now, in
order to demonstrate, if possible, that even this *status quo* is of
divine law. And this despite the fact that the whole historical development shows in its variability that here we are manifestly in the realm
of the human law. Only if one dares (which truly would not be harmful to the Church) to see the variability in the development can one
guard oneself from doing violence to the truth of historical development through anachronistic formal distinctions and *a priori* postulates.[77a]

[77a] Against Scheeben's view of the relationship between councils and the laity,
which is characteristic of many manuals on dogma, the following criticism is
made by L. Scheffczyk, "Die Lehranschauungen Matthias Joseph Scheebens
über das ökumenische Konzil," in *Tübinger theologische Quartalschrift* 141 (1961)
171f: "Here Scheeben arrived at a strongly emphasized 'hierarchic' conception of
a council of which, indeed, there had already been indications at an early stage
and which culminates in the assertion that a council is the representation only of
the teaching Church. This statement, formulated without any restrictions, is
lacking at least in the necessary counterweight. For it cannot be disputed that
bishops at a council also bear witness to the faith of their Church and thereby
represent the faithful even though this representation, obviously, does not come
about in a parliamentary way but is grounded in their office. But it is especially
groundless to speak of a representation of the teaching Church when the greater
part of the episcopate is assembled at a council. Such a council is no longer only
a representation of the teaching Church, but much more the teaching Church
herself. Thus the phrase 'representation of the whole Church' by a council cannot
exclusively refer to the teaching Church. Seemingly Scheeben, on the basis of the
apologetic front-line position—linked to the mental climate of the time—against
the extreme advocates of a democratic-collegiate constitution of the Church,
who wished to regard bishops at councils only as the representatives and witnesses
of the faith of their Church, arrived at a 'nay' without discussing the problem
along positive lines. That he did not engage in a disputation over the historically
verified fact of lay participation in the early councils and take up the theological
problems underlying it may likewise be due to the same reason. Even here he
contended himself with the brief antithesis that the general convocation of lay
persons did not mean that they became members of a council. Thus there was no
real incorporation of conciliar events into the organism of the whole Church,
although Scheeben had at least proclaimed such an attempt."

(*b*) The *universal priesthood of all believers* is the foundation that makes it possible for the laity to participate in an ecumenical council. The doctrine of the universal priesthood is part of the fundamental truths of Catholic ecclesiology. Our whole presentation up to now has been based upon this fact: we Catholics believe that *all* Christians are called to the ecumenical council by divine convocation, that they are called as "a chosen race, a royal priesthood, a holy nation" (I Pet. 2:9).[78] Hence when Luther raised the question of participation at councils with an appeal to the universal priesthood of all believers, he was setting forth an authentic Catholic point of view. He thereby raised an issue which for a long time had been a sore spot in the Church. It can hardly be denied that this basic truth had faded into oblivion, and often alarmingly so, in the Middle Ages, during the Reformation, and also thereafter. Nor can it be denied that very often ecclesiology had turned into a hierarchology. This trend had made its appearance with the first systematic treatises concerning the Church (James of Viterbo, "De regimine christiano"; Aegidius Romanus, "De ecclesiastica potestate"; Jean de Paris, "De potestate regia et papali"). Since these were occasioned by the quarrel between Boniface VIII and Philip the Fair, they dealt almost exclusively with issues concerning ecclesiastical authority, canon law, and the political power of the Church. These tendencies were intensified in the secular struggle against Gallicanism and conciliarism, Protestantism, Jansenism, and liberalism. "There was the danger of paving the way for a development in which the lay person no longer considered himself as an organic member of the whole Church and in which the Church was more and more understood and experienced as a Church of clerics. Thus the lay person was only to a slight degree aware of his responsibility for the whole Church. It would be an exaggeration, however, to assert that the lay person no longer had a voice in the modern Church. After the Church had again been interpreted as the Body of Christ by the Tübingen Theological School, Pope Pius X, through the promotion of eucharistic piety and especially through his communion decrees, ushered in a movement through which lay persons were again vigorously drawn back into the realm of the sacred. Popes Pius XI and Pius XII (the latter especially through the encyclicals 'Mystici Corporis' and 'Mediator Dei' as well as in many addresses) had most vigorously fostered the participation of the laity in divine worship. Theological science, especially liturgy and dogmatics, successfully clarified the problems that were cropping up, The place of the lay person in the Church emerged ever more clearly

[78] Cf. especially Chap. II,

even though it was not yet possible to achieve an ultimate clarity on the subject."[79]

Thus, in his address on February 20, 1946, to the newly appointed cardinals, Pope Pius said: "The faithful—more precisely, the laity—stand in the front line in the life of the Church; through them the Church proves herself to be the life-principle of human society. Hence it is they especially who must arrive at an ever-clearer awareness: we not only belong to the Church but *we are* the Church, the community of the faithful on earth under the common supreme head, the pope and the bishops united with him. They *are the Church.*"[80] And he was even more specific at the Second World Congress of the Laity in 1957: "It signified a distortion of the true nature of the Church and of her social character when on the one hand it was purposed to distinguish in her a purely active element, the ecclesiastical authorities, and on the other a purely passive element, the laity. All members, as we ourselves have said in the encyclical 'Mystici corporis Christi,' are called to co-operate in the edification and perfection of the mystical body of Christ. All are free persons and must be active . . ."[81] Both in practice and in theology, infinitely more still remains to be done in order that the priesthood of the laity may be granted the importance that is its due. Yves Congar's *Lay People in the Church* is the most comprehensive and truly pioneering work on the theology of the laity. He clearly poses and elaborates the fundamental question of the priestly, royal and prophetic mission of the laity, including its practical applicability.[82]

[79] M. Schmaus, *Katholische Dogmatik* (Munich 1958) 111/1, 732.
[80] *Acta Apostolicae Sedis* 38 (1946) 149.
[81] *Acta Apostolicae Sedis* 49 (1957) 925.
[82] Y. Congar, *Lay People in the Church* (London 1957). Concerning a theology of the laity, cf. further new Catholic works: J. M. Alonso, "Santo Tomás y el llamado sacerdocio de los fieles," in *XIII Semana Española de Teología* (Madrid 1954) 132–169; F. X. Arnold, "Die Stellung des Laien in der Kirche," in *Una Sancta* 9 (1954) 8–25; "Kirche und Laientum," in *Theologische Quartalschrift* 134 (1954) 263–289; H. U. von Balthasar, "Der Laie und die Kirche," in *Viele Ämter, ein Geist* ed. by H. Nüsse (Einsiedeln 1954), and in *Sponsa Verbi. Skizzen zur Theologie* II (Einsiedeln 1961) 332–348; G. Philips, *Role of the Laity in the Church* (Notre Dame, Ind. 1955) M. de la Bedoyère, *The Layman in the Church* (London 1955); K. Rahner, "Über das Laienapostolat," in *Schriften zur Theologie* (Einsiedeln 1955) II, 339–373 English, "Notes on the Lay Apostolate," *Theological Investigation* II, (London 1963) pp. 319–352; "Weihe des Laien zur Seelsorge," in *Schriften zur Theologie* (Einsiedeln 1956) III, 313–328; O. Semmelroth and L. Hofmann, *Der Laie in der Kirche* (Trier 1955); R. Spiazzi, *Il laicato nella Chiesa. Problemi e orientamenti di teologia dommatica* (Milan 1957); A. Sustar, "Der Laie in der Kirche," in *Fragen der Theologie heute*, ed. by J. Feiner, J. Trütsch, and F. Böckle (Einsiedeln 1957) 519–548; K. H. Schelkle, *Jüngerschaft und Apostelamt* (Freiburg ²1961); R. Tucci, "Recenti pubblicazioni sul 'Laici nella

The ecumenical council by human convocation is the representation of the ecumenical council by divine convocation, which is the Church. It is the representation of the *whole* Church, the representation of the *entire* royal and priestly people of God. Hence it may be said that no strictly theological and dogmatic reasons can be invoked to exclude *a priori* the participation of the laity in ecumenical councils by human convocation.[83]

(c) We justified the participation of lay persons in councils— in the light of the *Acts of the Apostles* and the first Church councils— on the basis of the universal priesthood of the faithful. Consequently we deliberately disregarded other justifications of lay participation that were formerly customary (in part connected with the concept of universal priesthood). Many points in the earlier justifications, especially those pertaining to the role of Christian princes, were determined by specific historical conditions. This applies, for instance, to the sacred character with which Byzantine emperors were invested, and the *ius in sacra* bound up with it. It also applies to the medieval emperors and kings (especially in the case of Charlemagne) whose interference in the ecclesiastical affairs of the territorial Churches can be compared only to the later interferences of the popes. The medieval body of Christians constituted a politico-religious unity with two branches, the spiritual and the secular authority. This cannot simply be equated with the modern concepts of Church and State, or of "religious" and "political." Spiritual and secular power—although separated at the apex of worldly power— were conjoined at their roots. In this symbiosis of powers the pope and the bishops also acquired a political character—just as, conversely, emperors, kings, and princes acquired a sacred character (consider the almost priestly position of the emperor and kings in the liturgy). In times of emergency it was possible for one of the authorities to assume the functions of the other (an interference of the pope in

Chiesa,' " in *Civiltà Cattolica* 109 (1958) 179–190; "Problemi di apostolato e di spiritualità dei laici," *ibid.* 398–406; K. Jahász, *Laien im Dienst der Seelsorge* (Münster 1960); H. Heimerl, *Kirche, Klerus und Laien* (Vienna 1961); Y. Congar, "Laie," in *Lexikon für Theologie und Kirche* (Freiburg i. Br. 1961) VI, 733–740.

[83] Concerning the whole council-laity problem area, cf. the bibliography cited at the beginning of the first chapter (Commentaries on the CIC, works dealing with the history of councils and with the position of councils in canon law and constitutional history). In addition, see especially G. Tangl, *Die Teilnehmer an den allgemeinen Konzilien des Mittelalters* (Weimar 1922); Y. Congar, *Lay People in the Church* (London 1957); P. Fransen, "Das Konzil und die Laien," in *Orientierung* 25 (1961) 1–5; H. Krüger, "Laien auf dem Konzil?", in *Frankfurter Hefte* 15 (1960) 29–36.

political matters whenever secular authorities had failed—and conversely an interference of secular authorities whenever there was a failure on the part of the popes or the bishops; for example, in connection with Church reform: *ius reformandi*). At the same time this was in part a matter of exercising rights that were valid at that time (recognized by the opposite side), which, of course, frequently led to illegal interferences and abuses—from both sides! By and large the princes respected the limits set by dogma and *iura divina*. It lies outside the scope of our investigation to pronounce a judgment on these conditions of medieval and, in part, post-Reformation times. What is important to our argument is the following: For the sacred and temporal powers *these* rights were a matter of *iura humana* which, after the dissolution of the medieval religio-political unity of *regnum* and *sacerdotium* (today divided in principle, in terms of secular state and spiritual Church), can no longer be emphasized in the same way. When the princes claimed special rights at councils, they meant human and not divine rights. And it was also a question of human right and not divine right when the ecclesiastical authorities, assuming a defensive attitude against the encroachments of the secular power, simply prohibited the participation of lay persons.[84]

(*d*) The position of Luther, who linked his argument of the priesthood of all believers with an appeal to the princes, was also determined by historical conditions. "One of the leading Lutheran scholars who is also a major authority on the whole Middle Ages (Boehmer) has made the following pertinent remarks concerning the territorial rulers' dominion over the Church at the time of the Reformation: 'It was not a creation of reformationist thought but a product of the late medieval politico-ecclesiastical law fertilized by the ideas of the old-Germanic private-Church (*Eigenkirche*) system.' Thus the unbroken link with the early Middle Ages can be established beyond doubt. The territorial Church adminstration of the Lutherans, at least in its fundamental theoretical and practical features, was altogether a legacy of the Middle Ages. Hence it can be unquestionably asserted that 'the institution of territorial Churches was already a creation of the Middle Ages.' As such it has nothing to do with the innovations of the Reformation. With its medieval

---

[84] On this question, cf. J. Hashagen, *Staat und Kirche vor der Reformation. Eine Untersuchung der vorreformatorischen Bedeutung des Laieneinflusses in der Kirche* (Essen 1931), and Y. Congar, *Lay People in the Church*, as well as the bibliography cited in these works.

peculiarities, it actually appears much more as an alien body within the frame of these innovations."[85]

Luther, starting out from the idea of the universal priesthood of all believers, increasingly favoured the territorial Church administration in questions of external Church organization: "It has been clearly and convincingly documented that even up to 1525 Luther had an essentially negative view of this competence of the secular authority, in so far as he was struggling against the ordinances of the old Church. An attempt has also been made to interpret Luther's genuine conception concerning the ecclesiastical activity of secular authority as in general completely negative: to explain the 'direct' government action in Church matters as deriving from secular sources and to limit the 'indirect' action to a minimum. Luther's actual and innermost convictions in this sphere may have been entirely negative. He may have had a particularly strongly felt inner aversion to the intrusion of the secular arm into internal Church affairs. Nevertheless, in the end he did not bring any of his habitual persuasive energy to bear upon the realization of these convictions. Rather, with 'the very rise of Protestant-minded communities,' Luther notably withdrew from his genuine positions. It was not long before he was again advocating 'that the Christian rulers should care for the salvation of their subjects' whereby at first the city, but soon also the territorial rulers were meant."[86]

The position of the Counter-Reformation theology is likewise historically conditioned. This holds true particularly for the exaggerated division of the Church into an active group of leaders and teachers and a passive group of mere followers and listeners, and despite the justified argument against the encroachment of secular authority in councils as well as against a completely democratic and parliamentary organization of these. Hence it is not strange that the theology of the Counter Reformation offered no theological appreciation of an active participation of the laity in the Church and the councils.[87] The previously cited words of Pius XII are applicable here: "It signified a distortion of the true nature of the Church and

---

[85] J. Hashagen, *op cit*. 558f.

[86] J. Hashagen, *op cit*. 562f.

[87] After the ecclesiological treatises of Torquemada and Cajetan cf. M. Canus, *De locis theologicis. De auctoritate conciliorum* (Padua 1762) 133–135; R. Bellarmine, *De conciliis, Opera omnia* (Paris 1870) XII, 217–222; F. Suarez, *Disputatio XI. De Conciliis, Opera Omnia* (Paris 1858) XII, 323–327; L. Thomassinus, *Dissertationum in concilia generalia et particularia tomus singularis* (Cologne 1784); C. Passaglia, *De conciliis oecumenicis* (ed. H. Schauf) (Rome 1961) 2–22, 80–106.

of her social character when on the one hand it was purposed to distinguish in her a purely active element, the ecclesiastical authorities and on the other a purely passive element, the laity. All members, as we ourselves had said in the Encyclical 'Mystici corporis Christi', are called to co-operate in the edification and perfection of the Mystical Body of Christ. All are free persons and must be active. . . ."[88]

(e) *In what ways* should lay persons participate in Church and conciliar affairs? In dealing with this question we must also take historical conditions into consideration. There were councils in which lay persons were *directly* represented, and others in which they were represented *indirectly*, namely by the ecclesiastical offices. It would not be fitting to declare only the former mode of representation as legitimate. What is noteworthy is the fact that even the reformers recognized the legitimacy of the first four ecumenical councils, which they esteemed highly, although they were predominantly episcopal synods without a direct representation of the laity (save for the emperor). Direct and indirect representation must also be conceded to the First Vatican Council.

No lengthy explanations are necessary to see why today not only an indirect but a direct representation of the laity is expected in broad circles of the Church. The oft-cited "hour of the laity"— the awakening of the laity to active participation in the liturgy and the apostolate is one of the most hopeful signs in the Church of our century—even with respect to ecumenical councils, must not remain a mere slogan by which one at best understands new duties but no new corresponding rights. Thus a prominent layman has declared: ". . . the 'gentle invitation' to the communities separated from the Church will be scarcely heard and believed as long as not even a sufficient number of seats, not to speak of votes, are made available in at least those commissions of councils which are to deal with matters that are essential to the laity. The Protestant, for example, with some justification draws the conclusion that he would have a hard time to defend his rightful cause in a Church which does not even give a voice to laymen, already belonging to the Church, during the preparatory discussions but urges them to let themselves be represented by 'laymen writ large' (that is, by clerics)."[89] And the professional theologian confirms this: "A council must be free. In this sense it means that in the first place it must be a gathering of

---

[88] *Acta Apostolicae Sedis* 49 (1957) 925f.
[89] F. Messerschmid, in *Wort und Wahrheit* 16 (1961) 635.

Christians, a concrete sign of God's act of salvation in Jesus Christ. It should not be misused as a panopticon of human power and pomp. It must gather in the Holy Spirit and according to the laws of the Spirit (according to the example of Acts 15). It must be a brotherly gathering, which excludes no one who belongs to Christ. Human barriers must be levelled. Priests *and* people, clergy *and* laity belong to a council, each with his full existence in Christ."[90]

(*f*) What are the *concrete possibilities* for a participation of the laity in Church and conciliar affairs? As P. Fransen has correctly pointed out, new institutions are necessary in order to make such lay participation possible today instead of old religious and social institutions and structures, which once had made the participation of the laity possible.[91] In this context Fransen correctly draws attention in the first place to the co-operation of laymen in the *news coverage* of councils. On this point precisely there is much to learn from the negative experiences of the First Vatican Council. "The news blackout that was imposed on the proceedings of the Vatican Council had far-reaching consequences. It was grist to the mill of those who had indulged in speculations about the Council, and it strengthened the suspicion of the enemies of Rome, as well as of interested observers of events, that this secretiveness was intended to shroud the aims and machinations of a specific faction. Thus the possibility of an objective and considered reportage of the Council was thwarted from the outset. On the other hand this very measure offered a wide field to the speculations and the untrammelled imagination of journalists."[92] Thus today leading Catholic publicists call for a positive, open co-operation of councils with the press in the interests of the councils themselves and of the Church.[93] P. Fransen lists the World Secretariat of the Lay Apostolate, the Pontifical Academy of Sciences, the great international and national Catholic organiza-

[90] W. Gruber, in *Wort und Wahrheit* 16 (1961) 596.
[91] P. Fransen, "Das Konzil und die Laien," in *Orientierung* 25 (1961) 3f.
[92] V. Conzemius, "Römische Briefe vom Konzil," in *Tübinger Theologische Quartalschrift* 140 (1960) 427.
[93] Cf. O. B. Roegele, "Die 'Nachrichtenpolitik' des Konzils," in his book: *Was erwarten wir vom Konzil?* (Osnabrück 1961) 46–54. Roegele also cites the joint resolution of the sixth World Congress of the Catholic Press (held July 1960 in Santander) at which twenty-six nations were represented: "The 400 participants . . . decided to give a very broad coverage to the preparations for the council. They expressed the wish to be informed about the proceedings at the council in accordance with the requirements of the modern means of mass communication, so that they could effectively prepare public opinion about this great event of the Church" (54)

tions, as further institutions that can make the participation of the laity possible.[94] During the council—as well as in its preparatory phase—a co-operation is possible in the deputations (commissions) that particularly affect the laity. Yet here we must pose the question as to whether lay participation may not also be possible in a stricter sense of the word.

(*g*) Is the lay person at a council entitled to the right of a final vote (a deliberative, decisive, and definitive *votum*) or only to an advisory vote (a consultative *votum*)? This question is linked to the question pertaining to the position of ecclesiastical offices at councils with which we shall soon be dealing. It would doubtless lead us too far afield were we to deal more closely with the interrelated question of the power of jurisdiction (the relationship between power of orders and pastoral power, or of the power to teach) and to open, say, a discussion on the problems connected with Canon 118, according to which only clerics can be granted power of orders and pastoral power (a distinction between clerics and lay persons on the basis of the tonsure and such matters). The following points must be borne in mind in our presentation: (1) Even canonists admit that in fact not only the earlier but also present law accords jurisdiction to lay persons (men and women) without changing these lay persons into clerics. Hence, Canon 118 is imprecise as regards jurisdiction.[95] (2) The history of canon law teaches us that far-reaching participation of the laity in pastoral authority was possible, not only at councils and through the princes, but also in the exercise of ecclesiastical authority by lay persons in administrative and judicial matters, and above all through the right of the people to the election of bishops (and of the pope) in the sense of agreement and approbation (the famous principle of Leo the Great: "Qui praefuturus est omnibus ab omnibus eligatur!") which has in part been preserved in a limited form in the Eastern Church until the present century.[96]

[94] P. Fransen, "Das Konzil und die Laien," in *Orientierung* 25 (1961) 4: "The fact that different theological faculties in Germany and in Austria in the first instance, however, did not receive an invitation to submit their votes deeply grieved all those who had expected an open, worldwide and therefore Catholic attitude from the Council."

[95] A. Szentirmai, "Jurisdiktion für Laien?", in *Tübinger Theologische Quartalschrift* 140 (1960) 423–426; regarding the position of lay persons in canon law, cf. also K. Mörsdorf, "Die Stellung der Laien in der Kirche," in *Revue de droit canonique* 10–11 (1960–61) 214–234; B. Panzram, "Die Teilnahme der Laien am Priesteramt, Lehramt und Hirtenamt im Rahmen des geltenden Kirchenrechts," in *Oberrheinisches Pastoralblatt* 62 (1961) 65–72.

[96] Y. Congar, *Lay People in the Church*.

In regard to the participants at councils, the law at present clearly establishes that in no way are bishops exclusively entitled to the right of a final vote. Non-bishops, cardinal-priests, cardinal-deacons, generals of the different Orders, too, are participants with the right to a final vote (Canon 223). It is altogether possible to extend the circle of invited persons having final vote even further to lay persons, no matter how a broadening of this kind may be justified and formulated in terms of canon law.[97]

Whatever the canonical regulation will eventually be, according to our presentation so far, a conclusive vote is ultimately to be justified *theologically*—on the basis of the desired representation of the universal priesthood at councils, according to the attestation of the book of Acts, which tells us of the share of the people in the decisions in the "Council of the Apostles," and following the tradition of the Church, which in many instances shows the participation of the laity in the decisions of councils. Up to now no one has convincingly proved that lay persons cannot be accorded a final vote on the grounds either of canon or of divine law. Even the practical difficulties that are cited against a representation of the laity can be easily solved with a modicum of good will. The election would have to reflect a fair representation of the individual territorial Churches as well as the catholicity of the Church. As one possibility, leading representatives of ecclesiastical lay organizations could be chosen from among persons prominent in Church life (though not associated with any organization in a binding way) who, as scientists, writers, educators, doctors, lay theologians, and other occupations, could act as representatives of the laity. Perhaps this could be done on the model of the appointments to the higher chamber of a bicameral system of government to which, in some countries, the head of the State can appoint leading personalities of public life in the capacity of Senators, Lords, etc.[98] In our day, lay representation becomes even easier since the theological education of many leading laymen is not inferior to that of many clerics. At the same time, however, the question of lay representation has become more pressing. There

[97] Even Cardinal J. de Torquemada observed: "Yet we do not deny that the pope, calling some notable persons of inferior status to the universal council, e.g., by minor prelate or other learned person, can graciously honour them by giving them authority even to have definitive vote with the bishops, as it is done with abbots." *Summa de Ecclesia* (Venice 1561) 289.

[98] In this connection it should be observed that R. Lombardi has proposed a representation of the laity at the highest level, corresponding to the College of Cardinals: "un Senato laico dell'Umanità." *Per un mondo nuovo* (Rome 1951) 305.

is scarcely a problem area in the Church—not the least of which is that of dogma—which would not also affect lay persons.[99]

(*h*) At this point we can no longer avoid a further question. Is, then, the ecumenical council by divine convocation, which is the Church, truly represented in a council by human convocation solely on the ground of the universal priesthood of all believers? Our answer in regard to the position of the laity at an ecumenical council by human convocation must remain essentially incomplete and somewhat ambiguous until this question is also answered. With firm determination we have tried thoroughly to understand Luther's concerns regarding a representation of the Church on the basis of the universal priesthood and also to show its fundamental importance to the structural frame of the Church. Now, with the same firmness, we must hand this question back to Luther: A representation of the the Church of Jesus Christ *exclusively* on the ground of the universal priesthood? We now come to the question that we have so far put off—the question concerning the representation of the *apostolic* Church. At the same time we must now face the difficulties that were already confronting us,[100] albeit somewhat more veiled but no less real, in the questions concerning the representation of the one, holy, catholic Church.

[99] It is interesting to see how in the questionnaire "Was erwarten Sie vom Konzil?" ("What do you expect from the Council?") in *Wort und Wahrheit* 16 (1961) 569–718, both clerics and lay people expressed wishes that to a great extent paralleled each other. In connection with the wishes of lay persons with respect to the Second Vatican Council, among others, cf. "Anregungen und Hoffnungen für das Zweite Vatikanische Konzil," in *Wort und Wahrheit* 15 (1960) 245ff, 325ff, 405ff; O. B. Roegele, *Was erwarten wir vom Konzil? Gedanken eines Laien* (Osnabrück 1961); V. Schurr, R. Baumann, M. Dirx, A. Lissner, *Konkrete Wünsche an das Konzil* (Kavelaer 1961); P. Bourgy, "Que pense-t-on, qu'attend-on du Concile?" (an inquiry), in *Qu'attendons-nous du Concile?* (Brussels–Paris 1960) 57–74.

[100] Cf. Chapt. IV, part 3.

VI

COUNCIL AND ECCLESIASTICAL OFFICES

1. WHO IS THE APOSTOLIC CHURCH?

To what extent is an ecumenical council by human convocation a representation of the *apostolic* Church? This question is dependent on another, namely: To what extent is the Church herself the *Ecclesia apostolica*? To what extent is the Church still the old Church, the Church originating from the apostles? A Church could be ever so impressively united, ever so encompassingly Catholic, ever so distinctly holy—yet if it were not the old Church, which goes back to the apostles, it would be a pious association, but never the Church of Jesus Christ.

(*a*) Luther was accused at an early age of having founded a new Church and thereby of falling away from the holy apostolic Church. Luther defended himself passionately against these accusations, which touched his most vulnerable spot. In the pamphlet "Wider Hans Worst" (1541),[1] written against the Catholic Duke Henry of Brunswick-Wolfenbüttel, he wrote the following: "Indeed, you say that we papists hold to the old Church, the Church which has hitherto existed, since the time of the apostles, hence we receive our rights from the old Church and we hold to them up to now. You, however, have become renegades and become a new Church against us. Answer: What, however, if I should prove that we hold to the true, real, old Church; nay, that we are the real, old Church, that you have become apostates from us, that is from the old Church, and erected a new Church against the old Church. That would be something to hear!"[2]

This question leads us directly to the very centre of the Catholic-Protestant dispute, a dispute—as the evidence shows again—over the true theoretical and practical concept of the Church. Luther's defensive polemic in the pamphlet quoted shows clearly that the question concerning the true apostolic Church is not merely one of abstract theological proof and ingenious apologetics. It is above all also a concrete question of credibility which cannot be separated

[1] *WA* 51, 469–572. [2] *WA* 51, 478f.

from the concrete history of the Church. Luther had good reasons to add to his theological reasons a detailed description of the conditions underlying the outbreak of the Reformation. The modern Catholic reader also will be ashamed to read[3] how through the political and financial traffic over indulgences, the bishopric of Mainz and St. St. Peter's Church, the apostolic Church was betrayed by all parties involved, because—as long before that—there had been a betrayal of the very *spirit* of the apostles. We cannot dwell upon this unsavoury matter here. Even today, however, the Catholic Church will have to acknowledge culpability in this matter. In this connection we must, however, take note that the apostolic character of the Church must be *credibly* presented and "not in the persuasive words of wisdom, but in the demonstration of the Spirit and of power, that your faith might rest, not on the wisdom of men, but on the power of God" (I Cor. 2:4f).

Luther presents a twofold argument for the theological clarification of the question as to which is the true apostolic Church. His first argument is positive. In it he proves that his Church shares the essential attributes of the old apostolic Church founded by Christ. According to Luther it is hardly deniable: (1) "That we just as much as the papists come from holy Baptism . . . the same old Baptism that Christ instituted, in which the apostles and the first Church and all Christians thereafter up to now have been baptized."[4] (2) "That we have the Holy Sacrament of the Altar, the selfsame one as Christ Himself instituted, and which the apostles and thereafter the whole of Christendom have used. And that we eat and drink therefore with the old and whole Christendom at the one table, and we receive along with them the selfsame Sacrament and have done nothing new or different therein."[5] (3) "That we have the true, old keys and need them only to bind and loose sins that have occurred against God's command, as they were instituted by Christ and used by the apostles and all Christendom up to now."[6] (4) "That we have the preaching office and teach and promote the word of God purely and abundantly without any additions of new, particular human teachings, just as Christ commanded and the apostles and the whole of Christendom have done."[7] (5) "That we hold, believe, sing, and profess the Apostles Creed, the old faith of the old Church, all things, just as you do. We have neither made nor added anything new thereto."[8] (6) "That

[3] *WA* 51, 537–544; cf. J. Lortz, *Die Reformation in Deutschland* (Freiburg i. Br. [3]1948) I, 193–263.

[4] *WA* 51, 479.   [5] *WA* 51, 480.
[6] *WA* 51, 480.   [7] *WA* 51, 481.
[8] *WA* 51, 482.

we have the same prayer, the same Our Father as the old Church, and have made up nothing new or different, that we sing the same psalms, praise and thank God with the same upright mouths and hearts, as Christ has taught, and the apostles and the old Church herself used and commanded us to follow according to their example."[9] (7) "That we teach and hold with the old Church that one must revere and not curse secular authorities nor force them to kiss the pope's feet."[10] (8) "That we praise and prize wedlock as a divine, blessed, and beneficent creation and ordinance, for the fruitfulness of the body and against carnal lust, and we have made up nothing new by ourselves."[11] (9) "That we have the same sufferings (as St. Peter says) that our brethren in the world have, that we are persecuted in all places, that we are strangled, drowned, hanged, and that all manners of vexations are laid upon us, and that it goes with us as it went with the old Church." [12] (10) "That we do not in turn also shed blood, murder, hang and take revenge as we no doubt could have done and still can do. Rather, just as Christ, the apostles and the old Church have done, we endure; the while admonishing, and praying for them, even publicly in the churches, in the litanies and sermons; all things, as Christ our Lord has done and taught, hence that which the old Church has done, too, since in this we hold steadfastly to the old nature of the old Church."[13]

Luther's second proof is negative. In it he argues that the Catholic Church has fallen away from the apostolic Church founded by Christ. The Catholic Church introduced numerous innovations: ". . . countless books, full of new discoveries which neither the old Church nor the apostles knew anything."[14] Luther lists the following examples: satisfaction through works, indulgences, holy water, pilgrimages, brotherhoods, innovations in the Sacrament of the Altar (understood as the priest's sacrifice, as an act of obedience, communion in one form), the power of the keys in secular matters (the deposition of kings and princes), the falsification of the sermon through the commands of men, the establishment of a bodily head in Christ's spiritual kingdom who accepts the titles of all-holiest and God on earth, idolatrous worship of the saints (canonization, fast days and feast days), the branding of the state of matrimony as unclean in regard to the special service of God, use of the "secular sword" and war as a means of achieving the Church's ends, purgatory, relics. . . .[15] Again and again Luther repeats: "Who has commanded

---

[9] *WA* 51, 482.   [10] *WA* 51, 482.

[11] *WA* 51, 483.   [12] *WA* 51, 484.

[13] *WA* 51, 485.   [14] *WA* 51, 498.   [15] *WA* 51, 487–497.

you thereto? Or where is it written? Where in the old Church do you find that you may make up such new Baptism and holiness? Who here is the heretical, apostate, new Church?"[16]

Luther's expositions, though frequently written with polemical fervour, certainly merit serious consideration. What, then, should the Catholic theologian do? With regard to the first argument, he must sincerely rejoice over that which unites us—despite all differences— it is more than that which separates us. With regard to Luther's second argument, the following is called for: (a) test everything fearlessly as the apostle demands in I Thessalonians 5:21; (b) sincerely regret, criticize, and struggle against everything that constitutes a deviation from the apostolic Church (for example, all types of attachment to "works," and of idolatry); (c) to find a reasonable explanation for specific historical phenomena which are not to be considered as belonging to the essence of the Catholic Church (for example, the direct power of the Church in temporal matters and the deposition of kings and princes); (d) a differentiated defence of what are genuine interpretations, fulfilments, and developments of the tradition of the apostolic Church.

All this, however, holds today in its own way also for the Protestant theologian. It can hardly be denied that the situation has greatly changed in the Catholic as well as in the Protestant sphere since Luther's Reformation. Many things that Luther praised are no longer restricted to the Protestant Church nor are those things he censured to be found exclusively in the Catholic Church. Neither Catholics nor Protestants can consider themselves exempt from making a continuous effort to model themselves upon the apostolic Church. Neither do appeals to Catholic tradition or to the Protestant Reformation release them from the obligation constantly to realize anew that which is the crucial factor, if one desires the designation "apostolic": namely, *objective harmony with the apostolic message.*

An ecumenical council by human convocation is a representation of the apostolic Church if it stands in a relation of *objective harmony* with the apostolic Church.[17] Objective harmony between a council and the apostolic Church is indeed the gift of the Holy Ghost, which has been certainly and irrevocably promised to the Church; but it is also the task and the object of the tireless concern of the Church herself. Hence, the difficult task facing an ecumenical council by

[16] *WA* 51, 488.

[17] This is not meant to give an adequate description of the apostolicity of an ecumenical council, but certainly to emphasize a necessary condition of the apostolicity of an ecumenical council.

human convocation is to represent *credibly* not only an outward and formal harmony, but also a harmony of inner content with the apostolic Church.

Unity, holiness, and catholicity are the unity, holiness, and catholicity of the Church of Jesus Christ only if they rest on the foundation on which Jesus Christ willed to found. His Church; foundation of the apostles (cf. Mt. 16:18; Eph. 2:20; Apoc. 21:14) who were the eyewitnesses of the risen Lord and as such the plenipotentiary heralds sent directly by Him to proclaim His message and to lead His flock. It is only in the testimony of the apostles that we perceive the glorified Lord. This is why the attestation of the apostles occupies a unique, lasting—and unrepeatable—normative position within the Church and *vis-à-vis* the Church. This is why a Church that claims the designation apostolic or a council that aspires to represent the apostolic Church requires a succession understood not only as historical, but as objective: in the spirit of the apostles, in the faith in their Gospel, and in obedience to their binding example.

(*b*) When is a council concretely in objective harmony with the apostles? Luther's answer to this question is: When it is in harmony with Scripture, transmitted to us by the apostolic Church, and the authority of which must stand above Church and council.

For Luther all the evil in the Catholic Church lies in the fact that the word of man has been placed on the same plane as that of God: ". . . that to them the word of God and the teachings of man have the same validity."[18] All the innovations in the Catholic Church have nothing to do with the word of God, but with human inventions. "Now let us see all the new elements one after the other which have emerged in the new Church of the pope. Thus we find that they are all without God's word, that is, without the way, truth, and life, and originating exclusively out of human devotion or discretion, or out of the pope's wickedness."[19]

The Church under the authority of the Word—together with the universal priesthood of all believers—is also the central concern in Luther's conciliar theology.[20] As early as 1512, on the occasion of a local synod of the diocese of Brandenburg in Ziesar, Luther declared in a sermon delivered for the prior of Leitzuau[21] that the council should apply itself to the preaching of the Gospel as its principal task.[22] If this were not done, the council would have met in

[18] *WA* 51, 509.   [19] *WA* 51, 515.
[20] Cf. the literature referred to in Chap. V, 1, footnote 1.
[21] *WA* 1, 10–17.   [22] *WA* 1, 13.

vain. The importance of the word of God for the council was then forcefully expressed at the eruption of the Reformation crisis: It was set forth in the controversy with Prierias in 1518[23] as well as in Luther's disputation with Eck in 1519: Holy Scripture is "the infallible word of God, the council merely the creature of this word."[24] Afterward he writes to the Elector Frederick that one should "believe more a layman who has Scripture than the pope and council without Scripture."[25] The assertion that councils should be subject to the authority of Scripture was already, after the dispute with Prierias, linked with the other assertion, that councils can err.[26] After the Leipzig Disputation, there was an even sharper tone and it was flatly declared that councils had in fact erred.[27] Luther thereby purposed to put Christ, as He speaks through Scripture, and not himself, above the authority of the council: "I do not raise myself above the doctors and councils, I raise Christ above all teachings and councils."[28]

Almost thirty years elapsed between the outbreak of the Reformation and the opening of a council. Through all these years of endless discussions Luther clung to his conviction that a council was subject to the authority of Scripture and not vice versa. This was the essential meaning of his repeated demands for a "free, Christian council": free of the pope and under the sole authority of Scripture. Councils should decide controversial questions, and to that extent Luther was sincerely in favour of councils; at the same time he maintained that councils should always submit to Holy Scripture—thereby contesting the establishment of an absolute conciliar authority. This was also the main tenor of his disputation theses. "De Potestate Concilii" of 1536,[29] and of his militant tract. "On the Councils and the Churches."[30] Here Luther expounds his position towards the question of councils in a detailed though highly polemical fashion. Nevertheless, a deep pessimism permeates this work. After having drafted the Articles of Smalcald[31] for the consideration of a council in Mantua as late as 1537—though with little hope for a serious reconciliation—Luther definitely buried all hopes for a council in his tract "On the Councils and the Churches," written in 1539. He was deeply disappointed and in despair over the fact that the pope, after the triple postponement of the council and persistent holding up of Church reform, obviously

[23] *WA* 1, 656, 658, 665, 685.   [24] *WA* 2, 288.
[25] *WA* (B) 2, 468, 472.   [26] *WA* 1, 656, 685.
[27] *WA* 2, 303, 308.   [28] *WA* 6, 581.
[29] *WA* 39, 1, 181–197.   [30] *WA* 50, 509–653.
[31] *WA* 50, 192–254.

did not want a council in any serious sense: "Ah, well! If we must despair of a council, let us commend the matter to our true judge, our merciful God."[32]

While Luther proceeded from the argument of the universal priesthood of all believers in his early "Address to the Christian Nobility," here his point of departure was the fundamental importance of Holy Scripture. Luther had made a careful study of the three-volume book on councils by Peter Crabbe, which had just been published:[33] Hence his treatise abounds with long historical expositions. In the entire first part[34] Luther attempts to show how councils were historically conditioned and determined and to show the contradictions in tradition. He points out that many conciliar prescriptions have been disregarded—beginning with the Apostolic Council, which prescribed abstention from the blood and meat of strangled animals. Scripture alone is the lasting foundation of councils: "In sum, you may put them all together, both fathers and councils, and you cannot extract the whole doctrine of Christian faith from them, though you keep extracting therefrom forever. . . . If Holy Scripture had not made and preserved the Church, she would not have remained for long because of the councils and fathers. . . . As evidence let me ask: Where do the councils and fathers get what they teach or discuss?"[35]

In the second part[36] Luther cites the four old "major councils" as models: True councils do not invent anything, they do not set up novelties, they only defend "as the highest judges and greatest bishops under Christ the old faith and the old, good works . . . according to Holy Scripture, save that they also deal with temporal, transient, changing things, in accordance with the needs of the times. This must also be done outside councils, in the parishes and schools."[37] It is the word of God, within the Church, which endows a council with the highest normative *teaching authority*. "Thus a council is naught else but a consistory or court in which the judges, after hearing the parties, render their verdict but with the appropriate humility, stating: 'On the basis of law our office is to pronounce anathema, to condemn, not according to our lights, or will, or a newly hatched law, but according to the old law that is held to be valid throughout the whole empire.' Thus a council condemns even a heretic not according to its own discretion but according to the imperial law, that

[32] *WA* 50, 623.

[33] P. Crabble, *Conciliorum omnium tam generalium quam particularium, quea iam inde ab apostolis in hunc usque diem celebrata*, vols. I–III (Cologne 1551).

[34] *WA* 50, 509–547.

[35] *WA* 50, 546f.

[36] *WA* 50, 547–624.

[37] *WA* 50, 606.

is, according to Holy Scripture, which they confess to be the law of the Church. Such a law, empire, and judge are to be truly feared on pain of eternal damnation, since such a law is the word of God, the empire is the Church of God, and the judge is the officer or servant of both."[38] Luther also compares the council to the Imperial Diet (Reichstag); but the Imperial Council being transient possesses only transient rights. "But in the empire of the Church the standing rule is: 'God abideth forever'; one must conform oneself according to it and not make up new or other words of God, or set up new or other articles of faith."[39]

Thus the apostolic character of an ecumenical council by human convocation stands or falls according to the strength of its fidelity to Holy Scripture. "I myself would not believe the council but say, 'they were men'; but Saint John the Evangelist and Saint Paul and Saint Peter, together with the other apostles, hold fast and give us a good ground and defence upon which to stand. For it was revealed to them by the Holy Spirit, publicly from heaven. The Church has it from them before this council, and the council as well had it from them."[40] This fidelity of the council to Holy Scripture is again stressed in Luther's last statement on the question of councils in the passionately polemical work, "Against the Papacy in Rome, Founded by the Devil," in 1545,[41] in which he again calls for "a free Christian, German council": "That means free, since the council is free, and Scripture, that is the Holy Spirit, is free."[42] Christian here has the meaning that one should "deal with Christian matters through Christian people and according to Scripture."[43] Luther did not live to see the convocation of such a free, Christian, "German" (that is, taking place on German territory) council. He died before this work reached the bishops convening in Trent. And he died without hope for a council or for the re-establishment of unity.

Luther's conception of Scripture as normative for councils was shared by the other Reformers. It was also self-evident to Luther's pupil Melanchthon, who as early as in his thesis of 1519 had defended the argument: "The authority of councils is under that of Scripture."[44] He contined to maintain this position steadfastly in all the various opinions he subsequently wrote for the princes on the question of Protestant participation in the council. Orthodox

[38] *WA* 50, 615f.
[39] *WA* 50, 617.
[40] *WA* 50, 552.
[41] *WA* 54, 211.
[42] *WA* 54, 211.   [43] *WA* 54, 212.
[44] Ph. Melanchthon, *Werke* (ed. by R. Stupperich (Gütersloh 1951)) I, 24.

Lutheranism takes the same position.[45] It is, however, interesting to note that the Lutheran Confessions that refer to the early Church councils express no opinion on the theology of councils (not even the prefaces to the Augsburg Confession, or the Articles of Smalcald). It is otherwise with the Lutheran Confessions of the *Reformed* Church (the Scottish Confession of 1560, *Confessio Helvetica Posterior* of 1561, the Irish Articles of 1615, and others). Actually they summarize Calvin's position on councils. Like Luther, Calvin maintained that the unqualified authority of Holy Scripture over councils is of fundamental importance. In the preface to the chapter "On Councils and Their Authority" of his Institutions, he states the following: "First, if I am rather severe on our adversaries here, it is not because I would allow the ancient councils less esteem than is due to them. I honour them with all my heart, and I desire that all esteem them and hold them in reverence. But here we must establish some measure, so that nothing is derogated from Christ. Now, it is the prerogative of Christ to preside over councils and to have no mortal man associated with Him in this dignity. But I hold that He presides in fact only where He governs the whole assembly by His

---

[45] At the time of Melanchthon's death, the main lines of the Lutheran conciliar theology appeared to be clear; neither Martin Chemnitz's *Loci theologici* (Frankfurt a. M. 1951) nor that of Matthias Hafenreffer (Tübingen 1609), nor Leonard Hutter's *Compendium* (Wittenberg 1610) or *Loci* (Wittenberg 1619) nor the *Loci* of Johann Gerhard (Jena 1610–25) produced a systematic doctrine of ecumenical councils. Certainly the Tridentive conclusions imposed a discussion, but it was only the detailed treatise on councils in Bellarmine's *Disputationes* (Ingolstadt 1586–93) which aroused men's minds and led to an abundance of controversial literature: Johannes Lampadius 1616, Heinrich Hoepfner 1620, Paul Röber 1631, Johann Gerhard's *Confessio Catholica* 1634–37 and, in connection with the desire for a Protestant council for reunion, above all, Georg Calixt. In the second half of the seventeenth century, the increasingly wide discussion of the problems posed by the councils led to the insertion of a new systematically structured theory of ecumenical councils into the Lutheran concept of the Church: this was the case with Freidrich König, Abraham Calov, Johann Andreas Quenstedt, Johann Wilhelm Baier. Here the normative character of scripture was strongly stressed throughout. With the decay of orthodoxy in the eighteenth century, there was a corresponding decay in the theology of ecumenical councils. The dogmatics of Johann Franz Budde. Franz Volkmar Reinhard, Karl von Hase up to Julius August Ludwig Wegscheider bear witness to this. Nor was there a renewal of the theology of ecumenical councils in the nineteenth century; the unfortunately phrased invitation to the Protestants did not lead to any deeper theological reflections regarding the nature of ecumenical councils. Only in 1927 did Werner Elert try to erect a bridge between ecumenical councils and the World Conference on Faith and Church Constitution in Lausanne. This whole development is described by M. Seils, "Das ökumenische Konzil in der lutherischen Theologie," in *Die ökumenischen Konzile der Christenheit*, ed. by H.-J. Margull (Stuttgart 1961) 339–359.

Word and Spirit."[46] Does that mean that councils possess no
authority? Calvin says, No: "What then? someone will say. Are the
decisions of councils to have no authority? I reply, Yes, indeed; for
I do not contend that all the councils must be rejected, all their acts
rescinded, or cancelled from one end to the other. But one will
reply that I degrade their authority, to the point of leaving it up to
each individual to receive or reject whatever a council shall have
determined. Not at all, but every time that a decree of some council
is brought forward, I would wish, first, that a diligent inquiry be
made with respect to what time, for what cause, and for what purpose it was held, and what kind of persons were in attendance. Second
that the matters discussed be examined according to the rule of
Scripture, and this in such a way that the determination of the
council should have its weight and be viewed as a precedent or case
formerly decided, but this should not prevent the aforementioned
examination."[47] In this argument Calvin refers to St. Augustine:
"I would like very much for one to observe that which St. Augustine
teaches in his third book against Maximinus. For, in order to silence
this heretic who was disputing the decrees of the councils, he says:
'I must not bring forward the Council of Nicaea and you must not
bring forward that of Ariminum, as if to prejudge the matter. For
you are not subject to the first, nor am I to the second. Let matter
dispute with matter, cause with cause, reason with reason. And let
all be based on the authority of Scripture, not that peculiar to either
one, but that common to both. Thus councils will once more have the
majesty that is their due and Scripture would maintain its pre-
eminence, so that everything may be subject to its standard." '[48]
Reformed orthodoxy has followed Calvin's teachings on councils:
All the most important dogmatists of the reformed Church (G.
Bucanus, F. Burmann, J. H. Heidegger, A. Polanus, F. Turretini,
J. A. Turretini, A. Walaeus, S. Werenfels, J. Wolleb, and others)
treat the question of *locus de conciliis* or *de synodis*[49] in great detail;
they all take it for granted that Holy Scripture is the only guide for
conciliar deliberations.[50]

[46] J. Calvin, Opera quae supersunt omnia. *Corpus reformatorum* (Brunswick
1834; hereafter designated as *CR*) 30, 858.

[47] *CR* 30, 861f.

[48] *CR* 30, 862.

[49] Cf. on the Calvinist tradition, J.-L. Leuba, "Das ökumenische Konzil in der
reformierten Theologie," in *Die ökumenischen Konzile der Christenheit* ed. by
H.-J. Margull (Stuttgart 1961) 376–386.

[50] As to the authority of Scripture in *reformed* theology, Leuba succinctly
notes the following: "From the theological standpoint, the decrees and definitions of a council fundamentally have authority only insofar as they are in accord-

According to what has been said up to now, the entire reform theology agrees that the apostolic character of the Church consists in objective harmony with the spirit of the apostles; this objective harmony with the apostles in the concrete is under the norms set by Scripture. Can the Catholic theologian concur with this view? We have seen earlier[51] that according also to the Catholic interpretation of this matter a council does not stand above the authority of Holy Scripture, but is subject to it. We must then carefully scrutinize this controversial theological problem. What does the above statement mean in the context of our earlier discussion? In contrast to all, including the most solemn, teachings of the Church it means that, according to the definition of the Vatican Council, Holy Scripture *alone* is God-inspired as the product of the apostolic preaching of the Gospel (*kerygma*), quickened and filled by the Spirit; God is its author. Thus the definitions arrived at by a council are not really the word of God as defined above. Definitions reached by councils are a word of *man* which confirms (*testatur, affirmat, confirmat, continet verbum Dei, non est verbum Dei*) God's revelation in human terms with the help (*assistentia,* not *inspiratio*) of the Holy Spirit. Conciliar definitions cannot be announcements of new revelations, but only new interpretations of the old revelation. Therefore ecumenical councils—especially in their exegetic and explanatory role—do not stand above, but below Holy Scripture. From this it follows that Holy Scripture is the primary norm for councils. It is binding both as regards doctrinal decisions and the spirit of the whole activity of a

---

ance with Holy Scripture. Authority, therefore, is indissolubly linked with legitimacy. An interpretation of Holy Scripture which is the result of reciprocal discussion among representatives of the greatest possible number of Churches, however, has more weight than the interpretation of a single believer or of a single local church. Hence all dogmatists more or less fully maintain that it is the duty of every believer to comply with the decree of a council. At the same time the French Calvinists differentiate in particular three kinds of conciliar definitions.

"(*a*) In matters of faith the councils are not actually to be regarded as judges but as mere witnesses and experts. They do not have to set forth the true teaching, which has indeed already been established in Holy Scripture. However, on the basis of the already established teaching, they have to unmask the false and heretical doctrine.

"(*b*) On the other hand they have to establish themselves as legislators in matters of discipline and Church government. Their determinations in this regard, therefore, are to be followed by the faithful because they concern things which could not put salvation into question.

"(*c*) Councils are actually judges with regard to those who obviously teach and live contrary to the word of God. They possess the right of censure and of excommunication. In contrast to the Independents it is assumed that councils exercise a legal right in the two last-named functions" (*op cit*. 381f).

[51] Cf. Chap. IV, 3.

council: the preliminary work, the choice of themes to be discussed, the order and the presidency of the proceedings, the manner and mode of discussion, the definitions and decrees. The framework of the council, its basic innermost attitude, conciliar decisions, in the cited words of Athanasius should all "breathe Holy Scripture." On all these counts one can agree with Luther and the Reformers; indeed, all this can be formulated more clearly and directly today when so much has been cleared up in the theological controversy and Protestants have recognized the importance of Church tradition.[52]

All this, however, is but one aspect of the truth. There is no difference of opinion on the question of the superiority of the word of God over a council. The question that the Catholic theologian must now pose to Luther asks: What is the situation as regards authority below the authority of the word of God? *All* Christians are subject to the word of God: Does this mean that the authority of all Christians below the authority of God's Word is the same? That of a bishop and that of an individual Christian, that of an ecumenical council and

---

[52] Besides the literature concerning Scripture and tradition cited in Chap. IV. 3, see the increasing number of Catholic works on the theology of the Word. In the field of exegesis, e.g., K. H. Schelkle, "Das Wort Gottes in der Kirche," in *Tübinger theologische Quartalschrift* 133 (1953) 287–293; *Jüngerschaft und Apostelamt* (Freiburg i. Br. ²1961) 58–84. "Heilige Schrift und Wort Gottes," in *Tübinger theologische Quartalschrift* 138 (1958) 257–274; J. Levie, *La Bible, parole humaine et message de Dieu* (Paris 1958; Eng. trans., by S. H. Treman, *The Bible, Word of God in Words of Man*, London 1961); H. Schlier, *Wort Gottes. Eine neutestamentliche Besinnung* (Würzburg 1958). In the field of patristics, various French works, above all, H. de Lubac, *Histoire et Esprit. L'intelligence de l'Écriture d'après Origène* (Paris 1950); *Der geistliche Sinn der Schrift* (Einsiedeln 1952); C. Mondésert, *Clément d'Alexandrie. Introduction à l'étude de sa pensée religieuse à partir de l'Écriture* (Paris 1944); M. Pontet, *l'Éxégèse de S. Augustin prédicateur* (Paris 1944); cf. also the various patristic works: H. U. von Balthasar's on Origen, Gregory of Nyssa, Maximus Confessor, and the excellent collection of texts, *Origenes: Geist und Feuer, ein Aufbau aus seinen Schriften* (Salzburg 1938; ²1953), as well as R. Gögler, *Das Wesen des biblischen Wortes nach Origenes* (Diss. Munich 1953). In the field of medieval theology: Th. Soiron, *Heilige Theologie* (Regensburg 1935; on Bonaventura); E. Eilers, *Gottes Wort, Eine Theologie der Predigt nach Bonaventura* (Freiburg 1941); Z. Alzeghy, "Die Theologie des Wortes Gottes bei den mittelalterlichen Theologen," in *Gregorianum* 39 (1958) 685–705. In the field of pastoral theology: J. A. Jungmann, *Die Frohbotschaft und unsere Glaubensverkündigung* (Regensburg 1936); F. X. Arnold, *Dienst am Glauben* (Freiburg 1948); *Glaubensverkündigung und Glaubensgemeinschaft* (Düsseldorf 1955). Syntheses are offered by: D. Barsotti, *Christliches Mysterium und Wort Gottes* (Einsiedeln 1957); the collection, *La Parole de Dieu en Jésus-Christ* (Cahiers de l'actualite religieuse 15 (Paris 1961); O. Semmelroth, *Wirkendes Wort. Zur Theologie der Verkündigung* (Frankfurt a. M. 1962). Cf. also my essay: "Karl Barths Lehre vom Wort Gottes als Frage an die katholische Theologie," in *Einsicht und Glaube*, ed. by J. Ratzinger and H. Fries, in a collection of articles (Festschrift) honouring G. Söhngen (Freiburg i. Br. 1962) 75–97.

that of a meeting of the congregation? Is there no *special* authority
below the Word of God? And if there were such an authority, from
whence would its special character derive?

To put the question differently: True, only that Church which is
inwardly, objectively in harmony with the apostles through succession in the apostolic spirit is truly an apostolic Church. True, only
that Church which is in conformity with the attestation that the
apostles have handed down to us is truly an apostolic Church,
through succession in the apostolic faith and confession. However—
and for us this is the crucial point—does the succession in the
apostolic spirit, in the apostolic faith and confession suffice? Does
not something else intervene here, something that emanates from the
apostolic attestation of Scripture, namely succession in the apostolic
office? Not, of course, in an ecclesiastical office for the exercise of
power, or in an office for self-glorification, but in an office of service,
of service in the apostolic spirit for the maintenance, defence,
and expansion of the apostolic faith and the apostolic confession?
And yet an office that is not merely an ecclesiastical officialdom
delegated by men, but an authority established and legitimatized
from above within the royal and priestly community, as a special
authority derived from a grace-dispensing apostolic vocation,
blessing and commission?

Applying this to the question of ecumenical councils, does it
suffice for *any* of the members of the various member Churches to
meet in council in the Word of God, for them to be in all-encompassing ecumenical representation of the Church herself, precisely as the
apostolic Church? What authority would a council of arbitrary
individual members have within the Church? Would it possess
special authority at all? What is Luther's theological argument
therefore with regard to the authority of ecumenical councils subject to Holy Scripture? Is theirs a special authority, or is it merely
the sum total of the authority possessed by the individual members?
The question at issue then is the following: What was Luther's
position with regard to ecclesiastical office and succession in ecclesiastical office? More specifically, what was his attitude towards the
position of ecclesiastical office at ecumenical councils?

2. THE MEANING OF ECCLESIASTICAL OFFICE

(*a*) In his "Address to the Christian Nobility," which is of
primary importance for an understanding of Luther's conciliar
theology, he started out, as we have seen, with the argument on the

universal priesthood of all believers.[1] A Catholic can have no objection against this argument. What, however, is Luther's position
with regard to ecclesiastical office? According to Luther all believers
in Christ are given "equal authority"[2] from above. Ordination by a
bishop, therefore, means that one is chosen from and for the community and charged with the exercise of this same authority for the
others. It is similar to the case of ten brothers, all of whom are princes
and heirs on an equal footing. They will elect one of the brothers to
manage the legacy for all. All ten brothers are kings with equal
authority, but they chose one to rule the kingdom for all of them.
From this example Luther deduces the following: If a small group of
pious laymen were taken prisoner in a desert and if there were no
episcopally ordained priest among them, they could choose one of
their number to whom they could delegate the offices of administering Baptism, of celebrating Mass, or of granting absolution and of
preaching. "He would be as truly a priest as if he had been ordained
by all the bishops and popes."[3] After all, this is the way bishops
(such as Augustine, Ambrose, Cyprian) and priests were formerly
chosen from the people and afterwards confirmed in office in a simple
form by other bishops.

Inasmuch as secular rulers are also baptized and share the same
faith and the same Scripture, they too are priests and bishops and
their office must be taken seriously as an office of the Christian
community. "Anyone who has been baptized may claim that he has
already been consecrated as a priest, bishop, or pope, although it is
not seemly for any one person to exercise this office arbitrarily.
Since we are all priests of equal status, no one must push himself
forward without our consent and election, and presume to do that for
which we all have the same authority. What belongs to all in common may not be claimed by any person without the consent and order
of the rest. And where it comes to pass that anyone abuses his
office and is deposed, he would return to the same status as before.
Hence the status of a priest in Christendom is nothing more than
that of an officeholder. For the reason that he is in office, he exercises
it; when he is removed therefrom, he is a peasant or burgher like the
rest. Truly, a priest is no longer a priest when he is deposed. But now
they have invented the claim to *Characteres indelebiles*, and declare
that a deposed priest is something different from a bad layman."[4]

What then is the difference between a priest and a layman? It is
not a difference of state but a difference in office, in duties, in the

---

[1] Cf. Chap. V, 1.   [2] *WA* 6, 407.
[3] *WA* 6, 408.   [4] *WA* 6, 408.

work for whose sake they exist. Just as temporal rulers, cobblers, blacksmiths, and peasants are consecrated priests and bishops through Baptism and have their office and work with which they serve others, so also do those who are now called ministers, priests, bishops, and popes have their work and office. "They have no further or greater dignity than other Christians save that they must preach the word of God and administer the Sacraments."[5]

Luther espoused similar views in his polemical tracts, "On the Papacy at Rome: An Answer to the Celebrated Romanist at Leipzig"[6] and "Against the Falsely Named spiritual Estate of the Pope and of the Bishops" in 1522.[7] Here he mercilessly exposed the abuses and subjected to the most severe criticism the entire conduct of the so unspiritual "spiritual estate." His most extensive work on this topic is his "De instituendis ministris Ecclesiae" in 1523[8] and the tract published in the same year entitled "The Right and Power of a Christian Congregation or Community to Judge and to Call, to Appoint and to Dismiss Teachers, Established and Proved on the Ground of Scripture."[9] Here Luther drew the logical consequences from his "Address to the German Nobility" and tried to set forth some principles for a community-constitution that could be freely adapted to fit local needs. For Luther a Christian community exists only where the pure Gospel is preached. Hence, bishops, foundations, and monasteries are not Christian in this sense, nor do they constitute a Christian community. In questions of doctrine, in the appointment or removal of teachers and pastors one should, therefore, be guided not by human prescriptions, no matter how venerable they might be, but only by the word of God.

[5] *WA* 6, 409.

[6] *WA* 6, 285–324.

[7] *WA* 10, II, 105–158.

[8] *WA* 12, 169–196. The following passage is especially characteristic of Luther's position; *WA* 12, 189: "It is of the common rights of Christians that we have been speaking. For since we have proved all of these things to be the common property of all Christians, no one individual can arise by his own authority and arrogate to himself alone what belongs to all. Lay hold, then, of this right and exercise it, where there is no one else who has the same rights. But the community rights demand that one, or as many as the community chooses, shall be chosen or approved who, in the name of all with these rights, shall perform these functions publicly. Otherwise, there might be shameful confusion among the people of God, and a kind of Babylon in the Church, where everything should be done in order, as the Apostle teaches. For it is one thing to exercise a right publicly; another to use it in time of emergency. Publicly one may not exercise a right without consent of the whole body or of the Church. In time of emergency each may use it as he deems best." (Luther, Martin: *Church and Ministry*. Vol. XL of Luther's Works, ed. by Helmut T. Lehmann. Philadelphia: Muhlenberg Press, 1958, p. 34).

[9] *WA* 11, 408–416.

That only bishops, scholars, and councils can pass judgment on doctrine is a convention instituted by man: "The word and teaching of man have decreed and ordained that the judgment of doctrine should be left solely to bishops, scholars, and councils. Whatever they decide, the whole world is duty bound to regard as law and as articles of faith, as is plentifully proved by their daily harping on the pope's spiritual power."[10] Against it, however, stands the word of Christ: "For Christ decrees the very opposite; He takes from the bishops, scholars, and councils both the right and the power to judge doctrine and bequeaths it to all men and to all Christians in particular. For in John 10, He says: 'The sheep know his voice.' In the same passage: 'But a stranger they will not follow, but will flee from him, because they do not know the voice of strangers.' And: 'All whoever have come are thieves and robbers; but the sheep have not heard them.' "[11] Bishops, popes, scholars and everybody else have the right to teach. It is up to the sheep, however, to decide whether they hear the voice of the Shepherd or that of a stranger. The word of God should not be thrust into the background before either bishops or councils. "Hence let bishop and councils decide and decree whatever they please, but when we have God's word on our side, it is up to us and not to them to say whether it is right or wrong, and they should yield to us and obey our word."[12] Luther documented the above utterance with various Gospel texts.

Two principles are drawn from the above argument: (1) A Christian community in possession of the Gospel not only has the right and the power but also the duty to shun or depose bishops and others who teach and govern contrary to the word of God. (2) Since there cannot be a Christian community without the word of God, and therefore without teachers and preachers, it must appoint suitable members from within the community itself, all of whom are anointed priests, and install them as preachers and teachers. Is it possible, however, for someone to preach without being *called* thereto? In relation to non-believers every Christian is called and anointed to preach (Acts 6:7 8:5; 18:25). The same applies among Christians in case of emergency. Under normal conditions, however, none should push himself forward among Christians. He should, rather, wait until called for by the congregation to take over the office and preach and teach in and by commission of the others.[13] Nevertheless a difficulty arises from the text of Holy Scripture: Did not Paul order Timothy and Titus (cf. also Acts 14:25) rather than

[10] *WA* 11, 409.   [11] *WA* 11, 409.
[12] *WA* 11, 409f.   [13] *WA* 12, 189; cf. note 8.

the congregations to install priests and thus demand an apostolic succession in office? Hence, does it not hold that "one must have the consent and commission of bishops, abbots, or other prelates who sit in the apostles' seat?"[14] Luther's reply thereto was that it could be done if bishops and abbots were really good successors to the apostles. But even then (except in case of emergency) election and appointment should be effected by the congregation: "If our bishops and abbots, and similar persons, sat in the apostles' seat, as they claim, one might say let them do what Titus and Timothy, Paul and Barnabas did when they appointed priests. But now they sit on the devil's seat and are wolves who neither preach the Gospel nor will suffer it to be preached, so that the office of preaching and pastoral care among Christians concerns them as much as it does Turks and Jews."[15]

Thus the point at issue is an emergency situation in which one must manage without successors of the apostles. "But since the need exists in our days and there is no bishop to provide evangelical preachers, the example of Titus and Timothy does not apply here. Rather, we must call a preacher out of the congregation, whether or not he be confirmed by Titus. For the people to whom Titus ministered would or should have done the same, had he refused to confirm their preachers or had no one else been there to appoint preachers. Hence these days are wholly unlike the days of Titus, since the apostles ruled and wanted the right sort of preachers. Now, however, our tyrants want only wolves and thieves."[16] Thus, in Luther's emergency measures of 1523 there was no provision for bishops; he did not go beyond the appointment of preachers and deacons. He did not treat of the whole Church, but only of individual congregations. He placed his whole trust in them.

In the same year, however, Luther had to intervene against the activities of the radical sectarians (Karlstadt, Müntzer, and others) who had also based themselves upon the Holy Spirit and the Gospel, but drew even more extreme conclusions therefrom, moving forward to demands for a Church reform that would be ever more radical. Luther appealed for help to the princes to suppress the sectarians. At the same time serious peasant revolts, which were likewise based on Luther's "The Freedom of Christian Man," also broke out. Thus it was no accident if in his preface to Melanchthon's "Instructions for the Visitors of Parish priests in the electorate of Saxony,"[17] in 1528, Luther perforce theologically sanctioned a

---

[14] *WA* 11, 413.
[15] *WA* 11, 413.
[16] *WA* 11, 414.
[17] *WA* 26, 195–201.

fateful new development in ecclesiastical organization, which already achieved a political breakthrough with the decree of the Imperial Diet in Speyer in 1526. This development, however, did not proceed according to Luther's earlier expectations;[18] that is, it did not come from below but from above, it did not emanate from the freely constituted congregations but from the power-wielding territorial princes.[19] On the one hand the new Protestant congregations could not perform the functions necessary for the maintenance of order and were therefore threatened by chaos, "strife, rioting and rebellion."[20] On the other hand, no one felt—for political and religious reasons——that he was called to the episcopal office of supervision: "Now that the Gospel has again mercifully come to us through the unspeakable grace of God or, indeed, has appeared for the first time, and thereby we have come to see how grievously Christendom is confused, scattered, and rent, we would have liked to see the true episcopal office and the office of visitation re-established because of urgent need. But, since none of us felt a call or a definite command thereto, and Saint Peter has not countenanced the creation of anything in Christendom unless we are certain that it is a creation of God, no one has dared to undertake it."[21] So there was nothing else to do but appeal to the territorial princes: "For what would happen if there were to be disunity and discord among us?"[22] According to Luther the territorial prince was to exercise this function of maintaining ecclesiastical order not as his princely right and coercive authority, but as his duty in the spirit of Christian charity: an extraordinary deed born of necessity and love. But who could not help noticing that the borderlines between all these fine distinctions had long since become fluid?

[18] Cf., e.g., *WA* Briefe 3, 373f; 4, 158.

[19] S. Grundmann: "Charles V had a negative attitude towards the Reformation. Then came the chain of compromise solutions, beginning with the recess of the Imperial Diet at Speyer in 1526, for overcoming the religious split which deeply shook the legal foundations of the old Empire and which were initiated with the federalization of the German State Church law. Thereupon arose the danger signs of fanatic sectarianism, iconoclasm, and anabaptism. On the basis of a radical spiritualization of the Church constitution, the latter elements most threateningly revealed the growing perils, the signal fires of the Peasants' War with the dissolution of every order, as well as the lack of adequate forces for a stable organized new ordering existing within the Church structure itself, with respect to the abolition of the traditional Church hierarchy with the papacy as focal point. All these factors compelled a close reliance on secular rulers, who in Germany as princes and dignitaries of the Imperial Diet, moreover, held the fate of the Reformation in their hands in terms of power politics in their territories." "Kirchenverfassung" (VI), in *Religion in Geschichte und Gegenwart* (Tübingen ³1959) III, 1571.

[20] *WA* 26, 200.   [21] *WA* 26, 197.   [22] *WA* 26, 201.

And that—although Luther had not wanted it so on the basis of his own theological principles—the doors had been opened to the administration of the Church by the territorial princes? We cannot discuss the whole historical and systematic complexity of this problem within the scope of this work. We must, however, examine more closely the theological causes of this development.

(*b*) The development leading away *from the congregations to the territorial princes* was not accidental. *The resistance of the bishops* to Luther's reformation made the shift to the territorial princes an obvious next step. True, at that time one could understandably have serious reasons for not taking part in Luther's reformation (both the denial of the infallibility of ecumenical councils and the questioning in principle of the Petrine office were of fundamental importance for the concept of the Church). The history of the Reformation, however, teaches us that the majority of the bishops (and the pope) opposed not only the Lutheran reformation, but any kind of serious reform of the Church, in theory and practice, in head and members. They, being also great worldly princes, opposed reform, not primarily for theological reasons, but for human—all-too-human—reasons. Their primary concern was the maintenance of their personal political and religious power and splendour. On the one hand they failed clearly to see the abuses growing out of structural defects; on the other hand, they were lacking in unselfish humility, in moral strength, and in an active will to conversion. In short, the personal life of most bishops was far from being an *apostolic life* in imitation of Christ, hence the lack of a serious *apostolic action in the Church* through the preaching of the Word and the administration of the Sacraments, through pastoral and missionary activities.[23]

In the face of the bishops' opposition to reform, Luther—deeply imbued with the centuries-old necessity for Church reform which he thought could now finally be carried out in the light of the Gospel —had to make a choice. And this was a choice that would not have presented itself in the way it did had the bishops shown a truly apostolic attitude—either Church reform without the bishops or no Church reform at all. In other words, either a succession of the apostles (therefore, an imitation of Christ) in the apostolic spirit and in apostolic life and activity, hence a serious Church reform in the light of the Gospel, *or else* a succession in the apostolic *office* (at that time lived in an utterly unspiritual way) and a renunciation of the apostolic spirit, of apostolic life and activity in the Church,

[23] J. Lortz, *Die Reformation in Deutschland*, Vols. I–II (Freiburg i. Br. ³1949).

which was tantamount to a renunciation of earnest Church reform. So, at least, did things look to Luther in *his* view.

In this terrible existential dilemma of an aroused Christian conscience, Luther saw no remedy in theological distinctions or apologetic arguments. This was an emergency situation. Time and again Luther repeated that necessity knows no law. And Luther decided in favour of the apostolic spirit, of apostolic life and activity, and against the apostolic office. At the same time he altogether hoped that this was only a choice of practical expediency and not of principle, merely provisional and not final. He hoped that in time the bishops would renew themselves in the apostolic spirit, that they would return to an apostolic way of life and work, that they would change from wolves into shepherds of Christ's flock: and that in the proclamation of the Gospel and the exercise of pastoral care they would once more turn into true successors to the apostles. Thus what he had written in 1523 in his "The Christian Community Has the Right and Power . . .," [24] what he repeated in the preface to his instructions on visitations in 1528,[25] and what he had also proposed in his "Address to the Christian Nobility" was full of suggestions for a strengthening of the episcopate through reform, and not for its abolition.

This idea was also incorporated somewhat later in the Lutheran Confessions. These called for a separation of the episcopate from domination, for the liberation of the episcopate from secular power, but they were clearly in favour of an episcopal constitution of the Church. In the Augsburg Confession of 1530 Melanchthon, whom Luther supported,[26] solemnly asserted the "divine right" of the

---

[24] *WA* 11, 413.

[25] *WA* 26, 197.

[26] Luther in 1530, again took up the distinction between officeholders (or title-holders) and the exercise of office, already prepared in the Resolutio Lutheriana super propositione sua decima tertia de potestate papae 1519) *WA* 11, 183–240), in his "Admonition to the Clergy Assembled in Augsburg." At the same time he admitted that on condition that the Gospel was allowed to be freely preached, one could also accept episcopal office (*WA* 30, 11, 341f.) His correspondence during the Augsburg negotiations likewise bears witness to this: "Indeed it is true, that where they would tolerate our teaching and no longer persecuted it, likewise would we not oppose their jurisdiction, dignity or however they call it. For we, of course, do not covet being either bishop or cardinal, but merely good Christians who should be poor. Matt. 5:27 and Luke 4:28" (*WA* Briefe 5, 535). According to Luther those who, like the Nurembergians, opposed the restitution of episcopal jurisdiction, proposed by Melanchthon, are "weak in faith": "They do not sufficiently understand the restitution of the episcopal jurisdiction, nor do they consider the attached circumstances. If only the bishops would accept it under those conditions" (*WA* Briefe 5, 618). Luther took a similar stand even during the negotiations for religious equality in 1531 (*WA* Briefe 6, 113).

episcopate against the opposition of various Lutherans[27] (especially the princes and the imperial cities): "When, therefore, it is asked about the jurisdiction of the bishops, we must distinguish power, from ecclesiastical jurisdiction. Hence, according to the Gospel, or as they say, by divine right, this jurisdiction is found in bishops as bishops, that is, in those to whom the ministry of the Word and the Sacraments is commissioned, to remit sins, to reject doctrine opposed to the Gospel, and to exclude from the communion of the Church the godless whose irreligion is well known, not by human force but by word. In this matter, necessarily and by divine right, they ought to render obedience to the Church according to the text, 'He who hears you, hears me.' "[28] The Apology for the Augsburg Confession expressly establishes an episcopal Church constitution (even with the qualifications that are set only for human authority): "Article 14. . . . in which we say the administration of the Sacraments and of the Word in the Church is given to no one, unless rightly called. However, they receive this right if we use canonical ordination. We have often testified in this convention that we most certainly desire to preserve the ecclesiastical polity and de-grees, even those established by human authority. We know that ecclesiastical discipline was determined in this manner by the Fathers through a good and useful plan, as the ancient statutes show."[29] Later it even speaks of a "willingness" to preserve Church order: "Therefore we again wish to clarify this, that we will gladly, pre-serve the ecclesiastical and canonical polity, if only the bishops cease to rage in our churches. In this matter, our aim will excuse us before God and before all peoples for future generations, so that we cannot be blamed for the weakening of the authority of the bishops, where men will read and hear that we, deprecating the unjust severity of the bishops, were able to accomplish nothing right."[30] This funda-

---

[27] Ph. Melanchthon to Luther on August 19, 1430 (*WA* Briefe 5, 598): "We are being reproached for restoring jurisdiction to the bishops. The people used to liberty, once having shaken off the yoke of the bishops, will find it hard to endure being put under this ancient burden. The ones who most hate this power are those in the imperial cities. They do nothing about religious doctrine and care only about ruling and liberty."

[28] *Confessio Augustana* XXVIII, 20–22 (The Confessional Writings of the Evangelical-Lutheran Church hereafter will be quoted according to the edition of the *Deutschen Evangelischen Kirchenausschusses* (Göttingen ⁴1959)). Cf. on the whole question, F. Haupt, *Der Episcopat der deutschen Reformation*, or Article 28 of the Confession of Augsburg, vol. I–II (Frankfurt a. M. 1863–66); P. Brunner, "Von Amt des Bischofs," in *Schriften des Theologischen Konvents Augsburgischen Bekenntnisses* 9 (Berlin 1955) 5–77.

[29] *Apology*, XIV, 1.

[30] *Apology*, XIV, 5.

mental position was also maintained in the Articles of Smalcald despite the denial of papal primacy: "Therefore the Church can no longer be governed and preserved unless we all live under one head, Christ, and the bishops all equally, according to their office (although they are unequal in gifts), stand together industriously in unanimous doctrine, faith (and) Sacraments, prayers and works of charity, and the like."[31]

The numerous statements on episcopacy made by Luther, Melanchthon, and the other Wittenbergers after the Articles of Smalcald and until Luther's death remained within this frame of reference.[32] Particularly important are the various opinions put forward for discussion at the conferences for the settlement of differences, which were held at that time.[33] Of these the "Wittenberg Reformation" of 1545[34] prepared for the Elector, or rather the Imperial Diet, the year before Luther's death, is by far the most significant and thorough. It was drafted by Melanchthon and signed by Luther, Bugenhagen, Cruciger, Major, and Melanchthon, and was the last joint deposition on this question.[35]

The episcopal office is viewed against the background of the preaching office (to which the administration of the Sacraments also belongs) appointed by God and continuously renewed by Him. This office is exercised by bishops, priests, ministers, or pastors: "Therefore a distinction is to be noted between the preaching office which

[31] Articles of Smalcald, Part 2, Art. 4; on the relationship between the Confession of Augsburg and the Articles of Smalcald concerning the question of bishops, see F. Haupt, *Der Episcopat der deutschen Reformation* (Frankfurt, a. M. 1866) II, 4–58.

[32] Cf. F. Haupt, *Der Episcopat der deutschen Reformation* (Frankfurt a. M. 1863) 1, 45–57.

[33] In connection with the negotiations at Regensburg in 1541, for example, Melanchthon, with Luther's approval, wrote as follows in his counter-draft: "But in order that everything in the Church be done in an orderly manner according to Paul's rules, and that the shepherds might be more linked to each other distributing the many burdens of governing and taking care to avoid quarrel and schism, this ordination proves useful, i.e., that a bishop be elected from the many presbyters, who will rule the Church, teaching the gospel, maintaining discipline, and presiding over the presbyters themselves. Several grades have been created, namely, archbishops and over these the Roman, Antiochean, and Alexandrian patriarchs. By this ordination, if these who preside do their duty, then they are useful to maintain unity in the Church, i.e., to call together synods, to contribute legitimate judgment upon doctrine, to amend the spreading of vices, of usury and other scandals, to improve laws and punish those who create scandal. But these who preside must serve their vocation, teach, watch over doctrine and morals of the Church over which they preside, correct error and vice, and exercise ecclesiastical judgments" (*CR* 4, 368f.)

[34] *CR* 5, 578–606.

[35] Cf. esp. *CR* 5, 595–603.

God has given to the Church for all time, and which out of grace He maintains for ever and ever, and episcopal high rank which is bound to great places, persons, and succession."[36] On the basis of practical considerations the episcopal office is separated from the general ministry: "In general it is stated of the preaching office, that is of all pastors, that each is rightly to accomplish his vocation in his place both in teaching and in the administration of the Sacraments. On this matter it is further said that there must accordingly be order among these pastors; all do not possess the same gifts they all cannot be judges concerning different articles of doctrine, they cannot all arrange and hold courts of justice. And because all kinds of frailties for ever and ever occur in this ailing nature, there must be special places where one may obtain advice and persons, who have supervision over others. And the same places must be provided with persons and support and be a permanent institution as much as is possible according to human foresight. Therefore bishops must be a rank above other priests, and they must have a settled administration, and do require many persons for orderly government, for the instruction of ordinands, for visitations, for courts, for counsel, for correspondence, for envoys and councils. As can be seen, Athanasius, Basilius, Ambrose, and Augustine had much to do in order to keep their own and other churches to the true teaching against all kinds of heretics. They required many persons, and had to dispatch many here and there for their work. Thus, if the present form of the episcopate should be rent asunder, a barbarism and devastation would ensue whose end no one could foresee. For the secular authorities and princes are burdened with other matters, and only a few of them pay any attention to the Church, or meditate upon doctrine."[37]

"Answer: we take no pleasure in viewing disorder and from our hearts we wish that the bishops and those persons collaborating with them would perform their episcopal office, and in this case we offer our obedience, namely, if they give up the persecution of Christian teaching and are not despots or murderers of our poor priests, but begin to implant the pure teaching of the Gospel, and the Christian administration of the Sacraments and help to administer them."[38]

[36] *CR* 5, 595.

[37] *CR* 5, 597f; in opposition to C. G. Bretschneider, F. Haupt, *Der Episcopat der deutschen Reformation* (Frankfurt a. M. 1863) I, 52f. and P. Brunner, *Vom Amt des Bischofs* (Berlin 1955) 56f, agree that here the question is not one of *obiectiones adversariorum*, but rather one of carefully and anonymously formulated ideas of Melanchthon and the Reformers themselves, with respect to secular princes and rulers, which they, at another time, frequently expressed and also took up in the "Answer" which directly followed.

[38] *CR* 5, 598.

From there on only one way is open for the reunification of the Church: "And in sum, there is no other way to Christian concord and unity than the following—that the bishops plant the true teaching and Christian use of the Sacraments, and that we thereupon will be subject to them as prelates of the Church, which we offer to do."[39]

What are the duties of the episcopal office renewed by the word of God within this frame of reference? Six episcopal functions are enumerated in the "Wittenberg Reformation" which more or less summarize the various pronouncements made by the Reformers in their confessional writings as well as in their private writings and opinions: (1) Responsibility for Preaching and Worship: ". . . the preaching office is to be set up properly by oneself or through others, and true Christian ceremonies are to be held. Therefore the bishops must appoint God-fearing learned men in their foundations and domains, who teach rightly. In addition they can certainly find beneficed clerics, whose will is good and Christian, and they should abolish abuses in the ceremonies."[40] (2) Instruction, Examination, and Ordination of Priests: "Bishops are to hold ordination with true earnestness, namely with suitable examination and instruction. The bishops themselves well know that in the past ordination was regarded as the single, special and proper work of the bishop, doubtless not without cause. Not alone for the enhancement of the estate, but even more for the reason that greater care might be taken with the examination and instruction so that unqualified persons were not admitted, but qualified persons only. As Saint Paul says in I Timothy 5, 'Do not lay hands hastily upon anyone.' " [41] (3) Visitations of Parish Priests: "Ever to have care that pastors and preachers teach and rule rightly. In addition, above all, to hold visitations as in the distant past, which are needed now even more."[42] (4) Ecclesiastical Court and Excommunication: "Ecclesiastical courts are to be held as Christ, in Matthew 18, and Paul, in I Timothy 5, taught; namely, that false teaching and vice are to be punished with excommunication, and true teaching and good discipline maintained."[43] (5) Convocation of Synods: "With many there is a great need to hold synods, and it is not a slight wisdom to note when they are to be held and how they are to be governed. For it is also not good to let stubborn, proud heads, or intriguers who can foment factions and mutinies come to the fore."[44] (6) Supervision of Education: "As the supervisors of teaching the bishops must zealously see to it that the uni-

---

[39] *CR* 5, 598.
[41] *CR* 5, 601; cf. 584–586.
[43] *CR* 5, 602; cf. 603–605.

[40] *CR* 5, 601.
[42] *CR* 5, 601.
[44] *CR* 5, 602.

versities and the special schools are properly organized and furnished. For the universities now, as were the first chapters and colleges in olden times, are the *custodes doctrinae*, who are to preserve Christian teaching, and be the witnesses from whence comes the teaching which they impart to the churches."[45]

So much for the "Wittenberg Reformation" as the last joint testimony of the Reformation. These reformatory depositions with regard to episcopal office, however, were substantiated by the actual organization of the Lutheran Churches of the Reformation period.[46] The Reformation with the explicitly stated retention of the episcopal constitution was introduced in the two Prussian bishoprics of Samland and Pomerania in 1525, in Sweden in 1527; after 1534 in Denmark, Norway, Silesia, Holstein, and Iceland; in 1535 in Pomerania, in 1539–40 in Mark-Brandenburg, in 1540 in Schwerin, in 1542 in Naumburg, in 1544 in Merseburg, and for a while, from 1542 to 1547, even in Cologne (with the Protestant archbishop Hermann von Wied).

Luther himself had jubilantly greeted the first Protestant bishop, Georg von Polentz (Samland) and similarly, in 1540, the Bishop of Brandenburg, Matthias von Jagow (they were rare exceptions: "May God grant us many more such bishops!"). Luther himself eventually consecrated two bishops. Nikolaus von Amsdorf, Bishop of Naumburg in 1542, and Prince George of Anhalt, Bishop of Merseburg in 1545, so that the episcopal office might remain intact in the bishoprics. The *name* of bishop and of episcopacy was dropped in places where, owing to the resistance of the emperor and of bishops, and to the difficulties arising from the imperial constitution, bishops could not be installed (in middle and south-west Germany). The Greek term was replaced by the Latin term *super-attendens* (*super-intendens*): thus the *office* was retained, inasmuch as the superintendent generally exercised the same authority and performed the same functions as the Protestant bishops in northern Germany. Episcopal constitutions, based on superintendency, were introduced in Braunschweig-Wolfenbüttel and Lüneburg, in Pomerania and Hesse; to Luther's great regret the superintendencies in Wittenberg and the Electorate of Saxony, of all places, were overshadowed at an early date by a consistory (the consistorial statutes of 1542 for the Electorate of Saxony), that is, the evangelical office of bishop was being eased out by a legal department. Summing up, then, the Lutheran

---

[45] *CR* 5, 602.
[46] On the following, cf. the summary in F. Haupt, *Der Episcopat der deutschen Reformation* (Frankfurt a. M. 1863) I, 57–117.

Reformers and their Churches were basically well disposed towards the apostolic office and especially towards the episcopal office (but not towards its unworthy holders). Both in principle and in practice they advocated its continuation or renewal. The Reformation would have taken a different turn if the bishops (and the pope) had taken a different, an *apostolic* attitude, at least after the spread of the Lutheran reformation; if they had espoused a serious Church reform.[47] This must be said even after due attention has been paid to the doctrinal difficulties arising from the very beginning (but not perceived precisely by the worldly princes of the Church), which pressingly called for a thorough renewal of the Church's all-too-neglected

[47] On the attitude of the German bishops in the Reformation period, J. Lortz, *Die Reformation in Deutschland* (Freiburg i. Br. [3]1948) states: "The concept and, even more, the ideal of the priesthood among the canons and the bishops had disappeared; with the bishops the notion of pastoral care had been immeasurably corroded from within. The lord who possess power and wields it for the sake of force and thereby enjoys life was *actually* the conception according to which the high ecclesiastics lived, to the point of a deplorable exploitation of ecclesiastical-spiritual matters for the most ordinary secular-financial purposes. In turn, this basic concept was infinitely more important and more dangerous than, for instance, an especially scandalous individual life. These prince-bishops were in fact not only priest-bishops, and also princes, dukes, and counts, they were predominantly only the latter" (I, 82f.)—"They were no leaders. All the crucial events of these first years resulted from their silence and their apathy. Their attitude with respect to the papal bull will make this evident. We are familiar with the generally valid picture of the sons of nobles and princes, to whom episcopal power was entrusted. The characteristic stamp, at least, is religious impotence, even if no worse ambiguity is discernible. They neither saw the danger nor took the trouble to discern it; nor were they ready to lend their support, if only by the disposition of material resources, generously and consistently, to those who faced up to the storm. When an excellent bishop (we shall become acquainted with several), such as Gabriel von Eichstätt, seriously perceived Lutheranism as a punishment from God, it was as punishment for the inactivity of the bishops: 'I have spoken with this and that bishop at Augsburg about it, but it doesn't seem to make any impression, nothing touches the heart' " (I, 259).— "Whether it was a question of the German or the Scandinavian bishops, in general they felt themselves religiously as well as theologically powerless against the new preaching. They showed an interest only in the preservation of their worldly possessions, not in the thousands of souls entrusted to them. The sense of sacrifice that characterized the Reformers stood in harsh contrast to them: 'The one lapsed Cologne Archbishop von Wied has expended more money and efforts on this problem in two years than all the German bishops together in twenty-five years. And nevertheless the bishops will lose their earthly goods' (Cochläus). . . . Cochläus' plea found 'drowsy shepherds' along the whole line, a judgment which we similarly perceive in von Eck, Herzog Georg, von Carafa, and many others. The first churchman of Germany, the Cardinal of Mainz, did nothing on his own initiative against the coming conflagration until 1524. When the reformation of the Brandenburg electorate affected his dioceses of Magdeburg and Halberstadt, he relinquished them indifferently, without a fight, to the new order" (I, 348f).

teaching. The decade-long, indeed century-long, predominantly un-apostolic behaviour of the bishops was a major cause of the Lutheran reformation. The continuous unapostolic attitude of the bishops, even after the outbreak of the Lutheran reformation, was responsible for the fact that the Reformation did not end to the advantage of the apostolic office (as Luther's intentions had been in principle). Instead, it ended to its detriment. The unapostolic behaviour of the bishops before and during the Lutheran reformation cost the apostolic office an enormous loss of reputation, an enormous loss of credibility. This is why Luther—when faced with serious difficulties caused by the wild outbreaks of Enthusiast movements, difficulties rooted in Luther's attempts to reform the Church on a congregational basis—looked for help to the powerful temporal princes and their secular authority rather than to the apostolic office (which viewed as a whole had, after all, rejected any kind of major Church reform). Would it not be easy, in the absence of a truly apostolic bishop, to turn the "emergency bishop" into a supreme bishop, *summus episcopus*?

Nevertheless, is this not, perhaps, only one side of the story? Was the failure of the bishops the cause of everything that happened? Was not Luther's failure also involved? In other words, is the structural element precisely of ecclesiastical office taken with sufficient seriousness in Luther's concept of the Church?

(c) The shift towards the temporal princes can also be explained by Luther's *devaluation of spiritual office*. Let us again repeat: Catholic theology convincingly supports the principle of universal priesthood of all believers. Each human being becomes a full member of the Body of Christ through the Gospel, through the Sacrament of Baptism, and through faith enlivened by the Spirit. He shares in the royal priesthood of Christ. He is born to the priesthood, chosen, sanctified, and consecrated; in short, he belongs to the holy people who had formerly not obtained mercy but now have it (I Pet. 2:9f). The universal priesthood is activated in the service of the word of God, which it is the duty of each Christian to proclaim, both in his private life and in the Church (Jn. 6:45; Acts 2:17f; I Pet. 2:9). It is activated also in the celebration of the Sacraments, among which Baptism (Mt. 28:19f; Mk. 16:15f) and participation in the Eucharist (I Cor. 11:23–25) are of fundamental importance to each Christian. Within the framework of the universal priesthood, which consists of service to the one body of the Church and to the world, spiritual office as such can only be understood as a special service (*minister-*

ium): as a special priestly ministry with specific authority over the public life of the Church.

After the clericalization of the medieval Church, the principle of the universal priesthood of all believers dawned on Luther like a great intuition. But had not his discovery also so dazzled him, perhaps with its true splendour, to the point where he could no longer perceive the *full* reality of the spiritual office within the structural framework of the Church? Consider for instance the previous quotation from Luther's great programmatic "Address to the Christian Nobility," where the "equal authority"[48] of all believers in Christ was expounded in such a way that the question arises as to whether the office instituted by Christ has not become superfluous. Here Luther actually justifies the office in sociological rather than in theological terms: The office exists for the sake of order in the congregation. The ordination of priest, then, means nothing more than the transfer of the rights of the many to the one in order to eliminate conflict among the many and make an orderly congregational life possible. The example of the ten princes with equal powers who delegate those powers to one among them clearly points up Luther's concept of the ecclesiastic office, so that one might ask whether it has the New Testament behind it. Thus conceived ecclesiastical office seems simply to be an office whose authority is delegated to it by the congregation. Does not this democratization of the concept of ecclesiastical office, however, signify its undermining?[49]

It would no doubt be unfair to see the whole Luther in these statements. We would then overlook what a great role[50]—as we have seen—the *rite vocatus* played in Luther and in the Lutheran Confessions.[51] According to the conception of the Lutheran Confessions this vocation to office is traceable back to a *ius divinum*, instituted not only by the Church, but like the proclamation of the Gospel and the celebration of the Sacraments, by Christ Himself.[52] Luther also traces the necessity of a special vocation and commission for the *public* exercise of a special priestly office (in the service of the Word

---

[48] *WA* 6, 407.

[49] Despite all the differences, cf. the similarity between Luther's conception of office and that of Marsilius of Padua, *Defensor Pacis* (ed. Kusch. Darmstadt 1958) II, Chap. XV, 594–615.

[50] P. Brunner, *Vom Amt des Bischofs* (Berlin 1955) 15–24, rightly attaches great importance thereto.

[51] Especially *CA* XIV; *Apol.* XIV, 1, 5.

[52] This is brought out in W. O. Münter's "Die Gestalt der Kirche 'nach göttlichem Recht.' Eine theologiegeschichtlichdogmatische Untersuchung zu den reformatorischen Bekenntnisschriften" (*Beiträge zur Evangelischen Theologie*, Vol. 5, Munich 1941) esp. 27–65.

and of the Sacraments) to an institution of Christ, in the tract "On the Councils and the Churches," which is especially important in our context: "Fifth, outwardly the Church is known by the fact that she consecrates or calls servants or has offices which they occupy. For we must have bishops, pastors, or preachers who publicly and privately give, administer, and use the above-mentioned four things or holy possessions (Prayer, Baptism, the Sacrament of the Altar, Absolution) for the sake of and in the name of the Church, or rather because of their institution by Christ as Saint Paul says in Ephesians 4: '*Dedit dona hominibus.*' He gave some to the apostles, prophets, evangelists, teachers, governors, and similar persons. Since the group cannot do these things, it must commission them, or allow them to be commissioned, to one person. What would happen if everyone wanted to speak or administer the Sacraments, and no one yield to another? One person must be commissioned and allowed to preach, baptize, give absolution, and administer the Sacraments. The others must be content and concur with this. Wherever you see this, be assured that God's people, the Christian holy people, is present."[53]

Vocation effects a distinction based on divine right between the universal priesthood and superiors in the Church: "Thus does it happen also in Christendom. Everyone must be a Christian and a born priest before he becomes a preacher or bishop. And no pope or other man can make him into a priest. But when he is born a priest, then comes the office which makes a distinction between him and other Christians. For some must be taken from the group of Christians to have supervision over others, to whom God gives special gifts and skilfulness, so that they rise to office. . . . Since although we are all priests, to be sure, nevertheless we all cannot and should not preach or teach and govern."[54] Peter Brunner has summarized the functions of this special ministry according to the Lutheran Confessions[55] in the following way: (1) The preaching of the Gospel and the teaching of God's word without and within, in a missionary as well as a parochial sense (2) Baptism. (3) Forgiveness of sins through absolution (4) Celebration and distribution of Holy Communion in the congregation. (5) The expulsion from the Church community (excommunication) of the godless, of those whose wickedness has become manifest; their reinstatement through absolution after their

[53] *WA* 50, 632f.
[54] *WA* 41, 209f.
[55] *Confessio Augustana* V; XIV; XXVIII, 5, 20f; *Apology* XXVIII, 13; *Articles of Smalcald*, Part 3, Art. 4; *Tractatus de potestate papae* 60; 65.

repentance. (6) Guarding the purity of doctrine by comparing it to the Gospel, rejecting that which contradicts it. (7) Co-operation in the vocation.[56]

On the basis of this divine law the superintendents of the Church may claim obedience and institute human ordinances. The one pastoral office, established by Christ, can be designated with different names: bishop, priest, or pastor. A development of this one office instituted by Christ is possible, of course. Nevertheless Luther regarded such a development—according to the testimony of Church history[57]—as human law. A development is possible either through a structural extension at the base, that is, the establishment of specific auxiliary services—or through a structural extension at the top, that is, the institution of a super-ordinated episcopal office. Thus bishops can be in the Church as higher pastors. Nevertheless, as an ecclesiastical institution, this function is based on human law even though they exercise their ministry, as all others called to be pastors, on the basis of divine law. We have already seen what the special tasks of an episcopal supreme pastor are.[58]

Can one simply speak of an undermining of ecclesiastical office in view of the positive statements of Luther and the Lutheran Confessions on the divine institution and the divine functions of ecclesiastical office, of its authority and the obedience due to it? Yet,

---

[56] P. Brunner, *Vom Amt des Bischofs* (Schriften des theologischen Konvents Augsburgischen Bekenntnisses, Berlin 1955) 26.

[57] As early as 1519 Luther quoted Jerome's letter to Evagrius, in which the original and basic equality of priest and bishop is espoused (*WA* 2, 228–230). Luther regarded this letter as of such importance that he published it himself in 1538 with a personal foreword (*WA* 50, 339–343).

[58] It can be doubted whether the *ius divinum* of ecclesiastical office in Lutheran and in Catholic theology does not, from the outset, mean the same. Luther speaks of an "Institution by Christ" and expressly designates the office as a gift of God, "donum dei" (*WA* 50, 632f.) What should be questioned and investigated more closely here is: What does this statement mean in the context of the whole structure of Lutheran ecclesiology? The Council of Trent declares: "Si quis dixerit, in ecclesia catholica non esse hierarchiam, divina ordinatione institutam, quae constat ex epicopis, presbyteris et ministris: A. S." ("If anyone says that in the Catholic Church there is no divinely instituted hierarchy consisting of bishops, priests, and ministers: let him be anathema") (Denz. 966). What should be questioned and investigated more closely is: What does "divina ordinatione institutam" mean? Does it refer to "ordinatio divina" as this seems to result from the wording of the text, or simply to the "hierarchia" in general or also—which does not seem to result from the text—to the institution of the individual offices as such and to their differentiation from one another? If the second is asserted, how is such a statement to be interpreted in the light of present-day exegesis? And how then do Denz. 966 and Denz 962 and 965 relate to each other? Do all these canons have a strict doctrinal character or do they have, in part, only a disciplinary character?

what one finds surprising are not so much these positive statements; insofar as they are positive they conform to the concept of ecclesiastical office found in the New Testament. What is surprising is how rapidly Lutheranism has, in effect, given up this position. So many of Luther's utterances on this question have never been realized. We have already mentioned that at the very centre of the Reformation, in Wittenberg, Luther personally was forced to witness the process whereby the constitution of the episcopal system of superintendents was superseded by the juridical consistorial administration. Many of Luther's angry outbursts against this development have come down to us, but he was helpless against it. This was not only owing to the influence of his princely advisors, but also—as F. Haupt[59] has correctly noted—to the fact that the visitational system of 1527 (introduced as emergency measures because of peasant and sectarian disorders) failed to gain control over the disorder and lack of discipline produced in the congregation by the Reformation. In reaction to this state of affairs, Church discipline was expected to be restored through the directives and penalties imposed by temporal legal authority (the consistory of Wittenberg was composed of seven lawyers and two theologians). Was this development accidental? Was it accidental that the consistory which Luther had at the beginning (1539) endowed with powers merely on matters of finances and legal disputes—but to which he wanted to deny a voice in matters of pastoral duties and Church visitations—had already since the consistorial statutes of 1542 taken over supervisory functions in all forms over the parish priest in preaching, doctrine, morals and in general Church discipline as well? Or was this a manifestation of the inner weakness of the Lutheran ecclesiastical office, which had been conceived and established all too much in the image of a civil service?

Luther at that time wrote to Dresden about the interference of princes' officials (*aule*) in affairs pertaining to ecclesiastical office. He used the bitter words that Satan remains Satan and that while formerly the Church under the pope interfered in the affairs of the state, the state now interfered in the affairs of the Church—which threatened to be even worse: "If it is to be that they wish to govern the Church for their own princely ambition, God will not bestow His blessing, and this latter condition will be worse than the first. Because what is done without faith is not good—for when there is no divine vocation undoubtedly there is no faith—and it is destroyed. There-

[59] F. Haupt, *Der Episcopat, der Deutschen Reformation* (Frankfurt a. M. 1863) I, 105.

fore either they must be pastors—preaching, baptizing, visiting the
sick, administering communion, and doing all ecclesiastical things—
or they are to stop confusing vocations, take care of their own courts,
leave the Church to those who are called to these things and who must
render an account to God. It is not to be said, as others claim, that
we are burdened with giving an account. We want to distinguish the
offices of the Church from those of the court or to desert both. Satan
remains Satan. Under the pope he involved the Church in politics;
in our time he wishes to mingle politics in the Church."[60] A year
before his death Luther also complained vehemently against the
consistory of Wittenberg in a letter written (January 18, 1545) to the
Elector Johann Friedrich.[61]

After Luther's death this development could no longer be contained. The statutes which already formed part of the resolutions
of the Diet at Speyer in 1526 became definitely binding with the
religious Peace Treaty of Augsburg in 1555. Thereby the Imperial
Estates had the right to determine the confessional adherence within
their territories and the *ius reformandi*. It was scarcely possible to
prevent the princes and magistrates from increasingly extending their
influence to the Church. In areas with an episcopal constitution the
Protestant bishops in general, could not be selected solely by the
prince. The superintendents and jurists of the consistories, however,
were predominantly chosen by the princes. The holders of ecclesiastical office appointed by princes and other secular authorities
increasingly fell into a state of complete and often downright unworthy dependency. The awesome prophecy of Melanchthon—who
in 1530 with the non-re-establishment of the episcopate had foreseen
the rise of a tyranny that would be much more intolerable than that
which had allegedly prevailed under the pope—was fully realized:
"How I wish I could certainly not confirm the domination, but restore the administration of the bishops. I see what kind of a Church
we shall have in the future when the public power (πολιτεία) of the
Church is destroyed. I see that the future tyranny will be far more
intolerable than it ever was before."[62]

Towards the end of the sixteenth century the collegial consistorial
system, in which the bishops and the superintendents, viewed as a
whole, were not allowed to exert personal influence on the Church
hierarchy, practically achieved absolute power in the Lutheran areas
of Germany. The territorial prince increasingly emerged in the place

[60] *WA* Briefe, 10, 436.
[61] *WA* Briefe 11, 22–25. Further evidence in F. Haupt, *op cit.* 107f.
[62] *CR* 2, 384.

of the bishops—considered only as an emergency bishop by Luther—
but who now as *praecipuum membrum Ecclesiae* assumed the rights
of the *summus episcopus* for four hundred years. What in the beginning was still episcopally grounded (the transfer of the bishop's
rights to the prince), during the seventeenth century was increasingly
derived simply from the prince's territorial authority. The influence
of the princes in internal Church matters reached its high point in
the period of late Absolutism and of the Enlightenment. To a great
extent the Church was integrated into the structure of the state. The
territorial Church administration remained intact in the nineteenth
century—despite certain modifications and the purely formal re-
introduction of the title of bishop by Frederick I of Prussia and Frederick Wilhelm III.

And here we must again ask the insistent question: Was all this
accidental? Whence comes the oft-deplored "lamentation over
constitutions"? Why in the interpretation of the Augsburg Confession does a "colossal, truly chaotic dispute rage in regard to the
meaning and content of our Article 28" (on the authority of
bishops)?[63] For some, the article refers only to pastors; for others,
to bishops (in the strict sense); for still others, to territorial princes.
Finally, there are some who think the article deals with the right
to self-determination of the congregation . . . ! How is it possible,
then, that both the proponents of a pastoral Church and those in
favour of an episcopal Church, both those favouring a democratically
organized Church and those favouring a presbyterial constitution of
the Church, those who want the territorial prince to be supreme
bishop—how is it possible then that they all can base themselves upon
Luther? Who then is the true Lutheran: the Orthodox with his
ministerial system, or Thomasius with his territorial system, or else
Pfaff with his collegial system? Or Rudolf Sohm, perhaps, who
maintains that, according to Luther, the constitution of the Church
should not be determined by the Church but by the secular authorities—although they do not possess "ecclesiastical authority" and
"ecclesiastical administrative power," they certainly have "the rights
of ecclesiastical sovereignty"? Or Karl Holl who maintains that,
according to Luther, the independent position of the Church should
be defended against the State and that there also exists a specific
form of Church constitution? From whence stem therefore these incomprehensible contradictions on the question of ecclesiastical office
within the one Lutheran Church? Is it essential or not for the Church
to have an external legal structure? Is ecclesiastical office necessary

[63] F. Haupt, *op cit.* I, 32.

for theological or for sociological reasons? Does the institution of ecclesiastical office originate with Christ or the Church? Is the episcopal office required in the Church or not? Is the episcopal office based on divine or human law? Does it include bishops in the strict sense of the word or does it merely refer to pastors? Is the desire for a Protestant episcopal office an expression of the consciousness of the Reformation or of political expediency? Is ecclesiastical office derived from election or from ordination? Is ordination an official legitimation (a confirmation of the vocation) or is it a "consecration" (an essential factor of the vocation itself)? Is ordination required by divine law or human law? Are the "rites "of ordination to be understood as Church ceremony or as a Sacrament of the Church? Is the office-holder an agent of God or of the congregation? It will require much patience on the part of the Catholic theologian to disentangle this confusion of mutually contradictory opinions.[64] This is particularly difficult because of the frequently superficial criticism of the Catholic doctrine of ecclesiastical office and Church constitution, which is bound up with the opinions expressed. This criticism implies, for example, that the Lutheran Church represents in fact the Church of the universal priesthood[65] whereas the Catholic Church is depicted as a clerical Church.[66] There are many other similarly oversimplified biased pronouncements.

Yet, in view of the history of ecclesiastical office in Lutheranism, we must ask further: Would all this—the depletion of the office first by the evangelical Enthusiast movements and then by the bureaucracy of the state Church—have happened in the same way if Luther, who was sincerely in favour of ecclesiastical office, had laid down a solid theological foundation for it? Did Luther have a theological understanding of the nature of a *spiritual* office at all?

---

[64] It is unnecessary to emphasize that it is not the task of this section to set forth historically, as well as systematically, the Lutheran (or for that matter the Catholic) conception of office.

[65] For an opposite view, see E. Sommerlath, *Amt und allgemeines Priestertum* (Schriften des Theologischen Konvents Augsburgischen Bekenntnisses No. 5. Berlin 1953) 40: "One indeed may venture the assertion that in no Church has the universal priesthood been so little realized as in the Church of the Lutheran Reformation."

[66] For an opposite view, see H. Asmussen, *Warum noch lutherische Kirche?* (Stuttgart 1949) 188: "How wrongly we in the Protestant sphere see most things will become clear according to the opinion that has the validity of a dogma, among us, namely that the Catholic Church is the priests' Church, whereas we allow opportunity for the laity. The fact is that in the Catholic Church—as history proves—opportunity is offered quite as a matter of course for far-reaching lay work in which the laity becomes very active. There are of course also areas in which the laity is little active as is also the case in many Protestant areas as well."

What theological relevance (not only a practical organization relevance) is left to ecclesiastical office if all Christians have "equal authority"—we are referring again to Luther's "Address to the Christian Nobility"—and are "all priests"? What remains of it if all Christians through Baptism are not only "priests" but also "consecrated bishops and pope"?[67] Could not some of the young Luther's statements on ecclesiastical office be easily interpreted as meaning that ecclesiastical office arises from organizational needs of the congregation, and that the officeholder is therefore a mere functionary of the congregation (for the sake of maintaining formal order)? Was there not something logical in the conduct of Carlstadt, a colleague of Luther who originally shared his opinions, when he shed his cassock as symbol of his designated office to don a peasant's smock; when he married and celebrated Christmas Mass for the first time publicly as a "layman" (without the canon of the Mass!) in 1521 in the chapel of the Wittenberg Castle? Could not the Enthusiasts justify their rejection of ecclesiastical office as a divine institution and assert the unlimited possibilities of the revelation of the spirit in the Church? Could they not, despite their dependence upon medieval ideas,[68] rightly base these assertions upon certain utterances made by *Luther*? And did not Luther himself after the outbreaks of the Enthusiast and peasant revolts realize the dangers of exaggerating the principle of the Christian community? (Thomas Müntzer seriously tried to apply Luther's radical ideas of "Vaters Leisetritt" and raised the revolutionary demands that "laymen must become prelates and pastors!")[69] Are these "democratic" principles of Luther not strangely out of balance with his other utterances?[70] Was it not made easy for

[67] *WA* 6, 407f.

[68] Cf. W. Maurer, *Luther und die Schwärmer* (Schriften des Theologischen Konvents Augsburgischen Bekenntnisses, No. 6, Berlin 1952).

[69] E. Wolf, "Luther," in *Evangelisches Kirchenlexikon* (Göttingen 1958) II, 1172: "In the biblical spiritualism and mysticism of the 'Schwärmer,' especially Müntzer's, which was partly no more than the logical consequence of his own basic ideas, Luther saw the same 'Enthusiasm' as in 'Rome' and in the humanist reform: the erection of a human autonomy in the act of God's salvation, disobedience against the self-binding of the Holy Spirit to the external word of the proclamation ('Wider die himmlischen Propheten von den Bildern und Sakrament,' 1525). Naturally one cannot avoid the impression that as a result of the radical Reformers and soon also as a result of the Peasants' War (1525), in which he was not able to intervene and even acquired a great distrust of the common man, an idea of order opened up to Luther which was in contradiction with the espoused freedom of the children of God."

[70] A two-lined approach is confirmed from the Lutheran quarter, for example, in W. Elert, *Morphologie des Luthertums* (Munich 1931) I, 299; in M. Doerne, *Lutherisches Pfarramt* (Leipzig 1937) 5f; E. Sommerlath, *op cit.* 50).

the tendencies within the Church towards democratization as they occurred later in the nineteenth century, for instance, to refer to Luther and his original reformatory intuition (partially in contradiction to his confessional writings)? Was it not easy to turn one of Luther's secondary arguments into a major principle? Hence is it an exaggeration to say that from this point on, in wide circles of the Lutheran Church, one no longer knew what the authentic concept of office was according to the Lutheran Confessions? And that therefore the ideas of the Enthusiasts on this subject widely prevailed?[71]

At any rate the opinions with regard to ecclesiastical office which were still held by the Reformers were not deepened but only minimally interpreted. To cite one well-known example: According to Melanchthon all those rites to which a *mandatum Dei* and a *promissio gratiae* are imputed in the New Testament must be called Sacraments.[72] Does this, however, not also apply to the spiritual office that fulfils its service in the proclamation of the Word and in the administration of Sacraments? Indeed, Melanchthon has no qualms about calling ordination a Sacrament in the above sense (not however in the sense of a Levitical sacrificial priesthood): ". . . not with difficulty do we call orders a Sacrament. For ministry of the word is a command of God and has rich promises. . . . If orders is understood in this sense, we have no trouble in calling the laying on of hands a Sacrament."[73] Why did these assertions made in the Apology for the Augsburg Confession remain without consequences? Why was it maintained soon afterward that ordination possessed no sacramental character? And what is the meaning of authority on the basis

[71] It is characteristic that, according to the above-mentioned report by W. Maurer, which sharply shows the dependency of the reformatory sectarians on medieval Enthusiasm, the discussion at the theological congress of the Augsburg Confession yielded the statement, "In the young Luther there were conceptions that could have found the way to Enthusiasm (but the very fact that Luther did not stumble into it must have some significance!). From Carlstadt up to the Antinomians one based himself on Luther. If these approaches were not at hand in the young Luther then he would have finished more quickly with Latomus and the Antinomians who understood him better than Melanchthon." (Schriften des Theologischen Konvents Augsburgischen Bekenntnisses, No. 6, Berlin 1952) 89. True, Luther had overcome these conceptions on the basis of experience in real decisions. Wholly? This is the question asked by Catholics. Does not what was said in the discussion about Enthusiasm aim at the real weakness in Luther himself? "But how is it then that Enthusiasm in fact triumphed over Luther? Perhaps the mode and manner in which the struggle against the Roman Church had been waged is considerably responsible for it. In the struggle against Rome essential facts therefore had not been given their full value because they were present in the Roman Catholic Church. Thereby the Church is susceptible to the opposite, and we do not notice how we are encircled" (*op cit.* 89).

[72] *Apology* XIII, 3.   [73] *Apology* XIII, 11–12.

of this ordination? Does not that same Apology maintain that ecclesiastical officeholders represent Christ Himself while preaching and administering the Sacraments? "Because they represent the person of Christ on account of their vocation in the Church, they do not represent themselves, for as Christ says, 'He who hears you, hears me.' When they offer the word of Christ, when they offer the Sacraments, they offer in the person and in the stead of Christ."[74] Obviously a way of thinking is adopted here as expressed in II Corinthians 5:18-20. Why were no conclusions drawn therefrom either?

Let us now turn to the question which lies at the very root of all other questions: Does Luther's concept of office really have the backing of the New Testament? It does indeed have many essential features of the New Testament; but does the New Testament stand *fully* behind Luther on this question? In his work, "The Christian Community Has the Right and Power to Appoint, Call and Depose Teachers . . ." (1523),[75] Luther observes that Titus, Timothy, Paul, and Barnabas installed priests. He frequently quotes the classical passages of the Pastoral Epistles dealing with ordination. But was Luther able to see in the ordination according to the New Testament more than an external appointment to office, a public confirmation and actualization of the calling, which has taken place previously within a small circle? It was of grave consequence that Luther—as it seems[76]—added the provision of *benediction* to the confirmation only in 1524.[77] Luther seems to have overlooked completely that through the addressing of words, along with the laying on of hands and prayer, even a charism of office is not only tested but *bestowed*, and that thereby the officeholder has been legitimized before the congregation: "Do not neglect the grace that is in thee, granted to thee by reason of prophecy with the laying on of hands of the presbyterate" (I Tim. 4:14). "For this reason I admonish thee to stir up the grace of God which is in thee by the laying on of my hands" (II Tim. 1:6).

Is not the very *essence* of ordination overlooked if we disregard the charismatic character of the office and its special spiritual message? Is it possible, if one takes the charismatic character of ecclesiastical office seriously, to view it, as Bugenhagen did with Luther's obvious approval, simply as an introduction, to be repeated with each new induction to office? Only after 1535[78] did Luther seem to distinguish between ordination and introduction. From then on he

[74] *Apology* VII, 28   [75] *WA* 11, 413f.
[76] Cf. P. Brunner, *Vom Amt des Bischofs* (Schriften des Theologischen Konvents Augsburgischen Bekenntnisses, No. 9, Berlin 1955) 15.
[77] *WA* 53, 257.
[78] Cf. *WA* 38, 401–433.

considered ordination as something that does not have to be repeated later at either the induction or the change of office. And if one takes the charism of ecclesiastical office seriously in those who are ordained and who even later can be parenthetically reminded of it, is it possible, then, to maintain lightly—as Luther has done in his polemic against the "invented *characteres indelibiles*"[79]—that a retired Church officeholder is like a layman and no different from any other retired officeholder?[80] Is it not the charism through which the Christian becomes the instrument and servant of God? Does the difference between universal priesthood and special priesthood consist solely in the functions and efficacy of the officeholder? Does not the difference also lie in the special God-given charism that is bestowed through ordination and not solely in the sociological differentiation of status? And does not this special charism have something to do with special authority? Hence is not the question one of spiritual office rather than one of clerical status? Would not the history of the Lutheran ecclesiastical office have been different if more theoretical and practical attention had been paid to it? Could it not, then, have fulfilled its functions quite differently—not only for the preservation of the apostolic character of the Church, but particularly also for the preservation of Church *unity*, which cannot be maintained without a theologically well-founded concept of ecclesiastical office? But let us not stop with this question. The last decades, after all, have paved the way for promising developments.

3. NEW BEGINNINGS

(*a*) As a result of the political upheavals of 1918, the Church organization under princes and municipalities was dissolved. For the

[79] *WA* 6, 408.

[80] In connection with I Tim. 4:14 and II Tim. 1:6 E. Schweizer, in *Gemeinde und Gemeindeordnung im Neuen Testament* (Zürich 1959) 190f, observes that there it not only involves an "installation" (appointment to a concrete service in the local community): "For in both passages the charism is recalled which has been conferred on the appointed person by the imposition of hands. Since with Timothy and Titus it is presupposed that they will again return to being apostles after service in the communities in which they are now working, it is difficult to think that the author should have conceived to limit the charism only with respect to the duration and uniqueness of this special concrete service. Historically speaking in his time only the imposition of hands on the part of the presbytery to a service in the local community may have existed. . . . In the installation of the Pastoral Epistles the whole tone is laid on the transmission of the Spirit, which in any case was not the central motive in the Jewish ordination, if it played a role at all at the time of the New Testament." Cf. E. Lohse, "Ordination (II: im NT)" in *Die Religion in Geschichte und Gegenwart* (Tübingen ³1960) IV, 1672f; *Die Ordination im Spätjudentum und im Neuen Testament* (Göttingen 1951).

Evangelical Church a free path opened up for a new ecclesiastical reorganization of the episcopal office. But it was only with time that a clearer theological picture of the episcopal office emerged. "The turn came in 1918 with the abolition of the princely *summus episcopus*, an office which despite its provisional character accorded to it by the Reformers had been occupied by an 'emergency' bishop for 400 years. Nevertheless, the *summus episcopus* was not immediately replaced everywhere by a bishop. Before 1933 there were 'territorial bishops' only in a few Lutheran Churches (Mecklenburg-Schwerin, the Free State of Saxony, Brunswick, Hanover, Schleswig-Holstein) and in the uniate Church of Nassau, which also once before (1817–76) had a territorial bishop, an exception among the territorial Churches. The synods of the Old Prussian Union especially, in several dramatic plebiscites, over and over again rejected the introduction of the episcopal office with slim majorities. The term 'territorial bishop,' based on the idea of the territorial Church, has in general remained. Nevertheless, today the designation 'bishop' (Oldenburg) is also current. After 1918 the office of the Bavarian 'Church President' also gained in pastoral scope and power according to the Church constitution of 1920. The title of 'Bishop' was conferred upon him only in 1933. Only in this year were bishops installed everywhere. This, however, was due to the influence—though not everywhere and not in all cases—of the 'leadership principle' which had become dominant."[1]

Just as the failure of the bishops at the time of the Reformation had been partially responsible for the devaluation and ultimately for the practical rejection of the episcopal office in the Protestant Church,

---

[1] H. Liermann, "Bischof" (III: im ev. Kirchenrecht), in *Religion in Geschichte und Gegenwart* (Tübingen ³1957) I, 1306. On the history and theology of the Protestant episcopal office in the post-Reformation time, cf. P. Schoen, "Der deutsche evengelische Bischof nach den evangelischen Kirchenverfassungen," in *Verw.-Arch.* 30 (Berlin 1925) 403–431; W. Elert, "Der bischöfliche Charakter der Superintendentur-Verfassung," in *Luthertum* 46 (1935) 353–367; H. Liermann, "Das evangelische Bischofsamt in Deutschland seit 1933," in *Zeitschrift für evangelisches Kirchenrecht* 3 (1953/54) 1–29; E. Benz, *Bischofsamt und apostolische Sukzession im deutschen Protestantismus* (Stuttgart 1953); E. Sommerlath, *Amt und Allgemeines Priestertum* (Schriften des Theologischen Konvents Augsburgischen Bekenntnisses, No. 5, Berlin 1953); P. Brunner, *Vom Amt des Bischofs (ibid.* No. 9, Berlin 1955); W. Maurer, *Das synodale evangelische Bischofsamt (ibid.* No. 10, Berlin 1955); J. Heubach, *Die Ordination zum Amt der Kirche* (Berlin 1956); "Erklärung des ökumenischen Ausschusses der VELKD zur Frage der apostolischen Sukzession vom 26. 11. 1957," in *Evangelisch-Lutherische Kirchenzeitung* No. 5 (Berlin 1958); E. Schlink, "Die apostolische Sukzession," in his collection *Der kommende Christus und die kirchlichen Traditionen* (Göttingen 1961) 160–195.

so (despite the failure of the political bishops) was the strong stand taken by individual Protestant bishops in the Church struggle against National Socialism (Wurm, Meiser) important for an upgrading of the episcopal office in the consciousness of the Church and for the maintenance or introduction of the episcopal office after 1945. Thus in present-day Germany (with the exception of Rhineland-Westphalia and Hesse-Nassau, which have been strongly influenced by the Calvinist tradition) the episcopal office has again been generally established. It exists even in the non-hierarchically organized congregations of the Moravian Brethren. Only the Reformed Churches reject the episcopal office in principle, although in Hungary, for instance, there are even Reformed bishops. This is the reason why the episcopal office is not grounded in the constitution of the German Evangelical Church, which includes the Reformed Churches, but in the constitution of the Lutheran Evangelical Church of Germany. According to the present-day constitutions the bishop, as a rule, has the following functions: "ordination, induction of provosts and deacons, supervision of the purity of doctrinal teaching, pastoral care for ministers, right of visitation, pulpit rights in all congregations, the issuance of 'pastoral letters,' the establishment of special feast days and days of penance, participation in the induction of bishops in neighbouring churches, and the chairmanship of the highest ecclesiastical and administrative bodies."[2] There is no doubt that the episcopal office in general has assumed an increasing importance in the Christian confessions today whether or not it stands within the framework of apostolic succession. This is true in the Catholic, in the Old Catholic, in the Orthodox, and in the Anglican and Methodist Churches, as well as in many independent Churches (Philippines, Africa). But even in non-episcopal missions in many cases an office corresponding to that of bishop, though bearing another name, has been established to meet the requirements of ecclesiastical life. The leanings of the young Churches of Asia and Africa towards an episcopal church constitution is unmistakable (cf. the South Indian Union, the Pan-African Lutheran Conference of Marango 1955, the Lutheran Church of New Guinea, and the efforts at unification in North India, Ceylon, and Nigeria).[3]

Hence—despite all differences—developments in Church history since World War I have in a new way emphasized the importance of

[2] P. Brunner, "Bischof," in *Lexikon für Theologie und Kirche* (Freiburg i. Br. ²1958) II, 506.

[3] Cf. S. C. Neill, "Bischof" (IV, in the early churches), in *Religion in Geschichte und Gegenwart* (Tübingen 1957) I, 1309–1311.

ecclesiastical office, and especially of the episcopal office. This has been the case also outside the Catholic Church and therefore it can be viewed as a new commitment and as a sign pointing to the growing agreement between separated Christians. With reference to our argument, the conclusion to be drawn is that whatever is of special importance for the Church, as the ecumenical council by divine convocation, is doubtless also of special importance for an ecumenical council by human convocation, which aims to represent the Church. Hence the role of ecclesiastical office must also be given full value at an ecumenical council by human convocation.

(*b*) A crucial impulse for the theology of ecclesiastical office emanates from New Testament exegesis. In this respect an extraordinarily important development for the understanding of the apostolic character of the Church can be discerned. Where does the defection from the apostolic Church, where does "Catholic decadence," begin, according to the Protestant view? Is it just coincidence that this point in time in the development of Church history is always being pushed further back under the pressure of the findings of historical research? Luther still felt himself at one with the old Church of the first millennium: for him "Catholic decadence" begins—at least in a crucial sense—with the Middle Ages. Later Protestantism identified itself only with the Church of the first centuries. For it "Catholic decadence" had its beginning after the "*consensus quinquesaecularis*" or, even earlier, after the conversion of Constantine. At the beginning of our century, A. von Harnack set the first century as the time when the apostolic Church ceased to exist: Catholic decadence begins with the influx of the Greek spirit into primitive apostolic Christendom: "The influx of Hellenism, of the Greek spirit, and the union of the Gospel with it, form the greatest fact in the history of the Church in the second century, and when the fact was established as a foundation it continued through the following centuries."[4] Hence, in the second century we can begin to observe "the Christian religion in its development into Catholicism."[5] This is the starting point for the discussion of the following decades about the Hellenistic-Catholic original sin which, after the apostolic period, ushered in the period of "early Catholicism." It is in this early Catholic period that the typical Catholic concept of ecclesiastic office began to crystallize: "The struggle with Gnosticism compelled the

[4] A von. Harnack, *What Is Christianity?* (Harper Torchbooks, New York, 1957) 200.
[5] A. von Harnack, *op cit.* 190.

Church to put its teaching, its worship, and its discipline into fixed forms and ordinances and to exclude everyone who would not yield them obedience. . . . If by 'Catholic' we mean the church of doctrine and of law, then the Catholic Church had its origin in the struggle with Gnosticism."[6]

Had not this continuous pushing back of the "Catholic decadence" practically reached the New Testament itself? Had not the borders between the New Testament and the post-New Testament writings become fluid for Harnack too? It is to the credit of the Bultmann school in particular that the specific problem raised herewith has been discussed with an unmitigated clarity: "Catholic decadence" begins even earlier; "early Catholicism" can be found in the New Testament itself! In order to appreciate the progress that has been made along this line of reasoning it suffices to compare the discussion of Church order in the Pastoral Epistles in the *Theology of the New Testament* by Paul Feine[7] and in *The Theology of the New Testament* by Rudolph Bultmann.[8]

Within the scope of our argument Ernst Käsemann has provided an excellent and comprehensive presentation of this problem area in his treatise concerning office and congregation in the New Testament.[9] He distinguishes sharply between the different concepts of organization underlying the Church structure in the Pauline epistles, on the one hand, and in the Pastoral Epistles and in Luke (Acts), on the other. In contrast to the charismatically determined Pauline congregation, the structural order of the congregation both in the Pastoral Epistles and in Luke is defined in terms of early Catholicism.

According to Käsemann, in the Pastoral Epistles the congregation was sorely put on the defensive by the Gnostic heresies. The resistance was led from a single centre: by the apostolic delegate and by the presbytery closely linked to him. In the *Pauline* epistles a *presbytery* is never addressed, although it would have been the logical body to

---

[6] A. von Harnack, *op cit.* 207.

[7] P. Feine, *Theologie des Neuen Testaments* (Leipzig [7]1936) 319–25.

[8] R. Bultmann, *Theologie des Neuen Testaments* (Tübingen [3]1958) 452–463; cf. W. Schmithals, "Pastoralbriefe," in *Die Religion in Geschichte und Gegenwart* (Tübingen [3]1961) V. 144–148.

[9] E. Käsemann, "Amt und Gemeinde im Neuen Testament," in *Exegetische Versuche und Besinnungen* (Göttingen 1960) I, 109–134. Cf. also, however, Ph. Vielhauer, "Der Paulinismus der Apostelgeschichte," in *Evangelische Theologie* 10 (1950/51) 1–15; G. Harbsmeier, "Unsere Predigt im Spiegel der Apostelgeschichte," in *Evangelische Theologie* 10 (10 1950/51) 352–368; W. Marxsen, *Der "Frühkatholizismus" im Neuen Testament* (Neukirchen 1958); H. Braun, *"Hebt die heutige neutestamentlich-exegetische Forschung den Kanon auf?* (Fuldaer Hefte 12, Berlin 1960.)

struggle against the heresies. Indeed, there was no presbyterium of such a kind in the Pauline congregations as had probably been established in the congregations of the Pastoral Epistles. Presumably *ordination* (I Tim. 4:14; 5:22; II Tim. 1:6) in the Pauline congregations derived from the Judeo-Christian tradition: "It had the same meaning as in Judaism, namely, the communication of the spirit and the authorization to administer the *depositum fidei* of 1 Tim. 6:20, which we may well interpret to be the tradition of Pauline teaching. This means, however, that an office confronting the rest of the congregation had become the actual bearer of the spirit and that the primitive Christian conception, according to which every Christian partakes of the spirit in Baptism, receded into the background and actually disappeared. Equally clear is that this no longer corresponded to the charism doctrine of Paul. The Pauline legacy receded before the Judaic, at least at a central point of the Church's message. Thus the word "charism" appears only in I Tim. 4:15 and in II Tim. 1:6, which is illuminating in connection with statements concerning ordination. This was the designation for the mandate of ordination and the authorization to administer the *depositum fidei*. Awkwardly but most appropriately one could speak of a spirit of office."[10]

Thus, according to Käsemann, all references to the apostolic legates (Titus, Timothy) in fact pertain to the *monarchical* bishops: "His task is the continuation of the apostolic office in the post-apostolic period. In other words, he stands in the apostolic succession exactly as the rabbi, in the succession of Moses and Joshua, receives and controls the doctrinal tradition and the administration of justice by divine right—namely, as empowered through the gift of the Spirit at ordination. This was how that concept of office which was to be the determining factor in the subsequent period was formed; at least, in fact, there existed a distinction between clerics and lay persons. A tacit principle of tradition and legitmacy safeguards the unmistakable foundation of congregational order vested in the authority of institutional office which, in the form of the presbytery, diaconate and widows' institutes, surrounded itself with executive organs."[11] This whole transformation was necessary in order to meet the enormous danger of the Gnostic radical sectarians.

The conception of the Church in the Acts of the Apostles is quite similar to that in the Pastoral Epistles. Here too we find mentioned

---

[10] E. Käsemann, *op cit*. I, 128f.

[11] E. Käsemann, *op cit*. I, 129; compare also to I Tim. 6:11–16. Käsemann's article: "Das Formular einer neutestamentlichen Ordinationsparänese," *op cit*. I, 101–108.

everywhere bishops, presbyteria, ordination, as well as the principle of tradition and legitimacy. "As far as we can see, Luke was the first to propagate the early Catholic theory of tradition and legitimacy. Even he did not engage upon this on his own but in order to defend the Church against the threatening danger. The historian can do nothing but admit that this theory proved to be the most effective weapon in the struggle against Enthusiasm and protected early Christianity from sinking into radical sectarianism. To that extent the recognition of Acts as canonical is understandable and well deserved as an expression of gratitude on the part of the Church."[12] Hence it is no longer a cause for surprise that also the presumably latest writing of the New Testament canon, the Second Epistle of Peter, according to Käsemann, bears the stamp of early Catholicism. "From beginning to end Second Peter is a document of early Catholic views and it is probably the most dubious of all the writings of the canon."[13] Chapter I, verse 20 may be viewed as the most characteristic utterance of the whole epistle. It means: "Personal exegesis is not permitted to the individual unless authorized and prescribed by the teaching office of the Church."[14]

All these statements (in their positive content) are, of course, not new to the Catholic theologian. What is new is that those statements are made by a *Protestant* theologian and made with the utmost clarity. The simple scriptural texts in question here were, in fact, always understood in this way by Catholic exegetes (if we here disregard certain of Käsemann's loaded formulations and their relationship to the great Pauline utterances). Indeed Catholic exegetes have repeatedly pointed out that the interpretation of early Catholic texts must be taken seriously. Actually Protestant exegetes often considered them non-existent[15] or did not extensively interpret them.[16]

[12] E. Käsemann, *op cit*. I, 132.
[13] E. Käsemann, "Eine Apologie der urchristlichen Estchatologie," *op cit*. I, 135.
[14] E. Käsemann, *op cit*. I, 153f.
[15] A characteristic example is furnished by P. Feine, who not only does not explain the three classical passages named above in connection with ordination in the Pastoral Epistles throughout his whole *Theologie des Neuen Testaments*, but does not even mention them. And relative to II Peter, E. Käsemann says: "One would almost like to call it symptomatic, that apart from the dutiful treatment in the commentaries, there is for the most part silence concerning our epistles" (*op cit*. I, 135).
[16] Thus the prohibition against "individual interpretation" in I Pet. 1:20 for R. Knopf means only that "Christians should go to the Old Testament prophets with reverence, discretion and modesty," and for G. Wohlenberg and A. Schlatter: prophecy receives its interpretation and fulfilment from history (according to E. Käsemann, *op cit*. I, 152f.) Another example is furnished by W. Fürst, *Kirche*

Käsemann, however, is soberly and clearly aware of the full importance of these passages; courageously and perceptively he sees the provocative nature of the question which his admission entails. At the end of his chapter on Second Peter he writes: "What is it about the canon in which Second Peter has its place as the clearest testimony to early Catholicism?"[17] In the treatise, "Is the unity of the Church founded on the New Testament Claim?" he first of all re-iterates the decisive facts: "Here (in Second Peter) the Spirit no longer wields His influence also through tradition, He has become one with tradition. Hence, as is already the case in the Pastoral Epistles and in Acts, the Church's teaching office is the possessor of the 'spirit of office,' and every non-authorized exegesis and interpretation of Scripture is forbidden as in the almost classic monitory passage in 2 Peter 1:20. Here ordination is an indicator of the principle of legiti-macy and succession. In short, one has stepped beyond the borders of primitive Christianity and established early Catholicism."[18] From it is drawn the important conclusion: "The time when one could confront Catholicism with the full text of Scripture is past beyond recall. Protestantism today can no longer apply the so-called formal principle without adopting an untenable position in terms of his-torical analysis. The New Testament canon does not stand between Judaism and early Christianity but provides in itself scope and foun-dation to both Judaism and early Catholicism."[19]

The dilemma of the Protestant theologian is obvious: either to accept early Catholicism as an element of the New Testament and thereby definitely embark on the road to "late Catholicism," or else to reject early Catholicism as an element of the New Testament and correct the canon accordingly. It is instructive to compare Käse-mann's decision with that of another prominent Bultmann scholar, with whom Käsemann's exegetical work is in a continuous latent and, in part, overt discussion.

Heinrich Schlier chose the first path. His investigation regarding the structural order of the Church according to the Pastoral Epistles, which appeared in 1948 in a collection of essays in honour of

---

oder Gnosis? Heinrich Schliers Absage an den Protestantismus (Munich 1961) 36: "Thus one will not, for instance, burden the Pastoral Epistles with their undoubtedly 'Catholic' concept of office and tradition, but will listen in them to the claim of the Word, to which Christendom standing and resting in such developments, is called."

[17] E. Käsemann, *op. cit.* I, 157.

[18] E. Käsemann, "Begründet der neutestamenthliche Kanon die Einheit der Kirche?" *op. cit.* II, 220f.

[19] E. Käsemann, *op cit.* I, 221f.

Friedrich Gogarten, led him to a conclusion with respect to the question of office which largely agreed with Käsemann: "(1) The structural order of the Church, 'which is the Church of the living God, the pillar and mainstay of the truth' (I Tim. 3:15) rests upon the 'office.' The 'authority,' the spiritual power, lies in the hands of specific officeholders who are called thereto, provided with the grace of office, and installed in a service. Thus they teach, and govern the Church, and transmit the office through the laying on of hands (ordination). The principle of office prevails. (2) This 'office' has its origin in the vocation and the installation of the apostles in the service of the Gospel through Christ Jesus. It is transmitted and expanded through the transmittal of the charism of office (and on the apostolic paradox) from the apostle to the disciple of the apostle and from him to the local presbyter-bishops. The principle of succession prevails. (3) The office contains specific gradations. It appears in the service of the disciple of an apostle in charge of a Church territory who, at the same time, acts there as apostolic delegate; and in the service of several 'presiding' elders or bishops in the local Church. In addition there is the service of the deacons and 'widows' both of whom exercise supporting functions. In its gradation the office exhibits a tendency towards a monarchical apex. The principle of primacy permeates it."[20] In 1955, after his conversion to the

---

[20] H. Schlier, *Die Zeit der Kirche. Exegetische Aufsätze und Vorträge* (Freiburg i. Br. 1955, ³1962) 146. For further elucidation, H. Schlier writes later in his epilogue: "The situation of the Church-struggle of the 'Confessional Church' had confronted every theologian who took part in the question of church government. The widespread synodal and presbyterial theory in Protestant circles and the historical theory—often fused with the former—of the charismatic constitution of the early Church seemed indeed to correspond incontrovertibly with the apostolic testimony of the New Testament. However, not only practice but, on closer perusal, the New Testament as well, raised noticeable objection. The New Testament recognizes the principle of formal delegation which includes the principle of succession. It generally recognizes the principle of ecclesiastical authority and canon law. And these principles were effective in the Church from the beginning. I tried to authenticate them, and in connection with them also, the principle of tradition in the New Testament, and to illuminate them somewhat at that point in the so-called Pastoral Epistles where these principles pressed for a conscious clarification, because the apostle who had, as it were, collected them in a body and espoused them in his office, had to leave the Church to his successors. It is interesting, from the point of view of method, that I was able to base my findings on the interpretations of the old liberal school, which historically was unconcerned *vis-à-vis* the content of the Pastoral Epistles, because they considered them products of the post-aspostolic time; while conservative Protestant exegesis (Schlatter's, for example) deprived the New Testament statements of their sharpness. However, in this connection, the First Epistle to the Corinthians had greater meaning for me."

Catholic Church. Schlier, basing himself[21] not only on the Pastoral Epistles but also on the Epistle to the Ephesians and especially on the great Pauline epistles (above all, First Corinthians) wrote: "The New Testament led me to inquire whether the Lutheran Confession and more specifically modern Protestant faith, which has so widely deviated from its original form, is in agreement with its own testimony. Gradually I became convinced that the Church which it had in mind was the Roman Catholic Church. Hence it was, if I may say so, an authentic Protestant path which took me to the Church; a path which is actually provided for in the Lutheran confessional writings, although naturally not expected. In that context I must still mention something else. What led me to the Church was the New Testament as it presented itself to unbiased historical interpretation."[22] And the collection of exegetical articles which was published in the same year, almost all of which derive from his Protestant period, purposed "to ask only one question" of the reader: "Whether what I have heard from the New Testament is not right, and whether the New Testament therefore—in a word—is not after all Catholic, whether Catholic principles are not after all the apostolic principles?"[23]

Ernst Käsemann chose the second path. He insists decisively upon the "discernment of spirits."[24] The discernment of spirits within the New Testament! "One will have to recognize the intimate connection and the distinction between the letter and the spirit. What Paul asserts in II Corinthians 3 over against the Old Testament should not remain limited to the Old Testament. Rather, it applies likewise to

[21] Cf. the remaining articles in Schlier's collection, and especially the Epilogue, *op cit.* 308–314.

[22] H. Schlier, "Kurze Rechenschaft," in *Bekenntnis zur katholischen Kirche,* ed. by K. Hardt (Würzburg 1955, [4]1956) 176f.

[23] H. Schlier, *Die Zeit der Kirche. Exegetische Aufsätze und Vorträge* (Freiburg i. Br. 1955, [3]1962) 308. On this, see W. Fürst, *Kirche oder Gnosis? Heinrich Schliers Absage an den Protestantismus* (München 1961) 30: "We were embarrassed particularly by the fact that Schlier is able to raise his principle of office to validity on the basis of the Pastoral Epistles, since it is there that the concept of *Kerygma* actually dominates as a formulated apostolic tradition to be handed down. Schlier thinks that the Pastoral Epistles had only 'raised to consciousness' what, on this basis, he already finds in I Corinthians." We have already pointed out that Fürst, who strangely enough never even mentions Schlier's "little justification," in opposing Schlier takes refuge in the underinterpretation of the text in question. Schlier's question remains in principle, even if we agree, for instance, with Käsemann in his criticism of various exegetical interpretations. Cf. E. Käsemann, "Das Interpretations-problem des Epheserbriefes," in *Theologische Literaturzeitung* 86 (1961) 1–8; cf. also the reviews quoted by Fürst (*op cit.* 6 by H. Conzelmann and U. Wilckens).

[24] E. Käsemann, "Begründet der neutestamentliche Kanon die Einheit der Kirche" in *Exegetische Verusche und Besinnungen* (Göttingen 1960) I, 221.

the New Testament canon."[25] Or to put it differently: "God is not pinned down in the New Testament either. Because the Jews mean by it the Law, Paul speaks of the Old Testament canon as the letter which kills. If we do not understand the New Testament differently, the same applies there. Merely in virtue of its existence, the canon is simply not God's word."[26]

What then is Käsemann's further objective? He wants to find the "Gospel" in the canon. For the canon is the Word of God only insofar as it is and becomes "Gospel." Scripture must be understood in terms of its objective centre, in terms of the Message of which it is the record; in short in terms of the "Gospel." And what is "Gospel"? Only the believer, convinced by the Spirit and hearkening to Scripture, is able to decide this. "The Bible is neither the Word of God in an objective sense, nor is it a doctrinal system. It is the record of the history of the proclamation of the message of primitive Christianity. The Church, which canonized it, asserts, however, that it is precisely in this way that she becomes the bearer of the Gospel. The Church maintains, and can maintain this position here only because she views history portrayed and manifesting itself in terms of the justification of the sinner. Since her claim, however, is an attestation and a confession, she thereby summons us to submit our own history to a scrutiny in terms of the justification of the sinner. Thus we would be forced to make a decision not only as to whether we wish to follow the above summons or not, but likewise as to whether the core of Scripture is correctly grasped by such a confession."[27]

Thus Käsemann, with great earnestness, pursues his way, which he regards as the middle road, as the way of the "Gospel," as it is above all proclaimed by Paul who understood it most deeply. It is the middle way, between sectarian Enthusiasm on the left, which sought to seize on the Gospel in by-passing Scripture, and traditional early Catholicism on the right, which fancies that the Gospel can simply be found and made accessible in Scripture, without having to hold up Scripture continuously against the critical authority of the Gospel. Thus Enthusiasm and early Catholicism are not eliminated from the canon. They do have a place in the authentic canon only as an undoubtedly instructive, but also obscure, programme that is to be rejected by contrast to the authentic Gospel which proclaims the justification of the sinner as an event. In this way a "canon in a canon" can be critically discerned.[28]

---

[25] E. Käsemann, *op. cit.* I, 221f.   [26] E. Käsemann, *op cit.* I, 222f.
[27] E. Käsemann, Zum Thema der Nichtobjektivierbarkeit, *ibid.* I, 232.
[28] Cf. also W. G. Kümmel, "Notwendigkeit und Grenze des neutestamentlichen

What is there to say about this second way? The exegetical findings on which Käsemann bases himself both in principle and especially in regard to the problematic aspects of office and congregation cannot be disputed despite the reservations one may have on questions of detail.[29] There is: (1) a great variability of the New Testament kerygma which derives, on the one hand, from the special character of the scriptural passages in the New Testament and the traditions used and, on the other hand, from the different theological attitudes of the writers themselves; (2) an extraordinary profusion of theological positions in early Christianity going beyond the New Testament which can be surmised, on the one hand, on the basis of the altogether fragmentary character of our knowledge of the history and message of early Christianity and, on the other hand, on the basis of the obviously conversational character of most New Testament utterances which were addressed to concrete situations; (3) increasingly apparent differentiations among the various positions which simply cannot be positively synchronized. It follows then that the New Testament is not a systematic *Summa theologica*, that it is not a uniform systematic doctrinal system which, apart from its character as a proclamation, can be simply taught by way of explication and grafted on by demonstration. The different texts stem from different individuals, arise out of different situations, and have different theological goals and leanings. They must, in turn, be transmitted to different individuals with different goals and leanings finding themselves in different situations. The ever-new task of the Church is to transmit and translate the kerygma from the original context into the context of the newly arising situations.

What does Käsemann achieve by his efforts? We must admit that his concentration on the kerygma, in a broader sense on the Pauline

Kanons," in *Zeitschrift für Theologie und Kirche* 47 (1950) 311f: "The actual limit of the canon therefore runs through the midst of the canon, and only where this circumstance is truly perceived and acknowledged can the appeal of Catholic or sectarian teachings to specific *individual* passages of the canon be parried with really substantial arguments." H. Braun, "Hebt die heutige neutestamentlich-exegetische Forschung den Kanon auf?" (*Fuldaer Hefte* 12. Berlin 1960) 23: "The exegesis which pays attention to the mesage, paralyses the dross in the canon and, as far as the particulars go, brings the limits of the canon into question. It doesn't say 'yes' to the canon as a whole, nor 'yes' because it is the canon. It takes it critically, but with the application of *that* objective criterion which stems from the New Testament itself. And therefore it sticks to the canon as far as its centre, as the basic phenomenon of the New Testament, is concerned. Indeed it has this only *in* the canon, and later not at all; even though what is in the canon is not pure and unalloyed."

[29] Cf. especially the already frequently quoted article: "Begründet der neutestamentliche Kanon die Einheit der Kirche?"

kerygma, is most impressive. In Käsemann's view Paul is the one who had the deepest understanding of the Gospel. And Paul in many respects certainly is more concentrated and therefore more impressive than the whole, and indeed very variable, New Testament. In what, however, does this concentration consist? It consists in reduction. In reduction to Holy Scripture insofar as it is the "Gospel," insofar as it proclaims the justification of the sinner. Käsemann doubtless means, not the *doctrine* of justification, but the *event* of justification. And the event of justification was not only proclaimed in the epistles to the Romans and Galatians but also in the sayings of Jesus, in a beatitude, and elsewhere. In short *everywhere* that it occurs it is a question of the "Gospel."

But it is here that we must pose our question: Does not the *whole* New Testament deal with the proclamation of the justification of sinners; is it not a question of the "Gospel" in the whole New Testament? It is precisely this that Käsemann cannot admit within the framework of his chosen argument. In his view there are clearly texts which do not proclaim the justification of sinners, which are therefore not of the "Gospel." Hence Käsemann's concentration simultaneously signifies reduction or—as one might also say—selection. A formal principle of interpretation is applied which then also turns out to be a mtaerial principle of selection, a principle of choice. Only thus can Käsemann declare as unevangelical, within the context of the New Testament, not only the sectarian Enthusiasm on the left and legalistic Judaism on the right, but also early Catholicism which, in the Catholic view, is already found in Paul.

What actually is at issue here? Nothing but the renunciation in principle of a comprehensive understanding and a serious acceptance of the *whole* New Testament in favour of a concentrated *selection*, that is, the rejection in principle of a "Catholic" understanding of Scripture in favour of "heresy."

This is the high price which is paid for the protest against early Catholicism. Käsemann's protest against early Catholicism is a protest against Catholicism in general; Käsemann himself would be the last to challenge this. This protest is directed against the Catholic *Church* and not against the un-Catholic aspects of the Catholic Church. This would be Catholic. Rather, it is directed against the Catholicism of the Catholic Church. And this is Protestant. We Catholics can understand, accept and, indeed, even participate in the former, never in the latter. Käsemann's chosen path, it would seem to us, could not lead anywhere but astray. In short: only aporia. For Käsemann's protest against the catholicity of the Church (as a

Protestant protest) necessarily becomes a protest against the catholicity of *Scripture* on which he bases himself exclusively in his protest against the catholicity of the Church! Thus the protest changes its originally corrective character (as Luther intended it to be) into a constitutive one (as intended by Protestantism of the most different shadings). The protest solidifies and cancels itself out by undermining the foundation on which it stands.

On what grounds does Käsemann claim that *his* selection from the New Testament specifically constitutes the "Gospel"? Certainly it is not simply on the basis of the New Testament because the New Testament, even according to Käsemann, includes more than just *his* "Gospel." Nor is his argument based on the "exegetic findings" which would tend towards an acceptance of the "Pauline median" as "Gospel." Indeed this is the very question: Why is Käsemann able to see only this "Pauline median" as "Gospel"? Can Käsemann base himself on anything more than on a Protestant preconception (unconsciously produced as a result of philosophical premises or of a scarcely credible presentation of Catholicism in history and at the present time)? Or, at a deeper level, upon a kind of ultimate option ("faith") in which perhaps we are confronted with more (Lutheran tradition?) than we had ourselves placed there? Hence a decision *prior* to all exegesis, a kind of Corinthian Enthusiasm—it is also this for which Schlier reproaches Käsemann. Is not this a position in which one can scarcely adduce reasons that could prevent others from making other choices and, on the basis of *another a priori* understanding, discover exegetically *another* median and another *Gospel*? One can no longer base oneself on the New Testament as a *whole* once its catholicity has been sacrificed to the protest.

What remains—against the will of its adherents—is a more or less great arbitrariness: "For Luther this median, from which he judged everything, was in fact Paul or, more precisely, his doctrine of justification by faith. On the other hand, for Luther the Gospel of John was the 'only tender, true main Gospel.' F. Schleiermacher likewise judged this Gospel to be the most essential one because of its spiritual content and defended it on these grounds. For critical historical theology at the beginning of our century the words of the Lord in the Synoptics was the measure of authenticity. But for R. Bultmann the Johannine Gospel is the testimony of the valid Gospel as the Gospel of the Word alone and of the present existential decision, even if allegedly later ecclesiastical additions concerning the Sacraments and the future eschatology must be discarded. Rather than measuring the New Testament on the basis of such a norm, would it not be more appropriate to weigh these critical standards against the wealth of the New Testament and, on this basis, ascribe to them at most a relative value.[30]

We know where this obviously subjectively determined selective attitude leads: Every selection refutes the others and is in turn refuted by them. The wrongly (!) understood *sola scriptura* leads to a *sola pars scripturae* and this in turn to a *sola pars Ecclesiae* (party); in short to a devastating chaos in the proclamation of the Gospel and to a progressive fragmentation of Protestantism. Even W. Fürst in his attempt at a Protestant reply to Heinrich Schlier freely admits: "Our own division should be the weak point at which Schlier's sceptical questioning should find us most sensitive. Are we united among ourselves, as we certainly ought to be according to the reformational 'Principle'? Do we at least agree with Schlier on those points on which we, according to all indications, should agree—namely, that the New Testament is the standard for all decisions? Schlier does not believe us, that behind the varied pronouncements that we make stands the one Scripture to which we all listen. And one can hardly blame him. Should not his conversion, which threateningly shakes all the foundations of our tradition, long ago have compelled us to catch up as rapidly as possible with the settlements that have over and over again been postponed among ourselves? So long as we do not attend to this, we shall scarcely be in a position to meet Schlier's challenge successfully. The effort that is to be undertaken

---

[30] K. H. Schelkle, *Die Petrusbriefe* (Herders Theologischer Kommentar zum Neuen Testament XIII, 2 (Freiburg–Basle–Vienna 1961)) 245. In his criticism of James, Luther formulated his hermeneutic criterion as follows: That also is the right touchstone to criticize all books: see whether or not they promote Christ." (*WA* Deutsche Bibel, 7, 385). Is there not already a subjective dissolution of the canon present here? W. Maurer asks in "Luthers Verstädis des neutestamentlichen Kanons" (*Fuldaer Hefte* 12, Berlin 1960) 76f: "The historical critical method relativizes the canon and places the apostolic testimony within the relativity of all history. The theological interpretation that Luther, in part, gives to the canon presupposes its existence and is unthinkable without it. His conception of the canon is derived from the relationship of the apostolic witness to Christ and brings it back to Christ's saving rule. Thus he bases the existence of the canon in God's establishment of salvation itself and binds the Christian faith indissolubly to it." On the other hand, cannot G. Ebeling ("Die Bedeutung der historisch-kritischen Methode für die protestantische Theologie und Kirche," in *Zeitschrift für Theologie und Kirche* 47 (1950) 16) rightfully reproach the Reformers for lacking consistency in their conception of the canon? The traditional view of Scripture "was most deeply shaken in the Reformation, but practically it was not thoroughly critically revised. The concentration of the Scriptural witnesses on Jesus Christ as *the* Word of God and the distinction between law and Gospel as the guiding thread of Scriptural interpretation established an unprecedented critical canon within the canon."

here stands under the burden of unfinished tasks and we must be aware of its provisional character even in this respect."[31]

The bold programme "canon in the canon" demands nothing but to be more biblical than the Bible, more New Testamentary than the New Testament, more evangelical than the Evangel and even more Pauline than Paul. If the intention is radical practice, a radical dissolution is the consequence. In contrast to all selectiveness, which in its self-absolutization unwittingly becomes hubris, a *Catholic* attitude seeks to preserve a full openness and freedom with respect to the *whole* of the New Testament. Often this seems to be less consistent and impressive than the powerful one-sided explication of *one* line. As has been indicated, Paul *alone* under certain circumstances can produce a more consistent and impressive effect than the whole New Testament, and under certain circumstances the Pauline Paul (purified of "sacramentalism" and "mysticism") in turn can produce a more consistent and impressive effect than the whole Paul. But the true Paul is the whole Paul and the true New Testament is the whole New Testament.

To be sure it is much more difficult to give full value exegetically to the *whole* instead of to a part only. Not only because *every* theologian as a human being is in danger of not perceiving in the New Testament precisely that which he should perceive, but also because in this Catholic approach the lofty exegetic art of differentiation and subtle distinction is particularly required. Hence, on the one hand, there is no streamlining and levelling of the different ecclesiological statements of the New Testament for reasons of methodological convenience which is too sluggish to go to the root of the different relative contradictions. And, on the other hand, there is no disassociation and reduction of those statements on the basis of a purely static, cumulative, comparative supercriticism, which takes more pleasure in ferreting out contradictions than in the detection of a deeper unity in the total context of Scriptures, which all ultimately aim to discuss—in whatever framework—Jesus Christ as the centre of the Gospel. Every attestation of the New Testament is an outcome of the history of the preaching of the message, in which the teaching and deeds of Jesus have been transmitted in manifold ways so that it may be believed that Jesus is the Lord.[32] Every ecclesiological testi-

---

[31] W. Fürst, *Kirche oder Gnosis: Heinrich Schliers Absage an den Protestantismus* (Munich 1961) 7.

[32] On the Protestant side, see H. Diem, *Dogmatik, Ihr Weg zwischen Historismus und Existentialismus* (Munich 1955, ²1957) 204–208, has excellently elaborated the importance of the situation of the proclamation.

mony of the New Testament, therefore, must be understood against the background of the whole history of the preaching of the Gospel, and of a definite situation to which the preaching is addressed.

Is not Käsemann's fear justified then—namely, that the *final* writing drawn from this preaching interprets the whole previous history and gives this its decisive character by virtue of the fact that it is the last testimony? In the Catholic view this New Testament attestation too must be taken seriously. As an evidence of early Catholicism it transmits the very link in the continuity necessary for the later Church—between the apostolic Church of the New Testament and the Church of the "Apostolic Fathers", in fact, the early Church altogether. Nevertheless this cannot mean that Second Peter is *the* crucial document, which must determine the interpretation of the whole New Testament. It should be kept in mind that the Petrine epistle is not an original but a *derived* testimony within the New Testament. Like the epistles of Jude and James, Second Peter also presupposes other New Testament writings and these, in turn, may conceivably presuppose still others, as for instance one or another saying of Jesus. The continually changing situation in which the Gospel was proclaimed necessitated an ever-new formulation of the original message in which the differences in character and theological orientation of the individual preacher of the message also played a great role. Hence, diversity within the New Testament was involved beforehand, as it were, by necessity. It is, after all, revealing that we have been handed down not only *one* Gospel or a Gospel-concordance, not even a biography, of Jesus, but different, often really divergent Gospels. In this whole complex development (which is not merely unilinear) it is understood that the original testimonies take precedence over the *derived* (in an objective and interpretive sense, but not—in view of inspiration—in a formal sense). The New Testament is, after all, not a kind of symposium of essays of equal rank (although not of equal worth), nor is the message of the New Testament the collective message of a group of writers to which each has contributed the conclusions of his independent research. The New Testament carries the message of Jesus Christ, of which all later testimonies can be, and aim to be, nothing more than interpretations. Hence, much as the derived testimonies of the New Testament are to be taken seriously, they are to be taken seriously as derivative and not as original attestations. Here not only the temporal proximity to the message of Jesus but also the inner objective proximity are important considerations. Apart from historical proximity to Jesus, the Epistle to the Romans may also be regarded as corresponding more closely to Jesus' message than, for instance, the Epistle of St. James. The further a testimony is removed from the original message the more will exegetes as well as dogmatists have to pay attention to the manner with which the testimony treats of the event of salvation in Jesus Christ. One will have to ascertain what kind of considerations play a part in the particular situation in which the Gospel was proclaimed; how the interpretation of the message was influenced by the personality of the preacher; how these secondary factors promoted, restricted, strengthened, weakened, exaggerated, or minimized the essential quality of the message. Thus every testimony in the whole of the New Testament must be understood in the terms of the message of Jesus and its original dominant issues. Hence, the later attestations should not overshadow the earlier ones; the Pastoral Epistles, for example, should not overshadow the Sermon on the Mount. It is hard to deny that Catholic ecclesiology for a time strongly overestimated precisely the Pastoral Epistles and thereby almost changed ecclesiology into a hierarchology. Nevertheless this misuse of the Pastoral Epistles provides no justification for discarding them as products of early Catholicism.

Throughout a turbulent history of the canon it is the Church, nevertheless, which has preserved for us the New Testament as a whole.[33] Without the Church there would be no New Testament. The Church also maintained that all parts of the New Testament were to be regarded as positive attestations of the message, deeds, and life of Jesus Christ—and not merely as partially negative contrasting presentations—and incorporated into the New Testament canon. The concrete relationship to the Church will also be a decisive factor today as to whether a theologian will or will not be able to accept with confidence, and yet at the same time critically, the whole New Testament as handed down and vouched for by the Church. We Catholics are convinced along with the early Church that we do right to consider the whole of the New Testament as a *conclusive* testimony of revelation as an event in Jesus Christ. We are, therefore, also convinced that recognition should be granted to every single testimony—as truly, but diversely oriented towards the event of salvation in Christ—and that each one of them should be accorded its full value, theologically as well as practically.

[33] In opposition to H. Diem (*ibid.* 179), H. Braun ("Hebt die heutige neutestamentlich-exegetische Forschung den Kanon auf?" [*Fuldaer Hefte* 12, Berlin 1960] 11) points out that the limitation of the canon has not simply prevailed in the Church, but was *decreed* in the final demarcations (Hebrews; a part of the Catholic Epistles and the Apocrypha): "The definitive character of this limitation is an ecclesiastical decree."

To summarize what has been said up to now we would like to quote K. H. Schelkle, the New Testament authority of the University of Tübingen, who has been specifically concerned with the problems presented by "early Catholicism": "Catholic theology will, naturally attach an all-embracing, different value to the attestations of early Catholicism in the New Testament than Protestant theology. Is it possible to narrow down the true New Testament message to the one hour, indeed to the mathematical point in time, say, of the Epistle to the Romans or the (demythologized) Johannine Gospel? The New Testament as a whole is the testimony of all-embracing, that is, catholic, truth in its fullness. To recognize only part of it means to choose, which means heresy. And if this New Testament in its later parts indicates a transition to early Catholicism then Catholic exegesis will attempt to show that in a truly historical sense this is not an inversion of truth and of the original message but an authentic and valid process of development. This will not prevent anyone from comparisons between the later and the earlier texts and from measuring the latter against the former, as all genuine critical theology— including the Catholic—always undertakes to do."[34]

What conclusions are to be drawn from this with respect to the significance accorded to ecclesiastical office in the New Testament? On the basis of the present-day state of exegetic problems, the Catholic view can be summarized in the following three statements (it is significant that competent Protestant witnesses can be cited in support, not of the whole, but certainly of each of the individual statements): (1) The New Testament encompasses "early Catholicism" and the "early Catholic" conception of ecclesiastical office.[35] (2) The *whole* New Testament must be given full value, though historically differentiated and translated in terms of the present.[36] (3) The

[34] K. H. Schelkle, *Die Petrusbriefe* (Herders Theologischer Kommentar zum Neuen Testament XIII, 2 [Freiburg–Basle–Vienna 1961]), 245.

[35] For E. Käsemann ("Begründet der neutestamentliche Kanon die Einheit der Kirche?" in *Exegetische Versuche und Besinnungen* [Göttingen 1960] I, 220f)— as is expounded in detail—"there is a going beyond the borders of primitive Christianity, and early Catholicism is established" within the New Testament.

[36] For example, H. Diem, *op cit.* 204: "The fact of the canon attests that the Church actually has clearly heard the proclamation of Jesus Christ in these witnesses and that therefore we too can hear and ought to hear them." 205: ". . . with every such situation-conditioned evaluation of the individual witness, attention is to be paid to the *limit* established through the fact of the canon. This demands the recognition that even that witness set back by us—within his conditioning historical frame, for how should be do otherwise?—executes the witness of Christ and therefore has found a hearing in the church, and therefore that he has spoken as one inspired by the Holy Ghost." W. Andersen, "Die Verbindlichkeit des Kanons" (*Fuldaer Hefte* 12, Berlin 1960) 44: "In the establishment of the canon

early Catholic testimonies regarding ecclesiastical office should not be placed in direct opposition to Paul and his doctrine of justification.[37]

Inasmuch as the whole set of problems could be presented here only in a sketchy and fragmentary way[37a] (we will immediately return to some of the problems raised), it should have become clear that a reorientation is taking place even in Protestant quarters in connection with the formulation of the New Testament problems and the positive as well as negative factors determining them. For some time now office in the Church has no longer been the centre of interest. But what, however, is important to the Church as the ecumenical council by divine convocation, is likewise of great significance to an ecumenical council by human convocation that aims to represent the Church. Within the framework of the New Testament it is equally urgent that ecclesiastical office be given its due consideration at an ecumenical council by human convocation since otherwise, as we have seen, the structural system of the Church will no longer be accorded the importance that is due to it.

(c) The impulses that had their point of departure in the general development in ecclesiastical history of the past fifty years and in

---

by the Church the latter makes a confessional decision on the content in that the Church states in what writings she believes she hears the apostolic attestation and to which, therefore, her life, her proclamation, and teaching ought to be subject, in short what are to be considered as canonical. In this way the Church has professed the historical uniqueness and finality of the revelation of God and recognized the normative character of the apostolic word, which endures as the word of origin in face of the being of the Church."

[37] For example, H. von Campenhausen, "Das Problem der Ordnung im Urchristentum und in der alten Kirche," in his collection, *Tradition und Leben* (Tübingen 1960) 162: "The early Church was practically much more strongly evangelically determined than one is frequently ready to admit, not only in her teaching but also in her understanding of order. I stress this expressly over against an unhistorical, fundamentally mistrustful, ultra-Protestant criticism that, wherever it does not find again its reformatory formulas, and wherever it encounters a naïve, uncritical adherence to order, already sees the authentic Christian-Evangelical character betrayed, and that not only brands all Fathers, including Augustine, with the concept of 'early Catholicism' formed in the light of this, but also broad parts of the New Testament, especially the writings of Luke, and that does not even call a halt at Paul. The most dangerous effect of such a pseudo-Protestant disputatiousness *vis-à-vis* its own origins lies much more in the fact that it arouses disgust and boredom by the immoderateness of its allegedly reformatory criticism, which taken as a whole creates an uncritical mistrust of the alleged one-sidedness of the Reformation as supposedly hostile to order. . . ."

[37a] I dealt with these same problems at the same time in a more general perspective (in a disputation not only with E. Käsemann, but also with H. Diem) in the article: "Der Frühkatholizismus in Neuen Testament als kontroverstheologisches Problem", in *Tübinger Theologische Quartalschrift* 142 (1962) No. 4.

New Testament research have also set in motion the *systematic theology* of ecclesiastical office. Today in many parts of the Protestant world there is an intensive questioning of the problem of Church structures taking place and much more work is being done towards the development of a more thorough theology of office. The question of apostolic succession in office has become a central issue. In the past few years many Protestant theologians have voiced a positive and constructive opinion about the question of apostolic succession. Among them have been the members of the Evangelische Michaelsbruderschaft (K. B. Ritter, W. Stählin, A. Köberle), the theologians of the *Sammlung* (H. Asmussen, M. Lackmann, R. Baumann), but also the reformed theologians and the Neuchatel journal *Verbum Caro* (not to be forgotten is the theologically active Reformed Brotherhood or Communauté of Taizé-les-Cluny in Burgundy) and the Lutheran theologians around the Heidelberg journal *Kerygma und Dogma* (a considerable influence was wielded by E. Schlink's *Theologie der lutherischen Bekenntnisschriften* and the publications of P. Brunner, to which we have frequently referred). Using the same point of departure the leading Lutheran theologians of the Theological Convention of the Augsburg Confession (Theologischer Konvent Augsburgischen Bekenntnisses) have also dealt thoroughly with these questions, especially in the years 1951–56 (cf. the reports of E. Kinder, O. Perels, E. Sommerlath, F. Hübner, H. Thimme, A. Kimme, W. Maurer, P. Brunner, H. Liermann, F. K. Schumann). On the basis of this intensive preparatory work the Convention, in October 1956, was able to agree unanimously upon an "Outline on the Organization of Ecclesiastical Office." prepared by the theologians P. Brunner, F. K. Schumann, H. Thimme, the church president D. Brunotte, and the vice-president D. Lücking.[38] This proposal enjoyed a wide and favourable response. Its influence reached into the doctrinal discussion on ecclesiastical office in South India.

At the same time the hierarchy of the United Evangelical Church of Germany commissioned in 1954 the ecumenical committee under the presidency of Bishop D. H. Meyer (Lübeck) to study the question of apostolic succession. In November, 1957, the committee presented the result of its labours that had stretched over a period of many years in a report entitled "A Declaration concerning the Apostolic Succession." The Church hierarchy approved the text. This official document[39] is impressive evidence of the progress that it has been

[38] Grundlinien für die Ordnung des Amtes in der Kirche (*Fuldaer Hefte* 11, Berlin 1960).

[39] "Erklärung zur Apostolischen Sukzession," in *Informationsdienst der Vereinigten Evangelisch-Lutherischen Kirche Deutschlands* (1958) 4–13.

possible to achieve in ecclesiastical and theological development of the last years. It is also symptomatic for the whole present development in the *ecumene*. The introduction of the report points to the following important events in theological and church history: (*a*) The ecumenical dialogue in recent years has concentrated on the theme of Christ. Thereby, the question of the catholicity and continuity of the Church has been raised anew from a different angle. (*b*) In the Protestant Church of the West, as well as in the Churches of Asia and Africa, questions concerning ecclesiastical office, ordination, offices, and services and the relationship between office and congregation have erupted on a broad scale. (*c*) In this context the Churches of Asia and Africa urgently raise the question of episcopal office and of its importance for the unity of the Church. For the sake of ecumenical union the Churches of the West therefore also have to seek an answer to this question. (d) In the resulting necessary discussion with the Roman Catholic Church the inevitable question regarding the justification of the apostolicity and authority of the Church presents itself to us. (*e*) As a Church of the Lutheran Confession we have every reason to strive for a strengthening of the ecumenical relationship with the Orthodox Churches of the East. In the discussions with them, however, it will be necessary to grant a prominent place to their statements concerning the wholeness and fullness of the Church, which has existed throughout the ages. This already poses a more specific question about apostolic succession in the stricter sense. (*f*) In recent decades the Church of England has been prominently engaged in efforts towards Church unity. She has also made efforts towards unity with the Lutheran, especially the Scandinavian Lutheran, Churches. In this connection it must be remembered that the Anglican Union attaches a great significance to the historical episcopate. (*g*) The Church of South India for years has been conducting a doctrinal discussion with her neighbouring Lutheran Church. She has not developed a theory of the historical episcopate but nevertheless determinedly clings to this as a never-to-be-surrendered gift bestowed upon the Church by the Holy Spirit. (*h*) Within the Lutheran Church of Sweden there is a noticeable increase of efforts directed at ascribing a special ecclesiastical and theological importance to the apostolic succession of her bishops, which formerly had been viewed as an historically given fact that was willingly preserved but was theologically irrelevant.[40]

There is no doubt that this report and the ecumenical developments that formed its background deserve full attention from us Catholics.

[40] "Erklärung zur Apostolischen Sukzession," *op cit.* 5f.

Various questions with which we Catholics had to confront Luther are answered here. At the same time, however, questions are raised here which it will not be easy for *us* to answer. The "Declaration" of the Evangelical Lutheran Church will require closer scrutiny with respect to the complex of questions regarding the relationship between ecclesiastical office and an ecumenical council.

4. THE APOSTOLIC SUCCESSION

(*a*) The "Declaration" is successful in its attempt to give earnest consideration to Luther's demands while interpreting and supplementing them against the richness of the New Testament background. Many ambiguities in Luther's theology of office, to which we have drawn attention, were cleared up in the "Declaration" and *several Catholic desiderata were fulfilled*. The following points seem especially important to us from a Catholic viewpoint.

(1) *A Democratic or Spiritual Concept of Office According to the New Testament?*
The democratic misunderstanding concerning spiritual office upheld by the young Luther (and later by Protestantism) is cleared away.[1] In the midst of the priesthood of *all* believers and their different spiritual gifts there are according to the New Testament, also "special and outstanding services which are then also formally imposed on their holders" (special missionary tasks, of founding and governing the Churches). These "are not functions of the congregation but a gift and an institution of God." For a vocation to these special services the determining factors are "not human utilitarian considerations but the will of God." "Through the special calling an already existent charism is put into service while the charism necessary to perform the service in its concrete sphere of action is also bestowed." This very important passage is expressly based on Romans 1:11 and 15:24, I Timothy 4:14, and II Timothy 1:6. The consummation of this calling "in the early community is often—although not universally—attested to by the imposition of hands." The fundamental and unique office of the apostles precedes all the special services in the Church.

(2) *The Theological Concept and Authority of Ecclesiastical Office*
The "Declaration" avoids a one-sided concentration on the proclamation of the Word and thereby also an inadequate presentation of

[1] "Erklärung zur Apostolischen Sukzession," I, 2–4, 6, *op cit.* 7f.

the pastoral authority of ecclesiastical office.[2] The service of the leaders of the congregation stands out among the variety of special services. "After the death of the apostles the functions of assembling and uniting the faithful for the sake of the Church and for the sake of service to the world had to be continued. Hence ecclesiastical office, in accordance with its nature, is to be defined as a pastoral office either in the individual congregation or in the community of congregations. The functions of this office are performed through the proclamation of the Gospel and through the administration of the Sacraments. All other tasks are subordinated to this task of the pastoral office, such as, for example, the teaching of doctrine, officiating at public worship, discernment of spirits, defence against heresy, maintenance of the ecumenical association of the communities, and inspiration and guidance of the missionary activity of the Church in the world." To the extent that the incumbents of ecclesiastical office "have taken over these tasks of the apostolic office their authority with regard to their congregation is like that of the apostles, that is, the authority of the representatives and messengers of Christ."

(3) *Is There an Apostolic Succession of the Church?*

The authors of the "Declaration" actually ventured to view the historical and the personal aspects of the apostolic succession.[3] "In the sense that Christendom is permanently linked with the ministry of the Apostles as founders and in permanent harmony with their decisive testimony . . . apostolic succession must be asserted without reserve as belonging to the essence of the Church. So it is acknowledged by us also with all Christendom, in the words of the Nicene creed: 'I believe in the one, holy, catholic, apostolic Church.' " The relationship of the whole Church as an apostolic Church to the apostles is not only of a spiritual but also of an *historical* character "because the Spirit moves in, with, and underneath the process of human tradition in which the canon of Holy Scripture, and hence specific contents of the preaching and deeds originating at the time of the early apostolic age, is handed down from generation to generation." This succession is not only a succession of faith and the profession of the creed but also "a succession of *persons* since there is no faith and no profession of a creed as such but only the faith and the profession of a creed of specific human beings. The faith of the later generations is the successor in relation to the faith and the testi-

[2] "Erklärung zur Apostolischen Sukzession," I, 7–9, *op cit.* 8f.
[3] "Erklärung zur Apostolischen Sukzession," III, 13–14, *op cit.* 10f.

mony to the faith of earlier generations reaching back to the apostles."

(4) *Is There an Apostolic Succession of Ecclesiastical Office?*

The particular apostolic succession of office is not neglected in the discussion of the apostolic succession of the Church in all her members.[4] "As a pastoral office for the community it occupies a special place in the line of succession and represents the pastoral office of the apostles. This apostolic succession of office is to be understood not only in functional but also in personal terms; it consists in the fact that persons who occupy this office succeed each other in the congregations."

(b) This positive approach to Catholic concerns makes it considerably easier for the Catholic theologian to present in turn in a precise and positive way the Catholic standpoint regarding the theology of office. Present-day Catholic theology of office, which no longer defines its position in terms of an anti-Protestant front but once again in terms of Scripture, can expressly confirm from a Catholic point of view many statements contained in the "Declaration."[5] The following points bearing closely on the "Declaration" will be raised here.

[4] "Erklärung zur Apostolischen Sukzession" III, 15, *op cit.* 11.

[5] We must leave it up to the reader himself to give an account of the catholicity of the assertions which follow, in the light of modern Catholic literature dealing with the theology of office. We are reproducing only a few typical examples in the following passages. However, cf.: F. M. Braun, *Neues Licht auf die Kirche* (Einsiedeln–Cologne 1946); F. X. Arnold, *Grundsätzlisches und Geschichtliches zur Theologie der Seelsorge* (Freiburg 1949); J. Brosch, *Charismen und Amter in der Urkirche* (Bonn 1951); J. Colson, *L'évêque dans les communautés primitives* (Paris 1951); *Les fonctions ecclésiales* (Paris 1956); Y. Congar, *The Mystery of the Church* (London 1960); *Lay People in the Church* (London 1957); "L'apostolicité de l'Église selon S. Thomas d'Aquin," in *Revue des sciences philosophiques et théologiques* 44 (1960) 209–224; O. Karrer, *Um die Einheit der Christen* (Frankfurt 1953); "Apostolische Nachfolge und Primat," in *Fragen der Theologie heute*, ed. by J. Feiner, J. Trütsch, F. Bökle (Einsiedeln–Zürich–Cologne 1957) 175–206; "Das kirchliche Amt in katholischer Sicht," in *Una Sancta* 14 (1959) 39–48; H. Schlier, *Die Zeit der Kirche* (Die Ordnung der Kirche nach den Pastoralbriefen [Freiburg i. Br. 1955, ³1962]) 129–147; M. Kaiser, *Die Einheit der Kirchengewalt nach dem Zeugnis des NT und der apostolischen Väter* (Munich 1956); K. Rahner, *The Dynamic Element in the Church* (London 1964); K. H. Schelkle, *Jüngerschaft und Apostelamt* (Freiburg i. Br. ²1961); O. Semmelroth, *Das geistliche Amt* (Frankfurt a. M. 1958); R. Schnackenburg, *God's Rule and Kingdom* (London 1963); *Die Kirche im Neuen Testament* (Freiburg–Basle–Vienna 1961); M. Löhrer, "Zur Theologie von geistlichem Amt und Gemeinde," in *Begegnung der Christen* (collection of essays honouring [*Festschrift*] O. Karrer, Frankfurt a. M.-Stuttgart ²1960) 210–233; *Die Kirche und ihre Amter und Stande* (Festschrift

(1) *The Priestly Ministry of Everyone in the Church*

The Catholic view also maintains that the ministry of Jesus Christ to the lost world also justifies, determines, and permeates the being and the ministry of His Church. Hence *all* believers in Christ are called to the royal priesthood through the outpouring of the Holy Spirit and Baptism. They are all commissioned and empowered to carry out and carry on the ministry of Christ to the world. Gifts are bestowed upon each member of the Church for this purpose, but they are not all the same kind of gifts. The bestowal of these gifts occurs through the freedom of the Spirit, the means of transmission not having been formally and absolutely laid down at the outset. There is a constant variation of special ministries in the Church.[6]

Kardinal Frings, Cologne 1960); H. U. von Balthasar, *Sponsa Verbi* (Nachfolge und Amt [Einsiedeln 1961]) 80–147; J. Ratzinger, "Primacy, Episcopate and Apostolic Succession," in *The Episcopate and the Primacy* (London 1962); H. Volk, *Gott alles in allem* (Das Wirken des Heiligen Geistes in den Gläubigen [Mainz 1961]) 86–112; O. Knoch, "Die Ausführungen des 1. Clemensbriefes über die kirchliche Verfassung im Spiegel der neueren Deutungen seit R. Sohm und A. Harnack," in *Tübinger Theologische Quartalschrift* 141 (1961) 385–407; *Das apostolische Amt* (French ed. Études sur le sacrement de l'ordre), ed. by J. Guyot (Mainz 1961).

[6] On the universal priesthood, cf. our Chaps II and V. The significance of the different ministries and gifts (charisms) was strongly emphasized by Pius XII in the Encyclical "Mystici corporis" (*Acta Apostolicae Sedis* [1943] 200ff): "Again as in nature a body is not formed by any haphazard grouping of members but must be constituted of organs, that is of members, that have not the same function and are arranged in due order; so for this reason above all the Church is called a body, that it is constituted by the coalescence of structurally united parts, and that it has a variety of members reciprocally dependent. It is thus the Apostle describes the Church when he writes: 'As in one body we have many members, but all the members have not the same office: so we being many are one body in Christ, and every one members one of another.' One must not think, however, that this ordered or 'organic' structure of the body of the Church contains only hierarchical elements and with them is complete: or, as an opposite opinion holds, that it is composed only of those who enjoy charismatic gifts—though members gifted with miraculous powers will never be lacking in the Church. That those who exercise sacred power in this Body are its first and chief members, must be maintained uncompromisingly. It is through them, by commission of the Divine Redeemer Himself, that Christ's apostolate as Teacher, King and Priest is to endure. At the same time, when the Fathers of the Church sing the praises of this Mystical Body of Christ, with its ministries, its variety of ranks, its officers, its conditions, its orders, its duties, they are thinking not only of those who have received Holy Orders, but of all those too, who, following the evangelical counsels, pass their lives either actively among men, or hidden in the silence of the cloister, or who aim at combining the active and contemplative life according to their Institute; as also of those who, though living in the world, consecrate themselves wholeheartedly to spiritual or corporal works of mercy, and of those who live in the state of holy matrimony. Indeed, let this be clearly understood, especially in these our days: fathers and mothers of families, those who are godparents through Baptism, and in particular those members of the laity who collaborate with the

(2) *The Fundamental Office of the Apostles*

The Catholic view also maintains that the office of the apostles precedes all other ministries in the Church. The apostles are those members of the original community to whom the resurrected Lord manifested Himself and whom He sent forth with the special commission to proclaim the Gospel that established and gathered the Church. Hence their proclamation is the fundamental and, for all time, standard-setting testimony of Jesus Christ. Therefore their office as a whole is by its very nature unique insofar as it encompasses the ever-fundamental eyewitness account of the Resurrection and the event of revelation, which the succeeding office can only preserve and interpret. On the basis of their calling they are the foundation and the uniting bond of the Church as it was coming into existence. On the one hand, the apostles, as representatives of Christ, stand

---

ecclesiastical hierarchy in spreading the Kingdom of the Divine Redeemer occupy an honourable, if often a lowly, place in the Christian community, and even they under the impulse of God and with His help, can reach the heights of supreme holiness, which, Jesus Christ has promised, will never be wanting to the Church. . . . Moreover He conferred a triple power on His Apostles and their successors, to teach, to govern, to lead men to holiness, making this power, defined by special ordinances, rights and obligations, the fundamental law of the whole Church. But our Divine Saviour governs and guides the Society which He founded directly and personally also. For it is He who reigns within the minds and hearts of men, and bends and subjects their wills to His good pleasure, even when rebellious. 'The heart of the King is in the hand of the Lord; whithersoever he will, he shall turn it.' By this interior guidance He, the 'Shepherd and Bishop of our souls,' not only watches over individuals but exercises His providence over the universal Church, whether by enlightening and giving courage to the Church's rulers for the loyal and effective performance of their respective duties, or by singling out from the body of the Church—especially when times are grave—men and women of conspicuous holiness, who may point the way for the rest of Christendom to the perfecting of His Mystical Body." (Vatican Translation as printed by the Tipografia Poliglotta Vaticana.) K. Rahner, in his work, *Das Dynamische in der Kirche* (Freiburg, 1958p. 46; English trans, *The Dynamic Element in the Church*, London 1964, pp. 51–52) which deals thoroughly with the charismatic side of the Church, states: "There are charismatic persons also outside the office in the Church They are not merely receivers of orders from the office, but can also be those through whom Christ 'directly' guides His Church. Naturally the office is thereby not abolished. . . . If, however, Christ also directly exerts influence in His Church outside the office, if therefore He governs and guides the Church through extra-official and in this sense extraordinary charisms, and if nevertheless there is a valid, irremovable office in the Church, then the harmony between both 'structures' of the Church, the institutional and the charismatic, is in the long run only guaranteed by the one Lord of both structures and by Him alone, hence again only charismatically." Cf. on relationship between charisms and office likewise, M. Löhrer, "Zur Theologie von Geistlichen Amt und Gemeinde," in *Begegnung der Christen* (collection of articles honouring [*Festschrift*] O. Karrer [Stuttgart–Frankfurt a. M. ²1960, 228–233.])

in a position of authority and freedom towards the world and the community. On the other hand, however, as members of the Church they stand *in* the Church and *under* Christ; they must appear before Christ's judgment and they are dependent on His grace. The actions of the apostles are always oriented towards the congregations and in communion with the other members of the Church and the services assigned to them. Their testimony is surrounded by the testimonies of all who received the Spirit. Just as the congregations need their testimony and their guidance, they, in turn, need the solace, the intercession, and the co-operation of the congregations.[7]

(3) *The Ministry of Ecclesiastical Office in the Church*

The Catholic view also maintains that ecclesiastical office must be distinguished from the unique office of the apostles. Nevertheless, after the death of the apostles the ecclesiastical office continues the functions of leadership (gathering and maintaining) in the apostolic Church by way of the pastoral office. The ecclesiastical pastoral office must be understood in terms of Christ as the centre of the manifold ministries. Hence it excludes neither the multiplicity of specific ministries nor the royal priesthood of *all* believers. With all the members of the Church, the office-holders also, like the apostles, are subordinate to Christ and continuously in need of the grace of the Holy Spirit and of the power and authority of the Word bestowed from above. Together with all the members of the later Church, the office-holders are also subject to the apostles to the extent that they are bound by the authority of the fundamental apostolic testimony. Together with all the members of the Church and with the other

[7] O. Karrer, "Apostolische Nachfolge und Primat," in *Fragen der Theologie heute*, ed. by J. Feiner, J. Trütsch and F. Böckle (Einsiedeln–Zurich–Cologne 1957) 178. "In the Catholic view, too, Christ Himself and alone is the absolute authority. His word is the norm for the Church and individuals. Revelation is laid down in Scripture, and one can say without hesitation that the whole of revelation is contained in Scripture. The Church and individuals know themselves to be bound to Scripture. There is no new revelation, to which the Church would be committed or could commit others. Scripture is the 'ultimate foundation' of all later traditions, and revelation was concluded with the apostles." H. Bacht, "Apostel," in *Lexikon für Theologie und Kirche* (Freiburg i. Br. 1957) I, 738: "As eye-witnesses of the resurrected Lord and as the foundation of the Church the apostles possess a uniqueness that is non-presentable and irreplaceable: from this point of view they can have no successors. To this extent the 'age of the apostles' is really essentially to be distinguished from the 'time of the Church' (O. Cullmann). But their office is not exhausted in these two functions. Next to the extraordinary powers, which neither could or should go further . . . stand the ordinary, transmittable powers: the administration of the Word and the care for the maintenance of its purity, the dispensation of the Sacraments, the leadership of the Church."

ministries, the office-holders should carry out their ministry. They too, like the apostles, are in need of the co-operation and intercession of their congregations for the performance of their own service. The transmission of ecclesiastical office must also in principle take place with the congregation and in co-operation with those who already hold a special office. Since it is the living Lord Himself who calls and empowers one to ecclesiastical office, this co-operation may take on different forms. Thus the ministry of Christ to the Church in the world is fully effected with all its manifold richness; it is effected through the unity and contradistinction of apostolic office and ecclesiastical office, of office and special ministries, of office and ministries on the one hand and of the congregation on the other, of congregation and congregation.[8]

[8] On the relationship between ecclesiastical office and the office of the apostles, and ecclesiastical office and universal priesthood, cf. the preceding witnesses. On the ministerial character of ecclesiastical office, cf. K. H. Schelkle, *Jüngerschaft und Apostelamt* (Freiburg i. Br. [2]1961) 36f: "In the New Testament διακονία is the all-embracing and deepest word for 'office'. To the New Testament it seems to be impossible to use as a designation of office in the Church the words otherwise frequently used in Greek for "office" (as ἀρχή, τιμή, τέλος). The New Testament knows these words, but it does not use them for the ecclesiastical sphere, but creates the word διακονία. In New Testament Greek ἀρχή is limited to the synagogal and governmental authoritity or angelic powers and τιμή to the dignity of office of the Old Testament high priest. This lexigraphic finding definitely states that office in the Church is essentially an order of ministration. The finding also makes manifest that the New Testament, government and law in the Church and in the world are obviously and essentially different. Therefore the same words could no longer be applied to them. These biblical ideas are developed further by O. Semmelroth, *Das geistliche Amt* (Frankfurt a. M. 1958) esp. 26–35, 50–57. In opposition to the curtailing of the spiritual in the concept of the Church of the Counter Reformation, the primacy of the office before the *Pneuma* and the clericalization of ecclesiastical activity, speaks with special clarity, the Tübingen pastoral theologian F. X. Arnold, *Grundsätzliches und Theologisches zur Theologie der Seelsorge* (Freiburg i. Br. 1949) 80–86. On the co-operation between office and community in the transmission of office, O. Karrer, *op cit.* 183, says: "In his 'Credo Ecclesiam,' A. D. Wendland expressly points out that according to the Acts of the Apostles (6:5ff), Didache (15) and Clement of Rome (44, 2) ordination is supposed to take place with the approval of the community—which in principle can scarcely be disputed. For the early Church saw bishop and people as a unity, the people, 'the pleroma of the bishop' (Chrysostom) and Clement of Rome at the same time wrote in the name of the Roman community which constituted a unity with him. This is doubtlessly valid at all times, only at the present time one should consider that the apostolic model itself left open different ways of co-operation between office-holders and community (after the Jewish model) and that the transmission of authority came about through election *and* ordination: *ordination* being always carried out by apostolic holders of authority as representing the whole Church, while in the *election* the holders of authority co-operated with the congregation as an 'unequal college.' "Calvin also observed, in his explanation of Acts 6:3: 'Nothing occurs without the agreement and assent

(4) *Apostolic Succession in the Church*

The Catholic view also maintains that the apostolicity of the Church consists in the enduring bond of the Church with the ministry of the apostles and in the abiding agreement with the apostolic testimony. Thus the apostolic succession first of all pertains to the whole Church in all her members. It manifests itself in manifold ways throughout the centuries and in all countries in the continuous process of baptizing and being baptized, in faith and in obedience to the apostolic testimony, in the community of worship and in the Eucharist, in the transmission of the apostolic testimony in the congregations, in missionary preaching to the world, in the fellowship and unity with the churches of the whole world. This interrelationship of the apostolic succession is not only of an historical but also of a spiritual character; the Holy Spirit continuously secures our encounter with the living Gospel and through it with Christ Himself in the apostolic witness to Christ. This interrelationship of the apostolic succession is not only a succession of persons either, but a succession of faith and its profession; it is after all primarily a question of again and again awakening the faith that was first awakened through the original testimony of the apostles and of making this faith known in the Church.[9]

---

of the people, but the shepherds hold the reins in their hands.' Indeed there are Protestant scholars, such as Headlam and Linton, who point out that the co-operation of the community is not to be conceived according to the modern example of a 'democratic majority vote.' With respect to Linton's inquiries, one can even ask whether the present-day scrutiny in the Catholic Church—with the careful testing of the candidates according to their spiritual predispositions—may not contain as much co-participation of the people as the early Christian assemblies of the congregation." Y. Congar, *Lay People in the Church* (London 1957), cites abundant historical material concerning the role of the laity in the appointment to office.

[9] O. Karrer, *op. cit.* 185: "Naturally 'succession in the apostolic confession' *exists* as a grace and duty for all—the question is whether thereby everything has been said regarding apostolic succession and whether the Church is 'apostolic' merely for this reason. In the sense of Scripture, can there not be an office in apostolic authority existing from one generation to the other? There exists even an inner connection between confessional succession and succession in office: this is posited for the sake of the confessional succession and is necessary for it." The apostolic succession of the whole Church is presupposed as obvious in Catholic ecclesiology rather than developed at length (cf. on the other hand, the exposition of apostolicity in K. Barth, *Church Dogmatics* [London] IV/1, 710–725). In the textbooks the *apostolicitas successionis* (in the office) is generally very exhaustively treated as a front-line position to be defended polemically. But the fundamental *apostolicitas originis* and *apostolicitas fidei* are at least always briefly mentioned.

(5) *The Apostolic Succession of Ecclesiastical Office*

The Catholic view also maintains that the succession of office occurs within the framework of the apostolic succession of the Church. Thus the office is and remains unconditionally subordinate to the unique authority of the apostles in regard to the decisive form of the attestation to Christ. On the other hand, the holders of pastoral office, even in the line of their apostolic succession, never occupy an exclusive position with respect to their congregations. Rather, as pastors to their communities they are also in need of the intercession and co-operation in succession to the apostles, of the royal priesthood of all believers and of the free charisms, all of which is an expression of the apostolic Church and all her members. Under normal circumstances the entry into the line of the apostolic succession occurs with the co-operation—which is possible in a variety of ways—of the office-holders and the congregation.[10]

(c) Obviously there is a far-reaching agreement between *present-day* Lutheran and *present-day* Catholic doctrine regarding ecclesiastical office. Does this mean then that all controversial issues in this area have been removed? Not at all. Indeed, the Lutheran document itself is not free of polemics. Even in the introduction we find it very clearly stated: "The separation from the papalistic formalization of the succession, which we undertook in the wake of the Reformation for the sake of the Gospel, was correct and necessary."[11] And in the concluding paragraph dealing with the apostolic succession of bishops through the chain of impositions of hands, it is clearly brought out what is constantly echoing throughout the "Declaration" and might be diversely interpreted.

Can this kind of *episcopal* succession be accepted by Lutheran theology? No objection can be raised against it as such. Episcopal

---

[10] O. Karrer, *op. cit.* 178f.: "The healing power of the Word and Sacrament comes only from Christ, from His spirit with which He blessed the bride. He 'dwells' in the Communion of Saints, who live in the grace of the spirit—the officeholders as such (insofar as they are not themselves among the saints) are only 'handymen' or 'wet nurses,' 'canals,' whether golden, silver, or clay, as Augustine often enlarges on this theme. The glorified Lord also through His Spirit, takes them also into His service; He baptizes also through sinners and heretics; He consecrates through saints and through sinners, and the same is true of preaching, absolution, anointing of the sick, etc.—without it being possible to speak of 'mechanical automatism' as the concept of *opus operatum* is often misunderstood." Compare, also, the above-mentioned works.

[11] "Erklärung zur Apostolischen Sukzession," in *Informationsdienst der Vereinigten Evangelisch-Lutherischen Kirche Deutschlands* (1958) 6.

succession can be respected "as a sign . . . of the real apostolic succession of the Church and of her office that even we would consider as appropriate in such Churches." But immediately a qualification is added: "appropriate but not objectively necessary."[12] Apart from the fact that the principle of an episcopal succession is expressed only relatively late in the early Catholic Church and that up to now no historical proof has been produced of a chain of episcopal succession, it must be rejected in two other circumstances:

(1) If episcopal succession is regarded as the *exclusive* means for the transmission of the full authority of office. Against this contention it must be argued "that the mission to a pastoral office cannot be established in a uniform way of transmission and succession from person to person, that a real mission and authorization thereto can be effected through the Holy Spirit by extraordinary means. Restriction of the transmission of authority to office-holders in the line of historical succession is contradictory to the sovereign freedom of the Holy Spirit in the Church and the frailty of the earthly existence of the Church. Moreover, it accentuates a separation of clergy and laity that is not in keeping with the reciprocity of the services between the spiritual authority of the special office and that given to all believers."[13] Hence, the principle of episcopal succession cannot be considered as the only and necessary means by which the transmission and authorization of all office-holders can be effected.

(2) If episcopal succession is regarded as a *guarantee* of the tradition of pure doctrine and of the preservation of the unity of the Church. Against this criterion it may be argued that: "No ecclesiasticel office as such as has been given the promise that its holders cannot lapse from the faith. It is true, no doubt, that the maintenance of the Church in the succession of the apostolic faith is also accomplished through the chain of services of those commissioned to a special pastoral service. But this chain can be continuously maintained by non-episcopal office-holders against the errors of episcopal office-holders. Indeed, the maintenance of the Church in the succession of apostolic faith can also be preserved by special acts of God, who in exceptional circumstances awakens true shepherds outside the institutional succession of offices in the Church. They carry on the pure apostolic preaching. Such free expressions of the Spirit do not abolish the responsibility of the Church for spiritual order."[14] Hence episcopal succession cannot be regarded as a *guarantee* of the purity of

---

[12] "Erklärung zur Apostolischen Sukzession IV, 21," *op cit.* 12.
[13] "Erklärung zur Apostolischen Sukzession IV, 19," *op cit.* 12.
[14] "Erklärung zur Apostolischen Sukzession IV, 20," *op cit.* 12.

apostolic tradition or as the *exclusive* means for the achievement and the preservation of Church unity.

These are the reasons why the Lutheran document can hold episcopal succession to be appropriate indeed but in no way as necessary. From this the following final conclusion is drawn: "We do not regard as necessary ... the further extension of such an episcopal succession to churches which do not already have it. Indeed such a policy could even be dangerous because it might give rise to the misunderstanding that ordination in churches without episcopal succession is not fully valid. At any rate we would first have to clarify the fundamental question of church community in all its broad dimensions and especially the question of vocation and ordination to office in the Church."[15]

(*d*) How is this criticism of the formalization of the apostolic succession to be answered from the Catholic view? We have already expressly pointed out that the reformers, through the fault of the officeholders who resisted every serious reform of the Church in *capite et membris*, created a tragic conflict. They were convinced that they had to choose between succession in apostolic spirit, life, and activity and succession in apostolic office. It cannot be denied that the succession in office of those bishops who were little concerned with the apostolic spirit, the apostolic life and activity, had in fact to a large extent been voided of its original significance and had therefore become formalized indeed. The reformers broke away from the episcopal succession only under compulsion, and the separation was regarded as an emergency solution by the reformers throughout their lives.

But is the Catholic doctrine of episcopal succession properly understood in the Lutheran document? Later we shall delve more deeply into this question of episcopal succession as the exclusive way of transmitting the authority of office. What, however, is the position with regard to the episcopal succession as a *guarantee* of the transmission of the pure doctrine and the preservation of Church unity? We Catholics, in fact, are convinced—as the Lutheran "Declaration" admits—that the "preservation of the Church in the succession of the apostolic faith is also carried out through the chain of ministry of those commissioned to special pastoral service."[16] Nor, in fact, does the Catholic think that episcopal succession in office is the *only* means of preserving the Church in the succession of the apostolic faith, of

---

[15] "Erklärung zur Apostolischen Sukzession IV, 21," *op. cit.* 12f.
[16] "Erklärung zur Apostolischen Sukzession IV, 20," *op. cit.* 12.

which the spirit of God makes use. It is, however, a misapprehension about Catholic teaching when it is considered necessary to raise against us the charge that "no ecclesiastical office as such has been given the promise that its holders cannot lapse from the faith."[17] This must be clearly and unequivocally answered: It is universal Catholic teaching that an "error of the episcopal office-holder" is altogether possible, indeed that even those standing in the line of the apostolic succession can lapse from the faith. Not only is an heretical bishop possible, but even an heretical pope—as we shall explain in more detail later. Apostolic succession offers no guarantee against this possibility: "To whom then does this promise apply? No doubt this was the intention of the Lord and was primarily given to the Church as an instrument of the kingdom of God in the world; hence the promise was given secondarily to ecclesiastical office—not in the main to the holders of office as such or for their own sakes, but for the sake of the Church so that she may fulfil her mission. Anyone can fail and because he can fail, he needs the supplication of Christ and of His saints. He is in need of the 'communion of saints,' as Augustine asserted against the Donatists. The communion of saints, with the one Mediator at the centre, according to I Timothy 2, and the great supplicant High Priest according to the Epistle to the Hebrews, together support the labourers of the kingdom of God through their intercessions and they also endure human shortcomings. In the last instance everyone is dependent upon the mercy of God. The testament of Pius XII addressed itself to our hearts because he left us while praying for the mercy of God."[18]

In the Catholic view apostolic succession is anything but a kind of mechanical formalism. And for the following reasons:

(1) In the first place apostolic succession is not an arbitrary human invention but a work of the Holy Spirit of Jesus Christ who sovereignly rules in the Church. The human imposition of hands is not the principal cause guaranteeing and insuring the transmission of spiritual authority. The main cause rather, is the Spirit of the glorified Lord, who is invoked during the laying on of hands and for whom the imposition of hands is only an instrument, a sacramental sign. Just

[17] *Ibid.* A similar misunderstanding in W. Joest, "Das Amt und die Einheit der Kirche," in *Una Sancta* 16 (1961) 248: "The institution of this succession is . . . tainted, in that in its origins it is bound up with the notion that the connection to the bishop standing in apostolic succession would guarantee the continuity in unity of the true Church, by virtue of a charism of the infallibility of right teaching bound up with this succession."

[18] O. Karrer, "Das kirchliche Amt in katholischer Sicht," in *Una Sancta* 14 (1959) 46; on the question of infallibility, cf. Chap. VIII.

as God in the Holy Spirit can baptize also through the unworthy, the sinful, and the heretical, so can He also ordain through the unworthy, the sinful, and the heretical representatives. Even ordination does not take place in the name of the ordaining minister, nor on the ground of his own virtue, but in the name and by virtue of Jesus Christ who has promised and sent us His spirit. The *opus operatum* is not an *opus operatum ministri*, but an *opus operatum* of Jesus Christ: "Everything which occurred in the history of the Church bearing upon our problem is not to be approved; this pertains particularly to the medieval 'legal' situation of ordination by feudal 'spiritual lords.' If, however, the Spirit is invoked through the lawful co-operation of the bishop and the people of the Church the ordination is not simply an externally transmitted form but—akin to God's becoming man—the expression of the mystery of the Church herself so that the gifts and the powers of the Spirit (here as also in the previous sacraments of consecration, Baptism and Confirmation) may be represented by an external sign. Thus it is not man but the Spirit who actually baptizes, ordinates, consecrates—the Spirit promised by the glorified Lord and invoked by the Church who works through men. The power of ordination is not handed down on a horizontal level from the past, although in the temporal dimension the man who received his ordination from his predecessors in turn ordains his successor. Rather, the power of ordination is passed down in the vertical dimension, from the Spirit, transcending time and space."[19] The following is to be taken into consideration with regard to the historical authenticity of the episcopal chain of succession: "As regards the list of bishops upon which, according to Barth, our ordination depends they signify nothing more for the life and consciousness of the Church than does a genealogical chart for a centuries old family; its life does not depend upon the genealogical chart of its ancestors; it is, however, important as a symbol reinforcing a certain spiritual attitude. Applied to the ecclesiastical realm, it serves as an admonition to the disciples in relation to those who bore witness before them, among whom there were many honourable blood-witnesses, going as far back as the 'glorious band of the apostles.' "[20]

(2) In the first place, the apostolic succession is not an individualistic mechanical succession of an individual to his predecessor but the entrance of an individual into a community. As a corporate

[19] O. Karrer, "Apostolische Nachfolge und Primat," in *Fragen der Theologie heute,* ed. by J. Feiner, J. Trütsch and F. Böckle (Einsiedeln–Zurich–Cologne 1957) 188.

[20] O. Karrer, "Das kirchliche Amt in katholischer Sicht," in *Una Sancta* 14 (1959) 44f.

body the college of bishops likewise succeeds the college of apostles as a corporate body. "It is not the individual bishop who is the successor of an individual apostle. He stands in the legal succession of an apostle only insofar as he belongs to the whole episcopate of the Church, which, in turn, as a whole succeeds the college of apostles as a corporate body."[21]

(3) The apostolic succession does not contradict the Word, but stands in the service of the Word. New Testament Scripture is a record of the living apostolic preaching. It aims to be regarded—even in the post-apostolic age, which is committed to the authority of Scripture—not only as a word that is read, but as the word that is preached. "It is precisely because the true *successio apostolica* is rooted in the Word that it cannot simply derive from a book but must be a *successio praedicantium* in terms of a *successio verbi*, which again cannot exist without a 'commission,' hence without a personal continuity going back to the apostles. A *viva successio* is required precisely for the sake of the Word, which should not be a dead letter in the New Covenant but a *viva vox*. With regard to this the New Testament theology of the Word and Scripture ultimately furnish a still more convincing confirmation of the early concept of succession as formulated by the early anti-Gnostic theology, based on the increasingly prevailing opinion that the rite of appointment to office through the imposition of hands, taken over from Judaism, must go back to the Jewish beginnings of Christianity."[22]

(4) The apostolic succession does not emerge "automatically" but under the presupposition of a completely devoted belief in the divine character of the call and commission of ecclesiastical office. According to the Council of Trent, faith is the foundation of Christian existence ". . . 'faith is the beginning of man's salvation,' the foundation and source of all justification, 'without which it is impossible to please God' (see Heb. 11:6) and to be counted as his sons."[23] Faith awakened by the grace of God is presupposed as a disposition of the person who is ordained in order for the ordination to be efficacious; this means that where faith is not present even in the sense of "intention" in the ordained person (namely, the serious

---

[21] K. Rahner, "In the Divine Right of the Episcopate," in *The Episcopate and the Primacy* (London 1962) 75; Rahner has fully called attention to the theoretical as well as to the practical consequences of this tenet.

[22] J. Ratzinger, "Primacy, Episcopate and Apostolic Succession," in *The Episcopate and the Primacy* (London, 1962) 53-54; Ratzinger refers here to the well-known book by E. Lohse, *Die Ordination im 'Spätjudentum und im Neuen Testament* (Göttingen 1951).

[23] Denz, 801,

desire to receive a Sacrament of the Church) all that occurs is nothing but a sacrilege. The Sacrament signifies the fulfilment of God's promise of grace only where it is received in true faith. Thus no pastoral authority is present in the Church where heresy is publicly acknowledged.[24]

(5) The apostolic succession does not bestow an office in which the holder could dispose of the Lord and of the Church according to his own discretion. Rather, it is an office that has to establish itself as an unselfish service of love. It does not grant an authority that glorifies the incumbent, imposing no obligations upon him, but an authority which demands an apostolic spirit, life, and activity from him. "Authority . . . is promised, given by God, but this does not means that one can dispose of what is divinely given according to one's own discretion. One is committed to conceive of the office in the spirit of Christ. And if one were to act or think in terms of self-glorification one would be at fault; this can possibly happen to human beings but nevertheless it is wrong. And every Christian according to his station is justified and called upon by the Spirit to take a position against this by publicly bearing witness to the truth, if he himself is not acting out of selfish considerations but in the spirit of truth and love."[25]

After these precise clarifications, supported by quotations of competent Catholic theologians, can one still speak so lightly about the "formalization" (mechanization and the like) of the apostolic succession? Can one—as does the Lutheran document—declare that the transmission of an apostolic succession, as understood above, to Churches which do not yet stand within the succession is simply unnecessary, indeed even "dangerous"?

(*e*) "It is indeed true that the succession of the episcopal ordination by the imposition of hands is to be regarded as a *sign* for the apostolic succession of offices and of the Church. It is a sign which brings out the fact that the Church is the Church of Christ only when she knows that her foundation rests upon the apostles. The continuous succession of the episcopal laying on of hands is thus the sign for both the unity and catholicity of the Church. For only the apostolic Church is the holy catholic Church. As a *sign* of the apostolic succession, ordination in the continuing succession of episcopal imposition of hands throughout the history of the Church is something to be welcomed

---

[24] Cf. O. Karrer, "Das kirchliche Amt in katholischer Sicht," *op cit*. 44.
[25] *Ibid*. 45.

and to be striven for where it is lacking."[26] Thus writes E. Schlink of Heidelberg, the leading systematic theologian of the World Council of Churches, in deliberate opposition to the "Declaration" of the Ecumenical Committee of the VELKD (United Evangelical Lutheran Church of Germany). Schlink thereby also compels Catholic theologians to reconsider the problem. The address that Schlink delivered in 1957 at the spring session of the above committee gives both a comprehensive and a precise theological justification for the "Declaration on Apostolic Succession" issued by the same committee in the fall of the same year. Schlink's report, which adroitly combines loyalty to fundamental Lutheran concerns with a genuine openness to ecumenicity, deals thoroughly with the problems that stand in the foreground of the "Declaration": (1) *Charisms and office:* The Church as a community of different gifts and ministries (important observations regarding the apostolic succession according to the Pauline lists of charisms), the general and specific calling and commissioning to the ministry (the importance of the imposition of hands), the dogmatic concept of ecclesiastical office (the differences and similarities between Paul's and Luke's early Catholic conception of service), charismatic ministry on the grounds of a special commission of pastoral office (functions and forms of the pastoral office). (2) *Apostolate and Church:* The concept of the apostolate (eyewitnessing and mission as constitutive factors, the commission thereto of the apostles), the apostles as the foundation of the Church (their unique function as founders) and as members of the Church (as justified sinners under the Lord in relation to the community), their service in the community with the other members of the Church. (3) *Church and Office:* The pastoral office in contradistinction to the apostolic office and in its continuation (the pastors in relation to the Church, as members of the Church, their service in the community of the Church), and finally apostolic succession.

Schlink's impressive presentation is of great importance on two counts above and beyond the "Declaration" of the Ecumenical Committee (1) As indicated, the positive importance of the imposition of hands is recognized more clearly here than in the "Declaration." (2) At the same time the possibility of other means for entering into the pastoral office is considered more precisely than in the "Declaration." On the first point Schlink is most accommodating to the Catholic position which, in the second point, enables him all the more effectively to ask critical questions on Catholic doctrine.

[26] E. Schlink, "Die apostolische Sukzession," in his collected works, *Der kommende Christus und die kirchlichen Traditionen* (Göttingen 1961) 194.

(1) *The Positive Meaning of the Imposition of Hands by Office-holders*

Schlink refers to concrete vocations, inductions, authorizations; in short, the special commission in the Acts of the Apostles and in the Pastoral Epistles. His position on this question is stated in the following words: "The commission of specific members of the Church to a specific ministry is often recorded in the New Testament as occurring by means of the laying on of hands. As is well known this refers to the question of adopting a custom already attested to in the Old Testament, which then was preserved in the ordination of Jewish scholars. Hence, it must be reckoned that callings and the imposition of hands had been carried out from the outset in the Palestinian early Christian communities and that the imposition of hands also took place in the case of callings where it is not expressly mentioned (for example, Acts 14:23)."[27]

These special commissions do not refer to any kind of ministries but are specifically concerned with the ministry of the establishment of missionary churches and of Church government as well as with auxiliary services connected with the founding of churches and Church government. This ministry corresponds to the ministry to which the apostles themselves were called. But if the apostles were called by Christ Himself, their successors in the ministry are appointed by human beings.

With reference to this special commission the following three factors are to be pointed out. (1) It is carried out by men but it is not left to the arbitrariness of human beings; it occurs, rather, under the guidance of the Spirit (hence also the fastings and the supplication for the descent of the Spirit on those about to be called). (2) In it words uttered by man, as well as human hands, serve only as the instrument of the summoning God. (3) God authorizes through the vocation; this authorization signifies not only the express acceptance into service of an already existing charism but, beyond and above this, the bestowal of a charism that fits one for pastoral ministry. "The commission to the concrete ministry also bequeaths upon the believer, who is driven by God's spirit, the concrete charism for the concrete ministry to which God calls him. The vocation is not a command of the law but of the Gospel. The Gospel, however, is the power of God. It is the unity of the deed and word of God. Thus the mission also is the power of God. It is a part of the nature of the New Testament imperative as such which, while based on objective facts, at the same time possesses the grace necessary for the fulfilment of what has been ordered. Thus the imposition of hands is

[27] *Ibid.* 166.

not an empty sign. Rather, by the laying on of hands that which is ordered by God and that which is sought from God are effectively appropriated. The imposition of hands in the case of a commission must of course be distinguished from the other kinds of laying on of hands, which are mentioned in the New Testament, for instance, for the purpose of healing, of benediction, of imparting the Spirit after Baptism. And as in the case of all these actions, according to the testimony of the New Testament, the request is granted through the laying on of hands, the charism is likewise bestowed for the concrete ministry to which a member of the community is sent forth through prayer and the imposition of hands. 'Ordination was not regarded as a mere form or as a symbolic action but as an act of the imparting of the Spirit' (J. Jeremias). On this basis it is possible to have confidence in ordination and in retrospect in the ordination once received. From this one gains that comforting certainty of being sent forth precisely by the external Word: I am called, I am sent, and indeed sent through the external word; 'for I can know that this external Word is not a word of the Law nor merely an empty word of promise, but one of great efficacy spiritually.' The person ordained can know that the charism of office will give him the power to proclaim the Gospel correctly and in this certainty he should 'stir up the grace of God which is in thee by the laying on of my hands' (II Tim. 1:6)."[28]

Thus Schlink arrives at the conclusion that ordination in the continuing succession of episcopal imposition of hands throughout the history of the Church as a sign of the apostolic succession of offices and of the Church and as a sign of Church unity and catholicity "should be welcomed and be striven for where it is lacking."[29] According to Schlink the whole development in the *ecumene* is leading in this direction and will make necessary a revision of this point in the "Declaration." "Within the framework of the whole ecumenical development no definitive importance should be ascribed to the more reticent 'Declaration of the Ecumenical Committee of the United Evangelical Lutheran Church of Germany of November 26, 1957' on the question of the apostolic succession."[30]

One cannot fail to see that Schlink has clarified and enriched the Lutheran position in the light of the New Testament and has provided safeguards for its weak points. In the light of the New Testament this in fact leads to a far-reaching accommodation with regard

[28] *Ibid.* 167.

[29] *Ibid.* 194.

[30] *Ibid.* 194; The protestant minister W. Richter, in "Apostolische Sukzession und die Vereinigte Evangelisch-Lutherische Kirche Deutschlands," in *Una Sancta* 14 (1959) 48–54, also criticizes the "Declaration" on this point.

to those questions which are of particular concern to Catholics.[31] But precisely thereby Catholic theology sees itself facing the questions that could be more easily answered if a more one-sided position (namely one of critical counter-questions) was adopted. These questions revolve around the problem that has already been raised by the Lutheran "Declaration" and that we have set aside previously, that is, the problem of episcopal succession as the *exclusive* means for transmitting the authority of office.

(2) *Are There Other Means Leading to Office?*

From the outset it must be noted that we shall not answer the questions that have been posed by Schlink and, albeit less clearly, by the Lutheran "Declaration." No ready-made answer to these questions is available. We therefore have to listen to the question first and to try to understand the difficulties involved.

Which human beings call others to office? Schlink freely admits that the New Testament reports of the accomplishment of the special commission through those persons who previously themselves had been sent to the ministry by a special vocation; the calling of office-holders by officeholders (Acts 14:23; Tit. 1:5; I Tim. 5:22; and most likely also in Acts 6:6). But at the same time he points out, significantly, that on the other hand the New Testament writings report of special commissions through persons who themselves had received no special mission; "So in Acts 13: If we hear of the commission of Paul and Barnabas by prophets and teachers in Antioch. For nowhere in the New Testament is there mention of an investiture of prophets through the imposition of hands. Even the investiture of the teachers involved here can hardly be presupposed. According to II Corinthians 8:19 Titus was called by the communities to work with Paul with no mention being made here of the appointed office-holders. According to I Timothy 4:14 Timothy was assigned to his special ministry by the imposition of hands of the presbyters and according to II Timothy 1:6 by the imposition of hands through Paul, whereas in the case of the presbyters it cannot be assumed out of hand that they themselves had been previously appointed to minister by the laying on of hands. Much is to be said in favour of the fact that the presbyters of the Pastoral Epistles were members of long standing if not the original members, of the community who

[31] Schlink also sees, however, the importance of this question for an ecumenical understanding with Anglican theology. He expressly calls attention to the far-reaching accord with different theologians, as they have expressed themselves in the symposium, *The Historic Episcopate*, edited by K. Carey, 1954.

had preserved their Christian faith by the purity and irreproachable character of their way of life, by their works of charity, and the like. Hence they were held in such high esteem in the community, without a prior special investiture of the office of presbyter having occurred. The investiture of presbyters mentioned in the Pastoral Epistles would then primarily be a matter of the investiture of presbyters as bishops."[32]

One might very well presuppose that the commission through officeholders was accomplished with the co-operation (or at least with the agreement) of the community and the commission through the communities or members of the community with the co-operation (or at least the recognition) of the office-holders (if they were present). There is no historical evidence, however, of a strict regulation— for instance, election by the congregation and the imposition of hands by the office-holders. "From what has been said it follows that in the New Testament writings there is no interest expressed in the chain of the imposition of hands, starting with the apostles and continuing by way of their collaborators and disciples down to the later local pastors of the congregation. Even where a chain of this kind can be presumed actually to have existed, the main concern clearly centres not on the succession of the imposition of hands but on the transmission of the pure doctrine (see, for example, II Tim. 2:2)."[33]

Doubtless it would be too simple to eliminate this problem by aprioristic interpretations (for example, that the presbyters who performed the imposition of hands were actually priests holding office, or that if it were a case of "community elders" their ordination was not a genuine ordination, or further that "congregation" was to be understood to mean office-holders, and so on). In the background here, indeed, stands the whole problem-complex that plays such a great role in the present research situation of the exegesis of the New Testament and which we have already discussed in connection with E. Käsemann, namely the differences between the undisputed Pauline epistles on the one hand and the Acts of the Apostles and the Pastoral Epistles on the other. The strength of Schlink's position lies in the fact that he does not merely try to get around the evidence produced by New Testament research or to explain it away dogmatically, but that he skilfully draws upon this evidence to justify his own contention. His point of departure is the Acts of the Apostles and the Pastoral Epistles in which the special commission plays a great role, whereas the manifoldness of special gifts of the Spirit

[32] E. Schlink, "Die apostolische Sukzession," *op cit*. 169.
[33] *Ibid*. 170.

and ministries given to every member of the community is not particularly stressed. Conversely, according to the great Pauline epistles
the Spirit is not only as according to the Acts and the Pastoral
Epistles given to every Christian—which could manifest itself in
bearing witness before the world—but the congregation itself is
presumed to be a community of manifold charismatic ministries,
a cosmos of different spiritual gifts and ministries, and it is addressed
as such. There is no mention of a special vocation to these ministries.
(apart from the apostles themselves and from the vocation of Titus
mentioned in II Cor. 8:19). It is especially striking that in the
Pauline epistles the ministry of ruling (1 Cor. 12:28) and presiding
(Rom. 12:8) is mentioned among the gifts that erupt out of the
freedom of the Spirit in the community without a special commission.
It is not the commission but the actual ministry that legitimizes the
obedience that the community owes its ministry. For the reason that
these who were the first fruits from the household of Stephen (according to I Cor. 16:15) began working and gathered a community together and served it, they should, according to Paul, be obeyed. Is
this not an example of how the early Christian Church expanded by
means of a spontaneous missionary activity?

Schlink's efforts in this direction actually do justice to both the
similarities and the differences of the two forms of service (the one
with and the one without a special vocation). First of all (in contradistinction to R. Sohm and E. Brunner and various exegetes of the
New Testament) he deals with the *similarities*: (1) The apostolic
office is fundamental to every ministry in the Church, hence the direct
vocation and authorization of the eyewitnesses of the Resurrection.
(2) The presupposition for every ministry is the complete surrender
of the individual to Christ in faith and Baptism. (3) The origin of
every ministry is rooted in the freedom of the Holy Spirit. (4)
Ministry on the basis of special commission is likewise a charismatic
ministry. (5) Equally the spontaneously arising charisms are not
simply utterances of an ecstatic frenzy in contrast to orderliness, or
impulses springing from person to person in contrast to personal
stability but, rather, in their effects they are akin to offices that have
been externally and firmly handed on. (6) The activities of the appointed minister are subject to the scrutiny and the judgment of the
community. (7) The ministry resulting without a special commission
is also endowed with the concrete word, based on the scrutiny and
judgment of the community and on the word of the apostles, recognizing this or demanding its recognition.

But precisely within these similarities, the *differences* have to be clearly recognized: (1) The "early Catholic" form of ministry (which originates from the communities conditioned by Jerusalem) is already a fact in the New Testament writings, but it must not be considered to be the only form of Church organization. "There is nothing to support the argument that an organization of presbyters or bishops by special vocation existed in the communities of Corinth or Rome at the time when Paul was writing to them. The generalization of the principle of commission begins with the First Letter of Clement and then was followed up in the early Church doctrine of office, common to both the Eastern and the Western Church and also prevalent among the Reformers, especially Calvin."[34] (2) The Pauline form of ministry (which was customary in the Pauline communities during the founding period) is supported by the evidence of the New Testament writings. Likewise, however, it cannot be considered as the only form of Church organization. "Nor is it possible to generalize the Pauline conception of ecclesiastical office in terms of a variety of spontaneously arising charisms, and using this as a point of departure to interpret the commission as a mere confirmation of the already present charism or to explain it as a sign of incipient Catholicism."[35]

From this it follows that "in the primitive Church we must from the outset reckon rather with the coexistence and overlapping of these different foundations and forms of ministry. The ministry of founding and guiding the Church was exercised partly on the basis of a special commission by the apostles or by others called to be the founders and leaders of the communities, partly on the ground of a commission by the community or by outstanding members assigned to office, but not on the basis of a special commission, and finally the ministry of founding and guiding the Church was also charismatically exercised without a special commission."[36] This finding is confirmed by the fact that New Testament writings do not point to a constant concept of ecclesiastical office but to a great variety of different and changing terms designating Church office. The dogmatic concept of ecclesiastical office must include, in a systematic representation, a variety of New Testament data.

It would be a total misunderstanding of Schlink if one were to assume that he advocates the coexistence of these three forms of Church organization for the present-day Church. This would represent a non-historical conception. Rather, Schlink strives to remain receptive to the Pauline view of the Church as well as to the dogmatic concept of ecclesiastical office, not in terms of the spontaneously

[34] *Ibid.* 173.   [35] *Ibid.*   [36] *Ibid.*

arising charismatic ministries but in terms of the special commission to ministry. Why does Schlink take this position? Not because the exercise of ecclesiastical office, in the development of Church history, was increasingly made dependent upon a prior vocation; the increasing repression of the free charismatic utterances could also be a sign of the narrowing and hardening of the ecclesiastical ministry. And also not because a degeneration of free charismatic utterances had set in at an early date (beginning with the eruption of Gnosticism and Montanism, and followed by the many medieval movements up to the radical sectarianism of the age of the Reformation). Those called to hold office could equally degenerate through a lust for power, heresy, and other factors. But the underlying fact remains: The *commission* in principle and necessarily achieved an *increasing importance with the increasing time interval that had elapsed from the Church-establishing ministry of the apostles:* "The Church can live only by remaining with the historical, the crucified and resurrected Christ as her present Lord. This means that she must stand by the testimony of the apostles, of those who were called to be the eye-witnesses of this Lord. With the growing time interval, the tradition of the apostolic message, doctrine, and orders—and, together with this, the commission to the ministry of the tradition—had to grow in importance. For indeed everything depends upon the unadulterated apostolic Word being always heard in the Church and all other voices that are raised in the Church remaining subordinate to it. It is in terms of the importance of the apostolic tradition that we can understand how the Church order of the Pastoral Epistles came to be placed under the authority of Paul."[37]

One will have to proceed with caution precisely because of the later development of the Pauline communities: "In view of the importance that Paul attributed to tradition in his unchallenged epistles, one cannot exclude the possibility that in his old age, in view of the further expansion of the Church, he promoted and supported by his authority an organization of ordination and office along the lines of the Pastoral Epistles. The relationship between the Word and the Spirit which underlies life in the Church and between the unique historical occurrence of the divine act of salvation and the constant work of salvation of the Spirit finds its appropriate expression in the emphases on the special commission. The Spirit acts as a reminder of the unique historical act of salvation of Jesus Christ and thereby refers back to the apostolic Word. Thus understood, the Spirit makes present the act of salvation. Hence Spirit and tradition are not

[37] *Ibid.* 176.

opposed to each other but belong together. At the same time one should not forget that the manifoldness of the charismatic expressions and spontaneously arising ministries in the Pauline communities had actually not remained without the guidance of an authority established by special commission, that is, it had not remained without the guidance of the apostles. The reports of Paul, on the basis of his special authority are indeed documents attesting to the concrete influence of the Apostle on the communities which he encouraged, admonished, recognized, but also warned while continuing to guide them. With the cessation of this highly concrete and ever-present guidance and ministry of the Apostle—despite the distance in space —the office based on a special commission perforce increased in importance, that is, the office of the charismatic leader who, grounding himself on this vocation, faced the community with an authority already given beforehand and not dependent, like that of other charismatics, on the subsequent recognition by the community."[38]

Given this premise, *ecclesiastical office* according to Schlink must be understood in a *twofold* context: (1) Ecclesiastical office must be understood as a charismatic ministry which, among the multiplicity of charisms and ministries, is grounded on a *special commission*; namely, on a special commission for the ministry of founding and guiding churches (and their auxiliary ministries); in short, a calling to *pastoral office.* Attention must be drawn to the great variety of functions of the pastoral office (concentrated on the two basic functions—guidance of the assemblies for worship and guidance of the missionary penetration of the world) and the many forms of pastoral office; the terms bishop, presbyter, elder, deacon, and others, were often used ambiguously and adapted to different situations, frequently overlapping each other. "The tripartite division of ecclesiastical offices which prevailed in the early Church, bishops, presbyters and deacons, cannot be assumed, on the basis of the New Testament, to have been the general basic order of the primitive Christian community."[39] Nevertheless the pointers are there, enabling us to deduce the most important potential forms of the pastoral office— the organization of offices into a relationship of superordination and subordination. The pastoral office of the local Church is the fundamental office which lacked nothing in authority but which did have to remain in communion with the other pastors. The differentiation in the ecclesiastical office was threefold: the highest ranking pastor, the various offices of deacons, and those holding limited commissions (visitations and the like). That which was not actually defined

[38] *Ibid.*   [39] *Ibid.* 179.

dogmatically had frequently to be settled later on by canon law as the definite structure of the Church order. No objections can be raised against this.

(2) This concept of the pastoral office at the same time must remain receptive to the Pauline concept of the Church as the community of charisms and must not exclude the *possibility of the spontaneously arising charisms* of founding and guiding a community. "If Paul recognized the spiritual gifts of directing, of presiding, and of the self-appointment of the first members without any special vocation and admonished the community to obey those engaged in this ministry, it was because this all took place in a missionary situation. The doctrine of the pastoral office must always remain open to the ever-present missionary situation on the frontiers of the organized Church. A Christian thrown into a purely pagan environment, calling all pagans to the faith, by virtue of bearing witness to Christ, baptizing them and celebrating the Lord's Supper with them, acts as a holder of the pastoral office if he performs all these activities according to apostolic doctrine and orders—even if he was not authorized for that task by a special mandate prior to being taken to the far-away pagan lands. In the isolation of a prison camp or in a forced-labour camp he, in fact, acts in harmony with the Church and her pastors, and the latter, when they come upon him and his congregation, can not refuse recognition to his pastoral office and his congregation. The charismatic ministry of the Christian does not rest exclusively on a special commission but, above everything else, on the apostolic Gospel, which the Lord wills to have preached to the whole world. The dogmatic teaching on ecclesiastical office must not exclude any possibility for the growth of the Church, which was a missionary reality in the period of expansion of the early Christian communities. Such freely arising ministries nevertheless remain dependent upon the approval of the Church and consequently also on the recognition of those called to be pastors."[40]

This definition of ecclesiastical office has the following consequences for the *apostolic succession* which is in the succession of obedience to the apostles as the appointed eyewitnesses of the resurrection of Jesus Christ. The apostolic succession of the *pastoral office* must be taken seriously within the apostolic succession of the Church and each of her members. This means that every pastor: (1) in his sermons, teachings, guidance, and administration is always to emulate the apostolic example; (2) is to stand *vis-à-vis* the Church, like the apostles, as the voice and representative of Christ; (3) like

[40] *Ibid.* 177.

every member of the community, is each day newly dependent upon Christ and His grace; and (4) is to be a shepherd to the Church in communion both with the other pastors and with the charismatic ministries.

And yet only when the relationship between apostle and Church finds its succession in the communion of reciprocal ministries and the common ministry to the world is the apostolic succession both of the Church and of office taken seriously. Schlink concludes from this that, in obedience to the apostolic activity, *three fundamental ways leading to the pastoral office* are discernible.

(1) "The commission to pastoral service through those who themselves have been sent forth as pastors before—with the recognition or, going beyond that, the co-operation of the Church and specifically of such Church members who themselves never received any kind of ordination."[41] Concerning this first way Schlink says quite clearly (and in this, as we have seen, he goes beyond the "Declaration") that today "it deserves priority and must be regarded as a rule. For with the increasing time span that separates us from the apostles the office itself, and a special training for office, perforce acquire a greater importance if the Church wishes to preserve the apostolic tradition. The idea of ordination at the hands of the already ordained quite justifiably prevailed in the Church."[42] Hence Schlink welcomes, as we likewise have seen, the continuous sequence of the imposition of hands in Church history as a sign of apostolic succession of the offices and of the unity and catholicity of the Church. And where it is lacking, one should strive for it. But in keeping with the two-fold aspect that Schlink ascribes in principle to ecclesiastical office, he is equally concerned to preserve, along with the rule of the apostolic succession of offices through the imposition of hands, the extraordinary ways so to speak which likewise are in keeping with the relationship between the apostles and the Church and upon which the Church likewise has grown. The ordination by the bishop through the imposition of hands is, no doubt, a sign but not absolutely a *condition* for the apostolic succession. There are two further ways leading to the ecclesiastical pastoral office.

(2) "Commission to pastoral ministry by the Church and by such members of the Church who themselves have not been sent forth as pastors. This latter with the recognition or, going beyond that, the co-operation of the appointed pastors."[43]

(3) "The recognition by the Church and those called to be pastors

[41] *Ibid.* 193.   [42] *Ibid.*
[43] *Ibid.*

of the fact of a pastoral ministry spontaneously arising in spiritual freedom."[44]

For Schlink, openness towards these other roads to office is "of considerable ecumenical importance. Without it many of the spiritual breakthroughs in Church history—whether they were missionary penetrations into the pagan world or movements of renewal within a Church that had become tired and self-righteous—would remain incomprehensible. Without this openness it would be impossible to heal the schisms which have arisen in Christendom."[45]

(f) It cannot be denied that Schlink puts forward his critical questions in regard to Catholic doctrine with great precision and urgency. By virtue of the fact that he accepts the apostolic succession of offices through the laying on of hands as the normally desirable procedure today, he takes the wind out of the sails of many Catholic objections to his own conception. By virtue of the fact that in accordance with scriptural guidance he insists on the validity of the two other ways leading to ecclesiastical office, he also presents the essential demands of the Reformation. At the beginning of this section, where the other ways leading to office were discussed, we stated we would not attempt to answer the questions raised here. Not only because this answer would itself require a book if it were to be adequate, but also, and above all, because there is no readily available answer to this question in Catholic theology. It is no shame to confess this; indeed it may rather be a cause for hope. What is necessary is not just a few aprioristic distinctions with which the existence of the problem is denied rather than solved, but a fundamental exegetic, historical, and dogmatic *discussion* of these questions. Perhaps then the difficulties that now still seem insurmountable may, at least in part, be diminished (with both sides co-operating).

The necessity of a fundamental theological discussion arises precisely from the pertinent decrees of the Council of Trent regarding the Sacraments in general—the Eucharist, Penance, Orders, and others. These decrees are obviously frequently opposed to Schlink's position; this pertains to the proclamation of the Word and the administration of Sacraments in general,[46] especially Penance,[47] Confirmation,[48] Anointing of the sick,[49] Ordination,[50] and the Eucharist.[51] For Catholics it goes without saying that a denial of

[44] *Ibid.*   [45] *Ibid.* 194.   [46] Denz. 853; cf. 1958.
[47] Denz. 902, 920; cf. 670, 753.
[48] Denz. 960; cf. 608, 697, 1458, 2147a.
[49] Denz. 910, 929; cf. 99, 700.
[50] Denz. 958, 960, 966, 967; cf. 305, 356, 548, 701.
[51] Cf. Denz. 424, 430, 574a.

these conciliar decrees is definitely out of the question. It is only a question of understanding them correctly. But conciliar decrees can be understood correctly—and today this should be the generally accepted view of Catholic theologians—only in terms of the prevailing historical conditions. Only thus can the positive meaning of their statements be understood. Only thus can we also understand their negative limitations. For no definition can be exhaustive. As a humanly limited statement a concilar decree—although it advocates truth and not error—with the assistance of the Holy Spirit promised to the Church, can also, according to the Encyclical *Humani generis*,[52] be interpreted, expanded, and perfected. Indeed, Augustine did not shrink from using the word *emendare* (that is, "to correct") in this connection. "But who can fail to be aware that the Councils themselves, which are held in the several districts and provinces, must yield, beyond all possibility of doubt, to the authority of universal Councils that are formed for the whole Christian world; and that even of the universal Councils, the earlier are often corrected by those which follow them, when, by some further experience, things are brought to light which were before concealed, and that is known which previously lay hid?"[53]

Hence it would be a matter of understanding the Tridentine definitions in their historical context and thereby of understanding them better today. Should it also not be possible for Protestant theologians to see the great positive questions with which the Tridentine definitions deal in their historical context? Was there not at that time the great danger that everything might be subverted in the Church, that all Church discipline might be dissolved and that the continuity with the old, the apostolic Church would be destroyed? Did not the Reformers too, faced with the overthrow of all Church government by the radical sectarians, have as many difficulties with them as with the Catholic Church? And have we not seen to what an extent at least the young Luther aided and abetted the radical sectarians? Indeed, had not Luther then called upon the secular rulers in order to cope with the radical sectarians? Is it not understandable from this vantage point that the Council of Trent too was forced to take vigorous defensive measures and thus pushed the special position of ecclesiastical office defensively and polemically into the forefront? Concern over the preservation of Church government as expressed in the

[52] *Acta Apostolicae Sedis* 42 (1950) 566.
[53] Augustine, *Writings in Connection with the Donatist Controversy*. Vol. III of The Works of Aurelius Augustine, ed. by M. Dods (Edinburgh: T. & T. Clark, 1872), p. 35.

fourth chapter of the "Orders" decree under the title "The Ecclesiastical Hierarchy and Ordination" stood in the background of many statements that for us today appear to be very one-sided: "But if anyone says that all Christians without exception are priests of the New Testament or are all-endowed with equal spiritual power, it is apparent that he upsets the ecclesiastical hierarchy (see 849, can. 6), which is like an army in battle array (see Cant. 6:3), as much as if, contrary to Paul's teaching, all were apostles, all prophets, all evangelists, all pastors and teachers (see I Cor. 12:29; Eph. 4:11)."[54] True, the negative consequence of these definitions and of the corresponding Church government was often a shockingly formalistic and legalistic rigidity. Protestant theology and the Protestant Church have not been reticent in their criticism on this score. But as a Catholic one may also permit oneself the question: "How would things often have looked in that same Protestant theology and Church (during the Enlightenment, during the liberalism of the nineteenth century) if the quiet countervailing influence of the (often all-too) rigidly organized Catholic Church had not existed?"

Concern over the preservation of the hierarchical structure of the Church was the subject of many of the canons devised in defence of ecclesiastical office. Another concern revolved around the spiritual character of church office. Was there not a great danger at that time that spiritual office would be reduced to a mere ecclesiastical bureaucracy and a democratic corps of functionaries? Has not the history of ecclesiastical office in the Protestant Church shown that this danger was not illusory? Is it not true that in broad circles, if not of Protestant laymen then of Protestant theologians, the specific spiritual character of ecclesiastical office has been ignored up to the present time in a way that pays little regard to Scripture? But did not Luther, too, simply neglect the most profound aspect of ordination, that is, the transmission of charism? Hence is it not obvious that the Council of Trent was forced to take vigorous defensive measures and thus emphatically concentrate attention upon the spiritual character of office? Concern over the spiritual character of office stood in the background of many canons that to us appear to be one-sided: "If anyone says that by holy ordination the Holy Spirit is not given and thus it is useless for bishops to say: 'Receive the Holy Spirit'; or if anyone says that no character is imprinted by ordination; or that he who was once a priest can become a layman again: let him be anathema."[55]

Thus, corresponding questions could be raised in the case of each

[54] Denz. 960.   [55] Denz. 964.

of the Tridentine decrees. Just as it is the task of Catholic theology to make an effort to understand the justified demands of the reformers likewise is it the task of Protestant theology to make an effort to understand the justified concerns underlying the decrees issued at Trent. Neither task is an easy one. It also requires a broad knowledge of the important progress that has been made since Luther and Trent in both Catholic and Protestant theology. Many ways that previously seemed to be closed by the Tridentine decrees have proved themselves to be quite viable in our century.

Compare the negative attitude of the Tridentine decrees concerning the idea of the universal priesthood of the laity and the importance of charisms and ministry in the Church with the positive statements of the Encyclical *Mystici corporis*.[56] Compare the negative statements regarding the active participation of all believers in the eucharistic worship with the positive statements of the Encyclical *Mediator Dei*.[57] Compare the Tridentine definition regarding the Vulgate with the statements of the Encyclical *Divino afflante Spiritu*[58] and the deviation from the text of the Vulgate in the official translation of the Psalms. Compare the Tridentine decrees with regard to the vernacular in the Mass with the present-day practice of the dialogue Mass (and the administration of the Sacraments) and the further reforms of the Mass that are expected soon. Who, immediately after the Council of Trent, would have ever expected a positive discussion at later councils of the chalice for lay persons and the new arrangements in regard to orders in the Church, of married deacons, and still other topics? Much that *seemed* to have been definitely settled and defined has changed. The general Council of Florence (along with Thomas Aquinas) decided in the binding decree for the Armenians that the matter of ordination consisted in transmission of the corresponding instruments hence for the priest the presentation of the chalice with the wine and the paten with the bread.[59] Pius XII ruled that the matter of Holy Orders (for deacon, priest, bishop) was the imposition of hands exclusively.[60]

In order to understand such doctrinal developments the following must be borne in mind: The limit to the meaning of a statement, objectively present even from the beginning, becomes clearly visible only when there emerges a new positive insight, on the basis of which the limitations of the old statement become apparent. Therefore we cannot simply say that the exact limitations of the radius of influence

---

[56] *Acta Apostolicae Sedis* 35 (1943) 200f.
[57] Denz. 2300.   [58] Denz. 2292.
[59] Denz. 701.   [60] Denz. 2301.

and applicability of the Trent declarations on ecclesiastical office in every respect are already discernible solely on the basis of the conciliar texts. The Fathers of the Council for example, did not consider the possibility that under certain conditions a priest can validly ordain another. They certainly did not deny such a possibility. But the fact that they did not do this, and the fact that this very silence does have a positive meaning—namely, that of leaving the question open to later positive answers—can be fully seen only in retrospect.

Will the door some day be opened to the possibilities of reaching an extraordinary route to ecclesiastical office? That cannot be predicted at the present time. What is certain, however, is that the definitions of the Trent decrees are completely valid for the normal case; normally admission to office occurs as it was laid down at Trent; namely, through the ordination of the officeholder. Schlink too considers this to be the ordinary procedure. In regard to eventual extraordinary ways, on the Catholic side, no more can be said at present than this: the question must be examined afresh in the light of the present state of the problems. The reception and the dispensation of Sacraments *in voto* has been theologically thoroughly investigated only with respect to Baptism. The new situation of an existential (and not only hypothetical) encounter with peoples of other continents in the age of the great discoveries had to arise in order for the full meaning and repercussions of the extraordinary means (as finally defined at Trent[61]) leading to Christian faith (Baptism *in voto*, Baptism by individual decision) to be grasped, although this doctrine had definitely existed since the twelfth century. So, perhaps the new situation of the existential (and not only hypothetical) encounter with peoples of other Christian confessions in the age of the ecumenical movement will bring into focus the extraordinary means of reaching office (*ordo in voto*, as might somewhat inaccurately be described).[62] A decision can hardly be made at the present time.

[61] Denz. 796.

[62] In Baptism *in voto* the circumstances are undoubtedly different: Here the question is whether the effect of the Sacraments can be rendered under certain circumstances without the established sign of the Sacrament. With an extraordinary means to office (*ordo "in voto"*) the question is, whether the effect of the Sacrament can be given with established signs in certain circumstances, although the person ordaining lacks legal authority. Baptism is necessary for salvation, Holy Order is not. Despite the distinction not every parallel can be rejected at the outset. It is precisely in the perspective of text-book theology and its understanding of the Sacrament and apostolic succession, that the question must be asked: What happens, for example, if the ordination of a bishop in a certain case is not validly administered (say because of a deficiency of the intention; because of a mistake in form), without this being noticed, indeed without the possibility of its

What is certain is that both exegesis and history teach us much that simply could not have been known at the time of Trent; thus with regard to the different and mixed usage of *episcopos* and *presbyteros*, for example, and of the historical development of the episcopate, as well as with regard to the variety of the apostolic Church order and the original importance of the universal priesthood of all believers. Here we can propose only a few questions for discussion.

(1) *Episcopoi, Presbyteroi, Diakonoi*

The present-day tripartite division of offices developed gradually and is not to be found quite clearly in that form in the apostolic Church of the New Testament. Alongside and among the apostles we encounter in the New Testament "further groups of persons who perform numerous ministries (charisms), but also those who have fixed offices in the service of the whole Church (apostles, prophets, evangelists) or in the ministry of the individual communities (bishops, presbyters, deacons, teachers, pastors). The relations between these office-holders and these offices is either co-ordinated or it is a relationship of superordination and subordination (I Cor. 12:28: first apostles, second prophets, third teachers; in Phil. 1:1: bishops and deacons; cf. I Tim. 3:2, 8). Gradually the leadership of a community is concentrated in the hands of the presbyters, or of bishops and deacons (Acts 14:23; 20:17; I Tim. 3). In the Pastoral Epistles the monarchical position of the bishops seems to be making its way. The shape of an hierarchical structure—bishop, presbyters, deacons—we meet for the first time in Ignatius of Antioch."[63] Thus the New Testament community displays a great variety; the different offices are not yet clearly and strictly distinguished as they are today—a development that took place only much later. Bishops and presbyters, particularly, cannot be distinguished in the same way as today: "Ἐπίσκοπος and πρεσβύτερος were more or less interchangeable terms, as the evidence of Acts 20:17-28 and Titus I:5-7 shows. Both functions can be performed by

---

being noticed? Is the whole "chain of ordination" and indeed the whole structure of "chains of ordination" arising out of this irreparably and unperceivedly demolished? Can the Catholic help himself in such a case only by the postulate that such a thing, at least on a large scale, will be prevented by Divine Providence? Or may he also assume in such a case, that *such* a consecration may nevertheless be valid and would be "completed" and lawfully "healed" by God himself; that it is correct in view of the wholeness and the unity of the Church: What is the logical conclusion if one is permitted to consider this second assumption as possible, since it is certainly not disavowed by any ecclesiastical pronouncement?

[63] J. Gewiess, "Hierarchie," in *Lexikon für Theologie und Kirche* (Freiburg i. Br. 1960) V, 322.

several persons in a community (Phil. 1:1; Tit. 1:5); the inherent meaning of the term ἐπίσκοπος refers more specifically to the office, whereas the term πρεσβύτερος refers more specifically to the dignity of ecclesiastical authority. Most, although not all, persons in the apostolic era who were designated as the ἐπίσκοπος or πρεσβύτερος are therefore priests in the present-day sense. The highest authority in the community was reserved to the apostles or to such trusted collaborators as Timothy or Titus (I Tim. 3:1–15; 5:22; Tit. 1:5) and others who emerged as founders of congregations and apostolic envoys, all of whom derived their authority directly from the apostles."[64] The questions to be discussed are the following: Office in the Church is doubtless *iuris divini*; but to what extent is the distribution of functions of this office *iuris divini*? Was not the head of the community in the early Church frequently also bishop and presbyter? Can the function of the supreme pastor (who is in charge of greater territories and several congregations) from the point of view of the New Testament not be understood as an upward branching-out from the one pastoral office or, conversely, the simple office of presbyter as the downward spread of the vast scope of functions of the episcopal pastoral office?[65] Is the *restriction* of certain functions to the supreme pastor a matter of divine or human law? Were there not also very often simple priests who themselves performed, and were allowed to perform, what were later the specific functions of a supreme pastor, such as Confirmation[66] and the ordination of priests?[67] Does this not all point to the unity of the pastoral office?

[64] H. Haag, "Bischof," in *Bibel-Lexikon* (Einsiedeln–Zurich–Cologne 1951) 246f; cf. "Hierarchie," *ibid*. 709f. cf. L. Marchal, "Évêques," in *Dictionnaire de la Bible, Supplément* (Paris 1934) II, 1297–1333.

[65] Cf. M. Schmaus, *Katholische Dogmatik* (Munich 1952) IV/1, 573f.

[66] In the Eastern Churches since the fourth century priests have been the regular ministers of confirmation (without, of course, any papal authority having been conferred). In the Western Church Confirmation has on occasion also been administered by ordinary priests. Today, by virtue of a general law, the administering of Confirmation is permitted to a great part of the priesthood. "A papal decree of September 14, 1946, gives all parish priests, all those in charge of a parish under a religious order, and parish administrators entitled to parish priests' rights, authority to administer emergency Confirmation within their parishes to the faithful who are dangerously ill, if the bishop or suffragan cannot be reached. This disposition is connected with the old Christian or Eastern Church tradition according to which priests who are not bishops also administered Confirmation. Hence the disposition remained in the framework of tradition, this all the more, when Scholastic thinking adduced as the reason for the bishops' prerogative of Confirmation the will of ecclesiastical authority is establishing law. It also stands in complete accord with the Church's earlier doctrinal reformations," (*op cit*. IV/I, 182). In order to explain all these weighty facts, theologians today generally maintain that the authority to administer Confirmation is conferred on *every*

(2) *Officeholders—Universal Priesthood*

This problem is much more difficult and complex than the one just mentioned. Nevertheless these problems, to which hitherto too little attention has been paid, must be considered thoroughly in all their aspects. It is not a question of what the Christian can do under normal circumstances (where the ecclesiastical office can perform its regular service) but a question of what he can do in an *emergency* or, rather (apart from the present legal situation in the Church), what he could do on the basis of *iure divino* proper. And when was the question more urgent than today when countless Christians are isolated in jails and concentration camps? In this case also the question must be thought through anew on the basis of the findings of the New Testament exegesis. There is no difficulty as regards emergency Baptism. Every Christian can baptize (indeed, since Baptism is the sign of *admission* into the community of the Church which does not already presuppose the existence of this community

---

priest at the time of his ordination; admittedly this authority is in the first place (by canon law) held back.

[67] L. Ott, *Grundriss der katholischen Dogmatik* (Freiburg–Basle–Vienna ⁵1961) 547 (English trans.: *The Fundamentals of Catholic Dogma* [Cork 1960] 459), has ably presented the historic and systematic difficulties: "Serious historical obstacles, however, confront this view (that a simple priest may not ordain to the priesthood): in accordance with the teaching of numerous medieval canonists (e.g. Huguccio [d. 1210]), Pope Boniface IX, by the Bull *Sacrae religionis* of February 1, 1400, granted to the abbot of the Augustine monastery St. Osytha in Essex (Diocese of London) and his successors the privilege of administering to their subjects both the minor orders and those of the subdiaconate, diaconate, and priesthood. On February 6, 1403, the privilege was revoked on the protest of the bishop of London. But the ordinations administered on the basis of the privilege were not declared invalid. Pope Martin V, in the Bull *Gerentes ad vos* of November 16, 1427, granted to the abbot of the Cistercian monastery Altzelle (Diocese of Meissen) the privilege of conferring to his monks and subordinates all orders, including the higher orders (subdiaconate, diaconate and priesthood) for the term of five years. By the Bull *Exposcit tuae devotionis* of April 9, 1489, Pope Innocent VIII granted to the abbot-general and the four protoabbots of the Cistercian order and their successors the privilege of conferring the orders of subdeacon and deacon on their subjects. In the seventeenth century, the Cistercian abbots were still making unhindered use of this. If one does not want to assume that the popes in question fell victim to an erroneous theological view of their time . . . then one must assume that the ordinary priest, in an analogous way, is the extraordinary minister of Holy Order in regard to diaconate and priesthood, just as he is the extraordinary minister of confirmation. According to the latter explanation, the necessary authority is contained within priest's power of order as *potestas ligata*. For the valid exercise of this power, whether by virtue of divine or ecclesiastical disposition, a special papal authorization is necessary." Cf. also K. A. Fink, "Zur Spendung der höheren Weihen durch den Priester," in *Zeitschrift für Schweizer Kirchengeschichte* 32 (1943) 506–508.

—anyone can baptize). According to the Catholic view the marriage partners also administer the Sacrament of Matrimony to themselves. What, however, is the situation with regard to an "emergency Eucharist"[68] and an "emergency absolution"?[69] It is a question that must be considered anew now that exegesis has shown us more clearly than before that the passages often quoted in this context, namely, Matthew 18:18 and Luke 22:19, do not refer exclusively to ecclesiastical office but to the whole of the Church. Nevertheless, according to Catholic theology (and in keeping with the unique position of ecclesiastical office) these texts also address themselves to the office so that these passages may not be considered *indifferenter et promiscue*—addressed, as it were, equally to all members of the community separately.[70]

In the case of *absolution* the following is to be noted: Matthew 18:18 is linked with a general instruction given to the disciples. Matthew 18 is one of the oldest community ordinances. The task of "binding and loosening" is assigned to all the disciples, to the whole Church, whereby the character and the degree of this "binding and loosening" is to be considered as corresponding to the functions of

---

[68] Compare to so-called "spiritual communion," Denz. 881.

[69] It is important that from the eleventh century up to Duns Scotus it was almost universally taught in the Catholic Church that the obligation lay confession in case of emergency was a realistic fulfilment of the *votum sacramenti*. (Albertus Magnus even ascribed an actual sacramental character to lay confession.) Cf. also K. Rahner, "Laienbeichte," in *Lexikon für Theologie und Kirche* (Freiburg i. Br. 1961) VI, 741 and the bibliographical references noted there. Y. Congar, *Lay People in the Church* (London 1957), 217–218, says the following on the question of lay confession: "A tradition that was then commonly accepted throughout the span of five centuries—from 800 to 1300 in the East, from 1000 to 1500 in the West—has permitted a practice that must be quite exceptional if it exists today, namely confession to lay members of the Church. St. Thomas who, among the theologians, maintained an exceptionally favourable position regarding confession to lay persons, expressly relates this point to that of the administration of baptism: in both cases the necessity for salvation seemed to him to justify the maximum freedom of action. St. Thomas did more than any other to attach great importance to sacramental action and to the role (instrumental) of priestly authority. Nevertheless, going far beyond many of his contemporaries he recognized a value, that in some manner was sacramental, in a confession made to a neighbour, no matter who he might be. For him the acts of the penitent (contrition and accusation) enter into the very constitution and into the essence of the sacrament. The fact that the absence of the priest deprives the faithful penitent of absolution and of doing properly sacramental penance does not prevent the confession, with respect to the subject, from being what it can be in the line of a sacramental confession, the minister being substituted by a lay person, and from meriting the qualification '*quodammodo sacramentalis*' on the basis of this reason."

[70] Cf. Denz. 902.

the individual in the community (as loosing in the synagogue).[71] In individual cases the disciples are represented by the assembly of the community that is to be viewed as structured, perhaps led by apostles or bishops. Even in this way the Church as a whole is charged with the task of pastoral care. According to Hebrews 13:15f, the Church must discharge this task by confession of faith, community and works of charity; according to Romans 1:9 through intercession; according to Romans 12:1 through self-sacrifice. To all it is said for all: "Edify each other."[72]

In the case of the *celebration of the Eucharist* it is to be borne in mind that "the celebration of the Lord's Supper was in all likelihood carried out in the circle of the Twelve, and they were the first to receive the command: 'Do this in remembrance of me' (Luke 22:19). The apostles also undertook this commission. But this order surely is one that also applies to the whole Church. Thus, up to the present day (according to the Codex Iuris Canonici, Canon 813, § 1) no priest may celebrate the Mass without at least one server being present, to represent the community of the Church which celebrates Mass together with the priest. And the celebration of the Sunday divine service is described in German as the "office" (*Amt*) or "high office" (*das hohe Amt*), certainly not the office of the celebrant but of the whole community. The Word that teaches and proclaims at the divine service is enjoined upon everyone. Paul tells the church of Corinth, which was assembled for worship: 'Whereas if, while *all* are prophesying, there should come in an unbeliever or uninstructed person, he is convicted by all, he is put on trial by all; the secrets of his heart are made manifest, and so, falling on his face, he will worship God, declaring that God is truly among you' (I Cor. 14:24–25). According to Matthew 28:19 the order to go and baptize all nations was also pronounced in the narrowest circle of the apostles. But in the Church it has always been understood as an order which can be carried out not only by the apostles but by any other person. Hence the order to preach the gospel, which is closely linked with the order to baptize, likewise applies not only to the narrow circle of the apostles but to the whole Church."[73]

---

[71] Cf. A. Vögtle, "Binden und Lösen," in *Lexikon für Theologie und Kirche* (Freiburg i. Br. ²1958) II, 480–482.

[72] Cf. K. H. Schelkle, *Jüngerschaft und Apostelamt* (Freiburg i. Br. ²1961) 119f.

[73] Cf. K. H. Schelkle, *op cit.* 120f. Clarification of the question of who celebrated the Eucharist at any given time in the spontaneously expanding early Christian mission (who celebrated it in the absence of Paul in Corinth, since, oddly enough, no presbytery is mentioned in First Corinthians?), would be important in this connection. Among others, O. Casel, "Prophetie und Eucharistie,"

These are statements concerning the universal priesthood of all believers, which naturally do not aim at questioning the office in the Church.[74] The question is whether these and other statements of the New Testament are already exhausted with respect to their concrete significance for theology and church life and how they can be applied to our problems. In this way under given circumstances decisive progress can be made toward an ecumenical encounter. Would it not be possible, on the basis of a more thorough exegetic and dogmatic exposition of the structures of the Church, to shift the accent in the traditional doctrine of the *"vestigia ecclesiae"* from *"vestigia"* to *"ecclesiae"*?

5. THE REPRESENTATION OF OFFICES AND COMMUNITIES

After these long expositions concerning Church and office we can apply them to an ecumenical council by human convocation with relative brevity.

(*a*) *Office:* We have seen that this ecumenical gathering of all the faithful who constitute the Church is not a conglomeration of believers who have democratically merged into an amorphous mass, but a structured community of manifold spiritual gifts, ministries, states and offices organized in different ways. It has become clear that within the universal priesthood of all believers a decisive role is assigned to the offices in the hierarchy of the Church. There is no Church without pastors; but everyone cannot be a pastor. Pastors, though not independent of the community, occupy a position of authority in the community and may demand obedience. Despite the ties of fellowship that link the pastors to their congregations, and

---

in *Jahrbuch für Liturgiewissenschaft* (1929) 1–19, has already referred to the celebration of the Eucharist by *prophets* which existed in primitive christianity: "The *liturgy* in which the spirit of the Christian community evolved into a solemn cult, we first of all see as held and led particularly by bearers of the spirit, especially the apostles and prophets. In Antioch, as reported to us by the Acts of the Apostles, prophets and doctors performed the liturgy. 'The prophets have the *Eucharistia* held as they want,' says the Didache (10,7); 'they are your high priests' (13,3). But as soon as the distinction between office and *pneuma* more strictly appears, the officeholders more exclusively take over the direction of divine service. We read further in the Didache (15): 'Ordain bishops and deacons . . . because they *also* perform the liturgy of the prophets and teachers for you. Therefore do not scorn them. They have the place of honour among you *with* the prophets and teachers' " (1f). Whether these prophets, as Casel feels, belong to the "primitive Christian hierarchy" is anyway more than questionable.

[74] K. H. Schelkle, *op. cit.* 121, 130–134.

despite all possible (and in part also necessary) co-operation of the community in their election and exercise of office, the pastors are not merely delegates and functionaries of the communities. They have not received their capacity and authority to minister as something delegated, democratically, by the people. Rather, in the line of the succession of the apostles they have been installed as pastors by the Holy Spirit of Jesus Christ Himself; it is from Him that they have received their authority as leaders over the whole flock: "Take heed to yourselves and to the whole flock in which the Holy Spirit has placed you as bishops, to rule the Church of God, which he has purchased with his own blood. I know that after my departure fierce wolves will get in among you, and will not spare the flock. And from among your own selves men will rise speaking perverse things, to draw away the disciples after them. Watch, therefore, and remember that for three years night and day I did not cease with tears to admonish every one of you" (Acts 20:28–31).

Just as the Church convoked by God is not an amorphous but a structured and ordered council, so must an ecumenical council by human convocation, especially if it really wants to represent the Church, also be not an amorphous association of random individual members but must reflect the ordered structure of the Church. Just as the ecumenical council by divine convocation, which is the Church, stands under the guidance of pastors, so must an ecumenical council by human convocation which truly wants to represent the Church stand under the guidance of pastors. An ecumenical council is not a gathering of enthusiastic sectarians but a gathering of the representatives of the whole Church coming together in the Holy Spirit. We have seen (and the first Christian synods which were held are impressive examples on this score) that these representatives need not only be office-holders; on the basis of the universal priesthood of all believers they can also be lay persons. But they cannot be lay persons *only*. As little as the Church is a democratically (charistmatically) organized society with legislative, executive, and judiciary organs, which are authorized (delegated) by herself, just as little is an ecumenical council by human convocation, which represents the Church, a Church parliament of delegates representing communities. Lay persons representing their communities (bishoprics, country, or continent) could be viewed as community delegates (in cases where a delegation is present) but office-holders as such could not. The latter do not derive their authority in the ministry from the community but from Christ and His Spirit. Hence they represent their communities at an ecumenical council by human convocation not as *representatives* (delegates) of their congregations (by authorization of the congregation) but in *representation* ("personification") of their congregations; as pastors appointed to their ministry, commissioned and empowered to it by the Spirit, who by virtue of the same Spirit and in serving their congregation, represent this in their own person. In elaborating on the theology of office as defined in the Acts of the Apostles and in the Pastoral Epistles, Cyprian offered the classical formulation that the officeholder is rooted in the congregation and that, conversely, the congregation is represented in the officeholder: "You must know that the bishop is in the Church and the Church in the bishop."[1]

In this way it is precisely the office-holders who represent their Churches at an ecumenical council by human convocation who also represent in a most excellent way the one, holy, catholic and apostolic Church. To the extent that the office-holders, as representatives of their Churches, stand in the line of the special apostolic succession, in the line of the succession not only of the apostolic faith and confession but also of the apostolic office. They represent at an ecumenical council by human convocation the *apostolicity* of the Church in a most excellent way. To the extent that office-holders, as representatives of all the Churches (congregations, dioceses, countries, continents) from the whole *ecumene* assemble in *one* place in order to take their decisions in the unanimity of the Spirit for the whole Church, they represent in an ecumenical council by human convocation the *unity* of the Church in a most excellent way. To the extent that the office-holders assembled as the representatives of the manifold countries and continents, of the manifold rites and languages, theologies and forms of piety of the *ecumene*, they represent in an ecumenical council by human convocation the *catholicity* of the Church in a most excellent way. To the extent that the office-holders gather in the Holy Spirit as the representatives of their spirit-filled Churches, on whom the charism of the Holy Spirit has been bestowed in a special way, they represent at an ecumenical council by human convocation the *holiness* of the Church in a most excellent way.

Here an illuminating insight is given on how the different attributes of the Church reciprocally promote and include each other and how the problems surrounding the representation of the apostolic Church are also those surrounding the representation of the one, holy, catholic Church. If the office-holders credibly represent the apostolic

---

[1] Cyprian, *Ep.* 66,8; *CSCL* 3,2, 732. Thus various interpreters explain the "angels" of the seven Churches in the Apocalypse as the "bishops" who represent these congregations as persons: the bishops as representatives of their congregations; cf. also A. Wikenhauser, *Offenbarung des Johannes* (Regensburg 1949) 32f.

Church, they also represent the one, holy, catholic Church. And they represent the apostolic Church credibly only if at the same time they also credibly represent the one, holy catholic Church.

Therefore representation of the one, holy, catholic Church at an ecumenical council by human convocation depends—not exclusively, but decisively—on the office-holders. As difficult as it is to determine in concrete detail the relationship between office-holders and the congregation (the laity) with respect to an ecumenical council by human convocation, the following principle must nevertheless be upheld on the basis of our expositions: An ecumenical council that would be held *against* the office-holders would not be an ecumenical council; an overriding or an exclusion of office-holders by representatives of the laity (say, by granting the laics a greater number of votes) would be contrary to the very nature of an ecumenical council by human convocation which truly aims to represent the Church to which office-holders, as the ruling pastors, essentially belong.

(*b*) *Office and Congregation:* The pastors at an ecumenical council by human convocation thus represent the Church in a specifically qualified way. They co-represent the laity (indirect representation of the laity by pastors), whereas lay persons by themselves do not co-represent the pastors. Nevertheless in this day and hour of the laity we have become sensitive to the fact that an ecumenical council by human convocation is a representation of the *Church*, which just as essentially (although in the same way) consists of both *lay persons* and office-holders. Therefore a *perfect* representation of the Church also calls for a direct, not only an indirect, representation of the laity. Such a call—as we have seen—is not only important because of the position accorded to the congregation in the New Testament and especially in the account of the "Council of the Apostles," but is likewise supported by the very history of the first Christian synods as well as of the later councils (albeit in a changing degree).[2]

---

[2] J. Ratzinger, "Zur Theologie des Konzils," in *Militärseelsorge* 3 (1961) 8–23, does not do justice to the very complex finding of the New Testament as well as of Conciliar history that has been pointed to. He involuntarily falls victim to a narrowing when he limits the collegiality of the *Church* to the collegiality of the *bishops*, and on this basis, suggests that my outline of a theology of ecumenical councils (cf. *Tübinger Theologische Quartalschrift* 141 [1961] 50–77) requires the insertion of a "connecting link" *between* the Church and an ecumenical council by human convocation. Ratzinger admits: "The lawfulness of the existence of the Church as such at the same time constitutes the lawfulness of the existence of the council. Thereby what is essential and correct is seen in fact. The Church as a whole is God's holy assembly in the world, and a council stands under the basic law, under which God had placed his people as a whole" (p. 13). We

also agree that the Church is structured "hierarchically" and that the collegiality of the bishops belongs to the nature of the Church as the apostolic Church, and that consequently it must absolutely be recognized at an ecumenical council by human convocation. (This has already been worked out clearly in the above-mentioned outline, cf. *op cit.* 70–77). But it is not only a question of dealing seriously only with the collegiality of the bishops and to overlook the collegiate character of the congregation as well as of the whole Church. Ratzinger rightly says: "According to its nature, the apostolic Church is structured along the lines of collegiality." What is not correct is the meaning he attaches to it: that it is a question *only* of the collegiality of the bishops. It is not correct that the "Church is and remains the apostolic Church only by virtue of this collegiality (of the bishops)" (15). The Church is and remains the apostolic Church by virtue of the collegiality of the entire Christian people. In regard to the realization of collegiality, Ratzinger says: "It has actually happened since earliest times that the bishops have come together, they have met one another as a college and thus have practised their communal fellowship concretely. *This coming together, however, we call a council*" (p. 15). The answer thereto is that precisely since "earliest times" not only have the bishops come together, but other members of the congregation participated with the bishops (often the whole congregation). They met in council with the bishops as a college and in this way have practised the communal fellowship (on different levels, but real) of *all* Christians. Here also the Acts of the Apostles, like the histories of the first Christian synods, provides an impressive picture and warns us against setting up later notions of the (often largely clericalized) Church as absolute. It belongs specifically to the nature of the college of apostles that it stands in organic connection with the congregation, but in the calling and in the imitation of the Lord. Here too it is narrowing to say exclusively of the college of apostles: "As such (*collegium*) they (the twelve) after Pentecost also constitute the first 'structure' of the Church" (p. 14). The first structure precisely of the primitive Church was constituted specifically by the college of apostles *and* the congregation. The strength of the college of twelve lay in the fact that at the command of the Apostles it did not raise itself autonomously above the congregation, but instead undertook its special *ministering* functions in and with the congregation. For further clarification of this answer compare the section on apostolic succession and the exposition which follows in this section on office and congregation. Here, meanwhile, we shall make the following brief remarks on Ratzinger's position: (*a*) The description of the Church as "the living presence of the Word of God in the world" (p. 9) is at least undifferentiated in its disregard of the essential confrontation of the Word of *God* and the Church made up of *human beings:* almost the same applies to the description of the Church as the "simple presence of the divine Word and the Body of Jesus Christ" (p. 13). Such definitions provide unnecessary pretexts for the objection that Catholic theology simply identifies the Church with her glorified Lord and overlooks the Church's human, all too human, misery. (*b*) On this basis one will also find the obvious deduction of the infallibility of the Church on the basis of the infallibility of the Word of God too simple and too undifferentiated: "For on the basis of the fact that the Church is the presence of the Divine Word and with it of the divine truth in this world, her infallibility in principle is completely self-evident." (p. 9). Therewith the actual problem is passed over, How, namely, the *human* word of the Church, which as such is able only to bear witness to the Word of God, can lay claim to the infallibility of the *divine* Word proclaimed by the human word? It would have to be shown: That the divine Word proclaims itself to be and to remain eschatologically victorious, and that it, itself, therefore creates and preserves the right hearing of this Word: that the message of Christ truly overcomes disbelief and heresy and thus creates the Church and, indeed, the tangible

Congregations and offices are mutually dependent. Neither congregations without offices nor offices without congregations constitute the Church. Neither should the office be raised above the congregations in a self-glorifying, autonomous way (this would be the absolutism of ecclesiastical office and the dissolution of the one Church)—nor should the office be overwhelmed by the congregations (that would be a radical sectarian democracy and likewise a dissolution of the one Church). Rather, the office under the Lord in the congregation must serve it in the proclamation of the Word, the administration of the Sacraments, and the direction of the Church. Thus the congregation and the offices serving in it *together* constitute the great ecumenical council of the Church. Thus the Church is over and over again (although not in the same way) built anew from above and from below—from above through the Holy Spirit of Jesus Christ and His gifts (to which through the Word and the Sacrament the office also belongs) and from below through the actively loving "Yea" of believers (to whom the office-holders also belong). The Church of Jesus Christ as the great assembly of all those who believe in Him exists in the personal polarity of the congregation and the office-holder. *Both* constitute the *essential structure* of the Church in which Church life is conducted—more or less imperfectly.

Two misunderstandings therefore have to be ruled out: (1) that which regards the congregation as preceding the office in time (we have seen quite clearly that the office is not a free democratic institution established by the community), and (2) that which regards the office as preceding the congregation in time. According to the Gospels and the Acts of the Apostles, even the primitive community had not simply been called into being by the apostles but apostolic college and community were both called into being by Christ. Thus in the post-apostolic age, too, the congregation was not simply called into being by the office-holders. The office-holders also had of course to be believers and, as such, *members* of the congregation with the rest of

Church of the truly faithful. The "infallibility of its binding teaching office first becomes understandable *to us*, if, of course, the Spirit effects the permanence of right understanding, precisely through the fact that He endows right teaching with a commission and assistance. (*c*) The ecumenical council by human convocation is more than a "council meeting" (p. 13); one may not view a gathering in the Holy Spirit merely as an organizational act. (*d*) In connection with the statement, elaborated in detail in my article in the *Tübinger Theologischen Quartalschrift:* "The whole Church appears as a great council of God in the world." Ratzinger refers to his own article: "Offenbarung-Schrift-Überlieferung" ("Revelation-Scripture-Tradition") in *Trierer Theologische Zeitschrift* 67 (1958) 13–27. The *Church* as "council," however, is not discussed in the latter.

the other Christians in order to hold an office. They too must *before* any teaching, be hearers in faith of the word of the Gospel, in which the Holy Spirit of Jesus Christ effects the work of salvation and creates the Church as the new people of God. They too *before* any official administration of the Sacraments must be *baptized* in faith and be reborn in this visible sign of grace and have been accepted into the people of God. No office-holder, therefore, can be a *dispenser* of the Gospel or of the Sacraments without previously having been a *receiver* of them. Karl Rahner correctly states: "It is indeed not as though the Church as the people of the redeemed and believers in Christ came into being only through the office merely recruited by officials like the followers of an ideology or members of an association who are herded together as a consequence of the proselytizing activities of its founding members. Thus the absolute, predetermining decision of God to create the Church as the community of believers, the redemption, and hence the objective sanctification of mankind in Jesus Christ and in His act of redemption, mankind as the consecrated people of God, all these precede in the same way the office and the individual believers. This divine act of salvation, which is the real reason for the Church, precedes both the human desire to socialization and the establishment of office, and likewise creates faith (at least among the office-holders to begin with) and office at one and the same time and links both factors into an ultimately inseparable unity. This can be seen in the fact that faith is oriented towards the common and ordered profession of this faith and derives from listening to the legitimate message from the lips of authorized messengers of the Gospel, and also in the fact that this ecclesiastical office has to converge only in a person (were he the pope himself) who is, at least in the sphere of public law, also one who professes the true faith. Thus faith and office can never completely fall apart (although for understandable reasons of juridical stability the authority of the individual office-holder in the Church is not dependent on his *inner* faith). Thereby, however, the office-holders are themselves necessarily believers, at least in the social sphere of the external profession of faith. In order to be office-holders they themselves belong to the believers who listen and obey. They and the people of the Church do not simply face each other as lords and subjects, as givers and receivers of orders. Both stand before God as believers *and* subjects; as those who share the same foundation— Jesus Christ and His act of redemption—and in His grace they are already one family of brothers and sisters, before, according to the will of Christ, this community of redemption and faith has branched out into the individual functions of the one Body of Christ. Whence have evolved the official charisms of teaching and ruling that are not allotted to each one in equal measure."[3]

With regard to ecclesiastical office (and with the institutional aspects of the Church in general) one must guard against abstract hypostatizing. It is precisely the important concepts of "structure" ("essence," "institution," and the like) and the fruitful conceptual distinction of "structure" and "life," which it is the great merit of Yves Congar to have applied to ecclesiology,[4] and which must not be misunderstood. It is not only the institutional features—besides the *depositum fidei* and the Sacraments, it is not only the hierarchy and the office—that should be reckoned as belonging to the structure, the essential texture of the Church, while the activities of the laity are relegated to the level of "life."[5] Office *and* community are essential as well as structural components of the Church. Therefore the institution may not be placed above or held up against the community in such a way that the very unity of the Church could be brought into question. This is what K. Mörsdorf fears: "Congar distinguishes between the Church as *institution* and as *community*. He designates the institution as something that 'stands before and above the faithful, before and above the communities which they constitute.' Congar sees in the institution the essential attribute of the Church, 'just as, for instance, as the picked troops, the service orders and the material constitute the substance of an army.' With the dual aspect of the Church as institution and community Congar combines two different principles of organization, the *hierarchical principle* and the *community principle*. It seems questionable to me that recourse must be had to contradictory principles of this kind in order to determine the place of lay persons in the Church, especially since at the same time it is not shown how the *unity* of the Church is to be preserved. The specific structural principle of the Church is that of unity of Head and Body. Both the Church as a whole and her separate communities are built according to this structural law. It is, however, not an institutional principle that confronts in advance the Church as community but a law of configuration inherent in the Church on the basis of her divine foundation. The Church is not partly an 'it' and partly a 'we' but a 'we' resting upon a divine foundation, the

---

[3] K. Rahner, "Zur Theologie des Konzils," in *Stimmen der Zeit* 87 (1961/62) 331.

[4] Especially in his work: *Lay People in the Church* (London 1957), but also already in *Vraie et fausse réforme dans l'Église* (Paris 1950).

[5] Cf. especially Y. Congar, *Lay People in the Church.*

new people of God living in an hierarchical order so as to bring about the kingdom of God on earth."[6]

(c) *The Ecumenical Task:* This whole chapter, dealing with the Church, council, and ecclesiastical office, has shown that in this sphere the Catholic Church as well as those Churches gathered in the World Council of Churches have a specific ecumenical task with respect to the reunion of separated Christians. This is the task of renewing the organization of the Church, which must be an order of unity within diversity, in the light of the New Testament and in the succession of the apostolic Church.

The specific task of the member Churches of the World Council of Churches concerns the function of office and thus the unity of the Church: The meetings of the World Council of Churches bear witness to the order of the apostolic Church to the extent that not only pastors but also the bearers of the free charisms and ministries are given abundant opportunities to express themselves. "It signifies a great richness that here the spiritual experiences and impulses, not only of the different Churches and countries but also of the different service spheres of evangelization, education, social work, political action, and the like, are assembled before the world for clarification, for exchange and for the common commitment to bear witness to Christ. Thus these gatherings are a representation of the community of offices and free charisms through which Christ manifests Himself before the world."[7] In connection with the position of ecclesiastical office in the Church, however, the assemblies of the World Council of Churches are far removed from the order of the apostolic Church. "The absence of the Lord's Supper already makes it clear that the ecumenical council of the Churches is not an ecclesiastical community of the New Testament. For the Church as the Body of Christ is built by the common reception of the sacramental Body of Christ. Separated Churches, which in part do not recognize each other as true Churches, pray, consult, and make decisions together in the assemblies of the World Council. This also means that in part these Churches also refuse recognition to the respective ecclesiastical offices. No doubt one must not underestimate the existing and steadily growing fellowship in Christ, but the divisions have not yet been breached and this certainly indicates that in each case one might bring into

[6] K. Mörsdorf, "Die Stellung der Laien in der Kirche," in *Revue de Droit Canonique* 10/11 (1960/61) 215f.
[7] E. Schlink, "Ökumenische Konzilien einst und heute," in his collection *Der kommende Christus und die kirchlichen Traditionen* (Göttingen 1961) 245.

question the participants as well as their common action."[8] Hence the reason also for the colourless character of many of the theological pronouncements of the World Council and the feeble authority of its decrees. This indicates the task that must be performed with respect to the function of office and of the unity of the Church. "The ecumenical council . . . would have to proceed from the incomplete and loose co-operation of the ecclesiastical offices of the different Churches to a reciprocal recognition and structuring of the same, whereby likewise the relationsip of the offices to the laity must be more clearly defined. By comparison the Roman Church has forcefully recognized the importance of this relationship and assigned specific responsibilities to laymen."[9] On this basis progress can also be made towards the necessary unity of worship, of Church organization, and of doctrine.

The specific ecumenical task of the *Catholic Church*, above all, is concerned with the function of the individual congregation and hence the manifoldness of the Church; the Catholic Church bears witness to the order of the apostolic Church to the extent that all her pastors can truly perform their authorized ministry and hence can provide effectively for the necessary unity of the Church in the faith, in the celebration of the Eucharist, and in the organization and direction of the Church. It is precisely an ecumenical council by human convocation that most impressively manifests this unity of the Catholic Church, or of the individual member Churches. Its theological pronouncements therefore are distinguished by their firmness and its decrees by the strength of their authority. Nevertheless one simultaneously notices in all spheres a very extensive uniformity and rigidity of doctrine, liturgy and Church organization, often experienced as oppressively totalitarian within as well as without the Church: a development that cannot claim to derive from the apostolic Church. At the modern councils of the Catholic Church particularly the manifold ministries and charisms of the laity and the lower clergy were mainly excluded although their functions were not contested in principle. Here too, then, the task to be performed with respect to the functions of the different ministers and gifts of the Spirit and of the universal priesthood of all believers and therefore of the whole catholic manifoldness of the Church becomes apparent. An ecumenical council in particular should consider the following: "Whether, and in what sense, and how, the pastors of the Church who assemble at a council have the duty (as it were, substantially democratic) to act in such a way that through their actions they may

8 *Ibid.* 250.　　　　　　　9 *Ibid.* 263.

represent the cause of all members of the one Church and that they may thereby act in the name of the people of the Church; whether they have the duty to pay attention, as it were, to the common good of the Church and thereby to the legitimate desires and tendencies of the people of the Church."[10] And above all, the question of the direct representation of the people, of the Church at a council, is to be given consideration: "If this substantial representation of the people is asserted by the hierarchy, it is thereby naturally not yet said that this fundamental representation cannot be expressed in different ways and carried out in the most varied forms for better *and* for worse. Still less is it denied that today also one could justifiably ponder on how and in what ways the influence of the people of the Church too could and should be made to prevail on an ecumenical council, which is altogether reconcilable with the divine constitution of the Church and the exclusive authority of the episcopate to rule. In this respect not every existing practice of the Church hierarchy need be equally ideal and equally adapted to the circumstances of the time.[11] On this basis progress could also be made towards the necessary variety of worship, Church organization, and doctrine.

These would be considerable advances towards reunion on both sides, in the light of the Gospel of Jesus Christ in the succession of the apostolic Church. But it is precisely through these efforts for a credible representation of the apostolic Church through office and community that an enormous difficulty repeatedly arises. To this we must now turn our attention.

[10] K. Rahner, "Zur Theologie des Konzils," in *Stimmen der Zeit* 87 (1961/1962) 330f.
[11] *Ibid.* 332.

VII

THE PETRINE OFFICE IN CHURCH AND COUNCIL

1. THE REPRESENTATION OF THE OFFICE OF PETER

ALL difficulties of a theological-dogmatic and practical-existential character that stand in the way of the reunion of separated Christians *and* in the way of a general council of the *whole* of Christendom converge and are rooted in the Petrine office. Here too lies the cardinal problem with respect to a *theology* of ecumenical councils. In connection with the ecumenical situation it often appears to us to be a problem with no hope of solution. "Whether one wants it or not, the primacy of the Pope stands out like a stumbling block on the road which ought to lead Christians, who sincerely yearn for unity, to Rome. The irony of fate: He who is the foundation of the Church sees himself charged with being mainly responsible for the continuation of the split among Christians! We must not be over-hasty in trying to come to terms with this paradoxical situation."[1]

All Christians outside the Catholic Church, even when they are motivated by good will and the best intentions, decidedly reject a Petrine office. Even those who are still in favour of the primacy of *Peter* are, notwithstanding, decidedly against the primacy of the *pope*. The problem of the Petrine office cannot be broached in its full extent here. The difficulties stretch from exegesis by way of the history of the Church, of Church constitution, and of dogma up to the present-day concrete presentation and exercise of the Petrine office. The whole discussion is overburdened by historical experiences and hardships, by anti-Protestant and anti-Roman emotions, by a host of extratheological factors. As long as all this is not at least to a certain extent cleared up, the exegetic and dogmatic discussions will make very limited progress. What, for the time being, are we expecting from our Protestant, Orthodox, Anglican, and Old Catholic partners in the dialogue is one thing above all—prudence and restraint in judgments. The Reformed theologian J.-L. Leuba has correctly put

[1] G. Dejaifve, "Der Erste unter den Bischöfen. Über den Zusammenhang von Primat und Bischofskollegium," in *Theologie und Glaube* 51 (1961) 2.

it as follows: "The Protestant Christian will not expect the abolition of the teaching office of the *pope*, that is, of the ecclesiastical structure, in accordance with which the teaching office has a crucial central position. And this again not just because such an abolition could happen only by a miracle, by which the Roman Catholic Church would cease to be her essential self, but because the Protestant consciousness is not yet at all in the position to pronounce a valid judgment as to whether a visible head of the Church is or is not an essential component of the divinely willed structure of the Church. There are, as is well known, certain Protestant Christians who are convinced that the question as to whether the Church should have a visible centre is not yet solved. The difficulty, however, consists in the fact that the question as to whether the existence of this centre, as such, is willed by God, is closely bound up with the question of *how* the centre, which up to now has claimed that it is this centre, has conducted itself. In this connection the rigidity of the Roman Catholic Church since the Reformation has made it difficult for Protestant Christians to see the justification of the papacy as such. On the other hand, Protestant Christians cannot conceive of what Christendom would be, what they themselves would be, if the Papal Church did not exist: for they have in fact been living in a state of constant discussion with the papal Church. And every debate means that one receives something of a decisive character from the other party to the discussion."[2]

Of special interest in this context is the declaration that accompanied Melanchthon's signature to the Smalcald Articles: "I, Philip Melanchthon, hold the articles above also to be true and Christian. As regards the pope, however, for the sake of the peace and the community of those Christians, even if they are also under him, and would like to be under him in the future, if he will admit the Gospel, I hold him to be superior to bishops, a superiority which he has by human law, which should also be admitted and granted by us."[3] Does it not follow from this passage, as even seems suggested by texts of the young Luther, that the original opposition of the Reformation was directed less against a Petrine office as an institution based on canon law than against the "claim to power" and the "heresy" of the papacy? Such a position would not be as far removed from that of the Eastern Church as it seems to be in view of Luther's utterances on the pope as Antichrist.

[2] J.-L. Leuba, "Was erwarten evangelische Christen vom ökumenischen Konzil?" in *Ökumenische Rundschau* 9 (1960) 80f.

[3] *Die Bekenntnisschriften der evangelisch-lutherischen Kirche* (Göttingen ⁴1959) 463f.

Accordingly our Catholic task—unconcerned about the outcome of the debate—is to present the Petrine office credibly again in order to make a meaningful exegetic and dogmatic dialogue possible or, in any case, to facilitate it. It is of little help to boast about such titles as "successor of Peter" and even "the vicar of Christ" *vis-à-vis* Christians outside the Catholic Church. In these titles Protestant Christians can see only high-flown claims without a correspondingly credible "proof of the spirit and of power." "Roman apparatus" and "Roman system," external unevangelical pomp and power, Byzantine court ceremonial, baroque forms of expression, and abso-lutist methods of governing make it very difficult for the Christians separated from us to recognize the fisherman of Galilee again in the pope, who claims to be his successor. The great tasks of Church renewal also present themselves here. Everything would depend on the Petrine office again being exemplarily set forth in a new, *credible* way—credible especially in accordance with the binding model of the Lord, whose sheep he should tend, and of Peter, in the line of whose humble, spiritual succession the office aims to stand. Thereby it would make it credible to people who do not approach a Petrine office in the Church from a secular point of view but from the Gospel of Jesus Christ.[4]

Such unrest about this credibility presents itself as a *new* task over and over again. The concept of credibility, to be sure, implies a relation to new people placed in ever-new historical situations with an ever-changing mentality. Credibility that is more than a possi-bility of recognizing the papal claims in a theoretical-abstract way thereby becomes a task ever to be fulfilled anew and, indeed, each time in a different way. An Alexander VI would certainly not be "credible" for the people of our time with respect to his claim to

[4] Recent Catholic literature on the question of the Petrine office: O. Karrer, *Um die Einheit der Christen. Die Petrusfrage* (Frankfurt 1953); "Apostolische Nachfolge und Primat," in *Fragen der Theologie heute* (Einsiedeln 1957) 175–190; "Das Petrusamt in der Frühkirche," in *Festgabe für J. Lortz* (Baden-Baden 1957), I, 507–525; R. Grosche and H. Asmussen, *Brauchen wir einen Papst? Ein Ges-präch zwischen den Konfessionen* (Cologne–Olten 1957); K. Rahner and J. Ratzinger, *The Episcopate and the Primacy* (London 1962). For works based on exegesis: J. Ludwig, *Die Primatsworte Mt 16 in der altkirchlichen Exegese* (Münster 1952); P. Gaechter, *Petrus und seine Zeit* (Innsbruck 1958); J. Schmid, "Petrus 'der Fels' und die Petrusgestalt der Urgemeinde," in *Begegnung der Christen. Festschrift O. Karrer* (Stuttgart–Frankfurt a. M. ²1960) 347–359; K. Hofstetter, *Das Petrusamt in der Kirche des 1–2 Jahrhunderts: Jerusalem-Rome* (*ibid.*) 373–389; J. Betz, "Christus-Petra-Petrus," in *Kirche und Überlieferung, Festschrift R. Geiselmann* (Freiburg i. Br. 1960) 1–21; F. Obrist, *Echtheitsfragen und Deutung der Primatstelle Mt 16, 18f. in der deutschen protestantischen Theologie der letzten 30 Jahre* (Münster 1961).

primacy. Despite the continuity of a recognizability *in principle* of his claim to primacy, he would provoke so many hindrances in people with respect to the *factual* recognition of his claim that with moral certainty one could say that the majority of non-Catholics (and perhaps of Catholics too), with no moral culpability to themselves, would not in fact comprehend the justification of his claim. At the same time it is not to be overlooked that a pope can obscure this credibility also without any actual personal culpability.

We must not expect everything all at once from the elucidation of the Petrine office. Great steps towards the evangelical renewal of the Petrine office have been made since the Renaissance-popes of Luther's time, up to the rulers of the Church State at the time of the First Vatican Council and finally up to the pastoral popes of the twentieth century. But it would be arrogant to believe we have come to the end of the programme of renewal. Great tasks still await us, to which theology must make its contribution. Its task is to circumscribe the position of the Petrine office exactly and carefully within the structure of the Church in terms of the New Testament and early traditions.

Despite all their objective correctness the notable weakness of the Vatican definitions with respect to the position of the pope in the Church is that they talk more in juridical than in biblical terms, that they speak in a marginal way of that which, according to the message of the New Testament, stands in the very centre of things—namely, that the Petrine office in the first place is a *ministry* in the Church and only on this basis is it an "authority" in the Church (but not *over* the Church). The Petrine office in the last resort should be concerned not with its rights, authority, and power but with ministering to the brethren: "For one is your Master, and *all* you are brothers" (Mt. 23:8). The special ministry of the Petrine office is the ministry of strengthening the faith, of charity, and of pastoral care for the unity of the Church.[5]

One could entertain the opinion that to a great extent we are still in the initial stages as regards a new ecumenical consideration of the true significance of the Petrine office in the Church, both in non-Catholic and in Catholic spheres, and here at a theoretical as well as at a practical level. No office in the Church bears the weight of its traditions as heavily as does this very office. It is very difficult to distinguish what really is essential and what is not essential to it. Not everything that one attributes to the "papacy" today is necessarily an essential component of the "Petrine office." The more the

[5] Cf. H. Küng, *The Council and Reunion* (London 1961).

"office of Peter" again comes to expression in the "papacy," the more will it gain, the more it will become credible.

This chapter is concerned with a segment only of the whole problem of the Petrine office; namely, with the relationship between pope and council, or between pope and Church.

This formulation of the question already presupposes that a council has something to do with the Petrine office. This results directly from the fact, which we Catholics believe, that the *Church* according to Matthew 16:18f; Luke 22:32; John 21:15–19, and according to the attestation of the Acts of the Apostles and the events of Church history has—and still has today—something to do with the Petrine office. According to the Catholic understanding of the faith Christ founded the Church on the rock of the Petrine office (and also the apostolic office)—the ecumenical council by divine convocation. If an ecumenical council by human convocation truly aims to represent the ecumenical council by divine convocation, it accordingly must reflect the basic structure of the Church and therefore make present—in whatever form—the Petrine office.

According to the Catholic view of the faith, the following, therefore, is valid: In the ecumenical council by divine convocation, which is the Church, the Petrine office has the special task of representing and guaranteeing the unity of the Church in the service of charity, of strengthening the faith, and of pastoral care. In this sense a special position must be ascribed in principle to the Petrine office also at ecumenical councils by human convocation.

But precisely here we are confronted with great difficulties: What does this mean concretely? The Councils of Nicaea, of Constance, and of the Vatican were all genuine ecumenical councils. Consequently, according to the Catholic assumption, there must have been an authentic representation of the Petrine office at all three. But how very different was this representation at these three ecumenical councils! Hence one can see that the representation of what the Petrine office implies at an ecumenical council by human convocation cannot be decided in a few words. And precisely with respect to the reunion of separated Christians it is a matter of pressing urgency today to investigate theologically what is essentially necessary to the representation of the Petrine office and what is time-conditioned. In the introductory chapter it was established that a *binding theology* of ecumenical councils cannot be simply deduced from the present regulations of the *Codex Iuris Canonici*. Yet it is *possible* that these regulations may contain a theology of ecumenical councils that is in fact binding. We shall begin our considerations precisely here.

2. THE PRIMACY AND ITS LIMITS
AT THE FIRST VATICAN COUNCIL

The towering importance of ecumenical councils by human convocation, which represent the Church, is set forth by Canon 228, § 1:
"An ecumenical council holds supreme power over the universal
Church." But another canon manifestly competes with this canon.
Canon 218, § 1, reads: "The Roman Pontiff, the successor to the
primacy of Saint Peter, not only has the primacy of honour but the
supreme and full juridical power over the universal Church in regard
to faith and morals as well as in what pertains to discipline and government of the Church which is spread through the whole world.
§ 2. This power is truly episcopal power, ordinary and immediate,
over each and every individual church as well as over each and every
one of the pastors and faithful, and independent of any human
authority."

According to the view of the Catholic Church, doubtless this canon
is not only concerned with a factual and practical legal principle (as,
for instance, with the right of convocation or the determination of
the agenda). For behind it stands the dogma of the First Vatican
Council of the primacy of the pope. This dogma (along with that of
papal infallibility) is vehemently rejected by all non-Catholics; for
many of them it was the reason why they did not believe in any new
council in the Catholic Church. It is necessary to keep the exact
text of the definition of primacy before us (we shall quote the important passages here): "And so We teach and declare that, in the
disposition of the Lord, the Roman Church holds the pre-eminence
of *ordinary* power over all the other churches; and that this power of
jurisdiction of the Roman Pontiff, which is truly *episcopal*, is *immediate*. Regarding this jurisdiction, pastors and faithful, of whatever rite and dignity, individually and collectively, are bound by a
duty of hierarchical subordination and of sincere obedience, and this
not only in matters that pertain to faith and morals, but also in
matters that pertain to the discipline and government of the Church
throughout the whole world. When, therefore, this bond of unity
with the Roman Pontiff is guarded both in community and in the
profession of the same faith, then the Church of Christ is one flock
under one supreme shepherd. This is the doctrine of Catholic truth;
and no one can deviate from this without losing his faith and his
salvation."[6] And the canon added by the Council reads: "And so, if
anyone says that the Roman Pontiff has only the office of inspection

[6] Denz. 1827.

or direction, but not the *full* and *supreme* power of *jurisdiction* over the *whole* Church, not only in matters that pertain to faith and morals, but also in matters that pertain to the discipline and government of the Church throughout the whole world, or if anyone says that he has only a more important part and not the complete *fullness* of this supreme power; or if anyone says that this power is not *ordinary* and *immediate* either over each and every Church or over each and every one of the pastors and the faithful: let him be anathema."[7]

From the theological standpoint, does this leave any scope for an ecumenical council? For an ecumenical council that is more than an advisory or an applauding organ of the pope? Are there any limits at all to the *potestas iurisdictionis episcopalis suprema plena, ordinaria, immediata, universalis* of the Pope?

The definition of papal doctrinal infallibility has very exactly circumscribed the conditions of the exercise of the infallible teaching office and thereby limited it to very clearly ascertainable cases. With the definition of the jurisdiction of the *primacy* the conditions of its exercise have not been more closely circumscribed. No doubt this has had negative effects. Even before the proclamation of the Second Vatican Council, E. Amann correctly wrote the following at the end of his long article on the First Vatican Council in the *Dictionnaire de Théologie Catholique*: "If there was one point in which a certain change was produced by the fact of the Council, regarding the position of the sovereign pontiff in relation to the Church, it occurred rather in the realm of pontifical primacy. The concentration of the struggle around the question of infallibility had masked the importance of the famous chapter III of the constitution *Pater aeternus*. By declaring the jurisdiction of the pope over each of the Churches 'ordinary, immediate, episcopal,' the Vatican Council certainly was making no innovation. Since the time of Gregory VII, the popes had claimed, sometimes with an energy that was extraordinary, this quasi-absolute and quasi-discretionary power over the episcopate. The great debates of the fifteenth and sixteenth centuries had led to the withdrawal of these ideas. For the reason that they had been only slightly reinforced at the beginning of the nineteenth century, they did not recover the force which they had had in the times of the 'pontifical monarchy.' Now there was a return to it. The years which followed the Council were to lead to a strengthening of the direct action of the pope in the dioceses and, let us not mince matters, to pontifical centralization. The problem of reconciling the divine rights of the episcopate with the divine rights of the pope unfortunately

[7] Denz. 1831.

could not come up for discussion. A well-balanced theology of the Church, nevertheless, demands that this question be posed, just as practical life requires that its application be regulated. Will this be the work of a Vatican Council II? This is the secret of the future."[8]

They particularly neglected to set forth just how the ordinary, immediate, episcopal power of the *pope* can be united with the ordinary and immediate power of the *bishops*. Indeed only the *first* dogmatic constitution on the Church of Christ was completed. The position, rights, and duties of the bishops were to have constituted the subject matter of a further *Constitutio*. As we know, it never followed because of the forced and sudden break-up or breaking-off of the Council. Nevertheless both the discussions and the definitions of the *Constitutio prima* provide us with valuable suggestions, which we shall utilize in the pages that follow.[9]

In the *Deputatio Fidei* there was opposition to the formulation of any kind of "limit" to the fullness of the pope's authority. It was still a matter of eradicating every form of Gallicanism. Despite this, one could not avoid admitting a limitation of the full authority in fact. For, according to the view of the Council, the pope no doubt possesses the fullness, and not only a part, of the ecclesiastical pastoral authority. But this authority is neither absolute nor arbitrary.

---

[8] E. Amann, "Concile du Vatican," in *Dictionnaire de Théologie Catholique* (Paris 1950) XV, 2583.

[9] On the discussions of the question of primacy at the Vatican Council, cf: U. Betti, "Natura e portata del Primato del Romano Pontefice secondo il Concilio Vaticano," in *Antonianum* 34 (1959) 161–244, 369–408; "La perpetuitá del primato di Pietro nei Romani Pontefici secondo il Concilio Vaticano," in *Divinitas* 3 (1959) 95–145; *La Costituzione Dommatica 'Pastor aeternus' del Concilio Vaticano I* (Rome 1961); R. Aubert, "L'ecclésiologie au Concile du Vatican," in *Le concile et les conciles* (Paris 1960) 245–284; G. Dejaifve, "Le premier des évêques," in *Nouvelle Revue théologique* 82 (1960) 561–579; "Conciliarité au concile du Vatican," in *Nouvelle Revue théologique* 82 (1960) 785–802; *Pape et évêques au premier Concile du Vatican* (Paris 1961); J. Leclerc, "L'oeuvre ecclésiologique du Concile du Vatican," in *Études* 302 (1960) 289–306; A. Chavasse, "L'ecclésiologie au Concile du Vatican, L'infaillibilité de l'Église," in *L'ecclesiologie au XIX siècle* (Paris 1960) 233–245; W. F. Dewan, "Preparation of the Vatican Council's Schema on the Power and Nature of the Primacy," in *Ephemerides theologicae Lovanienses* 36 (1960) 23–56; J. Hamer, "Note sur la collégialite épiscopale," in *Revue des sciences philosophiques et théologiques* 44 (1960) 40–50; "Le corps épiscopale uni au Pape, son autorité dans l'Église d'après les documents du premier concile du Vatican," in *Revue des sciences philosophiques et théologiques* 45 (1961) 21–31; G. Thils, *Primauté pontificale et prérogatives épiscopales. "Potestas ordinaria" au concile du Vatican* (Louvain 1961); "Parlera-t-on des évêques au concile?" in *Nouvelle Revue théologique* 93 (1961) 785–804; J. P. Torrel, *La théologie de l'épiscopat au premier Concile du Vatican* (Paris 1961); W. Kasper, "Primat und Episkopat nach dem Vatikanum I," in *Tübinger Theologische Quartalshcrift* 142 (1962) 47–83.

The authority of the pope is *not absolute*. Even the reporter of the one-sidedly composed Deputation on Faith, Bishop Zinelli, in a reply to an objection of the Melchite Patriarch of Antioch admitted: "If (the patriarch) understands that it is not absolutely monarchical because the form of Church-government was instituted by the divine founder himself and that even ecumenical councils could not abolish this form, he is certainly right. And no one who is sane can say that either the pope or the ecumenical council can destroy the episcopate and the other things determined by divine law in the Church."[10]

The authority of the pope is *not arbitrary*. Earlier, in the preparatory commission for theological-dogmatic questions, it was pointed out that in the formulation of the definition of primacy care should be taken so that the slanderous conclusion could not be drawn: ". . . that we, while asserting the free and independent authority of the Roman Pontiff, make it thereby arbitrary."[11] According to the Catholic conception, what Bishop Vérot wanted to strengthen through a condemnation, was so obvious as to need no "anathema sit": "If someone says that the authority of the Roman Pontiff in the Church be so full that he could dispose of all things according to his own will, let him be anathema," [12]

Thus there are "limits" also to papal authority. Even the reporter of the Deputation on Faith, Bishop Bartholomaeus d'Avanzo, spoke of a double "*limitatio*" in connection with the Petrine primacy: "Therefore does anyone say or has it been said, that in Peter inhered an all-embracing and full power without any limitation? Its limitation is twofold: one active, so to speak, and the other, passive."[13] The "active" limitation of the primacy comes from Christ: "Therefore Peter has as much power as Christ the Lord has given to him, not for the destruction, but for the building up of the body of Christ that is the Church."[14] And the "passive" limitation comes through Christ by way of the apostles: ". . . Christ himself designated the workmen whom Peter would use to build the Church, that is, the apostles present there. Peter was constituted the teacher in the second

---

[10] Mansi 52, 1114; cf. M. Schmaus, *Katholische Dogmatik* (Munich ⁵1958) III/I, 490: "The pope for his part is bound by the ordinance of Christ and also by the canon law promulgated by him."

[11] Mansi 49, 666f.

[12] Mansi 52, 591; cf. M. Schmaus, *op. cit.* III/1, 492: "The pope is bound to the will of Christ. He cannot do what he wills, he must do what Christ wills. The will of Christ aims at furthering the rule of God and the salvation of man bound up with it. By binding himself to the will of Christ in the execution of his power and by realizing the latter, the pope serves the furtherance of divine rule and thus of the salvation of man."

[13] Mansi 52, 715.   [14] Mansi 52, 715.

text in order to strengthen the others. But these others cannot be different from those whom Christ himself gave to Peter as brothers in the apostleship: strengthen your brothers; and he himself has chosen them as brothers: go to my brothers"[15] (whereby this limitation, however, means less a limitation than a support of the pope). Even in his decisive exposition before the voting, Bishop Zinelli, the reporter of the Deputation on Faith, spoke of a "*coarctatio*" of the fullness of papal authority: ". . . from all these sources of revelation it is clear that to Peter and his successors was given the truly full and supreme power in the Church, full in that it cannot be forced by any human power superior to her but only by natural and divine law."[16]

What are the concrete limits to the fullness of papal authority that are drawn by "divine law" in addition to all the limits of "natural law"?

(a) *The existence of the episcopate,* which the pope can neither abolish nor dissolve in its position or in its rights: "No one who is sane can say that either the pope or the ecumenical council can destroy the episcopate and the other things determined by divine law in the Church."[17] Therefore the Council too, following directly upon the definition of the ordinary and immediate episcopal jurisdiction of the pope, defined the ordinary and immediate episcopal jurisdiction of the bishops: "This power of the Supreme Pontiff is far from standing in the way of the power or *ordinary* and *immediate episcopal jurisdiction* by which the bishops who, under *appointment of the Holy Spirit, succeeded in the place of the apostles,* feed and rule individually, as *true shepherds,* the particular flock assigned to them. Rather this latter power is asserted, confirmed, and vindicated by this same supreme and universal shepherd in the words of St. Gregory the Great: 'My honour is the honour of the whole Church. My honour is the solid strength of my brothers. I am truly honoured when due honour is paid to each and every one.' "[18] This definition was meant to be the answer to certain fears of the bishops, as the reporter Zinelli declared: ". . . In order to satisfy the hundred-times-repeated objections of those who fear that by ascribing to the Roman pontiff real episcopal power, ordinary and immediate over each single diocese, the power of the individual bishop would be destroyed, the contrary had to be stated clearly, therefore. in the Vatican Council in order to rule out any wrong interpretation."[19]

---

[15] Mansi 52, 715.　　　　　　　[16] Mansi 52, 1108f.
[17] Mansi 52, 1114.　　　　　　　[18] Denz, 1828.
[19] Mansi 52, 1311.

The pope's power of jurisdiction was described as "truly episcopal" by the Council.[20] On the motion of Bishop Senestrey this term was later inserted into the schema in order to declare *vis-à-vis* certain teachings, that the pope's authority is not limited—as is also pronounced in the canon—to an office of inspection or direction but that it is a genuine jurisdictional authority. Nevertheless the pope is the "pastor supremus," while the bishops too are "veri pastores."[21] Thus "potestas episcopalis" in no way means that the pope is bishop of every place and of every believer, but that he possesses the "potestas pascendi agnos et oves." Thus *potestas episcopalis* does not mean simply "episcopal authority" but general "pastoral authority."[22] Nevertheless, this pastoral authority directly concerns all as well as each one directly, and not only indirectly by way of the bishops. This was the reason why Passaglia's proposal, which appeared in an anonymous work, "La causa di Sua Em. il Cardinale Girolamo d'Andrea" (Turin 1867), to substitute "episcopalis" by "primatialis" was rejected. But the reporter of the Deputation on Faith, Bishop Pie, firmly maintained that "episcopalis" was tantamount to "pastoralis" in meaning.[23] He clarified the co-operation between pope and bishops with a passage from Thomas Aquinas: "It would be incongruous for two pastors to be placed in the same way over two flocks, hence for there to be two bishops in one diocese. But it would not be incongruous if two bishops were thus placed in different ways (*inaequaliter*), as is the case with pope, bishop, and parish priest. Two causes for the same order cancel each other out but not two causes which are subordinated to each other, as is the case with pope and bishops."[24] The later reporter also of the Deputation on Faith, Bishop Zinelli, asserted that "episcopalis" is tantamount to "pastoralis" in meaning.[25] Nevertheless he saw no need to replace the ambiguous word "episcopalis" by "pontificiae"[26] or by "suprema"[27] because this had already been adequately expressed.

Nevertheless Zinelli's explanations are not felt to be especially elucidating in terms of present-day perspectives.[28] Further, the variety of misunderstandings that were called forth by its publication show that the *Constitutio* had not paid sufficient attention to the difficulties. These misunderstandings induced the German episco-

---

[20] Denz. 1827.
[21] Denz. 1828.
[22] Mansi 52, 10.
[23] Mansi 52, 32.
[24] Mansi 52, 33.
[25] Mansi 52, 1104.
[26] Mansi 52, 584, 1106.
[27] Mansi 52, 599, 1106.
[28] Cf. R. Aubert, "L'ecclésiologie au concile du Vatican," in *Le concile et les conciles* (Paris 1960) 283; G. Thils, *Primauté pontificale et prérogatives épiscopales* (Louvain 1961) 7–78.

pate to issue the famous collective declaration that was approved in a
solemn form by Pope Pius IX as the authentic exposition of Catholic
doctrine and of the doctrine of the Vatican Council.[29] From this
declaration it emerges clearly that the primacy of the pope is limited
by the existence of the episcopate. Among other things the declaration asserts: The pope cannot lay claim to the rights of the bishops
nor substitute his authority for theirs. Episcopal authority has not
been absorbed into the papal; as a result of the decisions of the Vatican Council the pope does not hold the whole of the bishops' rights
in his hands; he has not in principle taken the place of each individual
bishop and cannot at any given moment take the place of the bishop
in relation to governments; they have not become the tools of the
pope and even in relation to governments are not the officials of a
foreign sovereign. Leo XIII also says of the bishops: ". . . and one
must not consider them as vicars of the Roman pontiffs, since they
hold power which is proper to them. . . ."[30]

The question of the transmission of episcopal jurisdiction belongs
here: Does it occur directly through God or does it occur directly
through the pope? The First Vatican Council left the question
open: ". . . Do not think we are defining the question that was so
agitated in the Council of Trent about the derivation of the jurisdiction of the bishops, which some derive immediately from the supreme
pontiff, others immediately from Christ."[31] Thus it is not surprising
that this question is a controversial one in Catholic theology up to
the present day. A solution must be found here which would not
impair the rights of the primacy (which are not questioned by any
Catholic theologians) but which, on the other hand, would not do
violence to the facts of history "dogmatically," that is, by unproved
postulates or deductions made on the basis of the primatial authority.[32] Some of the things that exist today, at least in the Latin Church

---

[29] Text in *Der Katholik N. F.* 33 (1875) 209–213; cf. Neuner and Roos, *Der
Glaube der Kirche in den Urkunden der Lehrverkündigung* (Regensburg ⁵1958)
245–248.

[30] Leo XIII, "Encyclical 'Satis cognitum,' " in *Acta Apostolicae Sedis* 28
(1895/96) 723.

[31] Mansi 52, 1109; cf. 52, 1110.

[32] G. Thils in this connection makes the following fundamental assertion:
"What cannot be accepted, at any rate, is the reduction of the duality of the subjects by the suppression of one of the elements, whether these theories are
asserted clearly or in a veiled way to the advantage of the bishop alone (episcopalism, conciliarism), or to the advantage of the pope alone (papalism), by
voiding the prerogatives of the one or the other of all authentic substance. Such
is the case, it seems, when it is stated that there is no juridical prerogative save that
'communicated by a council' or that there is no juridical prerogative of the epis-

(the transmission of jurisdiction by the pope), cannot be postulated as divine law without certain proof.[33]

This first point leads directly to a second:

(*b*) *The orderly exercise of office by the bishops*, which the pope— as another bishop as it were—may not disturb through daily interferences (the principle of subsidiarity). No doubt the pope has *immediate* authority over all believers, which allows him to exercise his jurisdiction over every believer without the permission and the intermediacy of the duly qualified bishop.[34] But the following is also valid: "Certainly, if the supreme pontiff, since he has the right to perform every true episcopal action in any diocese, were to multiply himself so to speak, and nullify in each day's decision without consideration of the bishop what the latter has wisely ordered, then he would use his power not for building but for destruction."[35]

The long discussions concerning the "ordinary authority" (*potestas ordinaria*) of the pope have made clear how this ambiguous term is to be understood and how it is not to be understood according to the general view of the Council Fathers.[36] The papal exercise of office in

copal body save that 'communicated by the pope.' " ("Parlera-t-on des évêques au concile?" in *Nouvelle Revue théologique* 93 [1961] 800.)

[33] G, Dejaifve rightly draws attention to the difficulties which crop up here in the light of early Church history, especially that of the East: "Nevertheless one may ask oneself whether this doctrine, which we may call Roman, aims to regard this privilege of the pope as an essential feature of his primacy or as something connected with a state of affairs grounded in the concrete circumstances in which the primacy of the Latin Church is exercised. There is in fact no doubt that in the East since time immemorial ordained bishops obtained the independent jurisdiction of their office through the ordination itself, a circumstance which recently has been again accepted in the new Eastern code of canon law. For the Eastern bishops it sufficed to announce their election and the canonical carrying out of their ordination by letter to their joint brethren in the episcopate with whom their Church was in continuous contact in order to be recognized as legitimate bishops in the Church. According to the Eastern view the consecrating bishops seemed to be acting as persons tacitly commissioned to perform this act by the Church, that is by the whole 'community.' Although in the beginning there was no neat distinction between power of orders and power of jurisdiction we can assume that the consecrating bishops, who were in communion with the great apostolic sees, believed themselves to be legally qualified to transmit all canonical powers inherent in the episcopal office on the ground of a participation *in solidum* in the apostolic authority whose heirs they themselves were through their ordination. As is well known, prior approval by Rome was never requested in this whole procedure. This is a proven fact, and the Roman Church has adapted herself to it down through the centuries, even when in the person of the pope she clearly emerged as the binding centre of ecclesiastical unity." ("Der Erste unter den Bischöfen," in *Theologie und Glaube* 51 [1961] 17f.)

[34] Mansi 52, 1105.   [35] Mansi 52, 1105.

[36] On this important question, cf. the excellent clarifying historical inquiry by G. Thils, *Primauté pontificale et prérogatives épiscopales* (Louvain 1961).

the dioceses does not only occur *extraordinarie*, that is, only in extraordinary cases in the sense of Joseph Valentin Eybel (d. 1805) and Pietro Tamburini (d. 1827), a view which the Council had in mind. On the other hand, neither does it occur—see the above quotation—*quotidie*, that is, daily, ordinarily, habitually. It occurs—thus does Thils carefully seek to circumscribe the median between *extraordinarie* and *quotidie* in traditional terminology[37]—*in peculiaribus adiunctis*; in a special situation, during a special difficulty, under circumstances which are marked by *special, unusual, or distinct* features (which from the outset does not signify "rare").

Thus, according to the Council, there exists a crucial difference between the "ordinary" exercise of office of the bishops and the "ordinary" exercise of office of the pope. With the *bishops*, according to the general conviction of the Council Fathers, "ordinarie" means the day-to-day, the current, the usual, habitual pastoral activity of the "veri pastores." With the *pope* "ordinarie" means only an "adnexum officio," "ratione muneris," of the "pastor supremus" in contradistinction to a merely "delegated" extraordinary full authority. Thus Bishop Zinelli, in the name of the Deputation on Faith just before the voting declared: "By all advisers in law and doctors of canon law and in all Church documents there is a distinction made between ordinary and delegated power. All hold that ordinary power is that which belongs to someone by reason of his office, office bestowed on someone, whereas delegated power is not derived from one's office but is exercised in the name of another person, in whom the power is ordinary. The words having been explained, the Deputation considers the matter finished: is not the power attributed to the supreme pontiff in him by virtue of his office? If it is by virtue of office, then it is ordinary."[38] Thus whereas the non-delegated or ordinary authority of the *bishops* in their dioceses (and of the Roman bishop in his own Roman diocese!) ought to be exercised *ordinarie* (habitually, day-to-day in normal circumstances), likewise the non-delegated or ordinary authority of the *pope* is to be exercised only in *peculiaribus adiunctis* (in special, particular, unusual circumstances, hence *non-ordinarie*).

The Deputation on Faith made the following observation in regard to the improved schema "De Ecclesia Christi": "The supreme and universal shepherd and the subordinate and particular ones do not exclude one another; on the contrary, far from the power of the subordinate pastors being hindered by the supreme pontifical power, the lower pastors' power will rather be stabilized, strengthened, and

[37] Cf. G. Thils, *op. cit.* 98f.   [38] Mansi 52, 1105.

protected; and vice versa; the power of the supreme shepherd will not be hampered but will be fostered and affirmed by this power of the subordinate pastors."[39] The pope's duty is not only to impede, to suppress, or to override the orderly exercise of office of the bishops but, instead, to preserve and to promote it.

Is there a *criterion* with respect to the exercise of the papal pastoral office in the individual dioceses? In its militant anti-Gallican position the First Vatican Council was, understandably enough, not too interested beyond that which already has been said. Nevertherless post-Vatican theology developed a criterion: This is the *principle of subsidiarity* which, according to Pius XII, "is valid for social life in all its organizations, and also for the life of the *Church* without prejudice to her hierarchical structure."[40] What the individual can accomplish on his own power should not be done by the community, and what the subordinated community accomplishes should not be done by the superordinated community. The community must respect the individual, the superordinated community, the subordinated community. One could not formulate it more clearly than did Pius XI in the Encyclical *Quadragesimo Anno*: "It is, indeed, true as history clearly proves that owing to the change in social conditions, much that was formerly done by small bodies can nowadays be accomplished only by large corporations. Nonetheless, just as it is wrong to withdraw from the individual and commit to the community at large what private enterprise and industry can accomplish, so too is it an injustice, a grave evil and a disturbance of right order for a larger and higher organization to arrogate to itself functions which can be performed efficiently by smaller and lower bodies. This is a fundamental principle of social philosophy, unshaken and unchangeable and it retains its full truth today. Of its very nature the true aim of all social activity should be to help individual members of the social body, but never to destroy or absorb them."[41]

What, according to Pius XI, applies in the secular sphere to the relationship between the organizations of the highest level (the State) and organizations of a lower level is also applicable in the ecclesiastical sphere to the relationship between the Petrine and the episcopal offices, thus: "The state should leave to these smaller groups the settlement of questions of minor importance. It will thus

[39] Mansi 52, 11f; cf. also Denz. 1962.

[40] Pius XII, "Address to the Newly Appointed Cardinals," in *Acta Apostolicae Sedis* 38 (1946) 14f.

[41] Pius XI, "Encyclical 'Quadragesimo Anino,' " in *Acta Apostolicae Sedis* (1931) 203.

carry out with greater freedom, power, and success the tasks belonging to it, because it alone can effectively accomplish these, directing,
watching, stimulating and restraining, as circumstances suggest or
necessity demands. Let those in power, therefore, be convinced that
the more faithfully this principle be followed, and a graded hierarchical
order exist between the various 'subsidiary' organizations, the more
excellent will be both the authority and the efficiency of the social
organization as a whole and more prosperous the conditions of the
State."[42]

The principle of subsidiarity as a formulated legal principle is
of recent date.[43] The requirement formulated along with it, however,
has behind it not only Catholic tradition, especially of the first
millennium, but especially the still-binding model of the apostolic
Church. This model clearly excludes—what is possible even when the
episcopate is maintained in principle—a factual voiding of the
apostolic office of the bishop and the position of the faithful. A
monarchic-absolutist or even a dictatorial-totalitarian Church hierarchy is impossible according to the New Testament.[44] According to
the New Testament model it is manifestly not the meaning of the
Petrine guidance to accomplish all the tasks of the Church as far as
possible by its own activity (or by the activity of a bureaucratic
apparatus). Rather, its meaning is to make possible and to ensure by
its ministry the full efficacy of all the members of the Church, of the
bishops, priests, and lay persons. The Petrine office therefore may
never, like a totalitarian state, lay claim to attending to everything,
or at least to be empowered by law to attend to everything. This would
be a fateful misunderstanding of the Vatican definitions. Rather, the
principle of subsidiarity requires that the Petrine office leave to the
bishops, priests, and the people all that which can be carried out on
their own responsibility, whereby bishops, priests and people do not
require the co-operation of the Petrine office as such; and at the same
time it promotes the greatest possible participation in the direction
of the Church by bishops, priests, and the people.[45]

[42] Pius XI, *op. cit.* in *Acta Apostolicae Sedis* 23 (1931) 203 cf. also O. v. Nell-
Breuning and H. Sacher, *Zur christlichen Staatslehre* (Freiburg i. Br. 1948) 4,
53, 74, 96, 104; J. Messner, *Das Naturrecht. Handbuch der Gesellschaftsethik,
Staatsethik und Wirtschaftsethik* (Innsbruck–Vienna 1950) 199–202.

[43] On the application of the principle of subsidiarity to the Church cf. W.
Bertrams, "De principio subsidiaritatis in iure canonico," in *Periodica de re
morali, canonica, liturgica* 46 (1957) 3–65; "Vom Sinn des Subsidiaritätsgesetzes,"
in *Orientierung* 21 (1957) 76–79; "Das Subsidiaritätsprinzip in der Kirche," in
Stimmen der Zeit 160 (1957) 252–267.

[44] Cf. also remarks pertaining thereto in Chap. IV, 1–2.

[45] Here a distinction must be made between the pope's influence as a Roman

There need be no fear that the application of the principle of subsidiarity to the Petrine office would be harmful; on the contrary, in keeping with the above-mentioned quotation from Pius XI, here one can say: "The more perfectly a graded hierarchic order according to the principle of subsidiarity prevails in the different spheres of the Church's life, so much the more secure will be the authority and efficiency of the Petrine office and so much happier and more flourishing will be the state of the Church. Thus the Petrine office will not be diverted from its own great tasks but it will be able to carry out with greater freedom, power, and success all those tasks which are its exclusive concern, directing, watching, stimulating and restraining in *the* sphere of the universal Church, which surpasses the capacities of the bishops and their local Churches."

Obviously the principle of subsidiarity in the Church is not a principle that allows a *material* line to be drawn between the rights of the pope and those of the bishops, which would be valid once and for all, since "the pope has *fullness of power* and in individual cases one cannot adduce an individual full authority, as such, in the jurisdictional sphere of an individual bishop that the pope could not (for just reasons) take away from him (or forbid him to exercise)...."[46] Nevertheless the principle of subsidiarity, supported by the New Testament and by the apostolic Church, excludes the purely formal and external retention of episcopate. A pope who—despite all the external retention of the episcopal office—*in fact* so voided the episcopate as such (not only the episcopal office of an individual bishop for justifiable reasons[47]) so as to take all authority to himself and

---

bishop in the diocese of Rome, as a metropolitan in the Roman Church province, as a patriarch in the Latin Western Church, and as pope in the universal Church. F. Heiler's critical observations on this question should not be overlooked: "Different kinds of elements are symbolized in the tripartite division of the papal tiara: the office of *bishop of Rome*, who at the same time is metropolitan of the Roman Church province, the office of *patriarch* of the Western Latin Church— and the office of *primate* of all bishops. Many of the obstacles that stand in the way of a reunion of Christians are grounded in the combination of these three offices, in the extension of the authority of the sphere of the first office to the second and of the first two to the third. But if the primacy of the pope is viewed as such purely in its providential ecumenical function of unity and separated from the mutable functions of the Roman metropolitan and of the Western patriarch, the historical meaning, and the divine right of the papacy will then also become understandable to those who dispute it." *Eine Heilige Kirche* (Oct. 1953), quoted by O. Karrer, "Apostolische Nachfolge und Primat," in *Fragen der Theologie heute*, ed. by J. Feiner, J. Trütsch and F. Böckle (Einsiedeln 1957) 205.

[46] K. Rahner, *The Episcopate and the Primacy*, London, 1962, pp. 34–35.

[47] K. Rahner rightly emphasizes "that the limitation by the pope of the powers of an individual bishop, which can go as far as their practical removal, may not and cannot be extended in the same way by summation to the whole episcopate,

practically lower the bishops to the status of vicars apostolic would be doing precisely that which was sharply rejected by the Vatican Council: "Obstructing the power of ordinary and immediate episcopal jurisdiction by which the bishops who, under appointment of the Holy Spirit, succeeded in the place of the apostles, feed and rule individually, as true shepherds, the particular flock assigned to them."[48] Here, in fact, it could involve a "destruction of the episcopate"[49] in order to "reduce to nothing and to deny the authority of individual bishops."[50] "But who, even in a dream, could invent such an absurd hypothesis?" shouted the reporter of the commission, Zinelli, in this context[51] A pope who in practice so voided the position of the whole episcopate, so that the episcopate would remain only in name, would be setting himself against the constitution of the Church as willed by Christ, which is essentially and really (and not only apparently) episcopal. Such a pope who set himself against the essential structure of the Church willed by Christ would be an heretical or a schismatic pope. That the Church is not simply defencelessly surrendered to such a possibility (which was already earnestly pondered by theologians and canonists of the Middle Ages) and could hope only in the miracle of the Holy Spirit[52] will still have to be shown more thoroughly.

(c) *The aim of the pope's exercise of office:* The reporter of the

---

and that therefore the right of the pope *vis-à-vis* the whole episcopate is not simply the summation of his right *vis-à-vis* the individual bishops and that therefore, also conversely, the actual use of the papal right against an individual bishop has to observe *iure divino* that the right *iuris divini* of the whole episcopate, which the latter has as a college, is not abolished in practice or threatened in its essential character" (*op. cit.* 72).

[48] Denz. 1828.

[49] Mansi 52, 1114.   [50] Mansi 52, 1311.

[51] Mansi 52, 1105; cf. also in the same perspective, Mansi 52, 1108: "It is clear from all these sources of revelation that the full and supreme power in the Church was given to Peter and his successors and in such way that they cannot be restricted by any superior human power but only by the natural and divine law. Hence, vain and futile (excuse the word) are these cries, which can hardly be taken into serious consideration, that if full and supreme power were attributed to the pope, he could destroy the episcopate, which is of divine law in the Church, and that he then could turn upside down all the canonical sanctions which were laid down with wisdom and holiness by the apostles and by the Church. As if moral theology did not require that the legislator himself be subject to the directive power of laws, if not to their coercive power; or as if an obviously unjust but not harmful order could produce any obligation except that of avoiding scandal."

[52] Despite our approval of Rahner's basic concern, this must always be considered with respect to his solution. The questions posed by O. Karrer are justified: "Does the Spirit act as a kind of Deus ex machina *vis-à-vis* such conceivable (and in certain historical situations, as in the case of Boniface VIII, also undisputed transgressions of spiritual authority, or does God in such a case will to make use

Deputation on Faith declared the aim of the papal exercise of office was not the destruction but the edification of the Church.[53] Thus was it also formulated by the Council Fathers. Instead of the *aedificatio ecclesiae* they spoke also of the *salus* and *unitas ecclesiae*. Thus in the introduction of the council decree it was expressly stated that the primacy existed for the sake of the unity of the Church.[54] Hence primacy should serve the Church and her unity and not its own greatness and glory. It is on this basis that all concrete actions find both their meaning and their limits.[55] The Petrine office has the function of a clamp for the unity of the Church, which also holds the Church together externally; the clamp exists for the sake of the whole, not the whole for the sake of the clamping.

This involves nothing other than the *ministerial character* of every ecclesiastical office which, however, the Petrine office must make concretely visible in a most *outstanding way*. For "whoever wishes to become great shall be your servant" (Mark 10:43). Unfortunately this fundamental biblical aspect—never in the New Testament is the comprehensive word for "office" used in the secular juridical ordinance ($\dot{\alpha}\varrho\chi\acute{\eta}$, $\tau\iota\mu\acute{\eta}$ $\tau\acute{\epsilon}\lambda o\varsigma$), but $\delta\iota\alpha\varkappa o\nu\iota\alpha$, service—something

of the spiritual forces in the bosom of the Church as a corrective against threatening absolutism? Does the episcopal office—since it, no less than the Petrine office, is based on a divine apostolic commission—need any kind of *canonical* codicils at all in order to accomplish its mission directly in earnest decision? Is there not in the inspired New Testament a *de facto* approval, of the opposition of the 'last apostle' to a dangerous precaution of the 'first apostle'? Do the bishops represent the pope and not rather the apostolic college? Has the episcopal college its authority from Peter and not rather from Christ? And does the Church by virtue of divine law, hence *before* any canon law, rest merely on 'apostles' or also on the 'prophets'? Jesus *prayed* for Peter, that he might strengthen the brethren—and when he failed in Antioch, brother Paul knew himself summoned by the spirit to impose his admonition with apostolic authority. If, in the case assumed by K. Rahner, the bishops dutifully did the same would then a pope, who obstinately might wish to defend himself against the episcopate and the people, still be able to be regarded as a bearer of the Holy Spirit, in this attitude too, so that the Church could do nothing except wait for a miracle?" ("Okumenische Katholizität," in *Hochland* 51 [1959] 306f.)

[53] Mansi 52, 715, 1105, 1115f; cf. in the preparatory commissions on dogma, Mansi 49, 407.

[54] Denz. 1821.

[55] M. Schmaus, *Katholische Dogmatik* (Munich [5]1958) III/1, 492: "It would be a profound and fateful misunderstanding if one were to understand papal authority only according to its formal-jurisdical side and not in terms of its content and the meaning which it bears. Such an interpretation perforce leads to the view that the pope can prescribe anything arbitrarily and at his will. The truth is that (by nature) papal power is employed only for the furtherance of the rule of God and the salvation of mankind. Hence it is bound to Christ and His law. Only this justifies its exercise. Such an affirmation contains not only a moral duty, but a legal bond."

which was all too much neglected in the discussions and definitions of that time. People were all too much caught up in the toils of juridical thinking and all too little directly stirred by the word of Holy Scripture. This applied even to the mode of expression.[56] Therein the Council was dependent on the theology of its time.[57] At that time of the militant anti-Gallican position there was much talk about the duties of bishops but little about their rights and, conversely, much talk about the rights of the pope and little about his duties. Doubtless, however, what K. H. Schelkle has written about the office in the New Testament, which according to its nature is service, is eminently applicable here: "The New Testament brings this out even more prominently by describing its opposite as this occurs in the world: 'The kings of the Gentiles lord it over them, and they who exercise authority over them are called benefactors. But not so with you' (Luke 22:25f). Also applicable to the relationship between the apostle and believers must be the passages: 'For you have been called to liberty, brethren' (Gal. 5:13), and 'Do not become the slaves of men' (I Cor. 7:23), and 'What then is Apollos? What indeed is Paul? They are the servants of him whom you have believed' (I Cor. 3:5). Hence a community is not subordinated to its momentary apostles and teachers but always directly to Christ as the Lord. The apostle may not narrow the freedom of the Church by holding his disciples 'in check' (I Cor. 7:35) through his own prescriptions. Paul certainly fought for the communities in Corinth, Philippi, and Galatia. For what else did this homeless wanderer in the vast countries of the Mediterranean world, this man poor as a beggar, possess outside the brotherhoods that he had founded? But he did not bind the communities to himself. He can asseverate (II Cor. 11:2f) 'For I am jealous for you with a divine jealousy. For I betrothed you to one spouse, that I might present you a chaste virgin to Christ. But I fear lest, as the serpent seduced Eve by his guile, so your minds may be corrupted and fall from a single devotion to Christ.' Therefore Paul demanded that the pastoral service be really what the word says, a ministering and a teaching marked by simplicity, carefulness, and cheerfulness (Rom. 12:7-8)."[58]

[56] Cf. P. Parente, *Theologica Fundamentalis. De Ecclesia* (Rome 1954) 208: "A danger which was not always avoided by the theologians after the Council of Trent, who, having nearly forgotten the doctrine of the Mystical Body, indulged in juridical rather than theological skill in comprising this treatise."

[57] Cf. R. Aubert, "L'ecclésiologie au concile du Vatican," in *Le concile et les conciles* (Paris 1960) 260–262.

[58] K. H. Schelkle, *Jüngerschaft und Apostelamt. Eine biblische Auslegung des priesterlichen Dienstes* (Freiburg i. Br. ²1961) 36.

(*d*) *The mode and manner of the papal exercise of office:* The adjectives with which different Council Fathers in the discussions circumscribed the mode and the manner of the papal exercise of office were linked to the aim of the edification of the Church; it is to be non-arbitrary, non-inopportune, non-exaggerated, non-irregular. Or, positively expressed, the reasons for papal interventions must be rooted in an evident utility, and in necessity of the Church (*evidens utilitas, Ecclesiae necessitas*).[59]

Again it involves application of the principle of subsidiarity. Another formulation of this principle, as it is often given in the Catholic world, reads: As much freedom as possible, as much restraint as necessary! Hence, the principle of subsidiarity is all the better realized in the Church, the more the Petrine office, within the framework of essential and necessary Catholic unity, guides the Church through the *bishops* the more, therefore, decentralization and self-administration of the individual churches (of a diocese, a country, a language area, or a continent) are displayed, and the rarer are direct interventions on the part of the Petrine office.[60]

Here, too, a consideration of the biblical foundations with respect to the mode and manner of the exercise of office—precisely in connection with the credibility of office—would be of great value. Humility, modesty, mildness, compassion, faith, charity, are demanded there. Thus in I Tim. 4:12 we read: "Be thou an example

[59] Cf. G. Thils, *Primauté pontificale et prérogatives épiscopales* (Louvain 1961) 96.

[60] Cf. G. Thils, *op. cit.* 100f: "Even the reasons for pontifical intervention—*salus, bonum universitas, necessitas, evidens utilitas*—could be presented in an episcopal perspective. Actually, by reading the authors, it seems that the utility of the Church, her good, her health, her necessities always call for a more extended exercise of papal jurisdiction and hence for an increasing centralization. Now, in itself and in principle, it could be different. The utility, the good, the necessities of the Church could just as well call for a reduction of pontifical interventions and hence for a movement of decentralization. An ecclesiology centred on the episcopate could assert the same principles that justify pontifical interventions, but in an entirely different sense. Thus, one could ask, given the historical situation of the Church in the twentieth century, whether the *health* of the Church would not, in fact, call for a greater autonomy of the whole episcopate? whether the actual *good* of the universal Church would not be served by a certain movement in the direction of administrative decentralization, whether the present *necessities* of the Church do not call for a strengthening of episcopal prerogatives, whether the very *utility* of the Church of today would not call for certain declarations in favour of the variety and the plurality of rites, of customs, of canonical constitutions? Again, it is not necessary to revise principles but to see that they are applied also to an ecclesiology that is elaborated within the frame of episcopal prerogatives. The principles remain the same, they are immutable. But their application can be different, in accordance with the circumstances as they present themselves in fact."

to the faithful in speech, in conduct, in charity, in faith, in chastity."
On this basis many limits are also set to the Petrine office that can
be formulated in juridical terms only with great difficulty. Not everything that is "legal" or "legitimate" is for this reason necessarily
in keeping with the spirit of the Gospel. Here once again the words of
K. H. Schelkle can be applied to the Petrine office: "The presbyters
may not 'lord it over their charges' (I Pet. 5:3). This sentence recalls
the image of the rule of power in the world as it is given in Mark
10:42. Hence even the officeholders of the Church are tempted to act
according to the example of rulership customary in the world. The
superiors of the Church, however, must not assume their first places
in such a spirit. Rather must they hold them by setting a binding,
good example in that they are 'a pattern to the flock' (I Pet. 5:3)."[61]

According to the discussions and definitions of the First Vatican
Council four borderlines circumscribe the exercise of the papal office;
all are based on the nature of the Petrine office itself, the episcopal
office, and also precisely on the assembled people of God who, as a
priestly and royal race, are the Church, and whom the Petrine office
must serve in the cause of charity and of strengthening the faith for
the maintenance of unity.

How are we to view the *relationship between the pope and an
ecumenical council* against this background?

The First Vatican Council did not take an express position on this
question in its constitution. What we have elaborated on concerning
the relationship between primacy and the whole episcopacy would
also have to be applied to an ecumenical council. However, the
reporter of the commission, Zinelli, had to answer the question as to
whether the truly highest authority did not actually lie with an
ecumenical council. "Is not the surpreme and truly full power also
with an ecumenical council? Did not Christ promise all the apostles
he would be with them? Did he not tell the apostles: Whatever you
will bind on earth shall be bound in heaven and whatever you loose
on earth shall be loosed in heaven? Did he not say other things from
which it becomes clear that he wanted to give to his Church the
supreme and full power?"[62] While at the same time asserting the full
authority of the pope, Zinelli admitted all this: ". . . willingly we
admit that the ecumenical council, namely the bishops together with
their head, has the supreme ecclesiastical power over the faithful;
it corresponds best to the Church united with its head. The bishops
therefore gathered together with their head in the ecumenical council,
in which case they represent the whole Church, or the same, dis-

[61] K. H. Schelkle, *op cit.* 40.   [62] Mansi 52, 1109.

persed but together with their head, then constituting the Church itself, possess the full power."[63] And somewhat later he repeated even more clearly how this same full authority is found both in the pope and in an ecumenical council: ". . . we admit that the truly full and supreme power rests with the supreme pontiff as the head and that the same full and supreme power is also with the head joined with the members, i.e. the pontiff with the bishops, while maintaining inviolate and unshaken what we earlier asserted."[64] But even the reporter for the commission did not express himself in greater detail on the mode and manner of the coexistence between these two supreme authorities so that neither of the two might lose its authority. At any rate, in this context he did not enter seriously into the possibilities of conflict that have been presented here theoretically, but can be factually confirmed in the history of the Church.

3. CASE OF CONFLICT BETWEEN POPE AND CHURCH

Everything that we have said up to now on the declaration of the Vatican definitions of primacy will not be able to dispel the doubts and difficulties of Christians outside our Church (even the Eastern Orthodox Churches). For, so they say, *ultimately* the pope is still the absolutist ruler of the Church, and to the answer that the Vatican definition *the fullness of power* should not be misunderstood in an absolutistic way, they raise the objection: *ultimately* our Church, for better or worse, is surrendered to the popes, even if these popes live and teach against the Gospel. No doubt the Catholic Church has good popes at present but at one time she had (even very many) bad popes; and there is not the slightest guarantee that the Church cannot have such popes sooner or later. Finally, at the time of Leo the Great and Gregory the Great no one had imagined that thereafter a tenth century could follow which is generally known as the terrible *saeculum obscurum* of the papacy. And at the time of the greatest popes at the height of the Middle Ages no one had imagined that thereafter they could be followed by the age of the Renaissance popes. In a conflict between the Church and the pope, the Church— even though she would have the Gospel behind her—in any case would come out on the shorter end in view of the overpowering might of the pope and, as has come to pass, be delivered up for decades to popes who are bad and unworthy in every respect. Then nothing remains for the Catholic save to hope for a miracle of the Holy Spirit which, according to the witness of Church history, failed to

[63] Mansi 52, 1109. [64] Mansi 52, 1110; cf. 53, 310.

occur precisely during the *saecula obscura* of the papacy. The Catholic Church herself supposedly does not possess any legal means by which in an emergency to defend herself against a bad pope.

It is not easy for a Catholic to come up with a good answer to these doubts and questions. Naturally he cannot dispute that wherever there are human beings potential conflict exists, indeed even in the Church, even between pope and bishops, and between pope and ecumenical councils. Everywhere here, according to the evidence of Church history, there were serious and momentous conflicts and these could occur again; minor conflicts between a pope (or his organs) and a bishop are quite possible. All this belongs to the human and all-too-human aspects of the Church and cannot confuse the Catholic in his Catholic faith. Nevertheless the question remains: How are such conflict situations to be judged theologically?

We can give a satisfactory answer to this question only if we dare to look at the facts of Church history soberly, without embellishments of any kind. Abstract *theologumena*, which take no account of historical reality, are less convincing today than ever. And to keep silent about inconvenient historical facts is a sign of feeble faith. To be sure, in our context it would not be interesting to pursue any kind of historical or canonical curiosities, of which there is no lack, particularly in the history of the popes. Hence in this systematic view of the problem we cannot be concerned with conducting research into ecclesiastical or canonical history. Nevertheless typical conflict situations in Church history and in the history of canon law constitute typical borderline cases which, as such, in a most impressive way are able to shed light and clarity on the actual structure of the Church or on the forgotten lines of this structure. We shall now go further, soberly and cautiously, into this problem area, which is not at all an easy one and which unfortunately is all too seldom considered, in order precisely thereby to expound the ministerial character of the Petrine office in the Church more credibly, in its internal and external aspects.

Canon 1556 clearly states: "The first see is under judgment of nobody". Accordingly, no earthly, no state, and no ecclesiastical power or institution is recognized as competent to stand in judgment over the papacy. In Canon 1558 the competence of other judges is even designated as an absolute incompetence. Thus in general the "competence of competence" is ascribed to the pope even today.

The historical problematic aspect of the statement, "the first see is under judgment of nobody", is extremely difficult to grasp. For it cannot be denied that a very wide chasm yawns between papal claims and historical facts. This chasm is exhibited most drastically in the fact that depositions of popes have taken place in the course of Church history. The acts of violence carried out by pagans or later Arian tribunals, in which a power alien to the Church deposed the Bishop of Rome, exiling or sentencing him to death, are not theologically relevant in our context. What are especially important are the depositions of popes that took place in the Middle Ages. Up to now they have been only rarely considered together by historians, but recently H. Zimmermann has submitted them to a thorough historical investigation on which we shall base our discussion in the following pages.[1]

In agreement with Maassen, L. Duchesne, E. Caspar, A. Fliche and V. Martin, J. Haller, F. X. Seppelt, Zimmermann first of all establishes that the statement on the "prima sedes," which was also taken over into the present-day code of canon law from the *Decretum Gratiani*, clearly goes back to a sixth-century forgery (at the time of Pope Symmachus with reference to the apocryphal synodal documents of Sinuessa in 303). As early as the second half of the fourth century when charges were made against Pope Damasus I, a Roman synod simply proposed to Emperor Gratian and to Valentinian that in the future in criminal cases the pope was no longer to be subject to the jurisdiction of imperial officials but exclusively to the highest secular authority, namely the Emperor. According to all appearances this proposal was rejected. Only a hundred years later, when the emperor was too far away to be able to interfere in the negotiations, did members of the synod (as well as the Gothic ruler Theodoric) declare that it was not within the sphere of their competence to hold a trial against Pope Symmachus. "The forgeries which were produced at that time sought to justify the proceedings of the Council historically and to free the bearer of the papal dignity for all time from every secular and spiritual court. Thereby the climax of a long development was reached; the future had to prove whether the legal principle, *Prima sedes a nemine iudicatur*, had the opportunity of prevailing and of gaining general recognition."[2]

In any case, despite this legal determination and the steadily growing claims to primacy of jurisdiction, the history of the popes registers "from the earliest times up to the fifteenth century a whole series of

[1] H. Zimmermann, "Papstabsetzungen des Mittelalters," in *Mitteilungen des Instituts für Osterreichische Geschichtsforschung* 69 (1961) 1–84, 241–291; the most recent work relative to this subject, by S. W. Findlay, *Canonical Norms Governing the Deposition and Degradation of Clerics* (Washington 1941), contains nothing concerning the deposability of popes.

[2] H. Zimmermann, *op cit.* 5f.

'papal trials' to which the incumbents of the *prima sedes* were invited and where they were often even deposed."[3] The papal trials of the sixth and seventh centuries will give no evidence of any recognition of the legal principle *Prima sedes a nemine iudicatur*, although the principle was well known by then. And although this legal principle deriving from the Symmachian forgeries is found in compilations of law of the ninth century and was frequently used as an argument, trials of popes were also completely effective from the middle of the eighth century up to the dispute over investitutes. The participants in papal elections, the clergy and the people of Rome, as well as the emperor, also pronounced the sentences deposing the pontiffs.

A pope could be deposed under two conditions which absolved one from any consideration of the legal principle of the *Prima sedes*: (1) by public lapse from the faith; thus, in 869 Pope Hadrian II already had the principle declared at a Roman synod against the Byzantine patriarch Photius; in case of heresy a certain right of resistance against the pope was granted by citing the condemnation of Pope Honorius I;[4] and (2) if a pontificate was achieved through usurpation and was consequently illegitimate: "If the legitimacy of a pontificate from its beginning was seriously doubted because events of any kind during the election and elevation of the new pope did not conform with canonical prescriptions, the judges of such a pseudo pope would base their decision on the point that they were dealing, not at all with a real incumbent of the *Prima sedes*, in connection with whom the oft-cited principle was valid but, rather, with a usurper of the chair of Peter who was therefore punishable. The latter then must appear as a blasphemer against the immunity of the papacy, not him who calls him to account. Thus the word *invasio* crops up over and over again in the sources as a technical term for a pontificate that is to be judged as illegitimate, wholly apart from how long it has been in existence. . . . The charge of *invasio* in any case always refers to the beginning of the pontificate concerned and brands it as illegitimate, which absolves one from a consideration of the legal principle "Prima sedes a nemine iudicatur," no matter how much the accused invaders may have been convinced of the justification of their claims."[5]

At a deposition of a pope the guilt of the accused pope had to be expressly established by a lawful trial. In order for a papal deposition to be carried out, on the one hand, it had to be supported by the authority of the imperial protector, of the Patrician of the Romans, whose consensus was also required for the election. On the other

---

[3] *Ibid.* 6.   [4] Mansi 16, 126.
[5] H. Zimmermann, *op cit.* 78f.

hand, the authority of a synodal decree was required: "The synod, however, was the forum before which for centuries, even in the Frankish Empire, a member of the clergy and above all a bishop, had to answer. Thus the sources always also make mention of conciliar discussions whenever it involved pronouncing judgment against a pope. Thereby, seemingly with good reason, consideration was given to the Roman as well as to the universal character of the gathering. It appeared important that the Romans, that is to say, the electors of the pope, themselves should pronounce the verdict of guilty against their bishop. But since the latter at the same time was also viewed as the earthly head of the whole Catholic Church, the Christian world outside Rome, or at least a decisive part of it, had to approve the Roman judgment."[6]

Thus even here the synods must not be understood only as an administrative or judicative council meeting. "The synod convoked for such a reason, however, never appeared as a representation of certain circles of the people of the Church. It received its special authority by virtue of the fact that the participants felt themselves to be under the guidance of the divine Spirit and therefore removed from merely human contingency. God Himself was regarded as the judge, the sentence was pronounced in His name and thereby the divine right that had been violated was re-established. The assembly was held in a sanctified place, in the church and before the altar. The session was opened in the manner of a religious service with the solemn reception of the Holy Scripture and with the reading of the canons. During the consultations the participants supported their arguments by references to the Bible and early canon law. Finally, an invocation was placed at the head of the synodal protocol, to bear witness to later generations that not human wisdom but divine inspiration was solicited and was decisive in arriving at the verdict. Although all these were customary usage, practiced at every council and not only in the case of a papal trial, nevertheless their observance here appears to be especially important precisely when such thorny problems as the deposition of a pope had to be discussed. Even the conspirators against Leo III in April 799 felt it necessary to depose the pope, whom they rejected, from his dignity before the altar of a Roman church, hence, as it were, in the sight of God."[7] Attempts were made to avoid violence as much as possible in connection with depositions. Rather, there were attempts to induce the accused to renounce his dignity voluntarily, and thereby make acknowledgment of his guilt, in order to set forth indisputably the validity of the ver-

[6] *Ibid.* 81.   [7] *Ibid.* 81f.

dict of deposition that had been pronounced. When a pope was
actually deposed, the deposition was carried out and publicized not
only through a correspondingly formulated legal pronouncement but
at the same time by means of definite rites of deposition, which was
to make retraction of the elevation that had occurred, as it were,
through disrobing and a mock procession. Frequently all-too-human
motives played a role at these trials and depositions of popes which,
in the indescribable papal confusion of this time, often allowed recourse to none-too-fastidious practices.

Thus the papal history of that time had a considerable number of
depositions of popes. "From the Caroligian period, which may be
bracketed between the ascent to the throne of the major-domo Pepin,
effected with papal assistance on the one hand and the death of the
unfortunate Emperor Ludwig the Blind on the other, more than a
dozen pontificates can be named which in some way or other were
contested as illegitimate, which were interrupted by the violent removal of the pope from his seat, or which ended by deposition or the
murder of the pope. That not all these popes could today be considered
as legal holders of the *Prima sedes*, or lay claim to a consideration
of their immunity, is not a matter of importance according to that
reckoning. For, notwithstanding, we can assume that each one of
these bishops or antibishops of Rome was subjectively convinced of
the justification of his claims and must have felt the rejection first
of all as unjust."[8] It was even worse under the Ottos: "Not a single
pontificate was uncontested, and the number of elections of popes
almost balanced the number of depositions of popes."[9] The legal
claim of papal immunity was also known in the Otonian age.
Nevertheless even during this time reasons were adduced allowing for
the non-recognition of the legal principle "Prima sedes a nemine
iudicatur." The main reasons were *invasio*, simony, heresy; besides
these, often simply for purposes of strengthening the accusation,
perjury, ambition, sacrilege, adultery of the mystic marriage between
the legitimate pope and the Roman Church. "Only in a trial against a
pope whose elevation or whose exercise of office and way of life could
be characterized as irreconcilable with Christian dogma could one
disregard a consideration of papal immunity and consider oneself
justified to hold a new election to the papal throne judged to be
vacant."[10] Even in the Ottonian era in connection with "the lawful
procedure of the convocation of a synod it was felt necessary that it
be characterized as both Roman and universal by its participants
and that they felt themselves as being under the guidance of the

[8] *Ibid.* 241.   [9] *Ibid.* 243.   [10] *Ibid.* 287f.

Spirit of God and formulated its decrees on the basis of early canon law, regarded as the norm for such a process. Only thus did it seem possible to grapple with such important decisions as the deposition of a pope under charges, or the condemnation of an anti-pope."[11] Even here the deposition generally took place according to the symbolic rites of deposition.

In our context it is important to note that, despite the recognition of the legal principle "Prima sedes a nemine iudicatur," the Church of that time held a deposition of a pope to be justifiable under certain extraordinary circumstances. The clergy and people of Rome, as well as the emperor, pronounced the verdict of deposition.

A change first set in at the time of the dispute over investitures, towards the end of the eleventh century: "The sentences decreed against the Roman popes remained inoperative partly because the accused found help and support from foreign powers, especially among the Normans and in France. Now it was no longer decisive to find recognition in Rome. Rather, the whole of Christendom decided on the legitimacy of the holder of the see of Peter. It is by this time characteristic that the schism of Wilbert of Ravenna lasted until his death and that Pope Gregory VII and his successor could not overcome it either through the emperor or through the antipope."[12] The result was that hostile popes reciprocally condemned and excommunicated each other; but things did not reach the point of synodal negotiations resulting in a verdict of deposition—still less, in the execution of this verdict. In the twelfth and thirteenth centuries the usual way in which a pope or antipope during his lifetime lost his office and dignity was by resigning.

The depositions of the conciliar era of the fifteenth century in all their forms were based on the claim that a council stands above the pope and that consequently a council could also remove him under certain circumstances.[13] Later we shall accord a fuller treatment to conciliar theory. Here we shall note merely that, on the one hand, these depositions of popes are the last in papal history up to now and that, on the other hand, the possibility of further depositions of popes[14] was juridically always left open. This applies even to the period following the First Vatican Council.

[11] *Ibid.* 288f.

[12] *Ibid.* 10f.

[13] Concerning the different "emergency" theories at the time of the Western Schism, cf. B. Hübler, *Die Constanzer Reformation und die Condordate von 1418* (Leipzig 1867) 360–388.

[14] What can be understood *canonically* by the deposition of a pope (which is the legally operative cause, etc.) will become clear in what follows.

The legal situation in this respect was not changed by the definitions of the First Vatican Council. This is evident from the manuals of Catholic canon law which, even after the Vatican Council, treat of cessation of the power of the Roman pontiff in a more or less thorough fashion. Here we shall keep to the classic manual by F. X. Wernz, the famous Roman canonist, consultor of the Roman congregation and member of the codification commission for the CIC, and who as the rector of the papal Gregorian University was elected Jesuit General (1906 to 1914). His main work in six volumes has been newly revised by P. Vidal and deals in a relatively thorough way with the question of the cessation of the Roman pontiff's power, based on the classical teachings, mainly of Bellarmine and Suarez.[15]

When does the pope lose his office or his power of ruling? Five cases are to be distinguished:

(1) *Death:* "At death the spiritual and civil power of the Roman pontiff ceases. Although there is no obstacle to the *civil* power being exercised during the vacancy of the Apostolic See by another subject, the ordinary *spiritual* power of the Roman pontiff, however, similar to the ordinary power of a bishop, does *not* pass over to a chapter or the college of Cardinals as some commentators wrongly thought. . . . Hence the primacy of the spiritual jurisdiction of the Roman pontiff exists forever in the Church with a *continuity* that is only *moral*, not physical."[16]

(2) *Resignation:* "Upon resignation the Roman pontiff evidently loses his jurisdiction."[17] Just as the pope achieved the election of his office by free acceptance, so does he also lose it by a freely and publicly declared abdication. If bishops are allowed to abdicate—for the welfare of their souls and out of necessity or the good of their churches—all the more is this so in the case with the pope: "out of necessity or for the good of the universal Church."[18] The spiritual bond between pope and Church must not degenerate into a bond of iniquity, "from which the Roman pontiff and the Church would be freed only by death."[19] Wernz and Vidal thereby base their findings

[15] F. X. Wernz and P. Vidal, *Ius Canonicum* (3rd ed. P. Aguire, Rome 1943) II, 513–521.

[16] *Ibid.* 513f.

[17] *Ibid.* 515; cf. Canon 221: "When it happens that the Roman pontiff resigns there is no necessity of official acceptance of this resignation by the Cardinals or others."

[18] *Ibid.* 515.

[19] *Ibid.*

on the legal principle "Romanum Pontificem posse libere resignare" championed by Celestine V and which Boniface VIII included in his compilation of laws, and on the actual demissions of Celestine V and Gregory XII. Along with others Wernz and Vidal make the following observation with respect to the abdication of Gregory XII: "that Gregory XII restored peace and concord in the Church only by his legitimate and generous *resignation.*"[20]

We may then draw the following conclusion from the Wernz and Vidal presentation: There are extraordinary situations in Church history when a pope not only may resign but also must resign—"out of necessity or for the good of the universal Church and for the sake of peace and harmony in the Church."[21] The moral obligation arises from the fundamental structure of the Petrine office; the Petrine office does not exist in order to rule over the Church in an absolutist way, but in order *to serve* the Church and her unity. If a pope sees that his person—culpably or inculpably—is no longer able in a particular state of emergency to fulfil this fundamental function of the Petrine office, he is morally obliged to give up his office for the sake of the unity and peace of the Church, as well as for the sake of a more credible presentation of the Petrine office itself, and voluntarily make way for another pope who can more properly perform this fundamental function of the Petrine office.

[20] *Ibid,* 516.

[21] *Ibid.* 516—Divine Providence cannot be appealed to at the outset against the possibility of the mental illness of a pope. In the course of Church history the suspicion that a pope was mentally ill has cropped up in different ways. Even of a personage as significant in Church history as Boniface VIII, K. Biblmeyer and H. Tüchle write as follows in *Kirchengeschichte* (Paderborn [13]1952) II, 354: "One may perhaps think of a pathological mental state in connection with him." And F. X. Seppelt and G. Schwaiger, *Geschichte der Päpste* (Munich [2]1957), IV, 53: "If the question of whether Boniface was a heretic is to be answered negatively, one therefore cannot escape the impression that his selfconsciousness and his feeling for power on occasion were expressed in forms bearing marks of a pathological character and which can be explained only as a symptom of Caesar-madness. Let us recall that theatrical scene, which has been handed down to us in a thoroughly authenticated written report by the Aragon ambassador, in which Boniface, in alternating raiment as pope and emperor, appeared before the cardinals and bishops and cried out, 'I am pope, I am emperor.' " Urban VI, too, was regarded as mentally ill: "Since the pope refused all attempts at reconciliation, the king had him beseiged at Nocera. During the many months of siege Urban VI made himself ridiculous by having the bells rung several times, day after day, and by hurling anathemas at the besiegers while burning candles—a clear sign of his mental derangement" (F. X. Seppelt and G. Schwaiger, *op. cit.* IV, 205). Urban VI was also examined as a mentally ill person, and this was a reason why a large number of cardinals defected from him and elected a new pope. On the fact of the incapacity of this pope and the problems in terms of canon law arising therefrom, cf. O. Prerovsky, "L'elezione de Urbano

(3) *Mental Illness:* "Also through insanity, if it is *certain* and *permanent*, the Roman pontiff *ipso facto* loses the pontifical jurisdiction, as—according to Tanner—theologians also hold." Certain and permanent mental illness is even to be juridically equated with mental death. Further, no guidance of the Church is possible without the use of reason: "This is the reason why the raising of a child to pontifical dignity is by law invalid; therefore, similarly, the pope, if he is reduced to the condition of childhood, *ipso facto* loses jurisdiction."[22] Finally a man does not become pope on the basis of hereditary succession but on the basis of his personal qualities; thus in the exercise of his authority he cannot be fully and wholly replaced by any representative. "Since all these qualities in the case of certain and permanent insanity are no longer significant, when the basis of habitual use of reason of a Roman pontiff is destroyed, all jurisdiction is removed, for the *peace* and *necessity* of the Church."[23]

(4) *Heresy:* "By *heresy notoriously* and *openly* manifested, the Roman pontiff, if he lapses into this, is *ipso facto* deprived of his power of jurisdiction and without previous condemnation of the Church."[24] Wernz and Vidal characterize the view that a pope cannot lapse into heresy not only when he speaks *ex cathedra* but also otherwise (as *doctor privatus*) as *pia et probabilis*, but not as *certa et communis*.[25] They follow the view of Cardinal Bellarmine according

---

VI e l'insorgere dello scisma d'occidente" (*Miscellanea della società Romana di storia patria* vol. XX [Rome 1960]). The same authors state the following regarding Paul IV: "The intensifying anxiety and the pope's mistrust which degenerated into a pathological suspicion ultimately led to measures which must be appraised as the darkest pages in the pontificate of Paul IV." (*op. cit.* V, 86). It is certain that Paul IV "was dominated by the pathological anxiety that the cardinals whom he held in such great suspicion might one day occupy the Chair of Peter" (*ibid.*). "A chain of unfortunate events, blunders, errors, and extravagances extends through the pontificate of Paul IV. Apart from the extraordinarily difficult state of affairs, certainly the unbalanced, pathological character of the pope was itself to a great measure responsible for it" (*op. cit.* V, 88).

[22] F. X. Wernz and P. Vidal, *op. cit.* 516.

[23] *Ibid.*

[24] *Ibid*, 517.

[25] *Ibid.* E. F. Regatillo, *Institutiones Iuris Canonici* (Santander ⁴1951) I, 279. designates this view as "pia, sed parum fundata." Here, too, the history of the Church admonishes against an immoderate faith in Divine Providence. Church history also shows, of course, that the Church is in no way helplessly surrendered to an heretical pope and that in certain circumstances she can wage an effective and extremely vigorous opposition thereto. The classical case of an heretical pope is Honorius I and his doctrinal utterances in connection with the dispute over Monothelitism: "These unfortunate formulations became the occasion for the condemnation of Honorius by the sixth general council of Constantinople in 681.

to which the public heretic is no longer a member and consequently no longer the head of the whole Church. As a public heretic he is to

At the thirteenth session anathema was pronounced against the authors of the new heresy and Honorius, the bishop of old Rome, was expressly included 'because in a letter to Sergius we have found that he conforms to all his views and endorses his godless teachings.' In the subsequent period this condemnation was repeated by the Trullan Synod in 692 (Mansi 11, 938), and by the seventh (Mansi 13, 377) and eighth (Mansi 16, 181) general councils. Leo II, who accepted the decision of the sixth general council, modified Honorius' guilt by adverting to the fact that he (Honorius) was not concerned 'to preserve purely this apostolic Church with the teaching of the apostolic tradition, but had let the intact (Roman Church) become bespotted.' The account of the condemnation of Honorius found acceptance even in the 'Liber Diurnus.' Every newly elected pope had to condemn the author of the new heresy 'una cum Honorio, qui pravis eorum adsertionibus fomentum impendit.' Even the Book of the Popes and the Roman Breviary in the second nocturn on the feast of Pope Leo II reported on the condemnation without stressing the fact that Honorius referred to Pope Honorius. Thus it seems that the event had been forgotten in the high and late Middle Ages. It was only as a result of the translation of the works of Manuel Kalekas against the heresies of the Greeks by Ambrosius Traversari that the West again became aware of the condemnation of Honorius. Johannes de Turrecremata sought to solve this question by the assertion that the condemnation may have been an error on the part of the Easterners and had ensued on the basis of false information (*Summa de ecclesia*, vol. II, chap. 93). At the time of the Reformation, A. Pigge tried to cope with the difficulties arising from the condemnation of Honorius by means of the thesis that the condemnation of Honorius may have never actually happened but that it was falsely inserted by the Greeks in the acts of the Council. His thesis was gratefully received and expanded by Bellarmine and Baronius and it still had defenders in the nineteenth century, although M. Cano had already sharply opposed the hypothesis of falsification. The question of Honorius played an important role at the First Vatican Council (cf. C. J. von Hefele, *Causa Honorii papae* [Naples 1870]). The question as to whether the two Honorius letters are so-called decisions *ex cathedra*, which Hefele still affirmed in 1877 (cf. C. J. von Hefele, *Conciliengeschichte* III², 177) is denied today." R. Baumer, "Honorius I," in *Lexikon für Theologie und Kirche* (Freiburg i. Br. ²1961] V, 475. If one denies it and takes the interpretations of the councils and popes with the seriousness that is due to them, we then have a "classical case," in the sense of the theology of the Vatican Council, of a pope who was a heretic: without actually speaking *ex cathedra*, he had not only thought but also taught heretically. Even if one wished objectively to be more mild in his judgment of Honorius (obscurity of the point in dispute, etc.) there is still the crucial matter that councils and popes do reckon dispassionately with the possibility that a pope may teach heretical doctrine. Of importance, too, is the case of John XXII whose view was condemned by his successor, Benedict XII, in a solemn definition: John XXII "defended in several sermons since All Saints Day of 1331 the opinion that the souls of the righteous, even of Mary and the apostles, attain the vision of God (*visio beatifica*) only after the Last Judgment. This assertion called forth widespread opposition; even the University of Paris and part of the cardinals turned against the pope so that he found himself obliged to disavow that view on his deathbed." K. Biblmeyer and H. Tüchle, *Kirchengeschichte* (Paderborn ¹³1952) II, 366. Recent literature is cited in F. Wetter, *Die Lehre Benedikts XII. vom intensiven Wachstum der Gottesschau* (Diss. Rome 1959).

be shunned: "A public heretical pope is to be shunned as Christ and the apostles have ordained and because he is a danger for the Church. He must be deprived of his power, as nearly all admit."[26] Thus through heresy the pope *ipso facto* is ruled out as pope. Through its verdict a council merely establishes that the pope is a heretic, and thereby has separated himself from the Church and lost his authority: "The declaratory sentence of the crime, which must not be rejected as merely declaratory, does not judge the heresy of the pope but rather makes public that he is already judged, i.e. the general council declares the fact of the crime by which the heretical pope has separated himself from the Church and deprived himself of his dignity."[27] Suarez, on the contrary, holds the view that an heretical pope is not directly deposed by God Himself (in opposition to Torquemada, Augustine of Ancona, Paludanus, Driedo, Salmeron, and others) but that he ceases to be a pope only through a human verdict that establishes his guilt (in agreement with Cajetan, Melchior Cano, Dominic Soto, and others): "If the pope becomes an unrepentant heretic, after having passed on him the declaratory sentence of this crime by legitimate ecclesiastical jurisdiction, he ceases to be pope. This is common doctrine of the doctors, taken from the first letter of Clement I in which he says that Peter taught that a heretical pope was to be deposed. The reason for this is that it is a very grave harm for the Church to have such a shepherd and that she cannot undergo such grave danger. Furthermore, it is against the dignity of the Church to remain subject to a heretical pope without being able to remove him."[28]

(5) *Schism:* "Schism is rightly considered to be on the same level as heresy."[29] Hence a schismatic pope is to be judged and dealt with in the same way as a heretical one. Wernz and Vidal do not go further into this question. Here, too, more exact details are provided by Suarez who makes important utterances regarding the concept of schism.[30] From his expositions it emerges clearly that in connection with a schismatic pope it is not simply a question of an antipope. The latter is not at all a pope and therefore poses no problem in our context. For Suarez schism, in the specifically theological sense, is a cleavage in the one Church. A schism can eventuate even without heresy, namely when one does indeed retain the faith but in his ac-

26 F. X. Wernz and P. Vidal, *op. cit.* 518.

27 *Ibid.* 518.

28 F. Suarez, *De fide theologica, Disputatio X de Summo Pontifice, sectio VI* (Opera omnia, Paris 1858) 12, 317.

29 F. X. Wernz and P. Vidal, *op. cit.* 518.

30 F. Suarez, *op. cit.* 12, 733–736.

tions and in the character of his conduct is unwilling to maintain the unity of the Church. A schism is possible in two ways:[31] (1)By separating oneself from the pope; thereby one does not deny that the pope is the head of the Church (this would be a schism that is also a heresy). Rather, one denies it rashly in an individual case or conducts oneself towards him in such a way as though the pope were not the head (for example the election of an antipope, the convocation of a council without his authority). (2) By separating oneself from the rest of the body of the Church and by not desiring to share the communion of the Sacraments with it (as Epiphanius separated himself at worship from his Alexandrian patriarch Petrus, with whom he had a difference of opinion but no differences as regards the faith). In this way even the *pope* can be a *schismatic*; namely, when he does not maintain the necessary communion and bond with the whole body of the Church, or when he attempts to excommunicate the whole Church, or when he purposes to subvert Church usages protected by apostolic tradition: "And in this second way the pope can be a schismatic, if he does not want to have union and bond with the whole body of the Church as he should, if he attempts to excommunicate the whole Church, or if he wants to abolish all the ecclesiastical ceremonies which are confirmed by apostolic tradition as Cajetan remarks."[32] Just as it is the task of the Church to act in communion with the pope, so is it the task of the pope to maintain communion with the Church. A pope who schismatically cuts himself off

---

[31] Counter-Reformation theology often dealt only with the first type which perforce led to an improper and unhistorical narrowing of the concept of schism.

[32] F. Suarez, *De charitate, Disputatio XII de schismate, sectio I* (Opera omnia, Paris 1858) 12, 733f. The case of Pope Victor I is instructive. On account of the difference in the date of the feast of Easter he excommunicated the whole Church province of Asia to which probably more than one-quarter of all the faithful belonged: "Victor's harsh procedure called forth vigorous opposition from numerous bishops, above all from Irenaeus, the Bishop of Lyons, who on this account joined with numerous other bishops. Irenaeus, who himself was a native of Asia but who adhered to the Roman practice of Easter, addressed a letter to the Roman bishop in which he pointed out that his predecessors, above all Anicetus, had maintained communion with supporters of an Easter Feast deviating from the Roman practice, even though they themselves rejected the feast on the 14th Nisan for themselves and their congregation. Irenaeus warned Victor that he could not exclude whole communities of God that wished to hold fast to an old traditional practice. The success of the efforts of Irenaeus, of whom in this connection Eusebius said that he was a peacemaker in accordance with his name and attitude, is not clearly evident. Church fellowship was restored with the Asian congregations under his successors, if not under Victor, and in the course of the third century the Asian communities abandoned their particular custom with respect to the Easter feast" (F. X. Seppelt, *Geschichte der Päpste* (Munich 1954) I, 29f.

from the whole Church loses his office. A pope who excommunicates the whole Church would excommunicate himself out of the Church; he would place himself and not the Church in the wrong and burden himself with the guilt of schism.

All these cases dealt with by these canonists show how erroneous is that criticism directed against the Catholic Church, which holds that the Church is helplessly surrendered to popes who live and teach against the Gospel, In a conflict between the whole Church and a heretical, schismatic, or mentally ill pope the Church not only has the possibility but also the duty to take action against the pope. It is entirely unthinkable that the true faith, that the Church, could ever exist only in a single member, namely in the pope, while the whole Church, to which in the first place all the promises of the Lord have been given, should find itself in schism or heresy.

According to what has been said in such a conflict the pope would be morally obliged to resign of his own free will, as has happened in Church history. And the Church would be morally obliged to induce such a pope to resign of his own free will, as has also come to pass. If such a pope were to oppose a voluntary resignation then the Church must look for redress elsewhere. But there is the difficult question: Who judges? We have heard the answers that the canonists in general give: An ecumenical council; the bishops (formerly one also named the College of Cardinals); in any case it must always be a representation of the whole Church which effects a remedy. Suarez answered the question as to which is to pass judgment on such a pope as follows: "Some say he could be judged by the cardinals and the Church could put them in charge of this matter; but we do not read that they have hitherto been entrusted with this judgment. It must be said, therefore, that this is a matter for all the bishops of the Church: for since they are the ordinary shepherds and pillars of the Church, we must believe that a case of this kind concerns them. According to divine law there is no reason to attribute it to those more than to these, and since nothing about this is laid down to human law, it must be concluded that it concerns all and consequently the general council, and this is the common teaching of the doctors."[33]

What, however, if a heretical, schismatic, or mentally ill pope refuses to convoke a council? Suarez answers: Perhaps it may not be necessary to convoke an *ecumenical* council. It might suffice that archbishops or primates convoke provincial or national councils in

[33] F. Suarez, *De fide theologica, Disputatio X de Summo Pontifice, sectio VI* (Opera omnia, Paris 1858) 12, 317f.

the individual territories and that all these councils agree upon the same sentence. But what if particular councils do not suffice for this purpose and an ecumenical council against the will of the pope is required? Suarez answers: If an ecumenical council meets to decide on questions concerning faith or to issue general Church laws it must be convoked by the pope in a legitimate way. If, however, a council has to meet for a matter which concerns the pope in a special way and which, in some way, opposes him, such a council can therefore be convoked either by the College of Cardinals or by the consensus of the episcopate. Should the pope try to prevent such a council, he is not to be obeyed because in such a case his supreme pastoral authority is being misused against justice and the common welfare: "For this matter which concerns especially the pontiff and is somehow directed against him, the general council can be called together legitimately by the college of cardinals or by consent of the bishops. If the pontiff should try to impede such a convocation, one is under no obligation to obey him since he abuses his power against justice and the common welfare."[34]

On the basis of both historical facts and canon-law theory it has become obvious that the principle *Prima sedes a nemine iudicatur* has in fact its internal limits. Although the apocryphal origin of this principle is quite often passed over in silence[35] in the canon law manuals, in connection with the above-mentioned cases of the limits of papal authority it is nevertheless openly admited that a council may pronounce sentence (we shall soon have to determine what kind) against a pope and that under certain circumstances, it must do so. If today this legal principle is referred to by the CIC in connection with the interpretation of the primatial position of the pope (and it should not be denied) nevertheless, there must be an exact consideration of the sense in which this occurs, and to what extent. It is this principle that must be interpreted on the basis of the Petrine office in

[34] *Ibid.* 12, 318.

[35] During the whole Middle Ages there was no knowledge of the apocryphal character of the sources of this legal principle. Hincmar of Rheims was the only one to report it, in his ninth-century criticism; but it, however, again disappeared. That the acts of the Council of Sinuessa were of a questionable character was known even to Caesar Baronius as well as to Matthias Flacius Illyricus and the Centuriators of Magdelburg. Baronius rejected them as an invention of the Donatists. Their spuriousness was finally proved in 1721 by the Maurist, Pierre Coustant, who also assumed that they possibly arose during the period of the schism between Symmachus and Laurentius. Today there exists no further doubt that these acts are forgeries produced at that time. Cf. H. Zimmermann, "Päpstabesetzungen des Mittelalters," in *Mitteulungen des Instituts für Osterreichische Geschichtsforschung* 69 (1961) 4.

Scripture, and not the position of the Petrine office in Scripture on
the basis of this legal principle, which moreover is understood in a
purely abstract and formal way. Only thus does the ministerial
character of the Petrine office in the Church come to clear expression
in terms of theology and canon law.

Nevertheless we must now determine the character of this conciliar sentence more closely in the light of the definition of papal
primacy as enunciated at the First Vatican Council. We expressly
mentioned the *internal* limits of this principle. On the basis of Vatican
I a radical Gallicanism and conciliarism is impossible: this in principle
on the basis of the Church's constitution, superposes a higher juridical
authority on the pope as the legitimate pastor of the whole Church
and which, as an external competing factor, would limit papal
authority from case to case according to its decision and discretion.
But on the basis of Vatican I likewise, the following must be clearly
stated: Papal primacy does possess an *internal* limit, which of itself
inheres in papal authority as a finite-human authority established by
its Lord. Thus at the same time the legitimate possibility exists in the
Church that someone, distinct from the pope, is able to recognize this
limit and to act according to this recognition.

Naturally in a concrete historical situation it can be extraordinarily difficult to recognize whether or not this limit has been
transgressed. This difficulty is imminent in this whole problem to the
extent that the very posing of the problem involves a conflict between
a pope and the whole Church, and to the extent that an heretical,
schismatic, or mentally ill pope (if he really is any of these things
and obstinately also, as is presupposed by the canonists), *cannot* in
this situation acknowledge precisely that he is heretical, schismatic,
or mentally ill, and thereby that he has transgressed his limits.
According to the canonistic presentation of the problem no resolution of this conflict may be expected from the pope's understanding
of the matter. Naturally an extraordinary intervention of Divine
Providence must not be excluded at the outset in a momentous crisis
of this kind. Still less, however, must such divine intervention be
postulated at the outset—as a juridical solution, so to speak. It can
nevertheless, be precisely the intention of the Lord of the Church
that the Church, with the assistance of the Holy Spirit that has been
promised to her, herself master this situation by her *own* decision,
as she often has had to do, and has done, in Church history. On the
basis of the nature of the Church, it is, of course, not an individual
as an individual who is authorized to pronounce a definitive judgment in such a case. Rather, such a judgment is the concern and the

burden of the whole Church, as she is legitimately represented in an ecumenical council by human convocation. This is the meaning of the declarative sentence with which the canonists deal in this context. The concrete way in which this occurs in individual cases cannot in principle be predicted substantially in advance nor can it be derived concretely from the solutions that have been arrived at in the past. As a Church composed of human beings the Church cannot adequately master her history before it actually takes place.

Two things must be stressed in order rightly to understand the declarative sentence according to the meaning of present-day canonists: it is an authentic sentence and yet it is merely a declarative sentence. What does this mean? It is an *authentic* sentence—it is an authentic verdict with definite legal consequences. Concretely, it is a verdict declaring that this man, who was pope, can no longer be considered as pope; hence a new pope can be elected and the latter is then the generally acknowledged legitimate successor of his predecessor (still living to be sure but deprived of his office). Without such a sentence all this would not be known, or at least not generally known, in the Church. Since here it involves a decision that is of the greatest importance for the whole Church, only a legitimate representation of this whole Church, particularly an ecumenical council, is authorized to make it. Nevertheless this authentic sentence is merely a *declarative* sentence. It is a verdict which does not, as such, effect or bring into being the fact that has been judged; rather, as such, it merely makes public and authoritative declaration thereof. Hence it does not *effect* that this man, who was pope, is now no longer pope. Rather, it *establishes* that this man, who was pope, is now no longer pope, just as a death certificate—this is the example the canonists cite in this context—does not effect death but merely confirms its occurrence. It is not this declaration, but a fact that must be distinguished from this declaration, which constitutes the event really and essentially creating law—which makes a former pope no longer pope: the death of the pope, the loss of his mental faculties, his heresy, his schismatic separation from the whole of the Church.

To the extent therefore that the conciliar verdict is not the cause of the pope's loss of office, and the council therefore cannot remove his office from the pope as an external authority superposed upon him, but to the extent that the conciliar verdict is the legally valid confirmation of the pope's loss of office, and consequently the council, as a judging authority, makes this loss of office and all the consequences flowing therefrom legally effective publicly in the Church, to this extent and in this sense can we speak of a *superiority* of a council to be espoused in terms of Vatican I, without it thereby becoming the higher legal authority independent of the pope and which the pope would face simply as its subject.

Nevertheless we must discuss this "superiority" of a council in still greater detail. The Council of Constance provides a particular example which, on the one hand, shows that the considerations made regarding a "superiority" of a council can rightly base themselves on Constance and, on the other hand, as shown by the situation of the Western Schism, that they can also be of a great practical importance.

4. THE ECCLESIOLOGICAL IMPORTANCE OF THE COUNCIL OF CONSTANCE

That a council stands above the pope was defined by the ecumenical Council of Constance in the famous decree "Sacrosancta" of the fifth session (April 4, 1415). Here we have a classical case of conflict between Church and pope, which should also shed light on what has been said in the previous chapter. The whole of Christendom had been split only on account of its allegiance to the pope, or to different popes who were held to be legitimate popes by those who followed them at the time. As was said at that time the "nefarious papal duality" (the Roman obedience to Gregory XII; the Avignon obedience to Benedict XIII) had become an "accursed trinity"! (the Pisan obedience of Alexander V, or John XXIII). What is to be done in the Church when the Petrine office, whose meaning is the preservation of unity, in practice fails to accomplish this task and itself becomes the cause of cleavage? The preamble of the decree emphasizes that the aim of the definition is to remove the now forty-year-old schism and to re-establish Church unity and to promote Church reform in head and members: "This holy Synod of Constance, holding a general council in order to uproot the schism and to unite and reform God's Church in its head and members for the praise of almighty God and in the Holy Spirit, legitimately gathered together, and to achieve more securely and freely the union and reform of the Church of God, orders, decides and declares as follows."[1]

Then the Church gathering, as a legitimately assembled general council in the Holy Spirit that represented the whole Church, based itself on the authority directly bestowed by Christ, which everyone, even the pope, had to obey, insofar as it pertained to the faith, to removing the schism, and to Church reform: "It declares first that

[1] Mansi 27, 590.

being legitimately convoked in the Holy Spirit, forming a general council and representing the universal Church, it has immediate power from Christ, which every state and dignity, even if it be the papal dignity, must obey in what concerns faith, the eradication of the mentioned schism and the reformation of the said Church in head and members."[2]

Anyone—be it the pope himself—who persistently refuses obedience to the ordinances and decrees of this Council and of every lawful ecumenical council in points mentioned was to be duly punished: "Likewise, it declares that whoever of whatever condition, state, dignity, even the papal one, refuses persistently to obey the mandates, statutes and orders or prescripts of this sacred synod and of any other general council legitimately convened, above set out, or what pertains to them as done or to be done, will be penalized and duly punished with recourse if necessary to other means of law."[3]

After several directives aimed specifically at John XXIII, in the conclusion of the decree the complaint was made that John XXIII and all present were and remained in full liberty. A trial was opened against John XXIII, who had fled from Constance and who had been arrested before he could pass over into Burgundy, which led to the nullification of his dignity and to his removal from office (May 29, 1415). The other two popes were also expected to resign: Gregory refused, even after the right of convocation of the Council was formally granted to him (April 7, 1417), and Benedict XIII was formally deposed (July 26, 1417) after negotiations failed. The decree "Frequens" (October 9, 1417) called the "frequens generalium Conciliorum celebratio" the best means for achieving Church reform. On this basis the decree directed that the next council should take place five years after the close of the Council of Constance, the next one seven years later and that subsequent councils should be held at least decennially.[4] Finally Martin V was elected as the new pope.[5]

[2] Mansi 27, 590. The meaning of the decree must not be restricted: "The Fathers took care to make it very precise in the second paragraph of the decree, where it becomes evident that it was a question of the competence of *any* councils (*et cujuscumque alterius concilii generalis*) and of *everything* which closely or remotely touches upon matters of faith (*super praemissis*—that is to say, faith, reform and unity—*seu ad ea pertinentibus*). No other precise demarcation than this last one (*ad ea pertinentibus*) could give a broader meaning to the definition." P. de Vooght, "Le Conciliarisme aux conciles de Constance et de Bâle," in *Le concile et les conciles* (Paris 1960) 152.

[3] Mansi 27, 590.

[4] Mansi 27, 1159–1161.

[5] On the history of the Council of Constance, cf. the literature in K. A. Fink, "Konzil von Konstanz," in *Lexikon für Theologie und Kirche* (Freiburg i. Br. [2]1961) VI, 501–503.

The Council of Constance is the only ecumenical council in conciliar history which, after immense efforts (and with the substantial support of strong and sagacious lay authority in the person of King Sigismund), succeeded in overcoming a great split in the Church. The (traditionally understood) legitimacy of Martin V and all other subsequent popes up to the present day depends on the legitimacy of the Council of Constance and its procedure in the question of the popes. Despite this fact—apart from the condemnations of Wyclif and Huss—the Council enjoys no great favour in the dogmatic manuals. Doubtless this lies in a one-sided orientation of modern ecclesiology which, since John Torquemada, "Summa de Ecclesia," has been unable to deal in a positive sense with the decrees of Constance and which frequently merely cites them as difficulties standing in the way of certain ecclesiological theses. Some have not shrunk from pointing out the non-binding character of the Constance decrees, often with quite extraordinary, ostensibly historical arguments.[6] However, according to the most recent research in Church history, whose findings we shall briefly summarize here without interpreting them in terms of their dogmatic significance, it is not a question of insisting in the non-binding character of the decrees.[7] The findings are:

(1) The question concerning papal approbation must not be

[6] Only one example is presented here: "Many theologians, according to John Torquemada (D. Ioan. de Turrecremata, *Summa de Ecclesia*, Venice, 1951, I, II, c. 99, f. 236ʳ–237ʳ), have disputed the claim that the Assembly of Constance gave a general meaning to the decree of the fifth session. The fathers supposedly did not decree the superiority of the Council over the pope, but only the superiority of the Assembly of Constance over uncertain popes. This is manifestly the contrary to the very tenor of the decree. True, the latter cites the necessity of uniting and reforming the Church as the *reason* for its definition. But it is not from the reason which motivated the Fathers thereto that we shall ask the meaning of what they have defined, when this meaning leaves no doubt at all. Now the Fathers do not declare that in case of emergency the Council can depose the pope. Rather, they declare that the Council of Constance is legitimately convoked in the Holy Spirit, that it is a general council, that it represents the Church militant in her entirety, that it has its power directly from God, that every man, including the pope, owes its obedience etc." (P. de Vooght, *op. cit.* 153).

[7] Cf. K. A. Fink, "Papsttum und Kirchenreform nach dem Grossen Schisma," in *"Tübinger Theologische Quartalschrift* 126 (1946) 110–122; "Konzil von Konstanz," in *Lexikon für Theologie und Kirche* (Freiburg i. Br. ²1961) VI, 501–503; P. de Vooght, *op. cit.* 143–181; R. Bäumer, "Konstanzer Dekrete," in *Lexikon für Theologie und Kirche* (Freiburg i. Br. ²1961) VI, 503–505. They all confirm the basic work of B. Hübler, *Die Constanzer Reformation und die Concordate von 1418* (Leipzig 1867). C. J. von Hefele frequently had to revise his interpretation of the Council of Constance on the basis of Hübler's investigations. This revised interpretation was again corrected in Hübler's sense by F. X. Funk, "Martin V. und das Konzil von Konstanz," in *Kirchengeschichtliche Abhandlungen und Untersuchungen* (Paderborn 1897) I, 489–498.

posed anachronistically. An express approbation of the early councils by the pope is disputed by leading Church historians of today. The necessity for papal approbation was established in the papal general councils of the Middle Ages. But at the time of the Council of Constance an express papal approbation was not deemed necessary. Precisely because the Council derived its authority directly from Christ, precisely because the Council thereby stood above the pope (or the three popes), there was no question from the very beginning of a papal approbation; "Martin V closed the synod on April 24, 1418. A separate papal confirmation did not come into question and, viewed historically, it is not a matter of considering only the last three sessions under the new pope as ecumenical."[8] B. Hübler had already established that the wrong formulation of the question that developed only later between the Gallicans (who accepted an express approbation even for the decrees of the fourth and fifth sessions) and the Curialists (who limited an express approbation to the condemnation of the Wycliffian and Hussite heresies): "Both parties equally started out from false premises. In reality the synodal decrees of Constance did not require any papal approbation. In reality such papal approbation was never sought for; in reality Martin V neither refused nor gave it."[9] At the fifth session it had already been decided that the decrees should not be drawn up in the name of the pope, nor in the name of the Council and the pope, but exclusively in the name of the Council because the Council considered itself as standing above the pope. This was the procedure followed in all the decrees of the Council up to the election of Martin V. Because the Council considered itself as standing above the pope, in October 1417 an obligatory injunction to carrying out of Church reform (*cautio de fienda reformatione*) could be handed to the new pope, independent of his approval. Thus an actual guarantee was given to the Reform party. Because the Council considered itself as standing above the pope it could finally (by a purification resolution at the forty-third session) release the pope from his promise to institute reforms given before his election, for which the pope himself had

[8] K. A. Fink, "Konzil von Konstanz," *op cit.* VI, 503. For the essential inspirations of this chapter I thank my Tübingen colleague K. A. Fink, who, especially because of his studies over many years of the administrative acts of the pontificate of Martin V in connection with the Repertorium Germanicum, is probably the best authority on this period that has been little touched upon in terms of sources. Fink has further clarified the views presented here in an article: "Zur Beurteilung des Grossen Abendländischen Schismas," in *Zeitshcrift für Kirchengeschichte* 73 (1962) III/IV as well as in other publications.

[9] B. Hübler, *op cit.* 260; cf. R. Bäumer, *op cit.* VI, 504; P. de Vooght, *op cit.* 161.

petitioned. Hence there can be no question of a papal approbation by the new pope. And because the approbation was not necessary, neither was it asked for by the Council.[10]

(2) But did not Martin V pronounce an approbation at the closing session by declaring: "that he is willing to uphold and observe all and each matter determined, the conclusions and decrees on matters of faith passed in a conciliar way by the present sacred and general Council of Constance and that he would never act against it in any way."[11]

Just after the "Ite in pace," thereby pronouncing the official closing of the Council, the Poles complained that the condemnation of a heresy (of the German Dominican Johann of Falkenberg), which had been decreed as ready for presentation to the Council in the conciliar committees, had not been brought before the plenum by the pope as the president of the Council. In order to extricate himself from this matter, which to him was an embarrassing violation of the order of business, Martin V gave an evasive answer by rejecting the binding legal character of the full decrees on a national basis (in contrast to the decrees of the Council). He was bound by law to what the Council *as such* (*conciliariter*, hence not only *nationally*) had decreed, and he accepted it and purposed to uphold this, no more and no less. The Falkenberg affair, however, had been decided on a national basis, only *nationally* (not as a council decree, but as a department conclusion). There can be no question of any kind of *restriction* of approbation to matters of faith (in contrast to matters of reform and of union, which pertained to the superiority of the Council). "No great importance is to be accorded to the addition in *causa fidei* since it has no really determining meaning but is exclusively explanatory. The matter of the investigation against Johann of Falkenberg concerned the main intention or the principal purpose of the Sacred Council of Constance: the extermination of heresies. Accordingly it had been dealt with by the judges deputized for matters of faith, and the formulated preliminary decrees constituted *conclusa in materia fidei*. The complainants repeatedly referred to this *causa fidei* and papal acknowledgment is also based on it; thus Martin declared that "he purposed to uphold the decrees on faith

[10] B. Hübler, *op cit.* 261–263. Johannes de Torquemada, *Summa de Ecclesia* (Rome 1489, Venice 1560) Lib. II, cap. 99, p. 236, asserts: "After what was said before, the Council of Constance, after Pope Martin's election, asked humbly from him confirmation and approval of all they had done, following the custom of the ancient councils." There is no evidence for this assertion.

[11] Mansi 27, 1201.

of the synod, not the *conclusa* of faith of the nations. It was altogether only a question of matters of faith."[12] Characteristically the addition *in materia fidei* is wholly missing also in the Brunswick manuscript, written not later but in Constance itself, and which most carefully recorded the proceedings: "The pope . . . said he was willing to hold and observe all and each single act, fact and conclusion or other decrees passed in *conciliar manner by the general council,* and not others, nor those passed in other manners,"[13] Hence Hefele rightly says the following about the pope's declaration: "The pope therefore could not possibly have wanted to say that he would withhold confirmation from all other decrees of the Council which did not pertain to *matters of faith,* for otherwise indeed he would also have removed his confirmation from the reform decrees of the thirty-ninth session and thereby awkwardly cut the ground from under his own feet, since even the decrees through which John XXIII and Benedict XIII were deposed and which had ordered a new election did not deal with matters of faith."[14] What is involved in the pope's words therefore is not an attitude towards a specific matter (the Falkenberg case)[15] which had been delivered verbally and in an improvised manner; what is involved is a general approbation of the conciliar decrees, but not a formal approbation in the technical sense, which presupposed a sifting critique of the council's decrees.

(3) When the Poles, in the Falkenberg affair, threatened to appeal a *future* council, such recourse from the pope was declared as inadmissible: "An actual *bull* was certainly not published on the matter. Gerson, who is the only one who reports on the prohibition, speaks only about the draft (*minuta*) of such a bull which was to be read out *in consistorio.* . . . One seems also to have shrunk from an *open* violation of the new consitutional law. In consequence of the inadequate publication the decree was then also ignored. The Poles nonetheless registered their appeal. Even in the last days before the dissolution

---

[12] B. Hübler, *op. cit.* 266. P. de Vooght, *op. cit.* 153–155, takes a position towards the wrong interpretations of "conciliariter": 1. What concerns the Wycliffian and Hussite heresies (R. Bellarmine, M. Cano, etc.); 2. What was decided *re diligentur examinata* and not *tumultualiter* (R. Bellarmine, etc.); 3. What was decided with the approval of the cardinals (A. Baudrillart). Regarding these interpretations, P. de Vooght observes: "It must be acknowledged that all the pathetic attempts to void the word *conciliariter* of its meaning have remained futile" (155).

[13] Quoted according to B. Hübler, *op. cit.* 267.

[14] C. J. von Hefele, *Conciliengeschichte* (Freiburg i. Br. ²1873) I, 52.

[15] Thus, according to Hübler also, C. J. von Hefele, *op. cit.* I, 52; F. X. Funk, *op. cit.* I, 49; P. de Vooght, *op. cit.* 160.

of the Council Gerson wrote a special treatise on the appeals and—
what is especially important—neither Eugene IV nor Torquemada,
the great ecclesiastical legitimist of the fifteenth century, dared later
to make use of it."[16]

(4) In the Bull "Inter cunctas" (February 22, 1418) Martin V
vis-à-vis the Hussites demanded recognition of the Council of Constance in words of an unmistakable clarity: "In like manner whether
he believes, holds and asserts that any general council and also the
one of Constance represents the universal Church. In like manner
whether he believes that what the sacred Council of Constance
representing the universal Church has approved and approves in
favour of faith and salvation of souls and that then must be accepted
and be held by all Christian faithful. And what it has condemned and
condemns has to be held, believed and asserted as condemned. In
like manner whether he believes that the condemnation of John
Wyclif, John Hus and Jerome of Prague pronounced over their
persons, books and writings by the sacred general Council of Constance is right and just and by any Catholic as such as to be held and
firmly maintained."[17] A restrictive character has been ascribed to
the words "in the favour of faith and for the salvation of souls" by
individual theologians. F. X. Funk, on the other hand, rightly asserts:
"The words are in a document that was to serve for the conversion
or instruction of persons suspected of heresy. But if that is the character of the document, however, are we to assume that its author or
Martin V wanted to hint, if only faintly, that the pope and council
were not united on certain questions? The quoted passage is directly
preceded by the following: "whether he believes, holds and asserts
that every general council and also the one of Constance represents
the universal Church." The person under questioning, above all,
therefore, had to acknowledge the Council of Constance as a representation of the whole Church and after he had done this was he to
be given to understand, although only indirectly, that not all decrees
of the council were valid, but only those promulgated in "the favour

---

[16] B. Hübler, *op. cit.* 264; cf. P. de Vooght, *op. cit.* 157f. 161. Further accounts
in *Die Berichte der Generalprokuratoren des Deutschen Ordens an der Kurie*, vol.
II: Peter von Wormdith (1403–1419), arranged by H. Koeppen (=Veröffent-
lichungen der niedersächsischen Archivverwaltung, No. 13, Göttingen 1960)
490ff. No. 258: "do lies her lesen eyne minuten." No. 259 and No. 266 also contain accounts of the event. From this it shows clearly that Martin V's answer
concerned no universal decision of principle but a singular decision against the
Poles who had repeatedly harassed the pope vehemently.
[17] Mansi 27, 1211.

of faith and for the good of the souls? This is certainly very improbable. . . ."[18] Nevertheless Funk's further conclusion seems still to be too negatively formulated when he states: ". . . accordingly even this passage provides no explanation concerning Martin's position towards the Council of Constance or any proof that the pope did not reorganize all the decrees of the Council." P. de Vooght rightly observes: "Le sens obvie de ces trois paragraphes est une profession de foi dans le concile de Constance en tant que concile général et dans la valeur de ses décisions doctrinales." ["The obvious meaning of these three paragraphs is a profession of faith in the Council of Constance and in the importance of its doctrinal decisions."][19]

(5) Martin V's personal attitude to the Council: "If Odo Colonna had not been at least to a certain extent an exponent of conciliar theory, in the actual state of affairs at the council, he would never have become pope. Hence he too was—to use a term easily misunderstood—a 'conciliarist.' " Nevertheless, he was neither a professional theologian nor a writer but a cardinal and thus he belonged to the conservative wing of the exponents of the Council's superiority over the pope. This conservative wing asserted a "superiority" of the Council, but interpreted this restrictively. While the extreme exponents of the conciliar idea actually wanted to transfer the ordinary Church-government to the Council, the moderate exponents in turn wanted to transfer it to the pope and the cardinals. According to the view of these moderates the Council should intervene only in case of a crisis. No doubt they were also in favour of a limitation and control of the peope's power. But this control should in the first place belong not to the bishops but to the cardinals.

P. de Vooght has managed to make the seemingly contradictory behaviour of Martin V comprehensible in terms of this whole situation of the Council.[20] Cardinal Colonna had fled to Schaffhausen with John XXIII and he was not involved in the "Sacrosancta." But he did not in any way speak against it, for he too was in favour of the "superiority" of the Council. Subsequently he expressed himself in favour of the decree "Frequens," which laid down the periodicity of the councils. Nevertheless Colonna, along with other cardinals, was above all interested in electing a new pope as soon as possible and thereafter to set about reforming the Church under the leadership

[18] F. X. Funk, *op. cit.* I, 497.
[19] P. de Vooght, *op. cit.* 160.
[20] P. de Vooght, *op. cit.* 155–162.

of the pope. The council, although it was above the pope in a certain
certain sense, should intervene only in crisis situations. Nevertheless the opposition between the moderate and the radical wing of the
advocates of conciliar superiority had grown sharper after the deposition of the three popes. The radicals wanted to introduce a
universal conciliar Church-government to reform the Church before
any election of a pope. The compromise that was effected in 1417
on the one hand produced the promulgation of the reform decrees
(among them the decree "Frequens") and on the other hand the
election of a new pope. The "moderates" expected to lead radical
conciliarism along a safer channel than this. They were not disappointed. The very adroit Colonna pope did everything to strengthen
the position of the pope once more and to hold back the influence
of radical conciliarism. This was why he did not allow an appeal
from the pope in the first phase of the Falkenberg affair; this was also
why he did not deem useful a specification of the cases in which the
pope can be judged and deposed by the Church. But Martin in no
way denied the conciliar ideas, as they had been defined. For a
certain superiority of the Council over the pope in principle is one
thing—and the rights that appertain to the pope in the exercise of his
function are something else. The same Martin V could very well admit
a superiority of the Council in principle and, notwithstanding, reject
the appeal to a council against the decisions that he had issued within
the limits of his authority, as well as in the codification of a procedure
of deposition. In a certain sense he could very well acknowledge the
position of the Council over the pope in principle, nevertheless he
had an aversion to endless general conciliar discussions. All this does
not contradict that which clearly emerges from Martin V's actions—
his agreement with the conciliar definitions, which was officially expressed at the end of the Falkenberg affair and in the Bull "Inter
cunctas." To be sure, as we have seen, it has nothing to do with a
formal papal approbation; this Council had expected such approbation as little as had the ecumenical councils of Christian antiquity.
This says as little against the binding character of the decrees of
Constance as it does against the binding character of the decrees of
the early councils. In Nicaea as in Constance a general agreement of
the Roman bishop, without which no consensus of the Church is
possible, altogether sufficed for endowing decrees with a binding
character.

(6) The binding character of the Constance decrees is confirmed
by the fact that Martin V felt bound by the decres even after the
council, and carried them out loyally. He did not decide the (un-

decidable) question as to who was supposed to have been the true pope during the Great Schism: "Martin V also took seriously the attitude which excluded the epoch of the Western Schism and restored the link with 1378 (Gregory XI); and in his ordinances he treated all three former obediences equally, with slight preference for the Pisan obedience."[21]

At the same time the pope took pains to avoid any charges of disobedience towards conciliar decrees: "Martin stood formally upon the decisions of Constance; in fact the validity of his election was dependent on their binding force. The Antipope Benedict XIII obstinately maintained his pretensions at Peniscola. In spite of grave misgivings about its conciliar tendencies, Martin V sent legates to the General Council convened at Pavia in 1423 but soon transferred to Siena. When the Fathers of that feebly attended assembly began to squabble over the question of authority and reform, he dissolved it, on 7 March 1424. At the same time he sought to pacify the reformers by initiating a reform of the papal Caria. In this he was unsuccessful. By the time the Council summoned to meet at Basle in 1431 actually opened, and, after some delay, had been given a papal legate in the person of Cardinal Cesarini, the radicalism of the adherents of the conciliar theory was greatly increased and the call for reform became louder than ever."[22] Despite his recognition in principle and execution of the conciliar decrees, the pope, to be sure, very energetically also pursued curialist aims. During the very execution of the conciliar decrees he knew how most adroitly to render them practically ineffective, especially the decree "Frequens," and strengthen papal authority anew: "The new pope, who had been trained in law, knew what was legal in the Church's past. Thus in the field of actual Church reform along the lines of the changed Church constitution he managed, through astute ecclesiastical diplomacy with individual states, to deprive the 'Frequens' decree of its inner substance while externally seemingly carrying it out as much as possible, convoking to the very day and hour the synod scheduled to be held in Pavia and Siena, but dissolving it abruptly when it tried to deal with reform that was tantamount to changing the distribution of ecclesiastical authority. That this dissolution was accepted without ado, nevertheless, shows clearly enough how adroitly,

[21] K. A. Fink, "Konzil von Konstanz," in *Lexikon für Theologie und Kirche* (Freiburg i. Br. [2]1961) VI, 503.

[22] H. Jedin, *History of the Council of Trent* (Edinburgh 1961) I, 17; cf. K. A. Fink, "Papsttum und Kirchenreform nach dem Grossen Schisma," in *Tübinger Theologische Quartalschrift* 126 (1946) 110–122; "Martin V.," in *Lexikon für Theologie und Kirche* (Freiburg i. Br. [2]1962) vol. VII.

in the brief time span of five years, the Curia had worked for the re-
establishment of the political power of the papacy in the traditional
sense. The 'Frequens' decree then even served for rejecting the English-
French desire of shortening the periods between the convocations of
councils. By the very recognition and the literal interpretation of the
conciliar decrees the periodic supplementation of the general
council lost almost any importance in the hands of the newly
strengthened curialism, not only as a superposed or as a control
authority but as a synod altogether. Thereby the danger of this
setup was warded off and Church reform along the lines of Constance (superiority of the council to the pope, 'Frequens') was
practically shunted aside. In other words, the weight of regular
authority and permanent power triumphed over the extraordinary
setup. It was possible to achieve all this, however, only by exploitation of the desires and power ambitions of individual countries and
princes."[23]

(7) Directly after the close of the Council of Constance, at the
councils of Pavia and Siena up to the death of Martin V, there is no
question at all of any doubts being cast on the binding character of
the Constance decrees.[24] The Council of Basle, immediately after its
convocation, renewed the general decrees of the fourth and fifth
sessions of Constance. And the cardinal-delegate Julian Cesarini, who
was still entrusted with the presidency by Martin V, very clearly
declared in his letter of June 5, 1432, addressed to the newly elected
Pope Eugene IV, that the legitimacy of Martin V and of every subsequent pope depended on the validity of the decrees of the Council of
Constance: "Whether this council is legitimate depends on the
Council of Constance. If that was valid, this is too. No one seems,
however, to have doubted its legitimacy *and whatever it has decreed.*
For if one says the decrees of this Council are invalid, one has to
admit that the deposition of John XXIII, which was effected by
its decrees, was invalid. If this was invalid, then the election of Pope
Martin while the other was still in power does not hold. If Martin was
not Pope, then neither is Your Holiness who was elected by the
Cardinals made by him. No one, therefore, has more interest in
defending the decrees of that Council than Your Holiness. And if
any of that Council's decrees are called in doubt, for the same
reason could the rest of the decrees be revoked; with the same reasoning, the decrees of other councils are void since the cause that shakes

---

[23] K. A. Fink, *op. cit.* 116f.
[24] Cf. B. Hübler, *op. cit.* 269–277.

the faith of one council will make the others doubtful too."[25] Eugene IV also recognized, albeit in an emergency situation (which in any case in no way took away his freedom!), the binding character of the Constance decrees in the Bull "Ad ea ex debito" (February 5, 1547), with its express reference to the same view of his predecessor, Martin V: "We accept, embrace, and highly respect the general Council of Constance, the decree *Frequens* and its other decrees as well as the other councils representing the Church militant, her power, authority, dignity and eminence as all our predecessors from whose footsteps we never intend to deviate."[26]

Nevertheless the restoration of papal power had come about with an extraordinary swiftness. It was also expressed in the re-establishment of the earlier theory of Church constitution. K. A. Fink says the following on this subject: "Recent research has already pursued this question rather successfully. A systematic treatment of the reports and interpretations of this epoch, which I plan to make, will make it still clearer that even before the middle of the century the monarchic conception of the Church government and the absolute authority of the papacy, although not taught by the majority of the canonists, nevertheless again found notable exponents. As so often has been the case in history the 'via facti' had become crucial for theory. The pontificate of Martin V therefore produced nothing more than the consistent execution of the papal election at Constance, the determination, the tenacious will, and the personality of the new pope; the 'deductio ad absurdum' of the new theories concerning the Church constitution. Thus we can establish an altogether interesting development also in the area of the theory of Church constitution: under Martin V and in part also under Eugene IV, hence between Constance and Basle, the general view regarding Church constitution was still almost undisputedly conciliar; the canonistic doctrine followed the restoration introduced by Martin V only two decades later, that is, the theory did not accord at all with the actual conditions precisely in this important first half of the fifteenth century."[27]

With the strengthening of the curial power the popes proceeded ever more decisively in the renewal of their claims. Martin V (Eugene IV less so) at least formally still carried out the Constance decrees

[25] Quoted according to B. Hübler, *op. cit.* 269f.
[26] Quoted according to B. Hübler, *op. cit.* 270; P. de Vooght analyzed the Council of Basle on this basis and came to the conclusion: "I do not think that one can honestly escape the conclusion that Eugene IV approved, no doubt in a moment of depression, the superiority of the Council over the pope in the form extolled at Basle."
[27] K. A. Fink, *op. cit.* 119f.

and convoked councils. As regards councils, however, Nicholas V fundamentally pursued a policy of postponement; his successor Calixtus simply ignored them. Pius II was the first to dare, in 1460 in the Bull "Execrabilis," officially to forbid the appeal from a pope to a council and to punish such an appeal by excommunication. But the papal prohibitions could not prevail in the Church: "With the Bull *Execrabilis* the restoration Papacy dealt the conciliar theory its first blow. The result did not come up to expectations. In France and Germany it met with vigorous opposition and outside Rome it was not generally accepted. In spite of repeated prohibitions of appeals to a Council by Pius II in the Bull *Infructuosos palmites* of 2 November 1460, by Sixtus IV in the Bull *Qui monitis* of 15 July 1483, and by Julius II in the Bull *Suscepti regiminis* of 1 July 1509, secular princes as well as ecclesiastical bodies continued to use an appeal as a legitimate legal device."[28] The prohibitions of the pope were held to be measures of a curial policy and appeal continued to be made to the Constance decrees, which were vigorously defended outside Rome. They were defended by political powers and countless bishops and theologians not only in France (especially by the University of Paris) and in Germany (by the universities of Cologne, Vienna, Erfurt, Cracow) but also in Italy by canonists and jurists in Padua and Pavia, and even by curialists such as Giovanni Gozzadini at the court of Julius II. The latter defended the Constance decrees as late as 1511 as an article of faith and challenged the binding character of the prohibition of an appeal from the pope. According to him the relevant bull was void of any legal effect. Should the objection be raised that the appeal is directed to a wholly non-existent tribunal, the following must be taken into consideration: Even though no council is assembled, the authority of the Church nevertheless exists and should be considered greater than that of the pope. The "Frequens" decree especially makes obligatory the regular holding of councils and thereby guarantees a representation of the Church to which an appeal can be submitted. The fact that the popes had not implemented these decrees would be their fault, but this would change nothing in the law. Like Gozzadini, the bishop of Brescia, Mattia Ugoni, also defended the Constance decrees against Torquemada.

Thus to a great extent the Church of the fifteenth century, and also of the sixteenth century, was dominated by conciliar ideas. But the pope and the curia laboured tirelessly to push through their claims. At the Fifth Lateran Council, in 1516, Leo X had the following declaration made: ". . . the Roman Pontiff of the day, as having

[28] H. Jedin, *History of the Council of Trent* (Edinburgh 1961) I, 66–67.

authority over all Councils. . . ."[29] But objections were already raised against this Council, charging that it had been attended exclusively by Italians and that, as in the medieval general synods, it was wholly under the domination of the pope: "It met in Rome under the eyes of the Pope, and was almost exclusively attended by Italian bishops. Thus it conformed perfectly to the conception of a papal General Council which had taken shape in the course of the restoration period, The Pope himself settled the order of procedure and named the officials of the Council at its first session, 10 May 1512. His influence was decisive in determining the composition of the committees formed on 3 May 1513 and further expanded on 26 October 1516. The decrees were published in the form of papal Bulls."[30] Thus the ecumenicity of this Council was already strongly questioned. "It was characterized as an unfree council by the enemies of the pope. Nor did it meet with universal recognition at the Council of Trent."[31] In part there had been an appeal from the "conciliabulum Romanum" to a general council. Even Bellarmine replied with obvious reserve to the objections that were raised against the ecumenicity of the Fifth Lateran Council: "It can hardly be maintained that it was general."[32] And in connection with the statement that a pope stands above a council, he remarked: "Some doubt whether the Lateran Council, which defined this matter very clearly, was truly general; thus until today the question remains even among Catholics."[33]

No matter how we regard the question of the ecumenicity of the Fifth Lateran Council in detail, the Council, convoked for political reasons, must be viewed as a reaction to the Council of Pisa (1511–12). In view of the "irreformability" of the decrees of ecumenical councils!—it could in no way abolish the Constance decrees, which had the authority of the whole Church and of the pope behind them in a wholly different way than did the Fifth Lateran Synod. It is significant that the synod did not dare to propose a resolution that would declare the "superiority" decrees of Constance and Basle invalid, as was recommended by Ferdinand the Catholic in his instruction to his envoys at the Council. It is significant that the Council of Constance is not even mentioned in the papal bull, and the Council of Basle is rejected only from the time of the papal postponement. The statement that the pope stands above a council

[29] Denz. 740.
[30] H. Jedin, *op. cit.* I, 128.
[31] R. Bäumer, "Lateran-Synoden," in *Lexikon für Theologie und Kirche* (Freiburg i. Br. ²1961) VI, 818.
[32] R. Bellarmine, *De conciliis lib. II, cap.* 17 (Opera omnia, Paris, 1870) II, 271.
[33] R. Bellarmine, *De conciliis lib. II, cap.* 13 (*op. cit.*) II, 265.

was not made directly, but indirectly, namely as an argument for the other statements that the pope has the right to convoke, to transfer, and to dissolve councils. In any case neither Leo X nor any other pope of the restorationist period dared to abolish the decree "Sacrosancta" or to declare it not universally binding.

(8) The actual course of Church history, which was but little favourable to the Constance decrees, should not make us overlook the fact that the Constance decrees in no way claimed to be important and binding merely for that point in time. To describe them as "a means for overcoming the momentarily difficult situation"[34] corresponds neither with the text of the decrees nor with the intent of those who defined them. The binding character of the decrees (although not in the sense of a radical conciliar parliamentarianism, which was only *one* interpretation of the decrees) must be taken seriously: "Certainly not everything can be explained in terms of the emergency situation and thereby actually deprived of its importance, as a certain narrow and too dogmatic historiography is wont to assert. On the other hand it would be an excessive projection of our reflections into the historical consciousness of the time, if the dilemma is exaggeratedly formulated in terms of mutually exclusive alternatives—either a monarchical *or* parliamentary Church constitution. The questions were never posed so pointedly or felt as such."[35]

The binding character of the decrees of Constance is not to be evaded. The whole Church and the pope stood behind these decrees at that time with a great unanimity. Indeed, on the basis of these decrees the Church was able to settle the question of the three competing popes, and Church unity (at least in the West) was again restored. On the basis of these decrees the new pope was elected. On the one hand, the legitimacy of the new pope depended on the legitimacy of these decrees; on the other hand, according to the usual view, it is in turn the premise for the legitimacy of the popes in the last five hundred years. The Council was convinced that with the decrees it had provided a solution which had to be valid not only for this conflict between pope and Church, but also for future councils.

Summarizing the results of the Council in connection with our problem area, just what was actually defined at the Council of

[34] H. Hollensteiner, "Das Konstanzer Konzil in der Geschichte der christlichen Kirche," in *Mitteilungen des Österreichischen Instituts für Geschichtsforschung*. Supp. vol. XI (Innsbruck 1929) 414.

[35] K. A. Fink, "Papsttum und Kirchenreform nach dem Grossen Schisma," in *Tübinger Theologische Quartalschrift* 126 (1946) 112.

Constance? Conciliar parliamentarianism (along the lines of a radical conciliarism) was *not* defined; according to this the regular ordinary government of the Church would have been transferred from the pope to the Council and the pope reduced to a subordinate executive organ of the conciliar parliament. Doubtless this radical conciliarism was espoused by some at the Council. Nevertheless in no way was it the general view held by the Council Fathers nor therefore a universally binding interpretation of the Council. The moderates, above all from the College of Cardinals and the southern countries, and the newly elected pope stood opposed to the radicals. Therefore radical conciliarism could not prevail in the Church also as the genuine interpretation of the Constance decrees.

In any case, however, what was *defined* was a distinct kind of superiority of the council (along the lines of at least moderate "conciliar theory"), according to which an ecumenical council has the function of a "control authority," not only in connection with the emergency situation of that time but also for the future, on the premise that a possible future pope might again lapse into heresy, schism, or the like. *All* the participants at the Council, even the moderate Council Fathers and the pope, were in favour of the necessity of a certain control over the pope by an ecumenical council, viewed as the representation of the universal Church. The "Frequens" decree served the realization of the "Sacrosancta" decree, and served the undertaking of that conciliar "control function." Neither of the two decrees aimed at introducing a new Church constitution along the lines of parliamentarianism, wholly apart from the fact that the early Church constitution had not yet been expressly established in this respect. Thereafter it was perforce repeatedly to be admitted—as we shall see later—that a "control function" of this kind belongs in principle to an ecumenical council (although this need not take the form of the practical regulation of the "Frequens" decree, which undoubtedly is a human law). Admittedly curalist policy, dogmatics, and canon law took great pains to pass over this control function in silence as much as possible by a onesided absolutist emphasis on papal primacy and practically to reduce it to insignificance by an exclusive appeal to Divine Providence and to the impossibility of conflicts between pope and Church.

The Church might have been able to avoid many misfortunes after the Council of Constance had the fundamental position of the Constance Council—papal primacy *and* a definite "conciliar control"—been upheld. But just as Martin V and his successors strove, according to their powers, to reconquer the primatial authority

without regard to any control, likewise did the extremist conciliarists
in Basle, for their part, strive increasingly for a factual voiding of
the papal primacy in favour of a government of the Church in practice by the Council. Both parties at first formally and officially upheld the Constance decrees but they interpreted them in an extreme
sense in line with their own views—papalist or conciliarist. The
conciliarists wanted to grant the pope and the papalists only an
"honorary position" at a Council. If the conciliarists had the text
of the decree on their side, the papalists had the power of the papacy
on theirs. Extreme conciliarism without a genuine primatial Church
government led—along with many other factors—to the Basle
schism; extreme papalism without conciliar control—along with
many other factors—led to the abuse of office of the Renaissance
papacy and, indirectly, to the Lutheran Reformation. The moderates
of both sides, however, were much closer to each other than outer
appearances often indicated; even those who defended the full
authority of the pope did not without more ado deny the necessity
of a conciliar control, at least in certain cases (and in such cases the
council was in fact above the pope, himself in fact illegitimate);
and those who defended the control function of a council did not
without more ado deny the full authority of the legitimate pope in
the Church government (in which then the pope in fact stands above
a council).[36]

It cannot be overlooked that the definitions of Constance actually left many theoretical as well as practical questions wide open.
What was left open could not be easily and clearly established at
that time—for the Council Fathers held different opinions precisely

---

[36] P. de Vooght, "Le conciliarisme aux conciles de Constance et de Bâle," in
Le concile et les conciles (Paris 1960) 177f: "If the distance between the Basle
progressives of conciliarism and the Roman position was unbridgeable, it was
singularly reduced between the conciliarists who continued to give a discreet and
prudent interpretation to the Constance decrees, and the Roman theologians
who, like Torquemada, made a place—discreet to be sure, but not to be questioned
—for the control of the pope by the Church. Thus the real positions of those who
on the one side and the other did not content themselves only with repeating
slogans ("The Council is superior to the pope" or "The pope is superior to the
Council") seemed to be quite close. If the systematized ideologies (or theologies)
did not agree, the wisest in both camps thought that the *one* Church must be
governed by a single supreme head (in this sense the pope is above the Council),
but they also thought that in extreme cases the Church had the right to call even
the supreme head to order (in this sense, the pope is subordinate to the Council).
On these two essential points, the conciliarist Nicholas of Cusa and the papalist
Torquemada were agreed. Is it not this capital fact which, in the last analysis,
explains how Nicholas of Cusa could smoothly pass from conciliarism over to
papalism and become, as Aeneas Sylvius said, the Hercules of the Eugenists?"

on this matter. Thus, subsequently, further definitions of the relationship between pope and council were possible and perhaps necessary.
Had a radical conciliarism been defined, it would have left no room
for the definition of primacy formulated at the First Vatican Council.
Room for it was left by that particular kind of "superiority" of a council which was defined in Constance along the lines of moderate conciliar theory. Subsequently the kind of "superiority" that appertained
to a council was defined more exactly. Following present-day
canonist theory, we have in detail discussed the sense in which one
can speak of a "superiority" of a council over the pope, to be espoused in terms of the First Vatican Council. In the sense of possible,
declarative judgments operative in specific cases; namely, to the
extent that the conciliar verdict is not in fact the cause of the pope's
loss of office and a council, consequently, cannot remove his office
from the pope as a superposed authority coming from the outside:
but to the extent, however, that the conciliar verdict is the legally
valid confirmation of the pope's loss of office and consequently a
council as the judging authority makes it legally effective publicly in
the Church, with all the consequences flowing therefrom.

With all its justified emphasis on the superiority of the *pope* the
militant anti-conciliarist, anti-reformationist, and anti-Gallican position of the Church and of theology has at the same time frequently
made it unnecessarily difficult rightly to recognize and to take seriously the proper and traditional meaning of the superiority of a
council. Admittedly, in view of the present linguistic protocol of the
Church, it is very misleading to speak in an unqualified way of a
Council's superiority over a pope. A superiority of this kind, in
general, would be understood in the sense of an heretical extreme
conciliarism, and rightly rejected.

Although it is not disputed by anyone, today we are often too
little aware of the fact that this can also be understood in a thoroughly
orthodox way, namely along the lines of statements made by canonists
concerning the pope's loss of office and the confirmation of this fact
by a council. If our aim is not simply to drop the definitions of the
Council of Constance, which is not allowable to a Catholic according
to what has been set forth up to now, we cannot renounce the
affirmation of a rightly understood superiority that appertains to a
council. In any case the problems discussed here do not depend on the
word "superiority." This word can be correctly and incorrectly
understood, both with respect to a council and with respect to a
pope. In connection with both the correct determination of the
relationship between pope and council and the correct determination

of the relationship between the Council of Constance and Vatican I,[37] everything will depend upon not separating the factors pope and council, but viewing them together within the structure of the whole Church as a unity. On the basis of the nature of the Church we will then more deeply understand the relationship between pope and council if we grasp it not primarily as a relationship of superiority— understood along the lines of the one or the other tendency—but as a relationship that is reciprocally conditioned. Thus it is not to be understood as a relationship of superordination and subordination, but as a reciprocal ministerial relationship in the service of the Church under the one and only Lord.

We will acquire an even better understanding of the ecclesiological importance of the Council of Constance if we now consider the Constance decrees against the background of the whole development of ecclesiology and set forth the following two points: (1) The conciliar theory of the Council of Constance is not an invention of Marsilius of Padua and William of Ockham, but in its principles is rooted in the official canon law studies of the Middle Ages; and (2) The conciliar theory of the Council of Constance was not buried with the Council of Basle but, instead, it preserved its essential core even afterwards in the Church despite all opposition.

5. THE CONSTANCE DECREES IN ECCLESIOLOGICAL TRADITION

(a) *The Constance Decrees as a Product of Medieval Ecclesiology:* As the result of a dogmatic narrowness the attempt has been made in modern times superficially to brand all conciliar ideas, especially the conciliar theory that was developed during the Western Schism, as hereticizing "conciliarism." It became all the easier to make this point when—as a result of the work of K. Wenck,[1] A. Kneer,[2] and K. Hirsch,[3] at the turn of the century—the origin of conciliar ideas was seen generally (also in the manuals of Church History) as lying in Marsilius of Padua and William of Ockham. In this way the revolutionary secular-democratic, heretical origin and character of these ideas and the break with traditional ecclesiology seemed to be posited

---

[37] This will be discussed further in the following section.

[1] K. Wenck, "Konrad von Gelnhausen und die Quellen der konziliaren Theorie," in *Historische Zeitschrift* 76 (1896) 1–60.

[2] A. Kneer, *Kardinal Zabarella: Ein Beitrag zur Geschichte des grossen abendländischen Schisma* (Münster 1890).

[3] K. Hirsch, *Die Ausbildung der konziliaren Theorie* (Vienna 1903).

at the outset. Now the works of F. Bliemetzrieder,[4] A. Hauck,[5] and M. Siedlmayer[6] have shown the untenability of the thesis of the Ockhamite-Marsilian origin of conciliar theory and of the break with tradition. But B. Tierney[7]—inspired by W. Ullmann,[8] E. F. Jacob, and the prominent historian of canon law S. Kuttner—was the first to produce comprehensive and irrefutable proof that conciliar theories are grounded in the wholly orthodox and traditional ecclesiology of the twelfth and thirteenth centuries.[9] Tierney's work is deliberately restricted to the material of canon law (of which there is a tremendous amount, almost impossible to survey) in order, in the light of the work of the most important canonists of individual epochs to elaborate the outlines of those elements which could contribute to the growth of conciliar ideas.

Naturally, it would be important now to supplement this inquiry into medieval canon law with an inquiry into medieval theology.

[4] F. Bliemetzrieder, *Das Generalkonzil im grossen abendländischen Schisma* (Paderborn 1904).

[5] A. Hauck, "Die Rezeption und Umbildung der allgemeinen Synode im Mittelalter," in *Historische Vierteljahrschrift* 10 (1907) 465–482.

[6] M. Seidlmayer, *Die Anfänge des grossen abendländischen Schismas* . . . (Münster i. W. 1940).

[7] B. Tierney, *Foundations of the Conciliar Theory* (Cambridge 1955); by the same author: "A Conciliar Theory of the Thirteenth Century," in *Catholic Historical Review* 36 (1951) 415–440; "The Canonists and the Mediaeval State," in *Review of Politics* 15 (1953) 378–388; "Ockham, the Conciliar Theory, and the Canonists," in *Journal of the History of Ideas* 15 (1954) 40–70; "Pope and Council: Some New Decretist Texts," in *Mediaeval Studies* 19 (1957) 197–218. On the second problem complex, spiritual power versus secular power, closely connected with the problem complex of internal Church matters, cf. the important work by S. Mochi Onory, *Fonti canonistiche dell'idea moderna dello Stato* (Milano 1951).

[8] Cf. especially W. Ullmann, *The Origin of the Great Schism* (London 1948).

[9] Brian Tierney of Catholic University of America in Washington is the secretary of the Institute of Research and Study in Medieval Canon Law, directed by S. Kuttner, which has energetically begun to open up the enormous source material in the field of canon law. Tierney's work, which has been scarcely noticed by the dogmatists, has enjoyed wide recognition among historians; cf. especially the detailed review by M. Siedlmayer in *Zeitschrift der Savigny-Stiftung für Rechtsgeschichte, Kanonist,* Abt. 43 (1957) 374–387; furthermore H. Wolter, in *Scholastik* 31 (1956) 603f; R. Elze, in *Zeitschrift für Kirchengeschichte* 69 (1958) 353f; H. Jedin, *Ecumenical Councils of the Catholic Church* (New York 1960) 106f; "Konziliarismus," in *Lexikon für Theologie und Kirche* (Freiburg i. Br. ²1961) VI, 532–534; H. Schmidinger, in *Anima* 15 (1960) 308–318; Y. Congar, "La Primauté des quatre premiers conciles oecuméniques," in *Le concile et les conciles* (Paris 1960) 92–94; G. Fransen, "L'Ecclésiologie des conciles médiévaux," *ibid.* 139–141; P. de Vooght, "Le Conciliarisme aux conciles de Constance et de Bâle," *ibid.* 143–148; C. Andresen, "Geschichte der abendländischen Konzile des Mittelalters," in *Die ökuminischen Konzile der Christenheit* (Stuttgart 1961) 128, 137, 144; H. Fuhrmann, "Das Ökumenische Konzil und seine historischen Grundlagen," in *Geschichte in Wissenschaft und Unterricht* 12 (1961) 686–690.

There can certainly be no doubting the fact that the yield of a *theological* investigation in connection with our problems would not turn out to be nearly as abundant as that of Tierny's *inquiry into canon law*. Like the patristic theologians, medieval theologians also made many utterances concerning the Church, yet they had little interest in the systematic development of an ecclesiological treatise. As regards their ecclesiological views, most of the medieval theologians were above all influenced by the Church Fathers, especially by Augustine. The spiritual aspect of the Church was more important to them than the legal aspect. To a great extent they left the question of the Church constitution to canon law—which had already for some time enjoyed a leading position in Rome. It was from it that theology took theories, texts, and verifications when, since the middle of the thirteenth century and especially with Thomas Aquinas, it turned its attention more to the questions of Church constitution, thereby laying greater stress on the hierarchical factor and the jurisdictional position of the pope. The first systematic treatises concerning the Church—"De regimine christiano" by Jacob of Viterbo, "De ecclesiastica potestate" by Aegidius Romanus, and "De potestate regia et papali" by Jean de Paris—as was remarked previously, arose as a result of the dispute between Boniface VIII and Philip the Fair. From the outset, their content was originally determined less by theology than by canon law. If, therefore, in connection with the conciliar problems less material is to be expected from medieval theology than from medieval canon law, we must not, nevertheless, overlook the fact that certain basic propositions, which ultimately were of great importance for the development of conciliar ideas, are also to be found in both canon law and theology. This applies not only to the specific corporative ideas in the understanding of the nature of the Church, but quite generally in connection with the conception of the Church as a congregation of the faithful (*congregatio fidelium*). Even Thomas Aquinas, who in his ecclesiology thought along strong hierarchic lines, repeatedly started out from this traditional concept of the Church. It was on this basis, as we have seen,[10] that he explained the nature of the Church in his commentary on the Apostles' Creed.[11] A sifting of the problem, not only along canonico-

[10] Cf. Chap. II,

[11] Thomas Aquinas, *Expos. in Symb.* art 9: In regard to this, one has to know that *Ecclesia* [Church] means the same as congregation. Hence the holy Church is the same as the congregation of the faithful and every Christian is a member of the Church. Cf. *c. Gent.* IV, 78; *S. th.* I, p. 117, a. 2 obj. 1; III, q. 8 a. 4 ad 2; *De Ver.* q. 29 a. 4, obj. 8; *Comp. theol.* I, 147; in 1 *Cor.* c. 12 lect. 3; *in Hebr.* c. 3. lect. 1.

historical but also along theologico-historical lines, shows that the conciliar idea of the late Middle Ages is not only closely connected with the scholastic conception of the Church but also with the patristic conception of the Church (especially Augustine's) and even with the Scripture's conception of the Church as a *congregatio* of the faithful (and not as a "clerical Church") and of the office as service to and in the Church community. Our previous chapters should have led to some clarification of these things.

Tierney's brilliant study establishes the connection between conciliar ideas and medieval canon law with the greatest precision. During the Western Schism (and far beyond this) conciliar ideas were espoused everywhere in the Church (especially prominent in Germany were Konrad of Gelnhausen, Heinrich of Langenstein, and Dietrich of Niem; in France, Jean Gerson and Cardinal Pierre d'Ailly; in Spain, Andreas Randulf; and in Italy, Cardinal Francesco Zabarella). Tierney from the outset doubts that even the alarming situation created by the Great Schism would have temped so many pious and distinguished men of the Church from so many countries to subscribe to doctrines that had been fashioned by declared heretics only two generations before. Thus he rightly casts doubt on the tendency of the earlier research to consider the conciliar movement as something accidental, external, imposed upon the Church from the outside, instead of seeing it as the culmination of ideas that are imbedded in the very teaching and law of the Church.[12]

When Tierney investigates canon law from the twelfth century onward he is clearly persuaded that the leading canonists, for instance around the time of Innocent III, were not conciliarists in the sense of the fourteenth century. Nevertheless, he is convinced that he can extricate all the characteristic propositions of conciliar theory from the treatises of the papalist canonists of around 1200.[13] Tierney establishes three great periods of the development of conciliar ideas. Here we will summarize the statements that are of special importance to our themes:

[12] "The neglect of canonistic sources by most writers on the origins of the Conciliar Theory may also arise from a mistaken approach to the early history of conciliar thought. There has been a tendency to treat the Conciliar Movement as something accidental or external, thrust upon the Church from outside rather than as a logical culmination of ideas that were embedded in the law and doctrine of the Church itself. . . . But to understand the origins of a constitutional crisis in the Church we must surely turn to the background of constitutional law from which all parties in the crisis sought to defend their claims." B. Tierney, *Foundations of the Conciliar Theory* (Cambridge 1955) 13.

[13] "It would, for instance, be possible to extract from the canonistic treatises written around the year 1200 a series of assertions that seem to anticipate all the characteristic propositions of the Conciliar Theory." B. Tierney, *op. cit.* 19.

First Period: *Decretist Theories Concerning the Administration of the Church (1140 to 1220):* What do the commentators on the *Decretum Gratiani*, that compilation of canon law by Gratian which has, in fact, become official (among them Huguccio, bishop of Pisa, probably the greatest of the Decretists), teach about the relationships between pope and Church, pope and general council? For the Decretists around 1200, the superordination of a general council over the pope was not—as it was for the publicists around 1400—the most pressing ecclesiastico-political problem of the moment, but merely a theoretical question of harmonizing mutually contradictory texts from Gratian's *Decretum*. Hence they pursued all the different intricacies of the legal principles cited in the decrees with an untroubled freshness of approach, without concerning themselves overmuch with a systematic theory of Church constitution.

What do the Decretists teach about the relationship between *pope and Church*? The ambiguity that was found with respect to the nature of the Church in medieval writings was already contained in the interpretation of the Petrine passage Matthew 16:18 (next to Matthew 18:18 and Luke 22:32).[14] Whether Christ, Peter, or Peter's faith is the foundation of the Church was left open by most (as even by Huguccio). The keys were handed over to *all* the apostles. Peter thereby has the primacy but he stands—according to Augustine Gratian, and many Decretists—"symbolizing the Church," "signifies the Church"; it is the Church herself who is addressed in Peter in the passage, "I give thee the keys," as well as in the passage, "I have prayed for thee." On the basis of such Decretist utterances, which were linked to a strong emphasis on papal jurisdictional authority, different constitutional-legal conclusions could be drawn according to where the greater stress was laid: The pope embodies all the authority in the Church—or he exercises a limited authority, full authority remaining with the Church itself. The ambivalence of the utterances is especially revealed in connection with the question of inerrancy.[15] The Decretists teach the inerrancy of the "Romana Ecclesia" according to the Decretum. But they avoid or expressly reject a statement on the personal infallibility of the pope, who is recognized only as the highest judge in matters of faith: (Johannes Teutonicus: "It is certain that the pope can err. . . ."). The *Decretum* itself provides different cases of popes in error (after Marcellinius, above all Anastasus II). How do the Decretists resolve the dilemma that they themselves propound: inerrant Roman Church—heretical pope?

[14] Cf. B. Tierney, *op. cit.* 23–26.
[15] *Ibid.* 36–46.

Not by the modern Catholic distinction—not unknown to the Decretists either—between the pope as a private teacher and as an authoritative teacher—but by the ambivalent concept of the "Romana Ecclesia": the Roman local Church (pope and cardinals)[16] can err, but not the Roman Universal Church, which is the community of all the faithful. After Huguccio this distinction became the commonplace of the Decretists of the next generation. Hence not Ockham, but the Decretists—on the basis of a wholly different, unpolemical basic attitude—produced this distinction, which was to play an important role in conciliar theory. No system had been made out of it, but the raw material lay there in readiness for interpretation along different lines.

What do the Decretists teach about the relationship between *pope and general council*?[17] The fourth Lateran Council (in accordance with the pope's intention) in 1215, in fact, represented the all-embracing representation of the whole Church; it was not only a bishops' synod, but an assembly of the social estates of all Christendom. In this respect it could present the model council in the view of Konrad of Gelnhausen. Admittedly the Decretists did not make exact theoretical analysis of either the concept of representation or of the relationship between a general council and the whole Church, or of the relationship between conciliar representation and papal representation. For the Decretists there can be no council without a pope, and in their view the superiority of a council still consisted in the reunion of all the Churches with the Roman Church (and the pope). But what about cases involving a conflict between pope and council? Whereas Gratian had rejected a limitation of papal authority by a council, those who came later (especially the influential *Glossa ordinaria* of Johannes Teutonicus, which was important for the fourteenth century) in general accepted a twofold limitation: (1) A pope may not reject a council's decisions on faith: "In questions of faith the synod is above the pope."[18] As regards questions of faith (but then in regard also to other matters pertaining to the whole Church) the Decretists gave a decisive primacy to a council before merely papal decisions. This was justified on the grounds of the Roman legal principle, which was later taken over into the *regulae iuris*

[16] On the relationship between the pope and the cardinals, cf. B. Tierney, *op. cit.* 68–95. The real legal position of the college of cardinals, this youngest element in the direction of the Church, is still very weak: "The Decretist teaching on this point serves only to emphasize how very flimsy was the legal basis for the claims of the cardinals in 1378" (75f).

[17] Cf. B. Tierney, *op. cit.* 47–67.

[18] Cf. the text of Johannes Teutonicus in B. Tierney, *op. cit.* 250–254.

by Boniface VIII: "What concerns all is judged by all." And many took over from Gratian the idea that questions of faith are a general matter of common interest that concern not only clerics but also lay persons and all Christians altogether.[19] The pope, therefore, is bound to the decision of general councils. (2) A pope may not oppose the "generalis status ecclesiae." Here also Jerome's sentence "orbis maior est urbe" was quoted. The necessity to defend the *Status ecclesiae* led to the *limitation* of papal power rather than to the extension of its scope. Thereby "general establishment of the Church" is in no way a vague concept, but identical with the rules of Church life that are laid down in the laws of general councils, and confirmed by universal agreement. Here the concept of "general state of the Church" is transformed into the concept of "general statute of the Church."

Do the Decretists also teach anything about the possibility of a *deposition* of the pope?[20] Gratian leaves the legal principle "The pope can be judged by no one" inviolate up to the case, already set forth by Humbert a Silva Candida: "unless he is caught deviating from faith." This had tremendous consequences: From the twelfth to the fourteenth century the permissibility of judging and deposing a heretical pope remained the *sententia communis* of the canonists, and of the radical papalists too. At the same time it in no way remained limited to cases of heresy. The "Summa" of Rufinus (d. 1190) also includes schism among the heresies, namely, schism that has heresy as a consequence. Younger Decretists further ranged a series of sentenceable notorious crimes of a pope alongside that of heresy. Huguccio was the first to present a detailed discussion of this entire problem.[21] In this view the heresy cited in the *Decretum* is only an example of other notorious crimes (adultery, theft, sacrilege), which scandalize the Church and are equivalent to deliberate persistence in heresy. The welfare of the whole Church is the reason why the pope's immunity cannot be extended to these crimes "in order to avoid danger for the Church and general confusion in her." Huguccio also dealt thoroughly with the problem of holding a trial against a pope. The question was, above all, one of determining who can judge the

[19] "Which is universal, common to all and not only to the clergy but also to the laity and belongs to all Christians." B. Tierney, *op. cit.* 49.

[20] Tierney's discussions of this point shed an illuminating light in terms of canonics on our historical discussions concerning the legal principle "Prima sedes a nemine iudicatur," the depositions of popes in the Middle Ages and their juridical justification. Cf. Chap. VII 3.

[21] Cf. the full text of Huguccio's commentary on the words "unless he is caught deviating from faith" in Tierney, *op. cit.* 248–250.

pope, since according to the *Decretum* no one stands higher in authority than the pope. At this point Tierney criticizes the frequently
expounded modern view, namely that Huguccio or the medieval
canonists left the principle "Papa a nemine iudicatur" inviolate,
because in their view a heretical pope would automatically have
ceased to be pope. Tierney calls this modern theory an "over-simpli-
fication" of a complex question: Who then does decide *whether* a pope
is actually a heretic or not, whether he is actually pope or not?
Conscious of this difficulty, Huguccio took great pains to demonstrate the circumstances under which one might take legal action
against a pope in order thereby to exclude, as much as possible, the
holding of a trial against a person who is still truly pope. His qualified
position, however, was expounded with greater crudeness by the next
generation of Decretists, and many of the safeguards that he had
established were dropped. This particularly applies to Johannes
Teutonicus and his *Glossa ordinaria*, which exerted the greatest influence among the Decretist works of the fourteenth century (in it
we find the principle: "In matters of faith . . . the synod greater than
the pope"). Viewed as a whole the Decretists were much more interested in defending the Church against the abuse of papal power than
they were in upholding at all costs the theory of the judicial immunity
of the pope. Their arguments opened up an important breach in the
principle of papal supremacy understood in absolutist terms.[22] Although they did not expressly formulate the concept of the superiority
of a council, they nevertheless very obviously led thereto.

Second Period: *Papalism and the Canonistic Doctrine of the
Corporate Structure of the Church in the Thirteenth Century:* Unlike
the Decretists who espoused a limited papal monarchy, the Decretalists (the commentators of the countless papal decretals that came
into being especially from the time of Alexander III and Innocent
III) in the thirteenth century predominantly espoused an absolutist
papal monarchy.[23] Under Innocent III both tendencies existed simultaneously (sometimes in the same canonists). But the absolutist
tendency increasingly prevailed under Innocent III and his successors.
The pope appeared increasingly as the representative of God in the

---

[22] "In reading the Decretist sources one cannot escape the impression that
these writers were far more interested in defending the Church against abuses of
papal power than in upholding at all costs the doctrine of papal immunity from
judgment. Their arguments did open up an important breach in the principle of
papal supremacy." B. Tierney, *op. cit.* 66; cf. regarding this whole section also, the
same author's "Pope and Council: Some New Decretist Texts," in *Mediaeval
Studies* 19 (1957) 197–218.

[23] Cf. B. Tierney, *op. cit.* 87–95.

most literal sense, endowed with an absolute plentitude of power.[24] For a time the moderate teaching of the Decretists was half forgotten and nearly wholly ignored. Certain limitations of papal authority of dispensation (the welfare of the Church, of the "generalis status ecclesiae," articles of faith, definite concrete commandment) were discussed. Yet this occurred wholly on an abstract level and without any practical applications, since a human authority that in practice could limit papal authority of dispensation was not admitted. The idea that a council or cardinals could limit the pope's power was not so much rejected as ignored.

But paradoxically these very extreme papalists, in a field that was seemingly remote, unwittingly provided valuable material for the antipapalist theoreticians of the following century. In a thorough juridical analysis they applied the Scholastic theory of corporations to the *individual* Church (above all the diocese).[25]

Thirteenth-century studies in canon law ever more clearly expounded the concept of rights *vis-à-vis* the head within the ecclesiastical corporation. The view of Henry of Segusia, the cardinal-bishop of Ostia (Hostiensis, d. 1271 "source and only ruler over law") generally prevailed against the strict authoritarian view of the great jurist-pope Innocent IV. According to the former the authority of an ecclesiastical corporate body in principle lay not only in the head but likewise in its members; therefore in matters which concern the whole, the head requires the consensus of the members; the limit of his authority is the general welfare of the Church. The development of law in the thirteenth century produced a step-by-step extension and systematization of the rights of the members *vis-à-vis* the head; in the middle of the century it was established that the consent of the canons was necessary in connection with actions that pertained to their interests. At the end of the century they already had an extensive judicial and administrative authority for the time that an episcopal see was vacant. And the bishop, insofar as he acted for his whole Church *ex officio*, was understood as "proxy" and "administrator," whose administrative and jurisdictional authority was derived

---

[24] *Tancred:* "In these he represents God because he takes the place of Jesus Christ who is true God and true Man . . . in like manner he can make things out of nothing . . . equally he takes the place of God because he has the plentitude of power in Church matters . . . equally he can grant dispensation beyond the law or against the law . . . equally he can turn justice into injustice, correct laws and change them . . . there is no one who can question why he does so . . . Bernardus Palmensis: In everything he wants, his own will is the only norm of action." (In B. Tierney, *op. cit.* 88).

[25] Cf. B. Tierney, *op. cit.* 96–131.

not from his consecration but from his election. This theory constituted an important link between the concept of representation as a "personification" of the community prevalent in the twelfth century and the concept—which came to the fore in the fourteenth century—of representation on the basis of the express *delegation* of power by the community. Thus the source of authority lies with the community; in cases where the see was vacant (actually or "virtually": through imprisonment, heresy, schism, notorious crimes, indeed through negligence) most rights of the bishop's see devolved upon the members. It required little to apply such theories to the Great Schism. Although in the thirteenth century it involved only the relationship between bishops and canons, the older Catholic conception which views the Church as grounded not only on the prelates but as a "Church," as the "Universe of the faithful," as the mystical Body of all the faithful, was nevertheless not entirely forgotten in the background of these hypotheses.[26]

In order for the corporation theory to have consequences also in connection with the pope's plenitude of power, it needed merely to be carried over from the individual Churches to the whole Church. Tierney finds examples of this as early as in the thirteenth century.[27] The expression "plenitudo potestatis" is of especial importance here. This expression, which was generally customary among the Decretists from 1200, was originally used not only in regard to the pope but also in regard to other bishops, etc. Like the expressions "full power," "full authority," "plenary power," it had the meaning of an authorization and not that of an absolutist authority. In this latter meaning, the term now reserved to the pope, was applied by Innocent III and the subsequent popes and canonists. But a *conciliarist* meaning could be easily given precisely to this absolutist concept—remembering the originally moderate concept and in the lines of corporative thinking: *plenitudo potestatis* as a power that is *delegated* to the pope by the whole Church through authorization and which, under certain conditions, is also limited by the whole Church. How the corporative ideas in this paved the way for conciliar ideas is especially shown in the example of the great Hostiensis who applied the law

[26] "Yet there always remained in the background, never wholly forgotten, the older, more catholic view that the Church was not made up of prelates and higher clergy alone, but that the word 'ecclesia' in its fullest significance meant nothing less than the whole 'universitas fidelium,' the Mystical Body of Christ." B. Tierney, *op. cit.* 131.

[27] Cf. B. Tierney, *op. cit.* 132–149; M. Seidlmayer (*Zeitschrift der Savigny-Stiftung für Rechtsgeschichte, Kanonist*, Abt. 43 [1957] 382) finds Tierney's argumentation on this point, apart from Hostiensis, somewhat forced.

of the corporate body to the Roman Church (popes and cardinals).[28]

Hostiensis, himself a cardinal, juridically included the College of Cardinals, whose power had grown with the power of the pope, in the *plenitudo potestatis* of the "Roman ecclesia." At the death of a pope the College of Cardinals exercises his jurisdiction. But if none of the cardinals should remain, the election of a new pope devolved upon the Roman clergy, or—perhaps more justly the clergy and people of Rome must convoke a council: "et clerus et populus Romanus debent concilium convocare."[29] Thus the authority of the pope devolved upon the cardinals and from the latter by way of the clergy and people of Rome upon a general council: The way was not far from Hostiensis, the *monarcha juris* of the thirteenth century, to Konrad of Gelnhausen and Cardinal Zabarella in the time of the Great Schism. The congregation of the faithful which was treated more as a negative potency by the Decretists now—at least in times of emergency—had to be taken seriously as an active power.

Third Period: *The Conciliar Ideas in the Fourteenth Century:*[30] In our context there is no need to go into this period in any great detail. What is essential for us has already been clearly brought out: The conciliar ideas (and with them the Constance Decrees) are rooted in the traditional ecclesiology or canon law of the twelfth and thirteenth centuries and from there they can be traced still further back. The conciliar theory of the fourteenth century sprang from the fertilization of the Decretist ecclesiology of the twelfth century by the Decretalist corporation ideas of the thirteenth century: "The elaboration of conciliar systems of Church government in their more developed forms was made possible by the assimilation of these rather inchoate ideas of the Decretists into the framework of later corporation theory. . . . The Conciliar Theory, one might say, sprang from the impregnation of Decretist ecclesiology by Decretalist corporation concepts."[31]

Around the turn of the century Boniface VIII's dispute with the Colonna cardinals and France endowed the conciliar theme with an unexpected actuality. The great political theorist Jean de Paris,[32] who was not a professional canonist, combined the hitherto unconnected doctrines (above all of the Decretists, of the *Glossa ordinaria*,

[28] Cf. B. Tierney, *op. cit.* 149–153; and by the same author: "A Conciliar Theory of the Thirteenth Century," in *Catholic Historical Review* 36 (1951) 415–440.

[29] B. Tierney, *op. cit.* 152.

[30] Cf. B. Tierney, *op. cit.* 157–237.

[31] B. Tierney, *op. cit.* 245.

[32] Cf. B. Tierney, *op. cit.* 157–178.

and of Hostiensis) in a new and bold synthesis; the most coherent and complete formulation of the conciliar theory before the outbreak of the Great Schism. According to him every ecclesiastical authority, even that of the pope, rests upon divine institution *and* upon human co-operation (*cooperatio humana*)—that is, the transfer of office by election. The "universal community of the Church" is the mistress and proprietress of all the Church goods, the pope is only the "universal disposer and dispenser" thereof. On questions of faith the pope is dependent upon the co-operation of a council. All ecclesiastical authority is endowed not for the destruction ("destructio") but for the edification ("edificatio") of the Church. On the basis of the aforesaid, Jean de Paris cannot understand why a bearer of the papal office should be immune from judgment by any human tribunal. Just as God approves the election of a worthy pope, so would He approve the deposition of an unworthy one, who would be wholly useless.

After Jean de Paris, Tierney deals with Cardinal Johannes Monachus (an exponent of an oligarchic Church government), William Durantis (an exponent of an episcopally defined conciliar idea: a general council to be held every ten years!), and a series of academic canonists of the fourteenth century.[33] According to Tierney,[34] Ockham, where he had influence, was wholly dependent on the canonistic tradition. On the other hand his original ideas (evangelical freedom, denial of the infallibility of a general council, the position of the emperor) had no influence on the exponents of conciliar theory. Tierney deals in closing with Cardinal Zabarella as representative of the actual conciliar theoreticians of the Great Schism. Zabarella distinguished himself precisely by virtue of the fact that he grounded his conciliar theory exclusively in terms of canon law on the basis of old legal sources.[35]

We can see how wrong it is to seek the origin of conciliar ideas in the "revolutionary" and heretical ideas of Ockham and Marsilius and in this way place the Constance Decrees from the outset into a distorted light. On the basis of Tierney's book, the "Ockhamist conciliar theory" must finally give way. The conciliar idea—apart from the unique emergency situation of the time of schism that a rigid papalism proved incapable of mastering—actually grew out of ideas

---

[33] Cf. B. Tierney, *op. cit.* 179–219.

[34] Cf. B. Tierney, "Ockham, the Conciliar Theory, and the Canonists," in *Journal of History of Ideas* 15 (1954) 40–70.

[35] Cf. B. Tierney, *Foundations of the Conciliar Theory* (Cambridge 1955) 220–237.

that were imbedded in the very teaching and law of the Church—
at least as a possibility—and in the past of the Church herself.
"Verius est licet difficilius," as Hostiensis says.[36]

What Tierney says about the conciliar theory in general must also
be said about the *Constance Decrees* in particular. They are not "something accidental or external thrust upon the Church from the outside" but "a logical culmination of ideas that were imbedded in the
law and doctrine of the Church itself."[37] Obviously, they were not
only imbedded in the law and doctrine of the Church, for beside the
thrust of the conciliar tendency there was also that of the papal
tendency—which doubtless was stronger in the high Middle Ages.
Both presupposed "the ambivalence in canonistic doctrine."[38] Was
this the expression of a fruitful tension or the expression of a des-
tructive contradiction in the structure of the Church?

(*b*) *Conciliar Ideas After the Conciliar Epoch:* The conciliar ideas
were not buried with the Council of Basle. The end of the conciliar
epoch did not mean the end of conciliar ideas. "What is certain is
that both the strict conciliar theory and its moderate episcopalist
version continued to find exponents, and that the threat of the Council and the appeal to it were widely used as a means of bringing
pressure to bear on the Popes."[39] We have already remarked that the
Church of the fifteenth and sixteenth centuries was to a great extent
dominated by conciliar ideas.[40] The elaboration of the enormous un-
published material would show this even more clearly. These ideas
were very much alive in the subsequent centuries too; often they were
united with oppositionist tendencies within the Church. It is not
necessary to show the whole further development of conciliar ideas
in connection with our systematic purpose. It is more important to
show, through the available evidence of well-known theologians of the
papal restoration or later of the Counter-Reformation, that even
theologians of a papalist stamp, at least marginally, increasingly had
to admit that there were cases in which a pope can be derelict and in
which the Church, through a council, can and must stand in defence
against a pope.

With P. de Vooght we have already pointed out that after Constance, moderate "conciliarists" and moderate "papalists" to a large
extent fell in with each other and that both the proposition "the

---

[36] M. Siedlmayer, in *Zeitschrift der Savigny-Stiftung für Rechtsgeschichte,
Kanonist.* Abt. 43 (1957) 387.

[37] B. Tierney, *op. cit.* 13.   [38] *Ibid.* 241.

[39] H. Jedin, *History of the Council of Trent* (Edinburgh 1961) I, 32.

[40] H. Jedin, *op. cit.* I, 32–61.

pope stands above the council" and the proposition "the council stands above the pope" could have its proper meaning. The moderate "papalists," too, admitted the necessity of a certain control over a pope by the whole Church. In Basle, John of Tarentum in 1432 defended the papal plenitude of power; nevertheless in connection with the famous adage "The world is superior to the city," he also admitted that this pertained to a pope who should set himself apart from the faith of the Church: "The world is superior to the city . . . this is to be understood if the pope should disagree with the whole Church in the articles of faith."[41] Two further defenders of the pope, Johannes von Mella and the Abbot of St. Mary of Monaco, in 1433 declared that since Eugene IV's conduct was above reproach, the council had no reason to oppose the pope; thus tacitly they acknowledged that there can be reasons to oppose a pope.[42] For this reason even Nicholas of Cusa could easily turn from a "conciliarist" in to the "Hercules of the Eugenists" because this involved less a fundamental change of theory than it did a modification of his practical judgment.[43] "A papalist in the customary sense of the word he never became. Thus he continued to regard as fundamental the notion that the Pope exists for the building up of the Church—*aedificatio ecclesiae*—and he would not forgo guarantees against a possible misuse of the primacy. Pius II himself has left us a description of the dramatic scene when Nicholas championed with the utmost conviction the pretensions of the College of Cardinals. On the other hand his great journey through Germany as papal legate shows how seriously he took the work of reform to which the Pope was committed."[44]

The especially clear example, however, is the powerful and most influential champion of papal primacy in the fifteenth century, the Spanish cardinal Juan de Torquemada. It was from him that all the subsequent defenders of the primacy—from Domenico Jacobazzi and Cajetan, through Melchior Cano, Suarez, Gregory of Valencia, and Bellarmine, up to the theologians of the First Vatican Council[45]

[41] Mansi 39, 488.

[42] P. de Vooght, "Le Conciliarisme aux conciles de Constance et de Bale," in *Le concile et les conciles* (Paris 1960) 175f.

[43] M. von Steenberghe, *Nicolas of Cues* (Lille 1920) 65: "Hence Nicholas' about-face is explainable less in terms of motivations of an inner than of an outer character. On his part it implied less a change in theory than a modification of practical judgment . . . on the Council of Basle." (quoted in P. de Vooght *op. cit.* 178).

[44] H. Jedin, *op. cit.* I, 24; also see Jedin's comments on Piero da Monte and Antonio Roselli, *op. cit.* I, 26.

[45] K. Binder, *Wesen und Eigenchaften der Kirche bei Kardinal Juan de Torquemada O.P.* (Innsbruck–Vienna–Munich 1955) 196–207.

—have drawn their arguments. Although on the ground of Scripture and of history he defended the untenable thesis that the pope is supposedly the "una fontalis origo totius potestatis ecclesiasticae,"[46] and although, characteristically, there is practically no mention of reform tasks in his mighty *Summa de ecclesia*,[47] Torquemada in no way espoused a papal absolutism in everything. "However, it would be a mistake to see in Torquemada a blind absolutist and an opponent of the Council as such: for one thing he was too near to the agitated period of the Schism. He continues to regard the Council as 'the Church's last refuge in all her great needs,' as the ultimate authority to which it belongs to issue decisions in disputed questions of faith, to reform the pastoral ministry, and to check the arbitrariness of certain Popes."[48]

Torquemada attempted, in part with very dubious arguments, to restrict as much as possible the possibility of the Church taking action against a derelict pope. Unlike earlier canonists, in this respect he passed lightly over the real difficulties. But in his view too, it went without saying that a pope loses his office on account of *heresy*: "by heresy he ceases to be pope."[49] The reasons: (1) Whoever loses his faith is no longer a member of the Church; all the more is this so in the case of her (ministerial) head: "Having lost the faith by which the first union with the body of Christ, which is the Church, was established, he ceases to be a member of the Church and consequently ceases to be her head."[50] (2) The Church is built on the rock, that is, the belief in Christ (Mt. 16:18) without which even the pope cannot be pope. "The Church is founded upon the rock which is faith in Christ. Matt. 16. Upon this rock I will build my Church. Hence whoever notoriously falls away from the rock which is Christ or from his faith, both falls obstinately away from the Church of Christ and consequently from her authority which is called the papacy."[51]

[46] J. de Torquemada, "Oratio synodalis de primatu," ed. E. Candal, in *Concilium Florentinum, Documenta et Scriptores*, series B, vol. IV, fasc. II (Rome 1954) 26.

[47] H. Jedin, *op. cit.* I, 29: "The decrees *Sacrosancta* and *Frequens*, which were meant to inititiate and to ensure a reform of the Curia, remained a dead letter: the Popes reverted to the strict monarchical principle. By so doing they likewise assumed the task of reforming the Church. Was it not the duty, therefore, of the most distinguished exponent of the doctrine of papal authority to point out to those invested with it the heavy responsibility that was theirs?"

[48] H. Jedin, *op. cit.* I, 28.

[49] J. de Torquemada, *Summa de Ecclesia* (1448–1449. Venice 1560) lib. II, cap. 102, 241.

[50] *Ibid.*

[51] *Ibid.*

(3) According to Thomas Aquinas[52] schismatics lose their jurisdiction. (4) According to Thomas Aquinas [53] a pope through heresy would become less than any believer: "If the pope falls into heresy, he becomes subordinate to the faithful . . . this is a case in which the pope can bind a pope, in which the pope falls under the sentence of the canon *ipso facto* (*latae sententiae*)."[54] On the basis of these and other reasons it follows, for Torquemada, that a pope can be judged by the Church or he can be declared as one to be judged by God. "He can be judged by the Church or declared as judged by God."[55] And this occurs through a council: "Properly speaking, the pope is not deposed by the council because of heresy but rather he is declared not to be pope since he fell openly into heresy and remains hardened and obstinate in heresy."[56]

According to Torquemada a pope can become not only a heretic but also a schismatic. When does a pope become a schismatic? When he separates himself from the unity of the Church and from obedience to the head of the Church: "The pope can sinfully separate himself from the unity of the Church and from the obedience of the head of the Church."[57] How is this possible? In three ways: (1) When the pope separates himself from Christ, the Head of the Church and the guarantor of Church unity, through disobedience by not obeying the law of Jesus Christ or by prescribing something that is contrary to divine or natural law. "Because the pope can withdraw from Christ, the principal head of the Church, in respect to whom the unity of the Church is most secure, by disobedience to his law or by prescribing what is contrary to divine or natural law, and thereby separate himself from the body of Christ's Church, and in this way without doubt the pope can fall into heresy."[58] (2) When he wilfully separates himself from the body of the Church and from the College of Bishops by not observing what the whole Church observes according to the apostolic tradition or what is generally decreed by the general councils or the authority of the apostolic see (especially with respect to worship): ". . . the pope can separate himself without reason purely by his wilfulness from the body of the Church and from the college priests by not observing what the universal Church by apostolic

---

[52] Thomas Aquinas, *Summa theologica* II–II, q. 39, a. 3.

[53] Thomas Aquinas, *IV Sent. dist.* 19. a. 2.

[54] J. de Torquemada, *op. cit.* 241v.

[55] *Ibid.* 241.

[56] *Ibid.* 241v.; cf., on the question of *Papa haereticus* also lib. IV, pars II, cap. 18–20, 390v.–396v.

[57] J. de Torquemada, *op. cit.* lib. IV, pars I, cap. 11, 369v.

[58] *Ibid.*

tradition observes . . . or by non-observance of what was ordered universally by the universal councils or the apostolic see, especially in respect to the divine cult if he does not want to observe what concerns the universal state of the Church and the universal rite of the Church's worship."⁵⁹ According to Pope Innocent (IV?) the pope is to be obeyed except when he acts "contra universalem statum ecclesiae." (3) When several popes dispute over the papacy and the one who is the real pope—even though he is not recognized by all—conducts himself negligently and recalcitrantly towards reunion: "If several rivals dispute over the papacy and even if the one who is the real pope, although not recognized by some, acts negligently and obstinately in the fostering of union in the Church, and if he should not do what is in his power to bring about reunion, then he would appear to be a promoter of schisms."⁶⁰ Benedict XIII and Gregory XII were cited as examples.

To the objection that a pope could not separate himself by himself and therefore also could not fall into a schism, Torquemada answers as follows: "Schism need not only be understood as a separation from the pope; the pope himself in disobedience can separate himself from Christ, whose representative he is, and from the Church's tradition, and consequently he becomes schismatic." To the further objection that the pope is he in whom and with whom the Church supposedly is, Torquemada answers as follows: "The Church of Christ is truly with the pope only when he himself remains subject to the Head, Christ, in that he recognizes the dependency of his authority upon Christ, and shows Him due subordination and allows himself to be strengthened by the traditions of the whole Church, who is the Bride of Christ."⁶¹

Torquemada also posed the question of what is to be done with a pope who is undoubtedly the lawful pontiff but who is unable to prevail because of the outbreak of a schism. Torquemada espouses—save there is a better judgment—the opinion that such a lawful pope could doubtless not be forced to resign or be deposed (except if he is a heretic), but that he is in conscience morally bound to resign, although he be the lawful pope.⁶² The good shepherd is to give his life for his flock; thus for the sake of a reunion a pope should renounce his rights and office in order to make room for another who can effect reunion. Hence he should be more concerned about his eternal than

⁵⁹ *Ibid.*
⁶⁰ *Ibid.*
⁶¹ J. de Torquemada, *op. cit.* lib. IV, pars I, cap. 11, 369v–370.
⁶² J. de Torquemada, *op. cit.* lib. IV, pars I, cap. 13, 370v–372.

his temporal honour and avoid all scandal in the Church. In this connection Torquemada repeatedly cites Augustine: The prestige of a bishop should not stand in the way of the unity of Christians; the bishop is not bishop for his own sake, but for the sake of other Christians. Hence different humble bishops because of pious considerations had laid down their episcopal office in an entirely irreproachable, indeed praiseworthy, way. For the sake of unity, in imitation of Christ, the bishop should not hestitate to humble himself and step down from his chair. For the salvation of his soul it suffices that he be a believing and obedient Christian, and this he remains even without episcopal office. He is a bishop only for the sake of the Christian people, and he should do what serves the peace of the Christian people. Finally, even if he be a useless servant, the episcopal dignity would be more fruitful for him if it gathers the flock of Christ when it is *laid down* rather than when it is *retained* and scatters Christ's flock.[63]

A further characteristic feature of this conception is provided at the time of the Council of Trent by Melchior Cano, the great theologian of the Council. He ridicules the apologist Albert Pighius, who even at that time wanted to exonerate the heretical popes (Liberius, Marcellinus, Victor, Anastasius, Honorius) from heresy: "Dicit itaque ille (Pighius) multa multis locis de hac re quidem, sed aqua haeret, ut ajunt,"[64] ("There he is [Pighius] come to the end of his wisdom!") According to Cano it is not even necessary to dispute that a pope voicing his private opinion like any other theologian

[63] J. de Torquemada, *op. cit.* lib. IV, pars I, cap. 13, 370: "The dignitaries in the Church have to consider with careful vigilance that they do not act out of ambition and by this break through schism the connection of unity. For with what reason can we expect to receive honour in the future life from Christ if in this life we impede the Christian unity by ambition for honour?... Some humble and saintly men therefore have laid down the episcopal office, moved by pious consideration, in a manner not only without blame but, in truth, praiseworthy. ... Why do we hesitate to offer this sacrifice of humility to our Redeemer? Did he not descend from heaven into a human body so that we might form one body with him, and not members of this cruel division? It is sufficient for us, having stepped down from our chairs, to be simple, faithful Christians. This we will always remain, for we were ordained bishops for the good of the Christian people and we must therefore do with our episcopacy what helps the Christian people for the sake of peace. ... If we are useful servants, why do we not jealously look after the gain of the heavenly ruling instead of the worldly one? The episcopal dignity would be more fruitful if by giving it up the flock of Christ is gathered than by retaining it and scattering the flock." On the relationship between pope and council, cf. also J. de Torquemada, *Tractatus notabilis de potestate papae et concilii generalis* (Cologne 1480. Innsbruck 1871).

[64] M. Cano, *De locis theologicis* (Salamanca 1563, Padua 1732) lib. VI; de ecclesiae romanae auctoritate, cap. 8, 189.

(*doctor privatus*) can be heretical: "It cannot be denied that the pontiff can be a heretic, of which one or another example might be given."[65] By basing himself on the evidence of tradition he considers important precisely that which Pighius holds to be unimportant—namely, that heresy is a matter in which the flock may judge the shepherds: ". . . this one case in which the flock can judge its shepherd is that in which he has become heretical."[66] In this case the pope stands under the Church and her judgment: "The supreme pontiff committing the crime of heresy is subject to the judgment of the Church in the external forum, by divine institution."[67]

What Melchior Cano had ridiculed as a futile, unnecessary effort was performed anew by Robert Cardinal Bellarmine: Basing himself expressly on Pighius, he sought to prove that there had never been any heretical popes.[68] This was done with arguments that are no longer tenable according to the present status of ecclesiastico-historical research.[69] Bellarmine himself had to admit that this view was not certain and had common opinion against it: "Because it is not certain, and the common opinion is contrary, it would be interesting to see what the conclusion would be if the pope could be a heretic."[70] At any rate he was one of those who believed untenable any opinion that a pope might be deposed because of either hidden or overt heresy. In his view, the famous Distinctio 40 of the *Decretum Gratiani*, according to which a pope cannot be judged "*unless* he is found defected from the faith" speaks against this; against it also speak Innocent III's second *Sermo de consecratione pontificis* and the condemnation of Honorius by the sixth and eighth ecumenical councils as well as by Pope Hadrian II and the Roman synod: "Add to this the pitiful condition of the Church being forced to recognize the openly prowling wolf as her shepherd."[71] Hence Bellarmine's funda-

---

[65] M. Cano, *op. cit.* lib. VI, cap. 8, 190.

[66] *Ibid.*

[67] M. Cano, *Relectio de poenitentiae sacramento* (1547–48. Padua 1762), pars V. 497.

[68] R. Bellarmine, *De summo pontifice* (Inglostadt 1586–93. Paris 1870) lib. IV, cap. 6–14, II, 88–119.

[69] Cf., for example, on the classical case of Honorius, R. Bäumer, "Honorius I," in *Lexikon für Theologie und Kirche* (Freiburg i. Br. ²1961) V, 475: "At the time of the Reformation, A. Pigge tried to cope with the difficulties arising from the condemnation of Honorius by means of the thesis that the condemnation of Honorius may have never actually happened but was falsely inserted by the Greeks in the acts of the Council. His thesis found grateful reception or amplification with Bellarmine and Baronius and it still had defenders in the nineteenth century, although M. Cano had before then sharply opposed the hypothesis of falsification."

[70] R. Bellarmine, *op. cit.* lib. II, cap. 30, I, 608.

[71] *Ibid.*

mental conception is the following. "The manifestly heretical pope ceases *per se* to be pope and head as he ceases *per se* to be a Christian and member of the Church, and therefore he can be judged and punished by the Church. This is the teaching of all the early Fathers."[72]

Against Cajetan, Bellarmine had argued that a heretical pope would be directly deposed by God Himself. Cajetan was defended by F. Suarez who, together with M. Cano and D. Soto, upheld the necessity of a sentence of the Church or of a council: ". . . If the pope is an unrepentant heretic, he ceases to be pope once the declaratory sentence of his crime is passed by legitimate ecclesiastical jurisdiction."[73] We have previously referred to Suarez's extraordinarily clear discussions regarding a heretical pope and a schismatic pope.[74] We shall now conclude this testimony with that of L. Thomassinus, which was eagerly used particularly by theologians before the First Vatican Council. Thomassinus recognizes two cases in which a council can take steps against a pope and to which the popes should voluntarily subject themselves. Schism is one of them: "If the Church wavers in doubt because of two or more rivalling popes, it seems proper that the synod by its own judgment free itself from ambiguity; and it does not pronounce upon the primacy and apostolic see but upon the intruders."[75] Heresy is the second case: "Besides in the case of publicly professed heresy, the pope can be judged as all Catholic doctors teach."[76] He, too, based his argument on the condemnation of Pope Honorius and the *Decretum Gratiani*.

An appeal from the pope to a council was forbidden anew by the First Vatican Council.[77] This prohibition was taken over by the CIC.[78] Nevertheless the problems of conflict between pope and Church, which, as we have been able to follow them through the centuries in this chapter, have been dealt with by classical authors since the Middle Ages, were touched upon only briefly and not decisively. This extraordinarily important problem, as attested to by the whole of Catholic tradition, was passed over in a few sentences by Zinelli, the reporter of the Deputation on Faith.[79] the question of

[72] R. Bellarmine, *op. cit.* lib. II, cap. 30, I, 610.

[73] F. Suarez, *De fide theologica, Disputatio X de Summo Pontifice*, sectio VI (Coimbra 1621, Paris 1858) 12, 317.

[74] Cf. Chap. VII, 3.

[75] L. Thomassinus, *Dissertationum in concilia generalia et particularia tomus singularis* (Paris 1667, Cologne 1784) Diss. XV, 20, 418.

[76] L. Thomassinus, *op. cit.* Diss. XV, 20, 419.

[77] Denz. 1830.

[78] *CIC* can. 228 § 2, at the same time with § 1: "Concilium Oecumenicum suprema pollet in universam Ecclesiam potestate,"

[79] Mansi 52, 1109f,

Honorius and similar things are thoroughly discussed only in connection with papal *infallibility*. The prohibition of an appeal by the First Vatican Council just as little paralyzed theological and canonical discussions on what was to be held valid in case of the dereliction of a pope as had the previous prohibitions. This is testified to by the manuals of canon law which—as could be shown expressly by the available work of Wernz and Vidal—gave their attention, before and after, to situations of conflict between pope and Church, retaining the classical positions of the theologians before the First Vatican Council. The CIC itself offers no direct, concrete solutions for such cases of conflict. Nevertheless it expressly holds open the possibility of a voluntary resignation of the pope.[80] Besides this, it is generally established that all heretics and schismatics without exception are *ipso facto* excommunicated and after an admonition they lose their office and dignity in the Church; beyond that clerics are deposed after a repeated admonition: "Can. 2314: All apostates from the Christian faith and each and every heretic or schismatic: (1) incur *ipso facto* excommunication; (2) unless after being admonished they repent, they shall be deprived of benefices, dignity, pension, office or other position they had in the Church; they shall be branded with infamy; and clerics, after repeated warning, shall be deposed."[81] Catholic tradition says that even a pope, if he becomes heretical or schismatic, loses his office and that in such a case he cannot appeal to the legal principle: "No one can judge the first see." The question that the CIC does not answer is: Who is to judge? The answer of Catholic tradition and in particular that of the ecumenical Council of Constance is entireiy clear: The *Church* judges, the Church in her valid representation, the Church represented through an ecumenical council by human convocation.

(*c*) *Two Poles:* At the beginning of this section on conflict situations between pope and Church it was stated that it is not a question of discussing curiosities of an ecclesiastical-historical or ecclesiastical-canonical character on the margin of Church life. Now we must add: It is not a question of prophesying any kind of complications for the morrow. True, such complications often arrive unexpectedly (consider the sudden change under Boniface VIII: papal absolutism —exile and schism). And in a time where—as in Czechoslovakia, in Hungary, and in China—bishops and cardinals are arrested and forcibly separated from their churches for decades, in a time where

---

[80] *CIC* can. 221.
[81] *CIC* can. 2514 § 1; cf. can 188, 4.

elections are forced and bishops must act under political pressure, one must not nourish the smug illusion that from the outset such things cannot happen to the bishop of Rome. A political upheaval, an internment of the pope, and a papal election held under pressure and hence of doubtful legitimacy, could again today place the Church in the greatest peril. No century is immune from heresy and schism.[82] Despite all this no such fears lie at the root of our considerations, but the conviction rather that the borderline cases, as we have considered them, often most vividly shed light on the structures of the Church and make us aware of lines that are generally overlooked. What in everyday life is easily forgotten or taken for granted is taught by times of distress and emergency. And often it is disorder that first teaches us how important this or that factor is in the structural order itself.

Our historical considerations have shown how central in the life of the Church are the questions presented by those borderline cases. It has become clear that the Church, the great community of the faithful, is the ecumenical council of all believers, which God Himself has gathered in Christ and under Christ. There is only one Lord, Christ; all the others are brothers. Even the pope is not the Lord of the Church but her servant, the servant of all. He cannot be pope unless he is first of all and ever anew again, with all others, a humble, believing Christian man. If he is not this he acts and teaches against the gospel of Jesus Christ, and the Church is not delivered to him— as Protestant criticism holds—for better or for worse. Rather, the Church is morally bound to protect herself. Church history shows this is not only theory.

The history of the Church fluctuates over and over again, ever between the problems posed by Vatican I and the problems posed by the Council of Constance. Both are councils of the same Church; both teach what is necessary and exhibit the essential structures of the Church. Both can be wrongly understood and, instead of inter-

---

[82] G. Dejaifve, "Der Erste unter den Bischöfen in *Theologie und Glaube* 51 (1961) 21: "Jurisprudence which is fond of neat categories has scarcely as yet directed its attention to these interim situations, which escape precise regulations, and even less has it comprehended them legally. Church history has already provided us with more such cases that lead to very thorny juridical problems; consider, for instance, the Western Schism. It can place us before similar aporias in the future, indeed, it already does so since the local Churches that are in communion with Rome in reality have been cut off from every link with the centre of catholicity, to the extent that they could be led to continue to live for an indefinite time locked behind iron or bamboo curtains and be forced to organize an authentic Catholic life in a frame of autonomy which circumstances have forced upon them."

preting structures constructively, they can work destructively against their very intentions. If both these councils are understood in terms of the whole ecclesiastical reality, they manifest the fruitful tension between Peter and the community of the apostles, between Peter and the Church, the centre and the "periphery." If they are selectively (heretically) understood and absolutized, they do not express a fruitful living contrast but a contradiction having fatal effects for the Church. Neither council had any intention of exhibiting the whole structure of the Church and of formulating a comprehensive ecclesiology. This cannot be the task of councils. Both councils purposed simply to raise into prominence essential structures of the Church and to emphasize certain points in ecclesiology. Both are to be understood in terms of the whole of ecclesiology. Whoever constructs his ecclesiology exclusively from the Constance decrees does not end with the Petrine office in the sense of Holy Scripture, but at best with the chief official of a democratic-parliamentary Church association. Whoever constructs his ecclesiology exclusively from the decrees of the First Vatican Council glimpses the Church not as the great council of all the faithful, who according to Scripture are filled with the Spirit (Rom. 8) and are a royal priesthood (I Pet. 2:5–10), but at best an ecclesiastical subject people ruled in a totalitarian fashion by an absolute monarch (or his apparatus of officials).

The Council of Constance and Vatican I are respectively different emphases of the two poles to which all structures of the Church are directly or indirectly drawn without its being possible to trace them back either to the one or to the other: pope and Church. In the CIC we not only read (easily misunderstood theologically): "The Catholic Church and the apostolic see have the character of moral persons by divine institution."[83] The two poles can also be observed in both sayings of Jesus in which "Church" occurs (Mt. 16:18 and 18:17). On this basis Y. Congar has presented the history of ecclesiology as an interplay between pope and Church. His interpretation sheds much valuable light on our discussions up to now.[84]

According to Congar the Church's experience of faith in the first centuries was of a strong sacramental character and shaped by

[83] *CIC* can. 100 § 1.

[84] Y. Congar, "Geschichtliche Betrachtungen über Glaubensspaltung und Einheitsproblematik," in *Begegnung der Christen* (collection of essays honouring [*Festschrift*] O. Karrer, Stuttgart–Frankfurt a. M. ²1960) 405–429; cf. also, by the same author: "Conclusion," in *Le concile et les conciles* (Paris 1960) 329–334; *Lay People in the Church* (London 1957); "Bulletin d'ecclésiologie (1939–1946)," in *Revue des sciences philosophiques et théologiques* 31 (1947) 77–96, 272–296.

symbolism, a celestial-terrestial reality.[85] Here the "Church" pole, as the living community of the faithful in Christ, stands in the foreground of both theology and liturgy (the assembled Church as the subject of the liturgy). Here Peter and the Petrine office are less sources than they are signs of the unity of the Churches; Peter represents the Church (Cyprian and Augustine). Together with this view there existed at an early date the specific Roman ecclesiology—indirectly established by Clemens Romanus and Victor I, and increasingly more clearly expressed by Siricius, Innocent I, Boniface I, and above all by Leo I.[86] The genius of law and the apostle Peter were of especial importance for the elaboration of this ecclesiology; both factors were combined in the initial stages of the theory and practice of a primacy of divine right. Hence Roman ecclesiology, in contrast to the ecclesiology of the East, is an ecclesiology of a unified Church: a Church viewed not merely as a more or less federative community of local churches, but as the universal people of all believers in the legally grounded structure of an all-embracing corporate body under a central direction. This ecclesiology was first of all fostered by political circumstances: as opposed to the East, strongly marked with particularism, Latin Rome—even after the Fall of the Empire—possessed a strong unifying mystical power of attraction. Secondly it was fostered by theological circumstances: as opposed to the symbolic-sacramental thinking of the East, where canon law played no part in theological consciousness, the West learned to distinguish between the validity and efficacy of the sacraments, between power of orders and power of jurisdiction—a factor which made possible the distinction in the jurisdiction of pope and bishops. While thus the East and Africa (as well as broad circles in the West up to the ninth century) had a collegial and conciliary concept of the Church and also retained it, the West increasingly manifested an openness to the idea of a monarchic universal episcopate.

Since Nicholas I and John VIII, but especially since the Gregorian reform, the "pope" pole has increasingly assumed a decisive position in the West. Increasingly the organization of the whole life of the Church was derived from the "pope" pole. Cardinal Humbert equated the relationship "ecclesia"—papal authority to that between door and hinge, family and mother, building and foundation, river and source. Like the titles "pope" and "apostolic see," the title "vicar of Christ," previously peculiar to bishops, priests, and princes, was

---

[85] Y. Congar, "Geschichtliche Betrachtungen über Glaubensspaltung und Einheitsproblematik," *op. cit.* 405–408.

[86] Y. Congar, *op. cit.* 408–419.

reserved exclusively to the pope ever since the pontificate of Innocent III. Thus an important change in meaning was introduced.[87]
Canon law placed at the service of papal authority was an indispensable support for liberating the Church from the power of the
laity, which was assuming the upper hand in the early Middle Ages.
Yet often it led to a legalization (and consequently to a politicaliza-
tion) of originally spiritual concepts and to the far-reaching clericalization of the Church.

Still we must not overlook the fact that many forces in the Church
strongly emphasized the "Church" pole even during the Middle
Ages. The legitimacy of the old synodal and episcopal Church order
and the right of other ecclesiastical forms within the one Church
was not stressed only by the East (indeed precisely under Photius).
Even within the Roman Church there were pre-Gregorian canonists
(Burchard of Worms, Yves of Chartres, and others) alongside the
Roman canonists. And we have already seen in great detail[88] how,

---

[87] Y. Congar, *op. cit.* 415f: "The designation 'representative' or 'plenipotentiary
of Christ' did not as yet have the substantial meaning which it received later,
when the title was applied exclusively to the successors of Peter. Moreover, at
that time the Bishop of Rome was also called 'Vicarius Petri' or 'Successor of
Peter.' 'Vicarius' (representative), in a symbolic interconnection of the earthly
and the celestial, signified . . . the visible person who represented an invisible but
acting person, active even in an actual way (may we be excused for this necessary
pleonasm). The expression is more to be understood in the framework of an
intervention of Christ (God) or Peter or of the saints coming here and now from
above than as something relating to a temporal beginning, to the founding of the
Church or to an authority transmitted forever. Moreover, at that time this 'founding' itself was understood more as a repeated actual event than as an event which
occurred in the beginning, continuing thereafter to be operative for all time.
Conversely, the meaning 'representative' (*Vicarius*), because of the juridical mode
of thinking that had been introduced since the Gregorian reform by the lively
activity in canon law, *grosso modo* was more and more changed into the title of a
plenipotentiary that was transmitted to an authority as a personal qualification,
hence practically (at least with respect to papal power) to the title of a successor.
When the designation 'Vicarius Christi' became the peculiar title of the pope
and received the juridical meaning of a plenipotentiary of Christ, the old, actualis-
tic-symbolical idea was not thereby excluded. Rather, it was joined to the meaning
of the verb 'vices agere,' especially in the theology of the sacraments." Concerning the history of this expression, cf. further M. Maccarrone, *Vicarius Christi.
Storia del titolo papale* (Lateranum N. S. XVIII 1–4, Rome 1952). Cf. also the
work of O. Wüst, *Die stellvertretende göttliche Rechtsgewalt des Papstes. Eine
theologie-geschichtliche Untersuchung* (Diss. Pont. Univ. Gregoriana, Rome
1956): the author skilfully expounds how such far-reaching doctrines as that of
the *potestas vicaria Dei* came into being, in order subsequently to justify practical
measures (for instance, in the practice of papal dispensation) canonically. The
problems surrounding the argument current at that time, "The pope did it, therefore it is lawful," hereby become only too manifest.

[88] Chap. VII, 5a.

even with the Decretists of the twelfth century, the significance of
Ecclesia as a congregation of the faithful came to surprisingly clear
expression at certain moments, how later the corporative ideas of
the Decretalists of the thirteenth century decisively strengthened these
tendencies, and how finally these movements, produced the conciliar
ideas which largely dominated the Church in the fifteenth and sixteenth centuries asserted the claims of the "Church" pole.

All these theological, canonical, and practical strivings within the
Church, however, could not parry those movements which—starting
out from the spiritualistic sects of the twelfth century by way of
Ockham and Marsilius of Padua, Wyclif, and Huss and finally up
to the Reformation—all together conducted a radical anti-hierarchical
criticism against the concrete temporal-historical Church as a power
apparatus of a politically tainted institution and as a legal structure
for the transmission of salvation. At the same time, they strove to
project a more spiritual view of the Church as a congregation of the
faithful along the lines of the Gospel. In a counter-defence the
ecclesiological treatises, at the very moment of their appearance—
as we have already pointed out—were structured as a "hierarchology":
many texts simply equate "ecclesia" with the hierarchy, indeed many
even with the curia and with the pope.[89] Thus, to a great extent,
ecclesiology was formulated as a reaction to specific denials of claims
or to specific heresies.[90] The theology of the hierarchical, especially
of papal, power and the theology of the Church as an organized
kingdom was developed against Gallicanism and the Legists of the
French crown. Against the conciliar theories the theology of the
papal primacy was mainly developed. In opposition to Wycliffian
and Hussite spiritualism, stress was laid upon the ecclesiastical
and social character of the Christian message. In opposition to
the Reformers, stress was laid upon the objective importance of
the ecclesiastical means of grace (sacraments efficacious *ex opere
operato*), the importance of hierarchical authority, of the official
priesthood, of the episcopal office and, above all, of the Roman
primacy. Papal powers and rights were stressed all the more in

[89] Cf., for example, Aegidius of Rome: "The supreme pontiff who has the
triple crown of the Church and who can be called the Church." Petrus Amelii,
Cardinal of Embrun: "The pope and the reverend cardinals belong in such a way
to the Church that they are the Roman Church. . . ." Sylvester Prierias: "Virtually
the universal church is the Roman Church and the Roman Church representatively
in the college of cardinals, and virtually the supreme pontiff." (Quoted in Y.
Congar, *Lay People in the Church* [London 1957]).

[90] Cf. Y. Congar, "Bulletin d'ecclésiologie (1939–1946)," in *Revue des sciences
philosophiques et théologiques* 31 (1947) 77.

opposition to Jansenism, which was more or less linked with Gallicanism. In opposition to the laicism and the State absolutism of the nineteenth century there was an insistence upon the Church as a *societas perfecta*, provided with all rights and means. Finally, in opposition to modernism there was a vigorous elaboration of the prerogatives of the teaching Church. All this signified an often one-sided singling out of the pole "pope" *vis-à-vis* the Church.[91] Only too often indeed was this polemical ecclesiology in keeping with the deistic proposition, as Möhler lampooned it, "God created the hierarchy, and now the Church is more than enough taken care of until the end of the world."[92]

It goes without saying that there was also no lack of counter-tendencies in the Church of the modern age. We have seen that the conciliar ideas not only had an effect on Gallicans, Episcopalists, and Febrionists, but also on the great theologians of post-

---

[91] Unfortunately the complains over popolatry in so-called neo-ultramontanism were not unfounded about the time of the First Vatican Council. R. Aubert, "Le pontificat de Pie IX" (Fliche and Martin, *Histoire de l'Église*. Paris 1952) 302f, writes about it as follows: "The devotion to the pope sometimes also assumed very questionable forms which the Archbishop of Rheims denounced as 'idolatry of the papacy.' Some, for the purpose of better professing their belief that the pope was the vicar of God on earth—some called him 'the vice-God of mankind'—thought it proper to apply to the pope hymns which in the Breviary are addressed to God Himself.

> Rerum, *Pius*, tenax vigor,
> Immotus in te permanens
> Da verba vitae quae regant
> Agnos, oves et saeculum.

or again:

> A Pie IX, Pontife-Roi:
> Pater Pauperum
> Dator munerum
> Lumen cordium
> Emitte coelitus
> Lucis tuae radium.

Others hailed him with titles attributed to Christ by Holy Scripture. 'Pontifex sanctus, innocens, impollutus, segregatus a peccatoribus et excelsior coelis factus.' Now these embarrassing expressions were not only the outbursts of irresponsible persons. An article in *La Civiltà Cattolica*, the organ of the Roman Jesuits, explained 'that when the pope meditates, it is God who thinks in him.' One of the most prominent ultramontane bishops in France, Mgr. Bertaud de Tulle, presented the pope as 'the Word Incarnate which is continued.' And the bishop of Geneva, Mgr. Mermillod, did not hesitate to preach on 'the three incarnations of the Son of God': in the womb of a virgin, in the eucharist and in the old man of the Vatican."

[92] J. A. Möhler, "Review of Th. Katerkamp, Des ersten Zeitalters der Kirchengeschichte 1, Abt: Die Zeit der Verfolgungen (Münster 1823)" in *Tübinger Theologische Quartalschrift* 5 (1823) 497.

Reformation Scholasticism. The actual renewal of ecclesiology, which led to a broadening and deepening of the concept of the Church and, ultimately, to the Encyclical *Mystici corporis*, came especially from the Tübingen School in the nineteenth century. J. A. Möhler in ecclesiology in particular had deeply influenced the theologians of the Collegium Romanum (Perrone, Schrader, Passaglia) who were essentially responsible for the preparatory work in connection with the First Vatican Council.[93] The First Vatican Council stressed the pole "pope" in a maximal way. Nevertheless, it did not condemn only extreme episcopalism, but also extreme papalism.[94] Moreover, the Council purposed to have its exposition of the position of the pope be followed by a presentation of the position of the Church.[95]

Today Catholic theologians are busily at work in all fields in order to put the Church and her structures in a better light. This central ecumenical task presents enormous difficulties as our study should have shown in all the chapters. In any case, we are still far from the end of this task. Again and again it is a question of avoiding the extremes that aim to give full value only to one pole, and of taking the middle path which alone can give us a proper glimpse of the complex structure of the Catholic Church. Almost one hundred and fifty years ago, J. A. Möhler had rightly declared: "Two extremes, however, are possible in Church life and both are called egoism. Two extremes exist, namely when *everybody* or when *one individual* wants to be all. In the latter case the bond of unity becomes so tight and love so warm that one cannot ward off suffocation; in the former case everything so falls apart and it becomes so cold that one freezes to death. One form of egoism generates the other. But neither *everybody* nor *one individual* should want to be all. Only all can be all, and the unity of all can only be an all-encompassing whole. This is the idea of the Catholic Church."[96]

6. QUESTIONS OF HUMAN LAW

The history of the Church confirms what Möhler had to say about the two extremes. The Church *and* the Petrine office can be harmed

[93] Cf. W. Kasper, *Die Lehre von der Tradition in der Römischen Schule* (*Giovanni Perrone, Carlo Passaglia, Clemens Schrader*) (Diss. Tübingen 1961, Freiburg i. Br. 1962).

[94] Cf. J. Ratzinger, "Primacy, Episcopate and Apostolic Succession," in *The Episcopate and the Primary* (London 1962) 43–44.

[95] Cf. Chap. VII, 2.

[96] J. A. Möhler, *Die Einheit in der Kirche oder das Prinzip des Katholizismus* (Ed. by J. R. Geiselmann, Darmstadt 1957), 237.

in two ways: by ascribing too little or by ascribing too much to the Petrine office. The overgrown function of an organ harms an organism no less than regression. Too *little* is ascribed to the Petrine office when, at best, it is regarded as a human structure, as an establishment of human law, and the inner connection of the papacy with the Petrine government of the Church based in Scripture is not appreciated. And *too* much is attributed to the Petrine office when its ministerial character in the Church is not taken seriously and it is regarded as an absolutist ruling power and Church government and initiative is reduced as much as possible to the government and initiative of the Petrine office. It is questionable whether excessive or defective emphasis on the Petrine office has been more harmful to the Church. At any rate Möhler is right when he says that one form of egoism generates the other. Absolutist papalism was a prerequisite for democratic conciliarism; the latter in turn was the prerequisite for the reactionary restoration of an absolutist papalism. Today, at the end of the development briefly sketched in the previous section, probably the overgrown function of the Petrine office is the greater danger. Obviously we should not want to fall in to the anachronism of winding backwards, as it were, the position of the Petrine office in the twentieth century to the first or to the second century.

One should think in terms of historical development and recognize that the centralization process of the Gregorian reform, for instance, brought much good along in its train. The dependence on the princes was often much more oppressive than any dependence on Rome, and the shortcomings of the Germanic private Church system are universally known. On the other hand, one should not think in unhistorical terms in such a way as to identify certain historical forms of the Petrine office with its essential character and to declare them as necessary and unalterable for all time. As much as the essential character of the Petrine office, established by Christ, can be materialized only in specific historical forms, just as much—on the other hand —must one make a fundamental distinction between what is the work of God and what is the work of man in order not to lose sight of the perspective of the Gospel. The canonistic distinction between *ius divinum* and *ius humanum* (*ecclesiasticum*)[1] is not only a text-book distinction, but one that is grounded in the Gospel itself. In Mark 7:1–11 (cf. Mt. 15:1–9) it has been declared by Christ, in opposition to Pharisaic legalism that the word of God and the word of man are not one and the same. *That the word of God (proclaiming itself through the word of man) may not be made into a word of man,* by loosening

[1] Cf., for example, can. 6; can. 27 § 1.

the word of God through a human precept and tradition: " 'For, letting go the commandment of God, you hold fast the tradition of men, the washing of pots and of cups; and many other things you do like to these.' And he said to them, 'Well do you nullify the commandment of God, that you may keep your own tradition! For Moses said, "Honour thy father and thy mother"; and "Let him who curses father or mother be put to death." But you say, "Let a man say to his father or his mother, 'Any support thou mightest have had from me is Corban' (that is, given to God). And you do not allow him to do anything further for his father or mother. You make void the commandment of God by your tradition, which you have handed down; and many such-like things you do' " (Mark 7:8–13).

But conversely, *the word of man may not be made into the word of God* by extolling a human teaching and a human precept as the commandment of God. Here actually the same process is involved. If the word of God is debased to a word of man, thereby one also raises the word of man to the level of the word of God: "So the Pharisees and Scribes asked him, 'Why do not thy disciples walk according to the tradition of the ancients, instead of eating bread with defiled hands?' But answering he said to them. 'Well did Isaias prophesy of you hypocrites, as it is written, "This people honours me with their lips, but their heart is far from me; and in vain do they worship me, teaching as doctrine the precepts of men" ' " (Mark 7:5–7).[2]

If, therefore, the Church draws a sharp line between the word of .God and the word of man, the commandment of God and the commandment of man, and the law of God and the law of man, she speaks on the basis of the Gospel. The commandment of God is in principle absolute and inalterable. The commandment of man is in principle conditioned (it is perforce relative, related to the command-

---

[2] J. Schmid, *Das Evangelium nach Markus* (Regensburg ³1954) 134; "This 'tradition of the ancients' of which the laws on purity constituted only a part were declared by the scribes and their Pharisaical followers to be as holy and as binding as the law of Moses contained in the Old Testament, indeed as 'unwritten law' traceable to the revelation of God on Mount Sinai." J. Huby, *Evangile selon Saint Marc* (Paris 1948) 180: "It was not enough for the Pharisees to put the commandments of men before the precepts of God, to observe the former and neglect the latter. Rather, they nullified this divine Law, they reduced it to nothing. The complaint could appear paradoxical; did not the Pharisees vaunt that they had raised oral tradition like a 'protective hedge' of the written Law? Jesus was to submit the proofs of His accusation. No doubt, the Pharisees did not accept the contradictory character of the divine precept in order to erect it publicly into a rule for conduct: such a manner of doing things would no longer have been hypocrisy, but open revolt."

ment of God and superposed by it) and alterable (in the course of history it can be established and disestablished, formulated, spoiled, distorted, and newly formulated).

It is the task precisely also of theology and of canon law studies to elaborate this distinction between divine and human precepts in all important points of Church doctrine and practice, so that the word of man is not made into the word of God and then laid on man as a heavy burden. Here stand the Lord's words of warning: "And they bind together heavy and oppressive burdens, and lay them on men's shoulders; but not with one finger of their own do they choose to move them" (Mt. 23:4).

This distinction between divine law and human law is important precisely in the sphere of our set of problems: Petrine office versus ecumenical council. According to present regulations of canon law only the *pope* can convoke, transfer, adjourn, and close a council and endow its decrees with legal force, only the *pope* can preside at ecumenical councils and can determine the agenda and the order of business.[3] We have already explained in the first chapter that these determinations derive not from divine but from human law. Now this statement is to be made more precise, as has already been announced. The pope's right to convoke a council is sometimes understood as *ius divinum*, although for a long time it has not been directly designated as such. At any rate it is allowable to hold the opinion that this problem has not yet been sufficiently explored and differentiated. When it is said that the pope's right to convoke a council supposedly is *iuris divini*, then the following consideration must be pondered: Does this *ius divinum* refer to the *primatial full authority* factually operative in the convocation by the *pope* or to the *act of convocation as such*—which is possibly not formally identical with the act of primatial full authority? When in this statement the *ius divinum* refers to the primatial full authority factually operative in the convocation, a *ius divinum*, namely that of primacy, as defined at the First Vatican Council, must be correspondingly asserted. For when a pope actually convokes a council, he certainly does so as the *Primas* of the whole Church. But it in no way follows therefrom that, *iure divini*, only the *Primas* of the whole Church and otherwise no one else can convoke ecumenical councils, and that, therefore, the *exclusive* right to convoke a council is also posited along with the divine right of the primacy. It is indisputable from the outset that a pope can also possess the primacy of the Church, even though he alone cannot convoke councils. If one wants to dispute this, one must

[3] *CIC* can. 222.

from the outset assert that every action that is binding upon the whole Church must start out exclusively from the *supreme* pastor. In short, if one purposes to refer the *ius divinum* connected with a convocation by the pope not only to the factually operative primatial full authority but also to the act of convocation as such, one must be able to prove irrefutably this *ius divinum* on the basis of revelation. In terms of the situation surrounding the problem it turns out that it does not suffice to present a proof for the primacy of Peter or of the pope: indeed it is not simply a question of whether *primacy* belongs to the pope, but whether the *exclusive right of convocation* belongs to him on the basis of primacy. Moreover, one would have to prove irrefutably that primacy without the exclusive right of convocation could no longer be an authentic primacy in the sense of Holy Scripture (not in the sense, for instance, of a secular absolutism). Or, as we shall now inquire more closely, it is not simply a question of proving that a council must necessarily stand in unity with the pope (which Catholics accept as a matter of course) but of proving that the unity with the pope would exist only if *iure divino* the pope exclusively could convoke a council.

We hold the opinion that (*a*) the primatial full authority factually operative in the convocation by the pope is *iuris divini*, but that (*b*) the act of convocation as such is merely *iuris humani*. Consequently it is not necessarily posited only together with the primatial full authority as such. No one up to now has actually succeeded in proving that the act of convocation as such also pertains to the pope as his exclusive divine right, and in any case he would have the facts of conciliar history against him. Whereas a full clarity exists in the Church with respect to the first proposition, at least since the First Vatican Council, nothing of a binding character was laid down by the Church, nor by Vatican I, with respect to the second proposition. What is striking, in CIC, moreover, is that Canon 219, which deals with the transfer of the supreme power of jurisdiction to the newly elected pope, bases itself on a *ius divinum*. Canon 222, which deals with the convocation, adjournment, and similar matters of ecumenical councils by the pope, does not base itself on a *ius divinum*.

The legal principle, that every (not only the ecumenical) lawful synod requires papal convocation and direction, that their legislative and judicial acts require papal confirmation, stems from the false decretals, the Pseudo-Isidorian decretals.[4] The chief aim of the for-

---

[4] Pseudo-Isidore had already induced Pope Pelagius II to claim the right of convocation for the Roman See by suggesting the following: "Since the authority of the apostolic see to convoke a general synod was given to St. Peter as a singular

gery obviously was to secure *bishops* against the encroachments of secular rulers and against the towering influences of the Metropolitans and the provincial synods. The *heightening of the authority of the pope* served as a means to this end; he was designated as 'caput totius orbis'; and to him alone was arrogated the right to hold and to confirm synods, which heretofore had been exercised by the Frankish kings. Bishops under charges could appeal to him and, in general, all more important matters (*causae maiores*, that is, *episcoporum*) were to be brought before his court for final adjudication. State laws that contradict the canons and decrees of the pope were null and void."[5] E. Amann describes how, under Nicholas I (858–867), the forged legal principle was brought to Rome by Bishop Rothade of Soissons (deposed at a synod by Archbishop Hincmar of Rheims) where it was unhesitatingly accepted by the Roman curia.[6] From Pseudo-Isidore it then passed into the *Decretum Gratiani*, which shaped the whole medieval and modern development of law in the Western Church. Hence it was not surprising that subsequently the pope's right of convocation was viewed as an *exclusive* papal right and that the whole early history of Church canon law and of the Church constitution was interpreted according to an apriorist "dogmatic" schema. In connection with the influence of the Pseudo-Isidorian decretals, F. X. Seppelt has rightly observed

privilege, no synod was ever ratified unless it was done by apostolic authority, etc." Decretales Pseudoisidori, ed. Hinschius (Leipzig 1863) 721.

[5] K. Biblmayer and H. Tüchle, *Kirchengeschichte* (Paderborn 1952) II, 58f; cf. J. Lortz, *Geschichte der Kirche* (Münster [16]1950) 138; N. Jury, "Concile," in *Dictionnaire de Droit Canonique* (Paris 1942) III, 1289; H. E. Feine, *Kirchliche Rechtsgeschichte* (Weimar 1950) I, 271; H. Fuhrmann, "Das Ökumenische Konzil und seine historischen Grundlagen," in *Geschichte in Wissenschaft und Unterricht* 12 (1961) 684f; C. Andresen, "Geschichte der abendländischen Konzile des Mittelalters," in *Die ökumenischen Konzile der Christenheit*, ed. by H. J. Margull (Stuttgart 1961) 87–89.

[6] E. Amann: *L'époque carolingienne* (Fliche and Martin, *Histoire de l'Église* vol. 6. [Paris 1947] 387; "This was the principle which the pseudo-Isidorian decretals resolutely undertook to popularize. Although it did not create this principle, the collection of the mysterious Isidore set it off in singular prominence. Pope Nicholas and his advisers read with interest and curiosity this canonical collection, unknown till then, which Rothade had brought to them from beyond the mountains. Indeed, from this moment on, one was to see hitherto neglected ideas and arguments figure prominently in pontifical correspondence. Anastasius now redacted them nearly exclusively. 'There is no valid council,' it was repeated, 'if it has not been convoked by the authority of Rome; in all major legal suits, especially those in which bishops are involved, Rome reserves the right to restore the bishop to his goods and prerogatives; a renewed protest against all civil interference in ecclesiastical matters.' All that which the decretals of the very ancient popes had so clearly expressed was now to be found again in the documents of the Curia. Thenceforth the style took another turn."

"that the denial of the development of ideas in the history of the constitutional life of the Church, because of the antedating of many later definitions to an earlier time and the dragging in of ideas and demands of a Church party of the nineteenth century as far back as the post-apostolic time, has had the most baneful influence."[7]

General synods were first convoked by the pope in the twelfth century. "As a matter of fact the situation was quite different . . . in connection with the older synods. The Middle Ages, however, under the influence of the legal principle in usage and its scant knowledge of history, came to believe that it had always been so."[8] Thus Thomas Aquinas[9] speaks of the right of the pope to convoke general synods as if this were self-evident. The same was done by the Fifth Lateran Synod,[10] whose historical argument J. H. Hergenröther has in part submitted to a critical inquiry.[11] Admittedly serious doubts about the Pseudo-Isidorian decretals had already been expressed in the fifteenth century, among others by Nicholas of Cusa and by Torquemada. The Calvinist D. Blondel (1628) decidedly refuted the renewed defence of these decretals, which had been undertaken by the Jesuit F. Torres (1572) in opposition to the Centuriators of Magdeburg.

In systematic theology, accordingly, the conception remained very much alive that only the pope could convoke ecumenical councils (thus was the earlier quite general proposition later differently interpreted) and that he had also invoked them. Thus Bellarmine, also citing the Pseudo-Isidorian decretals, states: "The function of convoking general councils is proper to the Roman pontiff . . ., in this way, however, that someone else with the pontiff's consent can call the council, or it is sufficient that after the convocation is made the pope should ratify and confirm this."[12] And in a historical reference he unabashedly asserts: "A council convoked by the emperor alone without the consent and authority of the Roman pontiff is void."[13] He tried to verify this with respect to the first four ecumenical councils (and also with respect to the Council of Sardica).

Bellarmine's views (behind which also stand those of Torquemada,

---

[7] F. X. Seppelt, *Geschichte der Päpste* (Munich 1955) II, 238.
[8] F. X. Funk, *Kirchengeschictliche Abhandlungen und Untersuchungen* (Paderborn 1897) I, 39.
[9] Thomas Aquinas, *Summa theologiae* II–II, q. I, a. 10; cf. also ad 2; cf. *De potentia* q. 10, a. 4, ad 13.
[10] Mansi 32, 67.
[11] J. Hergenröther in the continuation of Hefele's *Conciliengeschichte* (Freiburg 1887) VIII, 713.
[12] R. Bellarmine, *De conciliis* (Paris 1870) lib. I, cap. 12, 211.
[13] *Ibid.* 214.

Cajetan, and Jacobazzi) were carried further by many others well up into the nineteenth century. "Theses de conciliis" by the Roman theologian Carlo Passaglia[14] are typical of these views. His theses can help us to clarify our standpoint so that we may arrive at a view which can be justified in both theology, and history. In Thesis II, Passaglia correctly asserts that, according to the norm of the Gospel, there can be no ecumenical council that would be separate and cut off from Peter and his successors: "According to the gospel and Christian tradition it cannot be, nor can it be conceived, that an ecumenical council should be separate or apart from Peter and his successors, the Roman pontiffs."[15] And for proof he has recourse to the classical idea of representation in a summarized form: "The ecumenical council represents in and by itself juridically the Church of Christ. The ecumenical council is truly the ἀνακεφαλαίωσις of Christ's Church. But according to the Gospel and Christian tradition it cannot represent the Church of Christ without its foundation, without its ecumenical shepherd who strengthens the brethren, without the visible head and centre of unity, i.e. without Peter and those in whom Peter lives and presides."[16] In this connection Passaglia does not go into the important traditional doctrine that a pope by himself cannot cut himself off and separate himself from the Church and from a council, namely, through heresy and schism. In his last thesis[17] he deals with the Council of Constance in a purely apologetic vein, adducing historical arguments that from the standpoint of modern research are no longer tenable.[18] Nevertheless this should not delay us here since Thesis II, as it stands, must be accepted in principle.

Passaglia's Thesis III ascribes the right of convocation to the pope: "Having established the distinction between *de jure* and *de facto*, we assert: (1) By the authority of Christ, the Roman pontiffs have the right to convoke the ecumenical councils (2) Neither the worldly

----

[14] H. Schauf is to be credited as the first to edit these theses and to provide them with copious annotations: *De conciliis oecumenicis. Theses Caroli Passaglia de conciliis deque habitu quo ad Romanos pontifices referuntur* (Rome–Freiburg i. Br.—Barcelona 1961). It would have been fruitful had the publisher of Passaglia's theses combined them with the work, *La causa di S. Em. il Cardinale G. d'Andrea* (Turin 1867) which appeared a few years later. This work would show that the responsibility of the episcopate in terms of the universal Church, of which there is barely a mention in the theses, is quite visible in Passaglia's theological thinking. Cf. on this point also, Passaglia's earlier work: *De Ecclesia Christi* (Regensburg 1853–56).

[15] C. Passaglia, *op. cit.* 16.

[16] *Ibid.*

[17] *Ibid.* 31–33.

[18] Cf. Chap. VII, 3–5.

rulers as a whole nor the emperors themselves in particular have this right. (3) The convocation by emperors is of a different order than a juridical convocation. (4) There are reasons why in the convocation of ecumenical councils emperors may be granted their part."[19] Thus in the first part of the thesis Passaglia asserts that the right to convoke ecumenical councils belongs to the Roman bishops by virtue of their investiture through Christ. This statement can be accepted in the following sense: To the extent that Peter, and thereby also his successors, have been commissioned to attend to the pastoral care of the whole Church as a service of charity, then the pastoral care (even more, one can say the pastoral duty) of convoking ecumenical councils, when necessary, also belongs to the successors of Peter in the service of the Church. Hence papal convocations of councils have their "legal foundation" since the twelfth century, hence the justification of Canon 222. Among Catholics all this is accepted today as a matter of course.

But does it follow from all this that the pope *exclusively* can convoke ecumenical councils? Canon 222 states this. Consequently it must be acknowledged that today, at least by church law (a human law), the right to convoke councils, in fact, belongs exclusively to the pope. This also is not contested among Catholics today. But the crucial question is: Must it be unconditionally so, and was it always so? Therefore, is an ecumenical council that no doubt was in unity with the pope (at least in a broadly understood sense) but which, at the same time, was not convoked by him, *not* an ecumenical council? Does the right to convoke councils, therefore, belong to the pope exclusively by *divine* law? It is not clear whether by "authority of Christ" Passaglia simply understands the pope's *right* of convocation (in this interpretation one must agree with his thesis) or whether by "authority of Christ" he also means the *restriction* of such a right to the pope alone. In general his statements are not exclusive, but simply formulated affirmatively; in another context Passaglia admits that many (presumably non-ecumenical) councils have been convoked "by the bishops in general."[20] But let us presuppose that Passaglia's statements are meant in an exclusive sense; are they covered by Passaglia's proofs? Apart from the argument of tradition, which in part we have already discussed and which will come up for further discussion, Passaglia brings forward two arguments:[21] (1) The pope has his *universalis iurisdictio ecclesiastica* (universal ecclesisatical jurisdiction) from Christ, hence he has the right to convoke councils.

---

[19] C. Passaglia, *op, cit.* 16f.

[20] *Ibid.* 18.   [21] *Ibid.* 17.

This argument is to be accepted. But does it therefore follow that the pope *exclusively* has the right? (2) The pope has the duty (*a*) to take care that the common cause of Christendom is not endangered, (*b*) to work towards the end that all appropriate means are utilized for the preservation of the Church and doctrinal unity; hence he has the right to convoke councils. This too is to be accepted. Does it follow, therefore, that the pope *exclusively* has this right?

That the *exclusive* right to convoke a council belongs to the pope by divine law cannot be derived from the reasons that are adduced by Passaglia. Curiously, in this context he never gets around to discussing the question of office, which could be taken into consideration here. He deals with princes and the emperor, but is silent concerning the episcopate. Now the episcopate is not only responsible for the care of individual dioceses but, at the same time, it is also responsible for the care of the whole Church. The bishops are in the Church not only as individuals but they are incorporated in the *College* of Bishops which, as such, is a successor to the College of the Apostles and to which, as such, the care of the whole Church has been transmitted, certainly not without, but with the pope, yet likewise by divine law.[22] Hence the episcopate assembled at an ecumenical council possesses an authority (*potestas*) not only over the respective individual dioceses, but in the whole Church (*universam ecclesiam*).[23] Hence what Passaglia states about the pope also applies to the episcopate, albeit in a different way. It too has a universal ecclesiastical jurisdiction; it too has the duty to take care that the common cause of Christendom is not endangered and to work towards the end that all appropriate means are utilized for the preservation of the Church and doctrinal unity. Hence there is a conceivable possibility (not provided in the present valid law) that under special circumstances the convocation of a council may also originate from the episcopate, that the episcopate of the different countries (thus the pope too) agree to meet together at a council. Thus there is a conceivable possibility that, in the case of an impediment of the pope (internment, imprisonment, or even mental illness), the episcopate would not be paralysed at such a time of extreme emergency in the Church and could convoke a council on its own. It would then in no way be "divided and separated from the successor of Peter"—to use Passaglia's expression—but in spiritual unity with him. As we have seen, Suarez goes significantly further. Although he defends the right of the pope to convoke a council, he clearly states: A pope who has separated himself from the body of

---

[22] Cf. Chap. VII, 2.   [23] *CIC* can. 228 § 1.

the Church in schism (for example, by trying to excommunicate the whole Church or to subvert the apostolic tradition), and who also tries to prevent the gathering of a council, is not to be obeyed because in such a case the pope would be using his pastoral full authority against righteousness and the welfare of the whole Church. Consequently under such circumstances the episcopate could assemble in an ecumenical council, notwithstanding.[24]

In times of emergencies and of Church crises one could not dispute, *ex iure divino*, even the right of lay persons to *convoke* a council for the welfare of the Church, assuming beforehand that they have the whole Church (that is, the episcopate with the pope), at least in principle behind them, without any formal commission, without any formal approbation, but certainly in the sense of at least tacit approbation, or however one might explain the process. This was how the early emperors effected convocations of councils. It is precisely these things which constitute a confirmation from history of the correctness of our conception, as we shall immediately see.

For the reason that an exclusive right of convocation of the pope cannot be proved *ex iure divino*, this right—otherwise than in the present code of canon law—could belong to others, or could have belonged to them formerly. Thus, if on the basis of historical findings, it should be shown that various councils generally acknowledged to be ecumenical were not convoked by a pope but by someone else, then we need neither throw doubt on historical facts, nor set forth juristic hypotheses by stating that this right had been delegated by the pope to these others (for instance the emperor)—although such a delegation is in no way provable, although it does turn out to be unlikely, indeed impossible. For it is unnecessary to turn facts upside down with aprioristic distinctions and to say that these others had convoked councils only *de facto*, but not *de iure*, only *materialiter*, but not *formaliter*, only *opitulative* but not *auctoritative*. All the juristic and canonical fictions that do violence to the facts become unnecessary in this case. We do not need to play the dogmatic method against the historical method and thereby actually make our dogmatics incredible in the eyes of the historians who have the facts behind them. Much rather, we can, without chipping away at the primacy, calmly take the facts as they are and build our theology upon facts.

For the reason that Passaglia started out from an unproved, in-

[24] F. Suarez, *De charitate, Disputatio XII de schismate*, sectio I (Opera omnia, Paris 1858) 12, 733f; *De fide theologica, Disputatio X de Summo Pontifice*, sectio VI (Opera omnia, Paris 1858) 12, 317f.

deed a wrong premise—at any rate that he did not make all the distinctions required—he was forced to take refuge in hypotheses and to do violence to historical facts. In order to prove his theses historically, he still based himself—in the middle of the nineteenth century—on the Pseudo-Isidorian decretals[25] and then in an aprioristic way he distinguished between *ius* and *factum*.[26] He tried to cast doubt on the convocation of the first ecumenical council by the emperor and purposed to prove, historically, that the convocation of the first ecumenical council depended on an order, an admonition, or an approbation of the Roman bishop: "Quite clearly it can be shown from the history of the councils that most of the councils up to the eighth, the convocation of which is attributed to the emperors, have not been summoned without order, admonition or consent of the Roman bishop."[27]

Yet we should not be unjust towards this important theologian. In many ecclesiological questions (especially those on the non-necessity of a papal Church state), he espoused many very progressive theses. The crucial ecclesiastico-historical clarification took place only after Passaglia's lectures in the 1850's. However, Bellarmine's historical argumentation, which also stood in the background of Passaglia's thinking (along with Thomassinus), had on the whole been retained by the historian of the councils, C. J. von Hefele, corrected of course in certain points.[28] Thereby Bellarmine's theory found widespread recognition. This conception had also been learned from Hefele himself and taken over by his pupil and successor in the chair for Church history, F. X. Funk, who espoused this view for a long time. As the result of dealing more closely with the old councils, doubts increasingly rose in Funk's mind so that he abandoned this theory as being contrary to facts. His historical inquiry showed him clearly that the emperors carried out the convocation of the council in such a way as to make it appear as though this were a right independently belonging to them, and that accordingly one could not strictly speak of a co-operation in the act or of a participation on the part of the popes. Funk first defended his changed view in Kraus's *Real-encyklopädie der christlichen Altertümer*.[29] He was attacked for this, and dealt with the subject anew in the *Tübinger*

---

[25] C. Passaglia, *op. cit.* 17.

[26] *Ibid.* 18.

[27] *Ibid.* 19.

[28] C. J. von Hefele, *Conciliengeschichte* (Freiburg i. Br. [2]1873) I, 5–15.

[29] F. X. Funk, "Concilien," in *Real-Encyclopädie der christlichen Altertümer* (Freiburg i. Br. 1882) I, 320–321.

Theologische Quartalschrift in 1882.[30] Later he remarked as follows on the matter: "I could not hope to make an immediate break-through with my view since it was not unknown to me that the pro-gress of the sciences up to now was accomplished only amidst difficult struggles, that hundreds of points, which were now regarded as established truths, had at first only gradually won acceptance, after they had been disavowed as erroneous for a long time. Indi-viduals and, to be sure, prominent scholars declared their agreement with me. Others, however, believed they should reject them."[31]

It was above all the great neo-Scholastic theologian M.-J. Schee-ben [32] who declared his opposition to Funk.[33] At the time of the First Vatican Council he wrote articles of a violent polemical-apologetical character against I. von Döllinger and J. Fr. von Schulte; then in a systematic theological testament took up a position in regard to conciliar theology,[34] in his "theological epistemology,[35] and in the article "Concil" in the *Kirchenlexikon*[36] and in the *Staatslexikon*.[37] Without going fundamentally into the historical question now posed, he again expressed himself in favour of Bellarmine's view: "Thus, the legal situation at that time was essentially as it is today, in that the pope exclusively convoked the councils in a juridical and authori-tative sense. The only difference is that the pope left the execution of the invitation and, at the same time, the organization of the required or appropriate measures for the material viability of the council (for example, the provision of means of travel and the installations involved at the assembly places) to the emperor. Admittedly then under certain circumstances in the bestowal of his authorization he

[30] F. X. Funk, "Der römische Stuhl und die allgemeinen Synoden des christli-chen Altertums," in *Tüberinger Theologische Quartalschrift* 65 (1882) 561–602.

[31] F. X. Funk, "Die Berufung der ökumenischen Synoden des Altertums," in his *Kirchengeschichtlichen Abhandlungen und Untersuchungen* (Paderborn 1807) I, 41.

[32] H. J. Hecker provides valuable information on Scheeben's biography and bibliography in *Chronik der Regenten, Dozenten und Ökonomen im Priesterseminar des Erzbistums Köln* 1615–1650 (Studien zur Kölner Kirchengeschichte I) (Düsseldorf 1952) 187–193.

[33] Especially in M.-J. Scheeben, "Concil," in *Kirchenlexikon* (ed. by Wetzer and Welte (Freiburg i. Br. ²1884]) III, 790f.

[34] M.-J. Scheeben, *Handbuch der katholischen Dogmatik I: Theologische Erkenntnislehre*, ed. by M. Grabmann (Ges. Schriften ed. by J. Höfer III. Frei-burg i. Br. ³1959) 242–261.

[35] Cf. L. Scheffczyk, "Die Lehranschauungen Matthias Joseph Scheebens über das ökumenische Konzil," in *Tübinger Theologische Quartalschrift* 141 (1961) 129–173.

[36] M.-J. Scheeben, "Concil," in *Kirchenlexikon* (*op. cit.*) III, 779–810.

[37] M.-J. Scheeben, "Concil" in *Staatslexikon* (Freiburg i. Br. 1899) I, 1475–1502.

saw himself induced to accommodate himself to the desires and proposals of the emperor, also with respect to the emergency situation
created by the emperor's encroachments."[38]

F. X. Funk commented as follows on Scheeben's exposition:
"The exposition leaves nothing to be desired in precision, and if the
reasons were as strong as the language is dependable, it would be
difficult to answer them. This premise, however, is in no way relevant. What is thus offered is not as much an historical proof as it is a
dogmatic, or rather a dialectical, construction since a dogma is not
under consideration. The difficulties opposed to the view that is
defended are simply brushed aside with the declaration that they are
not even to be taken seriously, or that logically it could not have been
so: as if our reason, or our modern view, were an absolute measure
for judging the past. And in order to give the thesis at least the appearance of justification a game is played with concepts which, in
itself, already betrays that an authentic proof cannot be provided.
In the beginning, wholly in harmony with the theory, mention is
made of a commissioning or authorization from the Apostolic
See which the emperor required for his action. But since this authorization simply cannot be proved, it is turned into an agreement, as if
this were the same thing; and since there are great difficulties in
proving even this, we end up with a mere presumption. Thus the view
against which historical evidence so strongly speaks, ultimately rests
on this presumption. Accordingly, the weakness of the argumentation
is obvious. With the same reason as that of a commission by the
pope, one could also talk of an authorization by the eastern Patriarchs
since the factors under consideration essentially can also be demonstrated with them. Thus one must also admit this as necessary or
acknowledge, if one will not make this admission, that the other is
not proved."[39]

Scheeben's reply, however (and J. Blötzer's position) induced
Funk to pursue the question of the convocation of councils—which
had never been dealt with methodically nor exhaustively—in all
its details. He first studied the numerous writs announcing convocations of councils[40] that are still preserved, then the four preserved imperial declarations to the synods, three letters and a
speech,[41] and finally the utterances of Constantine the Great re-

[38] M.-J. Scheeben, "Concil," in *Kirchenlexikon* (*op. cit.*) III, 791.

[39] F. X. Funk, "Die Berufung der ökumenischen Synoden des Altertums,"
in his *Kirchengeschichtlichen Abhandlungen und Untersuchungen* (Paderborn
1897) I, 42f.

[40] *Ibid.* I, 44–52.

[41] *Ibid.* I, 52–55.

garding the synod of Nicaea.[42] Funk concluded: "The emperors viewed the convocation of councils accordingly as a matter over which they had to decide independently, although they made use of the counsel of some bishops. They incorporated the act to the ἐκτὸς τῆς ἐκκλῆσίας, and in these matters they regarded themselves as bishops, as Constantine the Great had already expressly declared (Eusebius V, C. IV, 24). The idea that they required the acquiescence of a particular bishop, to be more precise, the pope, was far from their minds. The adduced writs of convocation and statements from other quarters show this with the greatest exactitude. This fact makes clear what we are to think of Scheeben's assertion, which holds that it is evident that in this matter the Christian emperors could not act independently or without the prior understanding of the pope. The alleged evidence of the impossibility of this rests upon an assumption that finds no support in the sources. Convocation of the councils was not only claimed by the emperors as a right, but this imperial right was acknowledged as such even by their contemporaries. This follows from the fact that the act on the whole was unanimously ascribed to the emperors by the ancients, in particular to the emperor exclusively without giving any thought to the co-operation of a third party or of the rights of a third party, to participate on the same level of authority."[43]

After Funk has thoroughly tested difficulties arrayed against this view,[44] he asserts: "According to these witnesses there can be no doubt that convocation of the ancient councils, claimed as a right by the emperors, recognized as such by contemporaries. Scheeben no doubt means that one would attribute an absurdity to the popes by making them act thus. Others do not find it so, and if he had studied the matter more carefully he would have judged otherwise. The questionable attitude is now once and for all a fact and it will remain so no matter how much one may still declare it an absurdity without substantiation. Nothing can be accomplished in the field of history with judgments of this kind. On the contrary they endanger the cause which they would serve, and instead of a defence an accusation actually results. In fact, a disavowal of this kind is not even required here. The imperial convocation does indeed contradict the status of the ecclesiastical law of a later time. But for this reason it is in no way an absurdity of such a kind that it would be simply inconceivable."[45]

[42] *Ibid.* I, 55f.   [43] *Ibid.* I, 56f.

[44] *Ibid.* I, 52–70.

[45] F. X. Funk, *op. cit.* I, 70; cf. also the discussions on pp. 70–75 which even more exactly circumscribe the position of the emperor at ecumenical councils; the epilogue to the quoted treatise on pp. 498–598, as well as finally the article:

Funk has clearly emerged the victor in this battle.[46] All competent historians agree with Funk against Scheeben (Kneller and others). Especially important is the evidence of the learned editor of the *Acta Conciliorum Oecumenicorum*, who writes: "Only the emperor has the right to convoke an imperial synod; in order to be legally valid their proceedings had to begin with the official reading of the imperial message, recorded with the minutes, which ordered them to assemble and assigned them the controversial questions which they had to resolve. The emperor was free to take part in the sessions personally or through his officials, indeed to preside over it. The attempt of Theodosius II to renounce the exercise of this right com-

---

"Zur Frage nach der Berufung der allgemeinen Synoden des Altertums," in his *Kirchengeschichtlichen Abhandlungen und Untersuchungen* (Paderborn 1907) III, 143–149; cf. 406–439.

[46] H. Schauf, in his detailed note 8 to C. Passaglia, *De conciliis oecumenicis* (Rome-Freiburg i. Br.–Barcelona 1961) 43–48, unfolds the battle backwards, as it were. He begins with Funk and ends with Scheeben, so that the conquered appears as the victor. On this point, as well as in many other passages, it would have been useful had the editors corrected the theses of the author on the basis of the present state of historiography, as this in part has happened. For example, the Tübingen dogmatist L. Scheffczyk in, "Die Lehranschauungen M.-J. Scheebens über das ökumenische Konzil," in *Tübinger Theologische Quartalschrift* 141 (1961) 164–166 has correctly posed Scheeben's theses in terms of historical criteria: "Thus it is fitting, in proceeding from the external to the internal state of affairs, to begin with a criticism of the historical proofs with which Scheeben underpins his discussions on dogma. Here one may not deny recognition to the effort also to give due weight to historical facts in the discussion of dogmas. But neither can one fail to recognize that the interpretation of historical facts is strongly coloured by the dogmatic idea of the nature of a council while the ambiguity of the development of this institution in the history of the Church is underestimated. Thus the assertion that the origin of the general councils is directly traceable to the Council of the Apostles is not historically convincing. Even the description of the relationships between popes and emperors in connection with the convocation of the early councils, in which Scheeben aims to preserve at least a presumption of agreement on the part of the popes, does not correspond with the facts. Likewise, the assertion that the older councils served above all for the execution, promulgation, and confirmation of papal decrees that had already been issued does not do justice to the differentiation that marked the relationship between the Roman Church and the general synods of the first century. This is shown by the very historical examples that Scheeben adduces in support of his assertion, namely the reference to the third and fourth General Council. In the case of the Council of Ephesus, for example, Scheeben completely passes over a fact to which Hefele clearly gave great prominence, namely, that at its first session that Council did not at all comprehend its task to be only an expression of its agreement with the Roman pronouncement concerning Nestorius, thereby introducing a new investigation of Nestorius' orthodoxy. Subsequently, admittedly, it gave its assent to the papal view. As regards Chalcedon, doubtlessly Leo the Great's doctrinal brief was accepted by the Council, but then a new formula of faith was set forth and proclaimed, even against the opposition of the papal legates, which constituted a progressive step *vis-à-vis* the papal formulations."

pletely miscarried and his successors, the imperial pair Pulcheria and Marcian, subjected the Chalcedonian synod to the direction of the highest imperial officials, whose energy left nothing to be desired. Justinian transmitted his order for an obedient adherence to the imperial Council of Constantinople. It is accordingly self-evident that the decisions adopted by the imperial synod required imperial confirmation. In no way was this merely a question of form. On the other hand the Church was to be governed by the Church herself."[47]

The historically correct conception is likewise maintained: for Nicaea by V. Grumel[48] and by G. Bardy,[49] for the councils of the whole fourth century by M. Goemans,[50] and for the early councils altogether by Fr. Dvornik.[51] The imperial synodal right has been investigated with particular care by A. Michel,[52] who amplifies in detail: "If through his right of nomination the emperor stood at the beginning of the most important pontificates, likewise did he also stand through his *synodal right* at the beginning, in the centre, and at the end of the most important synods. If he ruled there the individual offices, likewise his powerful influence here encompassed the totality of the Greek Church. For the synods, especially the so-called ecumenical ones, were the most important organ of ecclesiastical life, through which the hierarchy became effective *corporately* in the teaching office and in the pastoral office. . . ." The emperors claimed the right of *convocation of ecumenical councils* in their writs

[47] E. Schwartz, "Über die Reichskonzilien von Theodosius bis Justinian," in *Zeitschrift der Savigny-Stiftung für Rechtsgeschichte, Kanonist.* Abt. 11 (1921) 209.

[48] V. Grumel, "Le siege de Rome et le concile de Nicée. Convocation et présidence," in *Échos d'Orient* 28 (1925) 411–415.

[49] G. Bardy, "De la paix constantienne à la mort de Théodose" (Fliche and Martin, *Histoire de l'Église* 3 [Paris 1950]) 80, attests that the Council of Nicaea was clearly convoked by Constantine. In regard to the attempt to make a distinction between a "formal convocation" of the pope and a "material convocation" of the emperor, he observes: "Il y a là une subtilité bien inutile."

[50] M. Goemans, *Het algemeen concilie in de vierde eeuw* (Nijmegen-Utrecht 1945) 285: "The convocation of the general council [in the fourth century] was ordered by the Emperor and by him alone. He considered this his royal prerogative. He also could take independent decisions over it, without the help, approval or order of a second person, namely the Bishop of Rome. Further, contemporaries, the Council Fathers, and the popes, without exception, granted the Emperor's right to convoke councils as well as a general council. The Emperor also adjourned the council and allowed the Fathers to return to their homes."

[51] F. Dvornik, "De auctoritate civili in conciliis oecumenicis," in *Acta VI Conventas Velehradensis* (Olomucii 1953) 156–167; "Emperors, Popes and General Councils," in *Dumbarton Oaks Papers* 6 (Cambridge, Massachusetts 1951) 1–23.

[52] A. Michel, "Die Kaisermacht in der Ostkirche (843–1204)" in *Ostkirchliche Studien* 2 (1953) 1–35, 89–109; 3 (1954) 1–28, 133–163; 4 (1955) 1–42, 221–260; 5 (1956) 1–32.

without further ado but also without being contested. "It is my will," Constantine declared in his writ convoking the Council of Nicaea, "that all of you assemble without delay in the city mentioned." Convocations of this kind were feasible only for the emperors, hence no one disputed them; ultimately, they were exclusively ascribed to them and denied to the pope. Even such men as Athanasius and Leo the Great pressingly entreated the court to convoke the synod of Sardica and an Italian synod. When Leo's will changed with the circumstances, emperor Marcian, convinced of his exclusive competency in this matter, summoned the council, Nicaea and Chalcedon notwithstanding. Pope Vigilius, however, did not appear at the fifth ecumenical synod (553), as Patriarch Cerularius himself knew. As early as the sixth and seventh centuries, only those synods which had assembled at the emperor's orders were to be considered valid. Therefore the bishops of Quinisexta (691) in their address of thanks to Justinian II, stressed that the emperor "had convoked this holy, God-elected ecumenical synod." Empress Irene in the year 784 simply informed Pope Hadrian: "We have decided to hold a council."[53]

It is unnecessary to quote further witnesses. H. Jedin observes briefly: "The question whether the early councils were convened by the emperors with the previous assent of the Bishop of Rome, or even by commission, has been the subject of controversy from the time of the Reformation. More recently the question was once more vehemently debated between Scheeben, the theologian, and Funk, the Church historian. As far as the facts go, the question may be answered in the negative."[54] If divine and human direction, if the law of God and the law of man are carefully distinguished, and if not only dogmatic theologians but also historians—which for long has not always been the case—clearly see that questions of the convocation, direction, and confirmation of ecumenical councils from the outset concern questions of *human* law, the conflict between dogma and history can be avoided. Then neither the dogmatists need have a secret fear of the facts of history, nor the historians fear the censures of dogmatic theology.

Since it would lead us too far astray to go more closely into the problems of the direction of councils and the confirmation of councils in terms of an historical approach, we shall cite only two concluding witnesses in detail for the purpose of a general orientation:

(*a*) *Presidency and Direction:* "The *presidency* and *the determining direction* first of all of the *general synods* again belonged to the em-

---

[53] A. Michel, *op. cit.* 3 (1954) 1f.
[54] H. Jedin, *Ecumenical Councils of the Catholic Church* (New York 1960) 14.

perors by law, although they often commissioned prominent bishops or secular commissioners with this task. Thus a distinction can scarcely be made between internal and external Church matters. An imperial tribune presided at the synod against the Donatists in Carthage in 315; later emperor Constantine again presided personally at the impressive 'Encaenia ("dedication" of the basilica) Synod' in Antioch in 341. Such was also the case at the eighth anti-Photian council held in 869–70. After the imperially commissioned Dioscurus had steered the so-called Robbers' Synod (449) into heretical channels, Leo the Great did indeed consider it appropriate that his legates should preside at the council of Chalcedon (451), but he did not seriously reckon with it. The presidency was in fact conducted more energetically by the commissioner Candidian. The pope's vicars always 'sat,' however, 'in the first place' (*praesidebant*), and it was the popes each time who, by their previous attitude, compelled the orthodox course of most ecumenical councils but who also supervised them morally through writs and legates. The acclamations at the Council of Chalcedon, however, hailed Emperor Marcian as the teacher of the faith. Most of the sessions of the sixth general Council of Constantinople (680–81) were led by Emperor Constantine IV Pogonatus personally, and he had the official documents sent to the patriarchs. At the seventh ecumenical Council of Nicaea (787) the presiding officer was the Patriarch Tarasios, appointed by the Empress Irene to whom he had formerly been private secretary, although imperial commissioners were in attendance. At its conclusion, however, the empress herself appeared with her son Constantine. She presented the crucial question of the consensus and was the first to sign the decrees. At the eighth ecumenical council (869–70) Basilius I, to the extent that he was present, again acted as president as a 'matter of course,' where he had the credentials of the Roman legates examined once more, to their great chagrin. Further, he brought up the whole question of Photius once more and, instead of simply agreeing with the Roman council's decree of deposition, he ordered the opening speech to be read; he himself questioned the followers of Photius, established the consensus, and in his absence he handed over the presidency to his commissioners, especially to the patrician Baanes, who 'played an important role.' This is what the Alexandrian patriarch had expected when, in his address, he called the emperor 'the highest head and the teacher of the synod.' Thus the imperial 'leadership' had for a long time become 'a formal element' of ecumenical synods."[55]

[55] A. Michel, *op. cit.* 3 (1954) 7f.

(*b*) *Confirmation of Synods:* "None of the usual proofs adduced for papal approbation of the early synods, therefore, can stand up against a scientific test. The result shows, since the burden of proof falls on the exponents of the approbation theory, that this view is no longer tenable. The same, however, can also be proved more positively. Several synods made pronouncements concerning their decrees in a way that altogether excludes the idea of approbation. They consider the decrees, as such, valid in themselves. The circumstance that stands out at a synod is that the promulgation of decrees takes place before the alleged confirmation. However, this point merits closer consideration. Yet, as far as I can see, it has continued to be disregarded in Catholic literature; formerly it even escaped my attention. It is, however, of the greatest importance, and if my discussion should still leave any doubt, such doubts should vanish now. The facts speak for themselves. The procedure proves clearly and irrefutably that the validity of the decrees was not thought to depend upon subsequent confirmation by the Roman see. Otherwise the decrees could not have been published, and the emperor could not endow them with the force of law before such confirmation had been granted."[56]

What has been said in this section provides also a positive answer to Martin Luther's question *of principle* concerning the convocation of councils. Thereby, the fact that some aspects have been presented as of human or ecclesiastical law *in principle* also by us obviously does not mean that *in practice* all possibilities would be of equal validity or even merely desirable. What the practical modus of an eventual council for reunion could be today is not within the scope of our inquiry. However, with respect to the reunion of separated Christians it is a cause for rejoicing to see that the Constitution of the Catholic Church in no way closes all doors from the outset, but gives a great deal of scope for a serious ecumenical encounter. But we should entertain no illusions because of this. The way to reunion is long and arduous, not only in theology. The way to reunion requires patience, penance, a genuine renunciation on the part of all participants who indeed are not all without guilt, a renunciation—Constance can serve as teaching here—precisely of the Petrine office, too, as a service of charity for the sake of the unity of Christendom.

The following question, however, is immediately posed to us here from the Protestant side: Renunciation also in doctrine? What is the situation with respect to the infallibility of conciliar and papal decisions?

[56] F. X. Funk, "Die päpstliche Bestätigung der acht ersten allgemeinen Synoden," in his *Kirchengeschichtlichen Abhandlungen und Untersuchungen* (Paderborn 1897) I, 119, 121.

VIII

WHAT DOES INFALLIBILITY MEAN?

1. THE FALLIBILITY OF COUNCILS
ACCORDING TO LUTHER AND CALVIN

LUTHER'S first polemical exchanges with his adversaries—as has been pointed out—led him perforce to acknowledge that councils can err: "... the pope as well as the council can err" (Answer to Prieras, 1518[1]) And even more: Councils have erred: "I agree with the d. [divine] doctor that the statutes of the council must be upheld in what concerns the faith. Only this I reserve for myself, and it must be reserved, that councils have erred and can err, especially in matters not pertaining to faith, nor has a council the authority to make new articles of faith; otherwise, we have finally as many articles as opinions of men" (Disputation with Eck[2]). Luther was compelled by Eck to make this statement in connection with the condemnation of Huss by the Council of Constance. In his *Operationes in Psalmos* subsequently he most sharply assailed the "council of Satan" in Constance.[3] The assertion of the infallibility of councils (especially of the Council of Constance) then constituted the chief reason why Luther was dropped by the emperor and the princes at the Imperial Diet at Worms in 1521 and punished with the Imperial Ban.[4] At the hearing, the Chancellor of Trier, Johannes Eck, demanded that Luther should acknowledge the inerrancy of councils and disavow the propositions condemned by the Council of Constance. Hence Luther's clear refusal: "Unless I am convinced by the testimony of Scripture or by evidence of reason (for I do not believe the pope or the councils alone since it is proved that they have erred frequently and contradicted themselves), I am convicted by the scripture I have quoted and held prisoner by conscience in the words of God, I cannot revoke anything nor do I want to, for to act against conscience is neither safe nor honest."[5] This was the context of Luther's famous words: "I can do naught else, here I stand, may God help me, Amen!"[6]

[1] *WA* 1, 656, for Luther's position towards councils, see footnote 1 at the beginning of Chapter V, sec. 1.

[2] *WA* 2, 303. [3] *WA* 5, 451.

[4] Cf. J. Kolde, *Luthers Stellung zu Concil und Kirche bis zum Wormser Reichstag* 1521 (Gütersloh 1876).

[5] *WA* 7, 838. [6] *Ibid.*

The profession of faith that Luther made in Worms remained a guiding one for all the later years: He would bind his conscience only by the evidence of Scripture (or by evident grounds of reason) but not by councils when they do not have the word of God behind them. Councils have erred, they have erred often and they contradict each other.

Calvin, in his principal work *Institutio christianae religionis*, took a position towards the question of the authority of councils in a systematic and detailed way.[7] It would be eminently worth while to familiarize ourselves with his position. In his fourth book on the external means with which God calls us to communion with Christ and retains us in it, Calvin treats of the Church, her offices, and her authority. The eighth chapter is devoted to the authority of the Church in relation to dogmas. By way of introduction, Calvin refers to the words of Paul in 2 Corinthians 10:8 (or 13:10) that played a great role both in the theology of office and in medieval canon law studies and especially in the conciliar epoch. All ecclesiastical authority must be directed towards one aim: to build up and not to destroy, "ad aedificationem et non in destructionem."[8] Those who exercise authority should not regard themselves as more than servants of Christ and his people. The edification of the Church takes place only when the ministers take great pains to preserve to *Christ* His rightful authority. Of no one else but of Him alone it is written: "Hear Him" (Mt. 17:5). Two things were of concern to Calvin in his theology of office: on the one hand, that ecclesiastical authority be honoured without meanness, on the other hand, that this authority be kept within definite limits.[9] The authority of the Church is not unlimited, but subject to the word of the Lord and, as it were, included in it: "subiecta verbo Domini et in eo quasi inclusa."[10] Nothing else should be held to be the word of God other than what is contained in the law and in the prophets and in the apostolic writings. There is no other way of teaching aright in the Church than according to the prescriptions and standards of this Word.[11]

[7] We quote according to Calvin's last edition, published in 1559 (*CR* 30); cf. also the German edition by O. Weber, *Unterricht in der christlichen Religion* (Neukirchen 1955). On Calvin's ecclesiology, cf. the bibliography in W. Niesel, *Die Theologie Calvins* (Munich ²1957) 185. On the theory of councils espoused by Calvin and Calvinists, cf. J.-L. Leuba, "Das ökumenische Konzil in der reformierten Theologie," in *Die ökumenischen Konzile der Christenheit*, ed. by H. J. Margull (Stuttgart 1961) 373–392.

[8] *CR* 30, 846.

[9] *CR* 30, 847.

[10] *CR* 30, 848.

[11] *CR* 30, 850.

The true servant of the Church and the Church altogether must adhere to this Word and not fabricate new dogmas.[12]

Calvin takes a sharp stand against—as he understood it—the arbitrary teaching authority of the Catholic Church, to whose arbitrariness in promulgating decrees one simply had to subject oneself in blind belief.[13] The Catholic Church bases herself on the promises said to have been given to the Church, namely, that the Lord will never forsake her and that the Spirit would guide her in all truth. But, according to Calvin, these promises were given not only to the whole Church but to every individual believer. True, the same measure of wisdom has not been allotted in the same degree to each one, and it is allotted in a much greater and richer degree to the whole community. Despite all these promises that are given to them the believers are still short of the mark. They are still imperfect and they must, therefore, continue to march forward. But this also applies to the whole Church, to which certainly nothing necessary is wanting but which is not yet perfect. The Church is sanctified by Christ but only at the end of time will the Church be wholly without "spot or wrinkle" (Eph. 5:26ff). In the Church the truth of God is preserved through the preaching office, hence to the extent that the Church accomplishes this truly and purely she is "the pillar and mainstay of the truth" (I Tim. 3:15).[14]

Precisely here, according to Calvin, is the point on which the controversy turns and which must be kept in view: He too admits that the Church *cannot err* in things that are essential to salvation. Why? Because the Church renounces her own wisdom and opens herself to instruction by the Holy Spirit through the word of God. Hence the difference between Calvinist and the Catholic teaching does not lie in the fact that the former disputes the infallibility of the Church in matters of salvation and that the other asserts it. Rather, according to Calvin, the difference consists in the fact that the Catholics place the authority of the Church *outside* the word of God. According to them the Church can go along her way with certainty even without the word of God; whithersoever the Church goes, she can do naught else but think and speak the truth. Consequently when she determines anything outside or above the divine Word this is simply to be regarded as an unmistakable oracle of God.

Against this Calvin wants the authority of the Church *to be bound to the word of God* and the Church to be inseparable from it.[15]

---

[12] *CR* 30, 852.   [13] *CR* 30, 852f.   [14] *CR* 30, 854f.

[15] "Commenting on the statement that the Church cannot err, this seems to me the interpretation: when she is guided by God's Spirit, she can proceed safely

As the bride and disciple of Christ the Church should cling constantly and assiduously to His words. Hence the Church should not aim to be wise of herself; instead the Church should set a limit to her wisdom, where Christ Himself set a limit to His speaking. Even the Spirit does not proclaim new truths, but recalls all that Christ has said (Jn. 14:26). The Church is never governed *without* the word of the Holy Spirit.

Therefore the Church will distrust the inventions of her own reason. But in matters in which the Church can support herself on God's word, the Church will not waver with any distrust or hesitation, but will trust in God's word with greater certainty and unshaken constancy. The Church will trust in the amplitude of the promises given to her in order gloriously to preserve her faith, never doubting in the slightest that the Holy Spirit will always be at her side.[16] Hence no one will despise the unanimous consent of the Church, which accords with the truth of the word of God. We must hear the Church. Nevertheless the Church is not allowed to establish new doctrines. It would not do to declare what men have held to be true as a revelation of God.[17]

In the following chapter Calvin applies the teachings of Chapter 8 to the *authority of councils*. At the very beginning he observes that here he will be rather severe. But not for the reason that he esteemed the ancient councils less than they deserve. On the contrary: "Veneror enim ea ex animo, suoque in honore apud omnes esse cupio."[18] Yet a limit must be observed: Nothing must be derogated from Christ! He alone has the prerogative to the presidency of councils, and He has this presidency only when the whole assembly is ruled by His

---

without the word, and wherever it leads she cannot feel or utter anything but the truth. Further, it makes something outside or beyond the word of God to have no other foundation than a certain oracle of God. If we take the first, the Church cannot err in matters necessary for salvation, and the reason we give for this is that she lets herself be guided by the Holy Spirit and by the word of God and gives up all her own reasoning. In this lies the difference: these put the authority of the Church outside the word of God and we want it connected with the word, and we will not allow it to be separated from it." *CR* 30, 855.

[16] "The Church therefore does not reason or think anything of herself, but she sets the limit of her wisdom where she has put the end of speaking. She distrusts the things and the way of her own reasoning; but in so far as she rests on the word of God she is not disturbed by uncertainty and hesitation but remains undisturbed in great certitude and firmness. In this way, trusting in the great promises given to her, she will uphold the faith in clarity and she does not doubt that the Holy Spirit who is the best guide to the right way will be always with her." *CR* 30, 855.

[17] *CR* 30, 857.

[18] *CR* 30, 858.

word and by His spirit. Thus, on the one hand, Calvin aims to uphold the councils and, on the other, to keep them within bounds. Not he stresses, because he fears the ancient councils—indeed, the ancient councils provide him with abundant material over and above Scripture to use against the papacy—but for the sake of Christ and His word.

Calvin starts out from the premise that there can also be false as well as true councils. If one wants to learn what authority councils possess according to Scripture, one must meditate on the promise of the Lord: "For where two or three are gathered together for my sake, there am I in the midst of them" (Mt. 18:20). Christ here obviously did not promise to be at *all possible* councils, but only at those which are gathered in His name. The decisive thing is not that bishops are assembled, but that the assembly—whether it be a particular or a general council—is assembled *in the name of* Jesus Christ. Councils, then, are ruled by the Holy Spirit only when they are assembled in Christ's name. In any case, those not assembled in Christ's name are those councils which reject God's commandment, prohibiting any diminution of His word or the least addition to it (Deut. 4:2; Apoc. 22:18f), which then determine the one or the other according to their own discretion, which are not content with the words of revelation in Scripture and which concoct something new out of their own heads. But those which uphold Holy Scripture and are content with it are assembled in the name of Christ.[19]

Hence, according to Calvin, there are false councils and councils of bad bishops. The supposition that the truth remains in the Church only when the Church is under the pastors, or that the Church can exist only when she is presented in general councils, is far from correct. Rather, even the Old Testament reports of the ignominious dereliction of pastors and priests. And Christ as well as His apostles have sufficiently predicted that the greatest danger to the Church would come from her pastors (Mt. 24:11, 24). The second epistle of Peter (2:1) warns against false teachers and prophets. And Paul shows that the anti-Christ will have his seat nowhere but in the Temple of God (II Thess. 2:4). And even in the address to the bishops of Ephesus he warned against wolves and false teachers who will not spare the Church (Acts 20:29f). This is said to have been confirmed all too well in the subsequent centuries of Church history. The truth lives not only in the pastors; nor is the safety of the Church, fortunately, dependent upon the state of the pastors. True, the pastors should be the defenders of the peace and of the safety of the Church,

[19] *CR* 30, 858f.

but "aliud est praestare quod debeas, aliud, debere quod non praestes" ["it is one thing to perform a duty which we owe, and another to owe a duty which we do not perform"].[20]

The authority of the true pastor should in no way be weakened. But there must be an absolute distinction between those who are pastors and those who are merely called pastors. In view of the records of the Old Testament and the council which the chief priests of the Jews in the "Church" at that time convened against Christ (Jn. 11:47), under no circumstances is it to be conceded that the Church consists in the assembly of pastors. For nowhere has the Lord promised that pastors will always be good pastors, but He has certainly warned that, at times, they would be wicked.[21]

But there are also true councils. And according to Calvin, these may not be rejected, nor should their acts be rescinded or cancelled forthwith. In such cases, however, is it left arbitrarily to every individual to decide what he will accept or reject concerning conciliar decrees? By no means. According to Calvin one must first of all carefully consider the time a council was called, the reason for and the intention behind its convocation, and what kind of persons were present. The conclusions of the Council should then be measured against the standard of Scripture, in which the definition of a Council should have its weight, being considered only as a provisional judgment, as a *praeiudicium*, which should not hamper the examination itself. For this Calvin bases himself on Augustine. Augustine had immediately silenced the heretic Maximinus, who contested the decrees of the councils, by saying to him: "I must not bring forward the Council of Nicaea and you must not bring forward that of Ariminum (359), as if to prejudge the matter. For you are not subject to the first, nor am I to the second. Let matter dispute with matter, cause with cause, reason with reason. And let all be based on the authority of Scripture, not that peculiar to either one, but that common to both."[22]

Calvin's view therefore is the following: The councils must be accorded the majesty due to them. But Holy Scripture has primacy even over councils. All councils are subject to the guiding line of Holy Writ. Hence, Calvin unhesitatingly accepts the early councils (Nicaea, Constantinople, Ephesus, Chalcedon, and others); indeed, he reverences their dogmas as holy, for he claims they contain nothing but the pure original interpretation of Holy Scripture against the

[20] *CR* 30, 860.   [21] *CR* 30, 861.
[22] Augustine, *contra Maximinum*, lib. II, cap. 14, 3; quoted according to German edition of the *Institutio* by O. Weber (Neukirchen 1955) 797.

heretics. Calvin asserts the same even about some later councils. Yet, the subsequent period also showed him how councils—despite some good Council Fathers—can defect from the normative lines of Scripture.

Apart from all the human factors that are observed at councils,[23] according to Calvin, one council contradicts another even in matters of doctrine;[24] for example, the Council of Constantinople in 754 condemned the veneration of images, the Council of Nicaea in 787 confirmed it. Actually the second council prevailed; but would Augustine or Epiphanius, who opposed idolatry, have accepted these conciliar decrees? To declare one council as legitimate and the other as illegitimate is no solution; only on the ground of Holy Scripture is it possible to arrive at a sure judgment concerning a council's orthodoxy. On this basis one cannot avoid acknowledging that councils can err. Catholics do not want to admit this; all they can do in the case of erring councils is to forbid the truth from being discovered or to forbid people to assent to the errors. Calvin purposes to espouse a more realistic conception in opposition to this. From the fact that councils can err it follows that the Holy Spirit certainly governed the councils, which after all are pious and holy, but the Holy Spirit governs them in such a way that He allows them now and then to betray something of human frailty, so that we may not place our trust all too much in men.[25] Truth does not perish in the Church because it is oppressed at one council. Rather, the truth in the Church is wonderfully preserved by the Lord against the error of a council so that in its own time it again breaks forth and is victorious.[26] According to Calvin, such a view is much more favourable than that of Gregory of Nazianzus who declared that no council had ever turned out well. Such a claim would completely destroy the authority of councils.[27]

From the fact that the Holy Spirit, as is the case everywhere where men gather, allows errors even at councils, Calvin contends that no blind obedience is to be accorded to a council. Rather, Scripture has frequently and sharply warned us to test spirits, to see whether they are of God (I John 4:1), to guard ourselves against false prophets

---

[23] *CR* 30, 863f.   [24] *CR* 30, 286f.

[25] "I maintain only that one can conclude that the Holy Spirit speaks and guides the councils in this way, that he allows them to do something in human frailty in order that we should not trust unduly in men." *CR* 30, 864.

[26] "I confess and state that the truth cannot perish in the Church even when oppressed by one council, but it will miraculously be saved by God through his letting it emerge and perdure at the time set by him." *CR* 30, 866.

[27] *CR* 30, 864.

who come to us in sheep's clothing but who are inwardly ravenous wolves (Mt. 15:14), not to let the blind lead the blind so that both fall in the ditch (Mt. 15:14). Therefore, we should not be overawed by any titles and names, nor by councils of bishops or popes. Rather, we should test whether they are true shepherds and not blind or wicked shepherds; we should test their definitions against the guiding thread of the word of God in order to determine whether they are of God.[28]

Given these precarious circumstances is it altogether good that councils be held at all? Calvin answers this question in the affirmative: despite all difficulties a council of true bishops is the best means to settle a dispute over a dogma. There are three reasons for this: (1) A decision which the pastors of the Church unanimously adopt all together after an appeal to the spirit of Christ will have far greater weight than the decision of a single pastor or of some persons holding no office. (2) The assembly in the same place makes it easier to establish consensus regarding doctrine and to avoid the scandal of diversity in doctrine. (3) Paul prescribes this procedure (1 Cor. 14:29) and it is dictated by the feeling of piety as well; in difficult cases the churches in concert should take the judgment in their own hands. Thus, the doubts among the people can be removed by conciliar definition and ambitious, refractory persons be silenced. This is what happened at the early councils.[29]

Thus a great importance is ascribed to a council in connection with the interpretation of Scripture. Nevertheless, according to Calvin, this importance should not be attributed indiscriminately as the Catholics do. They declare *everything* which the councils have decided as an interpretation of Scripture, even things which are not in Scripture (purgatory, the intercession of saints, auricular confession, etc.), indeed, even things about which the very opposite is expressly written (prohibition of communion under two kinds, although according to Matthew 26, Christ commands that all should drink of the cup, or the prohibition of marriage for the whole priestly state, although according to I Timothy 4:1–3 the prohibition of marriage is an hypocrisy of evil spirits and according to Hebrews 13:4 the state of matrimony is holy for all).[30]

This is how far Calvin went in his chapters on "the power of the Church respecting articles of faith" and "on councils and their authority." His conception is marked by an impressive clarity and consistency. Thus Calvin strives positively to give full value to the strength and weakness of ecclesiastical offices and of councils under

---

[28] *CR* 30, 864f.   [29] Cf. *CR* 30, 865f
[30] *CR* 30, 866.

the word of God and thereby to uphold the infallibility of the Church in matters concerning salvation.

We have already answered some of the questions that arise here, namely those regarding offices and their authority in the Church,[31] and the question pertaining to the importance of Holy Scripture for the Church and councils.[32] On the basis of these discussions some of Calvin's misunderstandings regarding Catholic doctrine can be briefly set right. (1) In the Catholic view, too, the Church in the world is always a Church composed of human beings and sinful human beings; therefore, she is and remains imperfect until the end of time; over and over again there is a dereliction of the faithful and of pastors, there are false prophets and false teachings, against which the Church must defend herself. (2) In the Catholic view, too, office-holders are not rulers but servants of Christ, and of the Church. Their authority is in no way unlimited but bound to the Word and the commission of the Lord. They are not autonomous, but hold the office only in faith under the Holy Spirit over which they have no independent control. (3) In the Catholic view, too, the Church or a council cannot formulate definitions arbitrarily. If they purpose to stand under the Holy Spirit both must adhere to the Word of Christ as found in Holy Scripture. The definitions of the Church must be understood on the basis of Holy Scripture.

The gulf between Calvin and Catholic teaching is not as great as it seemed to Calvin at that time. It must also be admitted that in Calvin's time it was much more difficult to perceive Catholic teaching in all its purity than is the case today. Yet the real point of controversy cannot be overlooked. It does not at all concern—and careful attention must be paid to this—the continuation in principle of the *Church* in truth, but rather the continuation of the individual *councils* in the truth. In concerns the infallibility of councils which Calvin contested and which the Catholic Church upholds. But this very assertion of the infallibility of councils in no way occurs in such an undifferentiated, indiscriminate way as set forth by the Reformers and also often by present-day Protestant theologians. We must now turn our whole attention to this point by considering first the teaching of that council which dealt directly with the infallibility of the pope and thereby indirectly also with the infallibility of councils.

[31] Cf. Chaps. VI and VII.
[32] Cf. Chaps. IV, sec. 3 and VI, sec. 1.

2. THE LIMITS OF INFALLIBILITY
AT THE FIRST VATICAN COUNCIL

(*a*) *Karl Barth and Vatican I:* After some very heated discussions Pius IX, together with the First Vatican Council, formulated the definition that when the pope, in his capacity of pastor and teacher of all Christians and on the ground of his apostolic authority, declares a doctrine on faith or morals as binding for the whole Church, on the ground of the divine assistance which is promised in Peter, he possesses that infallibility with which the Divine Redeemer purposed to arm His Church in ultimate decisions in matters relating to faith and morals: "We, with the approval of the sacred council, teach and define that it is a divinely revealed dogma: that the Roman Pontiff, when he speaks *ex cathedra*, that is, when, acting in the office of shepherd and teacher of all Christians, he defines, by virtue of his supreme apostolic authority, doctrine concerning faith or morals to be held by the universal Church, possesses through the divine assistance promised to him in blessed Peter the infallibility with which the divine Redeemer willed his Church to be endowed in defining doctrine concerning faith or morals; and that such definitions of the Roman Pontiff are therefore irreformable of themselves, but not because of the agreement of the Church."[1]

For Catholic doctrine the infallibility of the Church and the infallibility of ecclesiastical office (of the pope and of the councils) are essentially connected. For the reason that Christ in His Spirit promised to preserve the Church, as a whole, from apostasy through His eschatologically triumphant grace, He will also preserve office as a whole in the Church from apostasy: from falling away from faith, from a substantial error which would destroy Christ's message. No dilemma exists between the Church of the faith of the apostles and the Church of the office of the apostles. To the extent that it concerns the binding teaching of the whole Church and to the extent that the task of office (of the pope and of councils) is to serve the doctrine that is binding upon the whole Church, this office with and in the Church is an infallible norm for the faith of the individual Christian. Thereby the office does not raise itself above Scripture as the apostolic witness to Christ, rather, in its authoritative teaching it actually exercises its own obedience with respect to the teaching of the apostles. This infallibility is not guaranteed by any kind of human characteristic or in a "competency" necessarily to be assumed in the bearer of the teaching office, but by the assistance promised to the

[1] Denz. 1859.

Church by the Holy Spirit. The Spirit exercises His counselling and guiding power according to His pleasure. And this is precisely the way in which the Spirit prevents the office, in its ultimate doctrinal decisions, from introducing human inventions into the binding witness to Christ.

Nowhere else do the enormous difficulties blocking the way to a reunion of separated Christians seem to be more difficult to overcome than on this very point. It seems impossible that Lutherans, Reformed, Anglicans, and Orthodox could ever accept such a dogma. The differences here should not be blotted out nor can they be blotted out. Nevertheless, Christians who are struggling to achieve unity are duty-bound to concern themselves with this seemingly hopeless cleavage, if only at least to narrow down the distance between both sides. The first step in this direction is the removal of mutual misunderstandings. We have just shown through Calvin (and also previously through Luther) that it would be a misunderstanding of reformationist doctrine if Catholic quarters should hold the belief that the Reformers were interested simply in undermining the authority of councils. Rather, the Reformers wanted to buttress the authority of councils on better ground by limiting their relationship to revelation both positively and negatively. Now we must turn to the misunderstandings to which the doctrines of Vatican I regarding the infallibility of the pope (and of the Church) are exposed.

The opposition which Luther and Calvin ushered in against the "arbitrariness" of the Catholic teaching office has been continued by Karl Barth even more sharply. Barth especially is even more severe in his criticism that the Catholic Church does not sufficiently distinguish between Church and Revelation. According to him the process of identification, which certainly did not first begin with the Council of Trent and its definition of tradition as a second source of revelation (cf. the references already in Irenaeus and later especially the *commonitorium* of Vincent of Lérins in 434),[2] has gone far beyond the Council of Trent. According to Barth, *vis-à-vis* the Reformationist doctrine, "it is no less essential and important for the Roman Catholic system that it should reject this alleged narrowing down of revelation to its biblical attestation, putting a definite element in Church life which is given the name of divine revelation, so-called tradition, side by side with Holy Scripture, then broadening this element more and more until the whole of the Church life seems to be included in it, then subordinating and co-ordinating Holy Scripture under and with this whole, and finally declaring this whole

[2] K. Barth, *Church Dogmatics,* I/2, 548–551.

and therefore itself to be identical with the revelation of God."[3]
Thus it works its revenge in the Catholic Church (and in another way
also in the neo-Protestantism which is all too closely related to the
Catholic conception)[4] in that the Church has not taken seriously the
uniqueness of Revelation as an event occurring once and for all in
time, and along with it the prophetic-apostolic situation: "By
usurping to itself what does not pertain to it, the Church shows itself
at once to be incapable of the relationship of obedience in which the
prophets and apostles stand to revelation. It will pervert this relationship of obedience into one in which it thinks that by virtue of
possession and knowledge and power it can evade God, Christ and
the Holy Spirit, in which it has not merely to obey but to control.
And inevitably it will more and more be the one who really controls.
Inevitably it will more and more approximate to that direct, absolute
and substantial authority, and finally proclaim itself more or less
directly identical with it. Inevitably it will become a Church which
rules itself under the pretext of obedience to revelation."[5]

In post-Tridentine Catholicism, unlike the discussion at the
Council of Trent which spoke of two sources of Christian know-
ledge, now there was mention of three sources: Scripture, Tradition
and—drawn out of tradition—the Church of the present time.[6]
Increasingly it became unnecessary to go back to the tradition of the
"Fathers," unnecessary to go back to the authority of the early
Church, otherwise so highly praised as against Protestant claims.
The Tridentine "pari pietatis affectu" was extended to more and more
authorities of the present-day Church. According to Barth this
development achieved its final point in nineteenth-century Catho-
licism, which was especially manifested in two events: in the Catholic
Tübingen School and in Vatican I.

"The first of these events is one to which not enough attention
has been paid, the existence of the Catholic so-called Tübingen
School."[7] According to Johann Michael Sailer, "The Tübinger J. S.
Drey tried to take up again the thesis of Sailer and overcome its
weakness by his view of the Church, i.e. of revelation as a living
organism, which has developed and still develops out of the life
principle within it under the guidance of the divine Spirit, so that in
its life the static principle, i.e. that which is originally given by God,
is continually moved and kept in progress by the dynamically living
principle—which is tradition."[8] Hence it follows that "Scripture,

---

[3] *Ibid.* I/2, 546.   [4] *Ibid.* I/2 545–547.
[5] *Ibid.* I/2 545.   [6] *Ibid.* I/2, 557f.
[7] *Ibid.* I/2, 560.   [8] *Ibid.* I/2, 560.

tradition and theology are the living movement and development of the Christian spirit in the Church who must be heard, just because this movement and development takes place in her—and in fact first and decisively in what is at any point of time the last stage of the development of that spirit: in the objectivity of the living faith of the present and in the subjectivity of the conceptual expression this faith creates for itself in its temporal and historical antithesis."[9] This teaching was given its classical form by one who is "rightly honoured as the father of modern German Catholicism, J. Adam Möhler."[10] Barth quotes Möhler, according to whom, the Church "is *the Son of God* continuing to appear among men in human form, always renewing Himself, always becoming young, *His continual becoming-flesh*, . . . it is His visible form, His continuing and eternally self-rejuvenating humanity, *His eternal revelation.*"[11] In this view it is evident that the Church is infallible, and must be infallible. Here too Barth quotes Möhler's *Symbolik:* "If the divine element is the living Christ and His Spirit in it is that which is inerrant and eternally infallible, then the human element is also infallible and inerrant, because the divine does not exist for us apart from the human; the human is not in itself divine, but the instrument and manifestation of the divine."[12] For Barth the equation here of the Church, her faith and her word, with the revelation which justifies them has finally come to light.[13] These views have made their way in Catholic theology: "It was along the lines and with different variations on the ideas of Drey and Möhler that their successors, J. Kuhn and Franz Anton Staudenmaier taught in Tübingen. The decisive positions of this school have become the common possession of Catholic theology, although that theology was to enter into a new relation to the 'earlier theology,' meaning especially Thomas Aquinas, more strongly in the second than in the first half of the nineteenth century. This development outwardly forced the elements

---

[9] *Ibid.* I/2, 560.　　　　　　　[10] *Ibid.* I/2, 561.
[11] *Ibid.* I/2, 561.　　　　　　　[12] *Ibid.* I/2, 562.
[13] *Ibid.* I/2 564–565: "Therefore the real importance of Möhler's thinking did not consist in his identifying of what ultimately became the complex of Scripture and tradition with revelation, with the incarnation of the Word, with Jesus Christ, but in his attempting to understand the whole divine dignity and authority ascribed to this complex only as a predicate of the Church, the present-day Church, as the living bearer of the apostolate, the representative of Jesus Christ. The Church it is into whose faith the Word of God has come and in whose faith it has in fact been absorbed. The Church has the Word; expounds it; is Revelation *in concreto*, not a new revelation, but the old revelation, self-enclosed and for that very reason perfect and complete. The Church is Jesus Christ, speaking, ruling, acting, deciding today."

taken over from German idealism more and more into the background because of their alien form."[14] To that extent Matthias Joseph Scheeben also "stands entirely on the shoulders of Möhler."[15]

At the First Vatican Council the teaching office itself brought the whole development to an end: "Again, in Möhler the question had not yet been finally made clear, where that Church which is identical with revelation, i.e. where that mouth which declares revelation, where that authority of the Church which is identical with the authority of the Word of God, has to be sought and heard in *concreto*. To this question Möhler still gave the traditional answer, which was correct but incomplete, that it has to be heard in the voice of the whole episcopate united to its papal centre, as the legal successor and bearer of the apostolate proved by unbroken succession, as the visible representative of Jesus Christ."[16] But it was impossible to remain within this dialectical juxtaposition of pope and episcopate: "Is the first word, that the visible Roman Catholic Church stands and speaks in the place of Jesus Christ, because it itself is the continually-living Jesus Christ Himself—is that first word a final word, is it really spoken in a way in which it can be received and believed, unless it is unreservedly transferred and applied to the official status and utterance which admittedly constitutes its organizing centre, the centre of its teaching office, the episcopate? Was not the whole transformation of the authority of Scripture into that of the Church, which had been the meaning of the development from Irenaeus to Möhler, quite futile, because that meaning was still equivocal and finally obscure, so long as there had not emerged as the last and concrete culmination of the incarnation of the Word *one* man, who as the living bearer of the tradition identical with revelation, and therefore himself revelation as it has to be heard today, represents the Church, that is, Christian humanity which has attained possession of revelation and executes its self-government? Could the insight which has been ripe for expression so long be suppressed any longer, that this is in fact the nature and function of the Roman Pope? Could it be left unsaid that the official decision of the Pope is quite unreserved and needs no confirmation; that as such and in itself it is the decision of the whole episcopate and therefore the decision of the infallible Church, the infallible decision of Scripture and tradition, the infallible declaration of revelation and therefore itself infallible revelation for the present age; that by virtue of his supreme authority and apostolic power according to the Lord's promise, and under the guidance of divine providence, the Pope will never speak

[14] *Ibid.* I/2, 564.   [15] *Ibid.* I/2, 564.   [16] *Ibid.* I/2, 565.

except out of the common consciousness of the infallible Church, and in his official speaking utterances will never say anything but infallible revelation for the present age? Could this be passed over in silence any longer when it had been true from the beginning and had for so long, although only partially at first, been known to be true?"[17] Thus for Barth the definition of infallibility as pronounced by the First Vatican Council is "the closing of that circle, the opening of which is marked by the dualistic formula of Iraenaeus (repeated at the Council of Trent), the continuation of the triad of Vincent of Lérins, and the culmination by the syntheses of Möhler. Since the Vatican council we can know what, after all this, had not been previously known, viz, where and who *in the concrete* is the Church which teaches revelation."[18]

This Barthian criticism appeared in 1939. Amazingly, little attention has been paid to it in Catholic literature up to now. Was this because its publication coincided with the outbreak of the Second World War, or was it because a reply to the Barthian objections could not have been easy? In fact the matter cannot be settled by referring, in response to Barth, to the Petrine passages in the New Testament which designate Peter as the foundation of the Church (Mt. 16:18), as its supreme shepherd (Jn. 21:15–17), and as the strengthener of the faith of the brethren (Lk. 22:31f) (incidentally passing over in silence the denial of Peter and his inconsistent behaviour in Antioch). Apart from all the difficult questions regarding the continuation of the Petrine primacy in the pope—it would be much more to the point to show that all these passages signify *infallibility*.[19] Calvin already had

[17] *Ibid* I/2, 566.

[18] *Ibid.* I/2, 567; also cf. Barth with G. Ebeling; *Die Geschichtlichkeit der Kirche und ihrer Verkündigung als theologisches Problem* (Tübingen 1954) 47: "While on the one hand a dam was erected against the innovators, the boldest innovation of all was readily accepted. The modernist, universal-historical idea of evolution was outdone by the ecclesiastico-historical idea of development. The problem of the relationship between revelation and history found a grandiose solution by coupling the ecclesiastico-historical idea with the pope's pronouncement on infallibility. The concept of tradition was fully mastered by the papalist concept of the Church. The normative authority was shifted from the past to the present. Loofs has very trenchantly formulated this process: 'At the Vatican Council what befell tradition—at least the real, historically ascertainable tradition—was similar to that which befell Holy Scripture at the Council of Trent. It was pushed into the background by another factor. This factor was the teaching Church. What Scripture teaches is shown by tradition. What tradition is is taught by the Church. This was the expressed will of the Vatican Council.' " Cf. further H. Rückert, *Schrift, Tradition und Kirche* (Lüneburg 1951) 14–22; W. von Loewenich, *Der moderne Katholizismus* (³1956) 155–166.

[19] G. Dejaifve, "Der Erste unter den Bischöfen," in *Theologie und Glaube* 51 (1961) 14: "The exegesis of Scriptural texts, as it was practised at the Council of

320 of the Church

asserted that the infallibility of an individual council does not necessarily follow from the assertion that the Church is the pillar and
mainstay of the truth. What is thus said about the Church could
apply even more to the pope. From the statement that Peter is the
foundation, it does not simply follow that Peter must be infallible.
Could not the miracle of the grace of God appear still greater if
Peter, like every man—since to err is human—could also err in faith
and nevertheless remain the foundation of the Church, and still
remain the shepherd (who knows the weakness of men) and who
precisely as such could thereby understandingly comfort his brethren? Would not the victory of grace be more complete if it perfected
its strength here in weakness too, if the truth of revelation, seemingly
defeated, again and again ultimately prevails victoriously over
human weakness and errors? Catholic theology has not yet given
Protestant theology an adequate answer to this and similar questions;
even less than in other cases can it base itself simply on infallible
definitions. Above and beyond all these difficult questions, however,
Barth's fundamental criticism nevertheless remains: the Catholic
Church identifies herself with the revelation of God, she presents herself as the revelation of God and acts accordingly.

This fundamental Barthian criticism could be answered adequately only in a large work far beyond the scope of this study.
Indeed some thorough inquiries of a theological-historical character
must first of all be made.[20] At the same time attention must once and

---

Trent and at the Vatican Council, in this area was somewhat of a 'situation'
exegesis and prompted by the thesis that it was intended to prove."

[20] Regarding J. A. Möhler's conception of the Church, W. Kasper, *Die
Lehre von der Tradition in der Römischen Schule* (Diss. Tübingen, Freiburg i.
Br. 1962) 141f correctly states: "In Möhler the statement that the Church is the
enduring incarnation of Christ in the first place is less, or not at all, a statement
on the nature of the Church in itself, but rather on Christ's continuing efficacy
in the sphere of the Church. According to Möhler the Redeemer lived 'not merely
eighteen hundred years ago, so that consequently He would have vanished since
then and we could remember only His historical character as we do that of any
other deceased person. Rather, He is eternally living in His Church and He makes
this perceptible in a comprehensible way to percipient man in the altar-sacra-
ment.' Similarly this also applies to the proclamation of the Word and to the
other Sacraments. Thus the actual definition of the Church that Möhler gives is
not that the visible Church of the Son of God continuing to appear among men
in human form is the enduring Incarnation of the same. Rather, according to
Möhler, this definition applies only to a particular, 'just developed point of view.'
What is this point of view? None other than the one which holds that Christ,
even after His ascension, continues to be efficacious precisely in the Church in a
visible way and with visible means. The Church is 'His establishment in which He
lives on, and continues to quicken with His spirit, and which eternally echoes the
Word spoken by Him.' " The aforementioned description of the nature of the

for all be paid to the fundamental aspects of this question—one could certainly not get around the ascertained fact that Catholic theologians at least have used, and perhaps still use, highly misleading formulations. This occurs, for example, when there is frequent mention of a *sensus fidelium* as though the faith of the faithful presented, attested to, and regulated Revelation rather than conversely, namely, that the faith of the believers is engendered and must regulate itself according to Revelation. (What would not have been defined in the different centuries, if this regulation had simply been according to the "sensus" of the faithful!) It must be regarded as a danger signal that the Encyclical *Mystici corporis* had to point out that a false mysticism had crept into the teaching of the mystical Body of Christ, which sought to remove the inalterable borders between head and body, between God and creature and thereby perverted Holy Scripture: ". . . falsus subrepit *mysticismus*, qui immobiles limites, removere conatus inter creatas res earumque Creatorem, Sacras Litteras adulterat."[21]

It must not be overlooked, however, that already at Vatican I the borders between Church and Revelation were preserved for ever in the definition of papal infallibility. The Vatican declaration not only contains no expressions that designate the Church as the "still living Christ," and the like; the council majority—bending rather excessively to the other side—had even refused to start out from the concept "Body of Christ" in the description of the Church.[22] As regards the relationship between revelation and the ecclesiastical teaching office it was expressly established that the pastoral task

---

Church applies only under this viewpoint. The Church is the continuously existing Christ only to the extent that Christ continues to live and be efficacious in her. Möhler's statement, in other words, is to be understood dialectically. The actual comprehensive definition that Möhler gives then reads altogether differently: "By the Church on earth Catholics understand the visible community of all believers, founded by Christ, in which the activities unfolded by Him during His earthly existence for the absolution and salvation of mankind under the direction of His Spirit, by means of an uninterrupted, continuous apostolate instituted by Him which in the course of the ages will lead all peoples back to God."

[21] Pius XII, Encyclical "Mystici corporis," in *Acta Apostolicae Sedis* 35 (1943) 197.

[22] Bishop Ketteler criticized the schema in that it should not begin with "What is different and mysterious; this should be put at the end" (Mansi 51, 745). Bishop Ramadie: "especially objected to the notion of the Church as the mystical body of Christ, which is very abstract and abstruse" (Mansi, 51, 741). Bishop Plase: "did not want to call the Church the mystical body of Christ; for whom is this good; one does not understand it" (Mansi 51, 755). Cf. also R. Aubert, "L'ecclésiologie au concile du Vatican," in *Le concile et les conciles* (Paris 1960) 252f.

(*munus pastorale*) of the Petrine office is responsible for spreading Christ's doctrine of salvation (*salutaris Christi doctrina*) among all peoples and for preserving it unimpaired and pure (*sincera et pura conservaretur*).[23] Hence it is neither the task of the Church nor that of the Petrine office to produce revelation, to replace or to absorb revelation. The task of the Church as well as of the Petrine office is that of serving revelation through the protective and preserving care of the pure doctrine of the Gospel.

Vatican I, however, did not state this only in this general way; the dogma of infallibility was expressly shielded against misinterpretations in the Barthian sense; the definition of a pope means precisely not a revealing; the Holy Spirit is not promised to Peter's successors so that they may reveal new doctrines through His revelation: "Neque enim Petri successoribus Spiritus Sanctus promissus est, ut eo revelante novam doctrinam patefacerent. . . ."[24] The definition of a pope signifies only an authoritative bearing of witness to the revelation that has occurred, the Holy Spirit is promised to the successors so that with His help the revelation, transmitted through the apostles, may be preserved holy and explained faithfully: "ut, eo assistente, traditam per Apostolos revelationem seu fidei depositum sancte custodirent et fideliter exponerent."[25] Therefore Catholic theology, following Vatican I, has elaborated the distinction between the revelation of God and the infallible word of the pope with a great conceptual acuteness. Unlike God's revelation the charism of infallibility bestowed on the successors of Peter by the Spirit signifies (*a*) not a new authoritative divine word, but only an explanation and a defence of the revelation that has already occurred; (*b*) the main cause always remains the human subject (the pope); (*c*) for it, the assistance of the Holy Spirit does not have the character of a special inner revelation, but only that of an external preservation from error; (*d*) hence it is not a divine word but only a human utterance about the word of God.[26]

Obviously it is not only possible, but even desirable—that Catholic theology deepen the aforementioned distinction made by Vatican

---

[23] Denz. 1836.   [24] Denz. 1836.   [25] Denz. 1836.

[26] S. Tromp, *De sacrae scripturae inspiratione* (Rome ⁴1945) 96: "That which makes the Roman pontiff as teacher *infallible*, very clearly differs from *revelation*. (*a*) There is no new authoritative speaking of God, but what he has spoken before is explained, unfolded, and defined (*b*) The principal cause speaking *ex cathedra* is and remains the Roman pontiff. (*c*) The infallibility of the pronouncement does not come from internal influence but out of external assistance presupposing the ordinary gifts of the Holy Spirit and human effort; God is prepared to correct if the pontiff should deviate from the truth. (*d*) The pontiff's speaking is not the word of God but about the word of God.

I between the revelation of God and the word of the Church. The First Vatican Council had its definite (anti-Gallican) alignment; the biblical perspectives could be given better expression in a more comprehensive view; as over against the revelation of God the Church and the teaching office stand in a relationship of obedience, in a concrete juxtaposition to the exalted Lord of the Church who authoritatively speaks to the Church down the centuries through His Gospel, demanding faith and obedience. This relationship of obedience is never subsequently dissolved into a relationship of master and servant in that the Church could exert control over Christ and His word. The Church never "possesses" the word of God, proclaiming itself in human utterance, as her property. Rather, the Church remains under the word of God, precisely thereby remaining the possession and the property of the Lord, precisely thereby remaining the κυριακή, belonging to the Lord. Despite the unity existing between the Church and Christ, the Church in juxtaposition to Christ, therefore, remains as the pupil to the master, the servant to the lord, the flock to the shepherd, the earthly body to the heavenly head.

Hence the teaching authority of the Church is never of a directly original character, but only one that is mediated through and derived from Christ and His word. The ground and, at the same time, the limit of the Church teaching authority is the word of God proclaiming itself in a human utterance. The exercise of Church teaching ing authority also can be understood only as an actualization of obedience *vis-à-vis* the superordinated word of God. God and His word above, the Church and her word below: here no reversal is possible—all commissioning, authorization comes from above. Nor is absorption of the word of God by the Church possible. God's authority can never be simply appropriated by the Church. The obedience of the Church can never become an obedience to herself, towards her own teaching authority. God's authority exclusively is autonomous, the Church's authority is and remains heteronomous. The Church could wreak no greater damage on her authentic teaching authority than to want to divinize and transcendentalize it. If this authority no longer has God and His word about it, it is therefore lacking in source and ground, and it cancels itself out. The Church cannot strengthen her teaching authority better than by subordinating her authority again and again, in the concrete, humbly, modestly and gratefully to the authority of God's word, by seeking simply to hear, to proclaim, to realize, not her own word, but God's.

Just as the prophets and apostles, then, their successors too are the bearers of the Church teaching office, in particular the pope, but only in obedience to the Spirit. The officeholder over and over again must hear, receive, and learn the word of God in the human utterance of Scripture, and he must always subject himself to it and regulate himself accordingly. He must allow what he receives from above to prevail, and he must be grateful for it. He will, however, not conceitedly boast about what he does not derive from himself, as though it were his own possession. He will not adorn himself with it and put on authoritarian airs, as though he could exert control over it. He will derive no self-glorification from the glory of Christ, no self-praise from the praise of Christ. Rather, as a poor, weak, human being and sinner he will live from the grace of God, even in his office.

As difficult as it is for a Protestant Christian to understand the infallibility of the pope, it can be understood only in the perspective that has just been sketched: not as a self-glorifying appropriation of divine revelation but as a humble, obedient, non-partisan service of interpretation, directed and protected by the Holy Ghost, that remains a human interpretation. All understanding of papal infallibility which, in one way or another, would amount to an identification of the Church with revelation, is a misunderstanding of papal infallibility.

Now Barth rightly makes the point that purely theoretical assertions of the distinction between Church and revelation, pope and revelation, are not enough to remove the difficulties. It is more a question, rather, of whether this distinction and everything that is tied up with it can still become *concrete* in the Catholic Church and in the teaching office of the pope. Whether the Catholic Church and the papal teaching office, even despite all theoretical assertions, actually do not nevertheless have revelation in them rather than over them, as their original possession, over which in fact they have absolute control. Whether Church and teaching office have not concretely incorporated, domesticated as it were, the apostolic attestation of Holy Scripture as a free power of God into their own plans. And whether the pope as the representative of Christ does not in fact actually replace Christ.

We would be succumbing to illusions if we did not see that the problem of papal infallibility in the ecumenical dialogue is also in no way an abstract theological problem, but at the same time a problem of a practical-existential character. It is right here that theology and life pass over into each other; it is right here that a whole throng of true, half-true, and untrue "prejudgments" come together. Everyone who participates in a living ecumenical dialogue observes that

Protestant Christians take exception to certain externals of the papal teaching office which prevents them even from merely discussing the meaning and value of such a teaching office earnestly. They take exception to the language of documents concerning the teaching office (the identification with Christ in different papal titles, for example, "Sanctissimus Dominus noster"; the often unbiblical philosophical, canon-law terminology, the curial style that often has the ring of self-glorification and lovelessness despite the pious wording, the self-assured boasting about one's own prerogatives and authority; the human glorification of the hierarchy, the difference in tone between the apostolic epistles and modern papal documents). They often take exception also to the inner basic attitude which more or less seems to lurk behind the exercise of the teaching authority (they assert that Holy Scripture is used frequently only as a basis for arguments and not taken seriously as a ruling and enjoining word of God in the whole teaching and ruling activity of the Church). Tradition is said to be greatly preferred to the witness of Holy Scripture and the divine and human are allegedly dangerously mixed in this tradition. Further, in tradition consideration is given only to that which suits the convenience of the *status quo*. Concrete supervision of doctrinal teaching allegedly has totalitarian features and does not give the Catholic Church the appearance of a sphere of freedom along the lines of Scripture. In some decrees, even in those that are not at all infallible, no justification is given and in such decrees there is never an acknowledgment of mistakes that have been committed. Even genuine theological discussions are supposedly paralysed in advance by drastic means. The system of censorship to which Catholic theologians are supposedly subjected, and the denunciations with which they allegedly must reckon, spread an atmosphere of fear and restraint *vis-à-vis* the whole truth and frequently paralyse creative theological accomplishments. In short, the concrete exercise of the teaching office is supposedly not in keeping with the Gospel.

The criticism that other Christians direct against the papal teaching office is often one-sided, unenlightened, unjust, protest for its own sake. But despite this who would dare to assert that it is all wrong? We Catholics can only harm the Petrine office when we pass such criticisms over in silence or lightly dismiss them. Indeed they are often pronounced by the very theologians who devote themselves to a constructive ecumenical dialogue and understanding with the Church.[27] We should not answer them critically with abstract dis-

[27] I have given several detailed examples in *The Council and Reunion* (London 1961) 196–203.

tinctions, for example, by disengaging the pure character of the papal teaching office from its historical manifestation. The people outside our Church can perceive the nature of the papal teaching office only in its historical manifestation and nowhere else. Even the Petrine teaching office is faced with the permanent task of elucidating its evangelical character ever anew before the Church and the world, and to present itself *credibly* as a service of charity and of the strengthening of the faith of the brethren, for the defence and the promotion of the freedom of the children of God, for which freedom Christ Himself has liberated us from the law (Gal. 5:1). It is also the task of the Petrine office ever anew to convince—"not in the persuasive words of wisdom but in the demonstration of the Spirit and of power" (I. Cor. 2:4).

In his *Church Dogmatics* Karl Barth, in connection with the apostolic succession, acknowledges: "Thus the difference between the evangelical and the Catholic view consists here too not in the matter of the *That* but in the matter of the *How*. And even in the matter of the *How* no protest in *principle* can be raised on our part either against the summation of the apostolate in Peter, nor yet against the possibility of a primacy in the Church, which in that case might very well be that of the Roman community."[28] But Barth has formulated the crucial objection in the dialogue once and for all: "I cannot hear the voice of the Good Shepherd from this 'Chair of Peter.' " Should not this give us Catholics food for thought?

(*b*) *Limited Infallibility:* The theological clarification of the problems involved is not made unnecessary by virtue of the fact that importance is attached to the concrete credibility of the Petrine office. Rather, it is concomitantly required. If we are not to fall victim to misunderstandings at the outset in this discussion, everything will depend upon an exact understanding of papal infallibility as it has been understood by *Vatican I*.[29] All too often outside the

[28] Karl Barth, *Church Dogmatics* (London) I/1, 116.

[29] With the literature on the discussions revolving around the question of primacy at Vatican I at the beginning of Chapter VII, cf. especially in connection with the question of infallibility at Vatican I: R. Aubert, "L'ecclésiologie au concile du Vatican," in *Le concile et les conciles* (Paris 1960) 245–284; A. Chavasse, "L'ecclésiologie au concile du Vatican. L'infaillibilité de l'Église," in *L'ecclésiologie au XIX siècle* (Paris 1960) 233–245; W. Caudron, "Magistère ordinarie et infallibilité pontificale d'après la constitution 'Dei Filius,' " in *Ephemerides Theologicae Lovanienses* 36 (1960) 393–431; O. Karrer, "Das ökumenische Konzil in der römisch-katholischen Kirche der Gegenwart," in *Die ökumenischen Konzile der Christenheit*, ed. by H. J. Margull (Stuttgart 1961) 237–284, esp. 241–264; G. Dejaifve, *Pape et évêques au premier concile du Vatican* (Paris 1961) 93–137;

Church the Vatican definition is considered as the insurpassable peak, of the concentration of teaching authority in the pope and as the establishment of an unlimited papal infallibility. At the same time it is a fact that this very definition signifies a very clear *limitation* by contrast with what was frequently asserted about the infallibility of the pope in the Catholic Church before the council. One could rightly view it as a victory for the council minority; or else, as did Cardinal John Henry Newman, as a disposition of Divine Providence. The latter "has ruled over Pius: I believe that he (Pius IX) would personally have desired a much more rigid dogma than he achieved,"[30] Compare—not to speak here of the already cited, unintended blasphemous hymns of neo-ultramontanists to Pius IX[31]—the for-

---

K. Rahner and Ratzinger, *Episcopate and the Primacy* (London 1962); G. Thils, "Parlera-t-on des évêques au concile?" in *Nouvelle Revue Théologique* 93 (1961) 785-804; J. P. Torrell, "L'infaillibilité pontificale est-elle un privilège 'personnel'? in *Revue des sciences philosophiques et théologiques* 45 (1961) 229-245; W. Kasper, "Primat und Episcopat nach dem Vaticanum I," in *Tübinger Theologische Quartalschrift* 142 (1962) 68-77.

[30] J. H. Newman, "To Miss Holmes," in Karrer and Newman, *Die Kirche* (Einsiedeln 1945) I, 399.

[31] Cf. the annotation at the end of Chapter VII, sec. 5. Regarding the question of infallibility in particular, two typical witnesses may be mentioned here: (1) W. G. Ward, owner and editor of the *Dublin Review*, the theological champion of the English group of the extreme Ultramontanists; his views were espoused in England particularly by Th. F. Knox, and Archbishop Manning of Westminster was more than inclined to accept them. Dom Cuthbert Butler, *The Vatican Council* (London 1930), I, 73-74, summarizes Ward's views as follows: "For him, all direct doctrinal instructions of all encyclicals, of all letters to individual bishops and allocutions, published by the Popes, are *ex cathedra* pronouncements and *ipso facto* infallible. He was not directly concerned with the Gallican controversy —whether the organ of infallibility be the Pope alone, or Pope and episcopate; his contention was concerned, as he expressed it, not with the 'subject' of the infallibility, but with the 'object,' the kind of pronouncements to which it extends. He held that the infallible element of bulls, encyclicals, etc., should not be restricted to their formal definitions, but ran through their entire doctrinal instructions; the decrees of the Roman Congregations, if adopted by the Pope and published by his authority, thereby were stamped with the mark of infallibility; in short, 'his every doctrinal pronouncement is infallibly directed by the Holy Ghost.' Pusey in the *Eirenicon* not unjustly objected that such a doctrine of infallibility went far beyond the inerrancy in defining matters of faith or morals guaranteed to the Pope by the special assistance of the Holy Ghost, as laid down by the standard Catholic theologians, and, in fact, practically amounted to inspiration: indeed Ward held explicitly that infallibility often amounts to 'a new inspiration,' instancing the condemnation of the Five Propositions of Jansenius (*Dublin Review*, October 1869, 479). He did not shrink from saying that bulls, as the 'Quanta Cura' of 1864, were to be accepted 'as the Word of God.' . . . And not only did he urge with merciless logic and great vehemence of language his own view as to the infallible character of this enormous and quite indefinite mass of *ex cathedra* teaching, to be dug out from the Bullarium and Papal Acts of the

mula proposed by Archbishop Manning with what was ultimately defined after the most heated discussions. Manning's formula spoke with the complete lack of differentiation of the infallibility of every papal pronouncement on matters of faith and morals: "The pronouncements uttered by the supreme pontiff about faith, morals or so-called dogmatic facts, or about truths concerning questions of faith and morals, are infallible."[32] But as we shall soon see, the Council laid down very definite conditions against it which in fact very strongly limited the infallibility of the pope.

(1) Absolute infallibility is ascribed to God exclusively: *in no respect is an absolute infallibility ascribed to the pope.* This was stated with all desirable clarity by the speaker of the Deputation on Faith, Bishop Gasser: "The question is in what sense the infallibility of the pope is absolute: I answer and firmly confess: in no sense is the pontifical infallibility absolute, for absolute infallibility corresponds to God only, the first and essential truth who can nowhere and never deceive or be deceived."[33] Infallibility is communicated to the pope only with respect to a definite end. It is wholly subject to definite *limits* and *conditions:* "Any other infallibility ever communicated has a certain end and limits and conditions under which it is given. This is the case also for the infallibility of the pope."[34] The infallibility of the pope is

---

past; he insisted with uncompromising assurance that his view was the only Catholic one, and must be accepted as the Catholic Faith necessary for salvation, only invincible ignorance excusing from mortal sin.

"(2) Louis Veuillot, whose newspaper *Univers* exerted a far-reaching influence in France on the clergy and enjoyed their strong backing. Veuillot dealt with papal infallibility 'as inspiration.' 'We all know certainly only one thing, that is that no man knows anything except the Man with whom God is for ever, the Man who carries the thought of God. We must unswervingly follow his inspired directions.' Writing from Rome during the Council Veuillot thus posed the question: 'Does the Church believe, or does she not believe, that her Head is inspired directly by God, that is to say, infallible in his decisions regarding faith and morals?' Consonant with such ideas is what I myself heard a survivor of the Veuillot school say: he did not like the definitions of the Council being spoken of as having been put into shape by the discussions at the Council; 'it is much simpler to think of them as whispered directly by the Holy Ghost into the Pope's ear.' Again, Veuillot said: 'We must affirm squarely the authority and omnipotence of the Pope, as the source of all authority, spiritual and temporal. The proclamation of the dogma of the infallibility of the Pope has no other object.' " C. Butler, *op. cit.* 75–76.

[32] Quoted in R. Aubert, "L'ecclésiologie au concile du Vatican," in *Le concile et les conciles* (Paris 1960) 280.

[33] Mansi 52, 1214: Bishop Gassner's report may be considered as the official interpretation of the decree on infallibility.

[34] Mansi 52, 1214.

wholly limited to the pastoral ministry to the whole Church (Mt. 16:18; Jn. 21:13–17): "Outside this relation to the universal Church, Peter in his successors does not enjoy this charisma of truth, granted by Christ in that promise."[35] Therefore the infallibility of the pope is limited in a threefold way: in relation to the *subject* (only when the pope as the universal teacher and supreme judge of the Church speaks *in cathedra*); in relation to the *object* (only when he speaks on matters of faith and morals); in relation to the *act* itself (only when he defines what is to be believed or rejected by all Christians): "In fact the infallibility of the Roman pontiff is restricted in respect to the *subject* when the pope speaks as teacher of the universal Church and as supreme judge in the chair of Peter, that is, constituted at the centre. It is restricted in respect to the *object* in so far as it concerns matters of faith and morals and when he defines explicitly what has to be upheld or rejected by all the faithful."[36]

Hence, when the pope speaks only as a private person or only as a private teacher he is not infallible.[37] Indeed, even when he simply speaks as the pope he is likewise not infallible.[38] Rather he is infallible *only* when, as the universal teacher and supreme judge of the Church, he purposes to define, in the strictest sense and with the claim of his whole authority, a final doctrinal decision in matters of faith and morals for the whole Church.[39] Gassner repeatedly emphasizes the word "only" (*solummodo*).[40] Thus all conditions without exception must be fulfilled and securely established before one can talk of an infallible definition.[41] Hence the CIC also defines: "Nothing is understood as dogmatically declared or defined, unless it is clearly established."[42]

[35] Mansi 52, 1214.   [36] Mansi 52, 1214.

[37] Mansi 52, 1212: "The personal infallibility of the pope must be accurately defined: it does not concern the Roman pontiff as a private person, nor as a private theologian, for in respect to these things he is like one of them. . . ."

[38] Mansi 52, 1213: "One cannot say that the pontiff is simply infallible on account of the papal authority but that he is certainly and indubitably under the guidance of divine assistance. For by his papal authority the pontiff is always the supreme judge in matters of faith and morals, and father and teacher of all Christians."

[39] Mansi 52, 1213: "He enjoys the promised divine assistance that he cannot err, only when he functions as supreme judge in controversies of faith and as teacher of the universal Church in the same matter. Hence the assertion, the Roman Pontiff is infallible, must not be rejected as false, since Christ promised it to the person of Peter and the persons of his predecessors. But it is only incomplete, since the pope is only infallible when he defines solemnly for the universal Church in matters of faith and morals."

[40] Cf. several times in Mansi 52, 1213.

[41] Cf. Mansi 52, 1212f. and 1225.

[42] *CIC* can. 1323 § 3.

(2) Therefore the pope is not *separate from the Church*. He is infallible only to the extent that he is the representative of the whole Church: ". . . We do not separate the pontiff from his well-ordered connection with the Church. The pope is infallible only when he exercises the office of teacher of all Christians and therefore representing the universal Church judges and defines what has to be believed or rejected by all."[43] In no sense is a co-operation on the part of the Church excluded: "He must not be separated from the universal Church which he has to support as a foundation does a building. We do not separate the pope who defines infallibly from the co-operation and agreement of the Church, at least in this sense that we do not exclude this co-operation and agreement."[44] The pope indeed possesses his infallibility only in relation to the whole Church, and he is dependent on the faith of the whole Church in so far as he draws from this the Church's understanding of revelation. Since the truth to be defined is neither revealed nor imparted as inspiration to the pope, the pope is duty-bound to apply means that are in keeping with the gravity of the matter in hand (councils, advice of the bishops, cardinals, theologians, and the rest) in order correctly to inquire into and appropriately to express the truth.[45] No doubt, there exists no absolute necessity for the pope to consult with the Church or the episcopate in a definite way, but there is certainly a relative necessity.[46] The consultation with the bishops is designated as a "medium ordinarium" and for an example of this reference is made to the definition of the "Immaculate Conception."[47]

For reasons of anti-Gallicanism, above all, at Manning's instigation the words "but not by consensus of the Church"[48] were inserted at the last minute in the formula that the infallible definitions of the pope are "irreformable of themselves." According to Gasser's authoritative commentary these words signify nothing more than an

[43] Mansi 52, 1213.

[44] *Ibid.*

[45] Mansi 52, 1213: "We therefore do not exclude this co-operation with the Church because infallibility is given to the Roman Pontiff not by way of inspiration or revelation but by way of divine assistance. Hence the pope must take the right means because of his office and the importance of the matter to find the truth and to announce it properly. Such means are the council and the advice of bishops, cardinals and theologians."

[46] Mansi 52, 1215: "In this strict and absolute necessity lies the point of our disagreement and not in the question of the opportunity or some relative necessity which has to be left entirely to the judgment of the Roman pontiff to weigh the matter and circumstances."

[47] Mansi 52, 1217.

[48] Mansi, 1317.

explanation of "ex sese"; the *ex cathedra* decisions of the pope have
a binding character by themselves, not on the ground of the consensus
of the Church or the episcopate.[49] Only the ground of law from which
the binding force derives, not the criterion on the basis of which the
pope produces the decision, is specified here. The necessity of a simultaneous or subsequent consensus of the episcopate is to be excluded,
yet it is not to be maintained that the pope can define a truth without
having already in principle the agreement of the Church.[50] No doubt
the pope does not require the formal consent of the Church for the
definition, nevertheless he may not define without the mind of the
Church.[51] At the same time, what Gasser stated still holds; that the
normal way (*medium ordinarium*) is the exercise of the teaching office
together with the Church and with the episcopate.[52]

(3) Following the discussions of the First Vatican Council the
question of whether there are two subjects or only one of ecclesiastical infallibility (pope and council or the pope alone) was studied by
theologians. Gasser, the reporter of the Deputation on Faith, considered the second theory, that all infallibility in the Church derives
from one actual subject, namely from the pope, as deplorable. He
criticized the view, ". . . from this pulpit—I say it with sorrow—it has
sometimes been suggested that all the infallibility of the Church rests
only in the pope and is from the pope channelled to the Church and
communicated to her."[53] According to K. Rahner, "we know from
positive sources that the council too has an active infallibility, that in

[49] *Ibid.*
[50] R. Aubert, "L'ecclésiologie au concile du Vatican," in *Le concile et les conciles* (Paris 1960) 271: "The whole context of the debates shows quite well that their idea involved excluding concomitant or further consent of the episco-pacy and not that of claiming that the pope can define a truth without having previously received the agreement of the Church on its essentials."
[51] R. Aubert, *op. cit.* 281: "Undeniably, the serious discussions which the Vatican definition occasioned have allowed a clearer perception of the distinction between the *sensus Ecclesiae* from which the pope, the vicar of tradition, can never exempt himself, and the *consensus Ecclesiae*, which is not necessary to him."
[52] G. Thils, "Parlera-t-on des éveques au concile?" in *Nouvelle revue théologique* 93 (1961) 791: "A kind of separated infallibility, normally exercised *without* any relation to the episcopate or the testimonies of tradition, has been wrongly concluded therefrom. On the contrary, the pontifical magisterium is exercised *normally* with the Church, in union with her organs, in communion with the testimonies of tradition, and, certainly, in perfect fidelity to the sources of revelation. But—and here is the point of the conciliar declaration—the pope, in well-defined conditions, can appeal to the charism of infallibility. In this case the act by which he defines is valid, infallible by itself, by virtue of this charism, and not by virtue of the consensus of the Church."
[53] Mansi 52, 1261.

Council the bishops together with the pope are *judges* in matters of
faith and not simply advisers to the pope or merely the first to express
their assent to a papal decision which the pope has reached independently, something which would not transcend the 'hearing' or passive
infallibility possessed by all members of the hearing Church. Past
councils, it must be admitted, never considered themselves to be mere
sounding boards or 'amplifiers' for papal infallibility. It would be
absurd to envisage the early councils thus and no less absurd in the
case of the later ones, even where no more doubts existed about the
supreme papal primacy of jurisdiction and so about the pope's
supreme magisterium. Many theologians (for example most recently,
Salaverri), even to the present day, point out that the promise of
Christ to the apostolic college seems to signify an *immediate* divine
assistance for the apostolic college as such (Mt. 18:18; 28:18–20;
Mk. 16:15; Jn. 14:16; 17:26; 20:21; cf. Mt. 10:40; Lk. 10:16), so
that this apostolic college must be infallible directly, not 'derivatively'
from Peter."[54] On the other hand, Rahner observes that a dual
supreme authority is impossible because ultimately it must lead to
two different corporate bodies.[55] But Rahner considers the whole
dilemma to be an unusual dilemma, the tacit assumption of which,
made by both sides, is incorrect: "the assumption that the infallibility
of the pope when he defines 'alone' is in no way also the infallibility
of the college of bishops. Grant the assumption, and either the pope
alone must possess the immediate active infallibility (if there can be
only one in the Church) or, if the council is also immediately infallible, then there must actually be two subjects of the infallible
teaching authority, since the pope is also infallible 'without' the
council or the episcopal college."[56] Against this Rahner rightly
espouses the view that "by conceiving only one subject of supreme
power from the start—the college of bishops united under the pope
as its head, so that an act of the pope 'alone' and an act of the council
are only different forms and modes of the activity of this one subject
of supreme ecclesiastical authority, but need not be derived from
two different subjects."[57] Thus, on the one hand, the act of the pope
is also included in the act of a council, and the act of a council is
always included in the act of the pope. This conception is completely
in keeping with Vatican I "out of the nature, not out of the consensus of the Church."[58]

[54] K. Rahner, *The Episcopate and the Primacy*, 94.
[55] *Ibid*. 93.
[56] *Ibid*. 95.
[57] *Ibid*.
[58] Cf. K. Rahner's further explanation, *op. cit.* 95–100.

(4) Despite all this can it not also be said that ultimately and finally the *pope exclusively* can define without the episcopate and Church, and that therefore he can define *arbitrarily*? True, he is to use his infallibility in relation to the whole Church,[59] but does not he alone define what is of benefit to the whole Church? True, the co-operation of the episcopate in some form is not excluded.[60] But does not the pope alone control whether this co-operation will be permitted? True, he should employ the necessary means for a definition.[61] But does not the pope alone decide whether they are to be laid claim to? True, the pope must proceed prudently and after due deliberation,[62] but according to the Vatican definition can anyone impede him if he will not do so? True, under certain circumstances he would be sinning, but would not his definitions be true and binding upon the whole Church?

Today Catholic theologians are taking great pains to expound, on the basis of the discussions at Vatican I, how the pope nevertheless is bound to the Church. But it must be seen clearly and sharply that, according to what was *said* at Vatican I, no possibility seems to exist of effectively preventing a pope from making arbitrary definitions (perhaps true, but under certain circumstances, nevertheless greatly harmful to the Church). If the pope merely wills it, he can do so ultimately even without the Church. The whole discussion between the majority and the minority sharpened on this point, upon which ultimately every compromise shipwrecked. This was the very point that the anti-Gallican majority wanted unconditionally to push through, and it was for this very reason that at the last moment the words "not by consent of the Church"[63] were inserted. One could expect everything from the council reporter Gasser (it is allegedly "opportune," "relatively necessary," etc.) save one thing: that it is *absolutely* necessary that the pope consult with the Church.[64]

It makes no sense to emasculate the definition. For the majority it really was a question of the pope and his exclusive teaching authority. At bottom the majority was little concerned about the *consensus ecclesiae*. Yet here it must be asked: Does it really follow therefrom that the pope *exclusively* can define *arbitrarily*? Here obviously Vatican I did not want to lay down any hard-and-fast definition. To the proposals of several Fathers who pointed out that, according to different theological treatises, additional conditions were required for the exercise of the infallible teaching authority of the pope,

---

[59] Mansi 52, 1213.
[60] *Ibid.*
[61] *Ibid.*
[62] Mansi 52, 1214.
[63] Mansi 52, 1317.
[64] Mansi 52, 1215.

especially "bona fides" and "diligentia in veritate indaganda et
enuntianda," Gasser replies hesitatingly, without answering in the
negative, that such conditions no doubt would bind the *conscience*
of the pope, but for this very reason they belong less to the dogmatic
than to the moral order: "they have to be attributed to the moral
rather than to the dogmatic order."[65] Therefore this question was not
dealt with further.

But Gasser thereby avoided precisely the question which, as we
have seen, played such a great role in Catholic dogmatics: Can the
pope proceed not only *without* but *against* the whole Church?
True, his definitions are not "irreformable by the consent of the
Church" (in this way his teaching authority over the whole Church
would be paralysed precisely at the crucial moments). But does this
mean that the pope could define a dogma (even if true in itself)
"*contra* consensum ecclesiae"? Under no circumstances. Despite all
emphasis on papal full authority Vatican I repeatedly attached a
great importance to the fact that no opposition could arise between
the pope and the Church (episcopate). Even the pope who formulates
a definition is morally obliged—hearkening to the voice of the
Church—to guard himself from a schism that might arise, "if he does
not want to have union with the whole body of the Church and be
connected with her as he should."[66]

(c) *"Infallible":* Although obvious, it is not entirely without
significance to note that "infallibility" does not mean "impeccability." In his commentary on the decree Gasser explained that in
German "infallibility" (*Unfehlbarkeit*) could be confused with
"impeccability" (*Makellosigkeit*): "for example, in German the word
infallibility could easily be confused with impeccability."[67] This
observation is important not so much for the reason that in popular
Protestantism one still is amazed over the fact that even the "holy
Father" has a father confessor. Rather, it is important because the
expression "infallibility" (*Unfehlbarkeit*) is ambiguous in German
and has a moralistic and often negative ring which the Latin *infallibilitas* in the sense of Vatican I does not have: If in German in
everyday speech we say that a person fancies himself "infallible," we
thereby mean a person who thinks that he is "errorless" (without
faults and shortcomings). Hence, when translating "infallibilitas," it

[65] Mansi 52, 1214.
[66] F. Suarez, *De charitate, Disputatio XII de schismate, sectio I* (Opera omnia,
Paris 1858) 12, 733f.
[67] Mansi 52, 1219.

would be a good thing to avoid this moral undertone which, willy-nilly, clings to it, and choose another expression instead of "*Unfehlbarkeit.*" But which?

At Vatican I "infallibilitas" was defined in general as "immunitas ab errore," hence, as "freedom from error."[68] This freedom from error does not mean a *de facto* but a *de iure* freedom of this kind: It is not only a "non errare" (does not err) but an "errare non posse" (not possible to err). In *ex cathedra* decisions the pope not only does not err in fact; but in *ex cathedra* decisions in principle cannot err. It would be a good thing, if in German the word for "freedom from error" (*Irrtumsfreiheit, Irrtumslosigkeit*) would gain currency instead of the ambiguous and frequently odious "infallibility" (*Unfehlbarkeit*). Now admittedly, theologically speaking, the definition of infallibility as "immunitas ab errore" still does not make it very clear. For it decisively depends on how one understands more closely the "freedom from error." This concept is in no way as unambiguous as it may seem at first glance. This question was not dealt with further at the Council; the concept was presupposed more as being self-evident rather than rendered precise in positive terms. The debates indeed clearly indicate that in most cases it was difficult to arrive at a generally acceptable formulation if one wanted to engage in a deep theological explanation. In such cases the limitation, even of ecumenical councils, is shown which can never replace theology with the help of a miraculously operating Holy Spirit. It is no accident that no conceptual clarification was given for the central concept of "infallibilitas" either in the constitution or in the actual definition. In fact, the formulation which closely circumscribed the infallibility of the pope in certain respects was merely a "solution to get out of a difficulty."[69] For the reason that no unanimity could be achieved with regard to a closer definition of the object of infallibility, it was decided to define the infallibility of the pope by the infallibility of the *Church:* "the Roman Pontiff . . . possesses the infallibility with which the divine Redeemer willed His Church to be endowed in defining doctrine concerning faith or morals."[70]

But now this very formula must be designated as a felicitous pronouncement; the interconnection of the freedom from error of the pope and the freedom from error of the Church is well expressed here. Indeed the infallibility of the pope is not self-contained but

---

[68] Cf. Mansi 52, 7, 14, 24, etc.; cf. in the Constitution itself: "ab errore illibata" (Denz. 1836).

[69] Mansi 52, 1226.

[70] Denz. 1839.

must serve the freedom from error of the Church. The important thing is the freedom from error of the Church whose organ (only one among several) is the infallibility of the pope. Still more clearly it can be said that the charism of a fundamental freedom from error has been given to the Church as it were in a permanent and abiding way, whereas it is ascribed to the pope only in extraordinary circumstances and provisionally. This is the reason why, according to Gasser, the statement, "The pope is free from error," must be designated certainly not simply as false, but indeed as incomplete because the pope is not always infallible, save when he pronounces definitions "ex cathedra."[71] The originally strong personally oriented title of the decree "De Romani pontificis infallibilitate" was replaced by "De Romani pontificis infallibili magisterio." [72] On this basis, in agreement with G. Thils, one can rightly speak—if the distinction is not drawn too sharply—of a freedom from error of the universal Church (*infallibilitas in credendo*) and from error of the college of bishops in general (*infallibilitas in docendo*) and of a freedom from error of the pope (and of ecumenical councils) in particular (*infallibilitas in definiendo*).[73]

3. REMARKS ON THE PROBLEMATIC ASPECTS OF THE QUESTION OF INFALLIBILITY

We have reported in great detail on the interpretation of the Vatican definition of infallibility. Thus it was made clear, in comparison to earlier ultramontane utterances, how papal infallibility was strictly defined at the First Vatican Council; how the pope was considered to stand *under* the word of God; how he had to maintain the relationship with the Church and the episcopate. This helps to clarify the discussion on ecumenical questions. True, often, these discussions among Catholics diverge from the difficulties inherent in the concept of infallibility and greatly overestimate the significance of the theologically defined terms mentioned earlier for the ecumenical debate. Let us have no illusions on this score: whether the in-

[71] Mansi 52, 1213; cf. R. Aubert, "L'écclesiologie au concile du Vatican." in *Le concile et les conciles* (Paris 1960) 282: "This method of procedure shows that the infallibility of the Church is primary therein and that the Sovereign Pontiff is only the organ, or rather one of the organs, of the Church. At best one might ask whether it would not have been desirable, in this same perspective, to add that the charism of infallibility resides in an endemic and permanent way in the Church, whereas the pope enjoys it only in a transitory and exceptional way."

[72] Mansi 52, 1218.

[73] G. Thils, "Parlera-t-on des éveques au concile?" in *Nouvelle revue théologique* 93 (1961) 797.

fallibility of the pope is exclusive or whether he shares it with the episcopate, whether or not he has to depend on support from other sources, whether infallibility extends only to matters of faith and morals or also to other areas, whether the infallible definition of the pope needs the consent of the Church, and so on, are all very secondary questions indeed for the Protestant Christian. To put it more sharply, it suffices that during the thousands of years of Church history one single pope at some particular moment pronounced with absolute certainty a single dogma of the Church as a pope infallible from the outset to see the whole significance of the problem: is a man who is not God infallible?

What applies to the *one* man also applies to *several* and to an ecumenical council, as well. In that respect the infallibility of a council poses exactly the same problem as the infallibility of a pope. The Protestants who consider the Pope to be a fallible human being, also regard a council of human beings as fallible. Hence it is of little use to base oneself on the charism of infallibility in discussions with Protestants. For them this is a mere postulate which despite the scriptural proof adduced by Catholic theology is without scriptural foundation. They regard it as a merely legal contrivance based on a specific biblical text ("if Peter is to be the rock, then he must also be or have this or that, or be able to do this or that, and so on").

True, according to Scripture, the existence and continuity of the Church is rooted in Christ; she remains in His truth, and the gates of hell shall not prevail against her. In this context—i.e. in terms of Jesus Christ and His preserving grace—Protestants too can speak of a Church whose *essence is indestructible, permanent, "infallible"*; maintained in her being by a gracious and faithful God who never simply surrenders, never simply abandons her.[1] But from the Protestant point of view, this does not make the Body of Christ incapable

---

[1] Thus according to the Reformers; it is very clearly expressed in Karl Barth; *Church Dogmatics*, IV/1, p. 689: "The community is holy because and as Jesus Christ is holy. But if this is true, then we can say of it that, as what it is as differentiated in essence from the world and all its *civitates*, it is indestructible. In this respect the older dogmatics called it infallible. What was meant by this expression in Evangelical dogmatics was that the separation in which it exists cannot be reversed, that it cannot lose its distinctness and separateness within the world. Because it is from Jesus Christ, because it is His body, it cannot cease to be this, it cannot become something else, it cannot be subjected to another law than that which is laid upon it. It has not taken it upon itself to be holy, and it cannot set aside its calling. It has it from God and no man can take it from it—just as Israel never could or can in any crisis of its history in the covenant of God with it cease to be the people elected and called and commissioned by God. The Church exists in unity with this people of the old covenant. The perennial nature of Israel as the people of Jesus Christ is that of the Church."

of sin. And if not of sin, then certainly not of error which is not a sin. The concrete history of the Church which, by the grace of Christ, in her essence is holy, indestructible, and infallible, in *all* its members is ever anew a history of sin and of error. This is demonstrated most strikingly precisely by a Church that arbitrarily attributes infallibility to herself.[2]

A Protestant Christian may in no way entertain any illusions; in terms of his *faith* he may in his own way take seriously both propositions: The Church which is *holy* in her essence *sins* in all her members! The Church which is *infallible* in her essence fails, errs in *all* her members! And although she sins and although she errs the Church is preserved and protected through Christ; through His promise and intercession—and through it alone: as the Body of Christ and as His Bride. The Lord does not abandon the Church which again and again abandons herself.[3]

[2] Karl Barth, *ibid.* pp. 689–690: "The community may sometimes be pushed to the wall, persecuted, suppressed and outwardly destroyed, as has actually happened to Israel in many of its historical forms both past and present. What is worse, it may, like Israel, be guilty of failure and error. It may deny its Lord and fall from Him. It may degenerate. Indeed it has never existed anywhere as a Church which has not degenerated to a greater or lesser, a more serious or a less serious degree: not even in the New Testament period and certainly not according to the records of Church history, and, worst of all, where it has been most conscious and boasted most loudly of its purity—just as, according to the Old Testament, Israel does not seem at any time to have been—and, least of all, in the times of supreme self-consciousness—what it was ordained to be in faithfulness to its faithful God. The Church stands in the fire of the criticism of the Lord. It is also exposed to the criticism of the world and this criticism has never been altogether false and unjust. It has always needed, and it always will need, self-examination and self-correction. It cannot exist except as *ecclesia semper reformanda*—if only it had always understood itself in this light and acted accordingly! Its acts and achievements, its confessions and orders, its theology and the ethics advocated by it and lived out by its members, never were and never are infallible at any point; and, again, they are most fallible where there is the arbitrary attempt to deck them out with infallibility."

[3] Karl Barth, *ibid.* pp. 690–691: "But in face of all that has come and still comes upon the Church, in face of all that can be said concerning it and against it, *credo sanctam ecclesiam.* The *credo* is obviously indispensable. We cannot say this except as a confession of faith. But it belongs to the confession of faith to say it. . . . The body of Jesus Christ may well be sick or wounded. When has it not been? But as the body of this Head it cannot die. The faith of the community may waver, its love grow cold, its hope may become dreadfully tenuous, but the foundations of its faith and love and hope, and with it itself, are unaffected. The reflection of what the Holy Spirit was in eternity and will be in eternity does not cease to fall on it. It finds itself on a way which is not of its own seeking. It has not set itself on this way, and it cannot leave it. No one can arrest it on this way, nor can it halt of itself. It may limp on it and stumble and fall. It may lie on it apparently dead, like the man who fell among thieves on the way from Jerusalem to Jericho. But death is behind it. 'Being born again, not of corruptible seed, but

Therefore, even when a council errs in a question of faith, even when—were there to be one—a pope errs in questions of faith, the Church—through God's abundant grace in the Holy Spirit—nevertheless continues to exist permanently in Christ; she remains within His truth, and it is precisely then that the gates of hell will not prevail against her. It is indeed the spirit of Jesus Christ that guides the Church, which makes her strong and preserves her, despite—and against—all human weakness. Men, even the holders of office at all times, are and remain weak, fallible, and sinful—erring human beings. An infallible man is a *contradictio in adiecto*. For Protestant Christians the postulate of human infallibility is an expression of a lack of faith in the power of the Holy Spirit in the Church: he who does not believe, but who avidly expects miracles demands an extraordinary, miraculous intervention of a *deus ex machina* who grants infallibility; who is expected to overcome the human condition of man through a miracle in order to save the Church. But he who in accordance with the word of the Lord has no desire to see miracles and who nevertheless believes, trusts firmly that the Holy Spirit—acting unobtrusively—permits the humanity of man and of the Church their sinfulness and their fallibility unto the end of time. And it is precisely thus that the Lord remains with the Church, that His Spirit time and again helps truth and grace to come through victoriously in the Church as well as individual cases. For Protestant Christians the continuity and indestructibility of the Church does not depend upon the infallibility of certain utterances but upon the Spirit, which operatively permeates the frailty and fallibility of human beings as well as their utterances: "lavans quod est sordidum, rigans

---

of incorruptible, by the word of God, which liveth and abideth for ever' (I Pet. 1:23) it cannot again fall victim to it. It has always risen again, and it always will rise again, beaten down justly by God or justly or unjustly by man, but not cut off from the world, perishing in the one form to begin again with new power in another, almost or altogether extinguished in one place to build itself up the more joyfully as a young Church in another. Its authority and effects and influence and successes may be small, very small. They may threaten to disappear almost or altogether. But the authority and power of God are behind it and it will never fail. It may become a beggar, it may act like a shopkeeper, it may make itself a harlot, as has happened and still does happen, yet it is always the bride of Jesus Christ. Its existence may be a travesty of His, but as His earthly-historical form of existence it can never perish. It can as little lose its being as He can lose His. What saves it and makes it indestructible is not that it does not basically forsake Him—who can say how deeply and basically it has often enough forsaken Him and still does?—nor is it this or that good that it may be or do, but the fact that He does not forsake it, any more than Yahweh would forsake His people Israel in all His judgments."

quod est aridum, sanans quod est saucium; flectens quod est rigi-
dum, fovens quod est frigidum, regens quod est devium. . . ."

It is impossible to deny the sincerity of deep faith inherent in the
conception of the Church and of the Holy Spirit as we have observed
it in Luther, Calvin, and Barth. Contrary to the frequently un-
informed Catholic opinion in these matters, the denial of the infallibility of ecumenical councils has nothing to do with rationalism
and poverty of faith. Would it be presumptuous to admit that since
the First Vatican Council it has become difficult to cope with this
question? The Fathers of that Council were not aware of *these*
difficulties. They were concerned with the extirpation of Gallicanism
root and branch. Most of the main discussions revolved around
certain modalities of infallibility and around opportuneness of a
definition of infallibility. On this point the views of the Reformers
were not at issue and infallibility as such was not directly discussed.
The theological text-books also, written wholly within the scope of
the problems posed by the First Vatican Council, and the few modern
investigations of these problems do not furnish a comprehensive
answer to the difficulties that have just been outlined.

Hence one will forgive us if—within the framework of this book—
we limit ourselves to offering these questions for discussion. Here
indeed we are concerned with the structures of the *Church*; the problems just touched upon go far beyond this frame of reference. However, it is something of an achievement if these problems are realized
and that they no longer remain within the narrow confines of a
treatment which revolves more around modalities than around the
essence of an authoritative doctrinal utterance. The question of an
infallible doctrinal utterance is a question about the structure of the
dogma, and at the same time a question about theological truth
and theological utterances of truth in general. Catholic theology,
however, so far has not attempted to relate in the first place—on the
basis of the New Testament—the structure of dogma with related
basic forms of theological statement; nor has it attempted to establish the similarities and differences between the structure of dogma
and that of prayer, doxology, of attestation, of creeds, of teaching;
to trace the different structural changes and structural shiftings of
dogma. Catholic theology has also neglected to analyse the basic
different given forms of human cognition in relation to human environment and in relation to man himself which have been explored
by philosophy, psychology, sociology, etc. It has also failed to analyse
the given basic forms of thought processes which are of paramount
importance for the structure of theological cognition. It would be

necessary to profit from the findings and methodological concepts of the different sciences (not only of epistemology, logic, and ontology but also of philology and philosophy, of psychology, anthropology, sociology, and of history) in order to arrive at a comprehensive presentation of what constitutes a dogmatic utterance in all its manifoldness and in all its historical connotations. It might thus become possible to move on to the question about the truth of dogma from a fresh angle.[4]

One can imagine that after such a comprehensive elaboration of the whole problem area which no doubt will still require the efforts of many theologians, the question of infallibility will appear in a different and in a more hopeful light from an ecumenical perspective. Our theology has still a long way ahead of it before reaching the summit from which the horizon can be marked out showing to other Christians also how obviously this dogma belongs to the structure of the Church. For the moment we cannot do more than smooth the way patiently, step by step, and remove obstructing misunderstandings. The following remarks on the problems involved should be viewed in this spirit. Their intention is neither to deal exclusively with the questions nor do they purport to be definitive statements on the subject. Rather, the intention is to stimulate further questions.

(*a*) *The Teaching Authority of the Church and Conscience:* Is the teaching authority of the Catholic Church, as is often observed or tacitly presupposed, a violation of Christian conscience which excludes all personal responsibility and decisions? In answer to this it must be said that even the teaching authority of the Catholic Church does not eliminate the freedom of Christian conscience. According to the general conception of Catholic moral theology conscience in *each* case is the direct norm of action. "Since conscience is the final court of appeal for personal morality, its dictates must be followed. This also applies in cases where the personal scale of values is inculpably false (the so-called erroneous conscience). Not to follow the dictates of one's conscience is a sin."[5] Hence subjective conscience possesses a genuine primacy over any objective norm. This is not an autonomous independence from objective norms, but the capacity and duty to act according to the subjectively certain judgment of

---

[4] Cf. the valuable and stimulating suggestions in E. Schlink, "Die Struktur der dogmatischen Aussage als ökumenisches Problem," in his collection of essays: *Der kommende Christus und die kirchlichen Traditionen* (Göttingen 1961) 24–79.

[5] J. Stelzenberger, *Lehrbuch der Moraltheologie, die Sittlichkeitslehre der Königsherrschaft Gottes* (Paderborn 1953), 97; cf. F. Hürth and P. M. Abellán, *De principiis, de virtutibus et praeceptis* (Rome 1948) I, 124.

conscience, even when objectively it is insurmountably erroneous.[6]

Obviously all this also applies to infallible papal decisions. Karl Adam rightly says: ". . . In Lutheranism, too, Christian consciences are not absolutely sovereign, but bound to the doctrinal word of their Church. Indeed, one can go even further and say that even though the Protestant conscience may not be bound as firmly as that of the Catholic, it is, nevertheless, not differently bound. In the last analysis for Catholics also it is not the objective norm of doctrinal teaching but the subjective dictate of *conscience* which ultimately must decide upon the faithful acceptance of the truth of Revelation set forth by ecclesiastical authority. Truly, it is not as though the faith of the Catholic is exhausted in servile obedience to an inflexible ecclesiastical law. His faith, too, is much more a wholly personal act, an act of reflective thinking as well as of moral volition stemming from innermost freedom, in short an act of decision. It too is consummated nowhere else save in the conscience of the individual alone. Indeed, where the conscience of the individual out of subjectively compelling grounds is entangled in invincible error and sees itself forced to utter its 'nay' to ecclesiastical doctrine, according to the Catholic view, it is not only justified but even morally bound to draw the conclusion from this 'nay' and to leave the Church. Indeed, the most esteemed teacher of Catholic theology, Saint Thomas Aquinas, expressly declares that for reasons of conscience one is obligated to leave the Christian community if one can no longer believe in the divinity of Christ. Thus both confessions similarly agree upon recognition of an ecclesiastical doctrinal authority as well as upon bestowing the highest esteem to the dictate of conscience."[7]

It is the view of classical theology and canon law that even the threat of excommunication should not keep a Christian from following the orders of his conscience. If he should find himself involved in such a tragic conflict precisely as a believing Christian he would have to bear with faith the excommunication, no matter how much this

---

[6] F. Hürth and P. M. Abellán *ibid.* I, 139: "The supremacy or 'primacy' of the subjective conscience as an objective norm is thus to be understood: the faculty and obligation to act according to the dictate of the subjective conscience, even if it is objectively invincibly erroneous (or the norm from which directly depends the subjective honesty and responsibility of man), has to be rightly maintained and admitted."

[7] K. Adam, *Una sancta in katholischer Sicht* (Düsseldorf 1948) 60f; cf. *Das Wesen des Katholizismus* (Düsseldorf [11]1948) 230–236. (English trans.: *One and Holy* [London and New York 1954], 40; cf. *The Spirit of Catholicism* [London 1938]. 232–237.

might test his loyalty to the Church. Referring to the words of Paul rightly quoted in such cases, "for all that is not from faith is sin" (Rom. 14:23), Innocent III gave this answer: "What is not from faith is sin and what is done against the conscience leads to hell . . . since this (person) has no obligation to obey this judgment against God's will; he has rather to bear humbly the excommunication."[8] S. Merkle, dealing with these views, remarks thereto: "Accordingly even Saint Thomas, the greatest teacher of the Order of Preachers. and with him a series of other scholastics taught that a person excommunicated on the basis of erroneous presuppositions ought to die in this state rather than obey the mistaken instructions—according to his knowledge of the matter—of his superiors. 'For this would be against the truth (*contra veritatem vitae*), *which one may not abandon even because of a possible scandal.*'[9] And the long Commentary on the Sentences likewise attributed to Saint Thomas, which today it is customary to ascribe to the Dominican Cardinal Anibaldo degli Anibaldeschi (d. 1272), contains the description of a situation (1.4, D. 38) in which one may not follow an order of the Church if one has a more reliable knowledge of the facts in question 'even when it is purposed to force one thereto by the threat of excommunication. The Church, namely, judges according to outside appearance; conscience, on the other hand, is bound to the word of God who sees into the heart. Hence one must remain true to conscience, no matter how strong the external pressure applied by the Church may be.' "[10] Even Cardinal Bellarmine, with all the emphasis he puts on the authority of the pope, had to admit: Just as one may resist the pope if he attacks one physically, so likewise one may resist him if he attacks souls, if he throws the State into turmoil, and especially if he seeks to destroy the Church; one may resist passively by not carrying out his orders, and also actively by preventing the fulfilment of his will.[11] According to Bellarmine the Church would be in a sorry state if she had to recognize an openly raging "wolf" as "shepherd."[12]

All this shows that in the Catholic Church, too, one reckons with the fallibility and frailty of men and their words under the word of God, and that one does not in any way hand over completely the

---

[8] *Corpus Iuris Canonici*, ed. A. Friedberg (Leipzig 1881) II, 287; cf. II, 908.

[9] Thomas Aquinas, in IV Sent. dist. 38, expos. textus in fine.

[10] S. Merkle, "Der Streit um Savonarola," in *Hochland* 25 (1928), 472f; cf. also Y. Congar, *Vraise et fausse réforme dans l'église* (Paris 1950) 531–536.

[11] R. Bellarmine, *De summo pontifice* (Ingolstadt 1586–1593). Paris 1870).

[12] R. Bellarmine, *ibid.* Book II, chap. 30, I, 608.

individual Christian and his conscience to any sort of teaching authority, not even to one that is indeed infallible in specific cases.

(b) *Faith and Formulation of Faith:* The distinction between faith and formulation of faith is of fundamental importance. In Scripture already it is evident that the *one* faith can exist under *different* formulations. The one Gospel is recorded in very different ways by the four Evangelists, the one Lord designated by very different adjectives of sublimity and lowliness, the one form of words instituting the Eucharist has been transmitted in many different ways. The New Testament, indeed, contains numerous formal elements yet no definite formula which was used word for word by all the early Christian witnesses for the testimony of the death and resurrection of Jesus Christ. Christian faith has a historical character and is expressed in ever-new formulations. Thus during the centuries following the New Testament there existed in the different communities often quite varied formulations of the creed, which were mutually recognized. It was only from the fourth century on that more and more attempts were made to have one formulation prevail in the whole Church. But fundamentally one remained convinced that no single formula can suffice to fully describe the faith in its fullness, and that differences in formulations must not necessarily forthwith be regarded as a difference of faith.

The oft-quoted example of dogmatic openness of even the medieval Church is the "filoque" at the Council of Florence. "Even discussions on already defined doctrinal truths had been permitted there, as on the "filoque" (on the procession of the Holy Spirit from the Father and Son), in order to determine whether objective differences existed or whether it was only a question of different modes of expression, shifting emphases, or an examination of the same truth from different points of view. The decree on union demonstrated the results of these discussions; the full recognition also of the Greek way of viewing the mystery and defining it: 'Attestations from Holy Scripture and from many holy Church teachers of the East and of the West were produced. Some of them spoke about the procession of the Holy Ghost from the Father *and* the Son, others of the procession of the Father *through* the Son. All meant the same though they expressed it in different words.' "[13] The Catholic Church demanded the recognition of the "filioque" by the Eastern Church, but did not demand its incorporation in the profession of faith of the Eastern Church.

[13] V. de Vries, *Wegbereitung zur Einheit der Christen aus ostkirchlicher Sicht* (Recklinghausen–Gelsenkirchen 1961) 22.

The councils of Nicaea and Sardica and many Fathers presupposed that there was *one* hypostasis in God; the first Council of Constantinople, the Council of Chalcedon and many others presupposed that there were *three* hypostases in God. This was not only a question of a simple substitution of word (or different word = definitions). Rather, behind it stood a highly complicated process of dogmatic and intellectual history, the disentanglement of which requires a great effort on the part of the historian of dogma.[14]

From all this it can be seen that faith as a gift of the word of God is not simply identical with a particular formulation of faith.[15] There is *one* faith, but many formulations of faith. One in keeping with the tradition of Nicaea and Sardica asserts: There is only one hypostasis in God. The other in keeping with the Council of Constantinople asserts: There are three hypostases in God. Both of them may have—which cannot be denied offhand—under the different formulations, also a different faith. But they can also be—which may be presumed among Christians in an *interpretatio benigna*—different expressions of the *one and same* faith in the one creative God. In the course of the history of the Church, of dogma and of theology many similar examples, far more difficult to elucidate, can be enumerated in Christology (the unity of Christ in person—in nature); in the doctrine of justification (justification through faith alone—not through faith alone; *simul peccator et iustus—olim peccator nunc iustus*); in the doctrine of the Eucharist (the bread remains—does not remain—in the Eucharist); and so on.

The faith can be the same, the formulations different, indeed contradictory. Behind such formulations of faith stand different ideas and mental images, concepts, judgments, and conclusions, and different forms of perception, feeling, thinking, volition, speaking, describing, acting, different forms of consciousness of existence and of the objective world, different physiological, psychological, aesthetic linguistic, logical, ethnological, historical, ideological, philosophical, and religious presuppositions, different individual and collective

[14] A. Michel, "Hypostase," in *Dictionnaire de théologie catholique* (Paris 1922) VII, 369–437; P. Galtier, *De SS. Trinitate in se et in nobis* (Paris 1933) 45–119; H. Diepen, "Hypostase," in *Lexikon für Theologie und Kirche* (Freiburg i. Br. ²1960) V, 78f (Lit.).

[15] No lengthy explanation is necessary to make clear thar our remarks are not to be misunderstood in a modern sense. The issue here is the faith bestowed by the grace of God, not, however, "*the religious sense*, which through *vital* immanence comes forth from the hiding places of the subconsciousness," etc (Denz. 2077; cf. 2078–2080, 2087–2089); for modern literature on the development of dogma, see H. Küng, *Justification. The Doctrine of Karl Barth and a Catholic Reflection* (New York 1963) 111.

experiences, languages, world views, environmental structures, conception of human nature, and the different traditions of individual peoples, of theological schools, of universities, and of Orders.

Is it any wonder that Christians of *one* faith often do not understand each other, that they were separated where they could have been united? It often happened that in the statements of the others one saw only what was missing, and in oneself only what was there; and that one saw the truth only in one's own formulation and only the lack of truth in the formulations of others. In our time of ecumenical encounter it would be of the greatest importance that all Christians become newly aware of the imperfection, the incompleteness, and of the fragmentary character of their formulations of faith. The Church will certainly not be indifferent towards the formulations of faith for it is through them that faith itself is expressed. Certainly, the Church will rightly maintain that not anybody at any time can formulate anything, if misunderstandings, disorder, quarrels, splits, indeed chaos, are not to grip the Church. The Church will, therefore, in the service of the one faith, certainly impose regulations for linguistic usage and at times forbid or commend the use of certain formulations. The Church, from her conviction that the Church of earlier centuries also professed the same faith because of the assurance and intercession of the Lord, will certainly respect the formulations of this earlier Church as utterances of the one and same faith. She will not reject and condemn them even though they seem to be formulated differently, conversely and perhaps even distortedly. Among all the different formulations of the different centuries, the Church will always certainly discern and uphold one and the same faith. Despite all, however, the Church—in the present line of ecumenical encounter, together with other Christian communions—will direct her efforts to the discovery of the one and same faith among the different and contradictory formulations of the others. Thus, with the greatest possible openness and readiness to understand, she will grant the others their different formulations as long at least as they have the same faith.

In this way, material progress can be made towards mutual understanding without the formal question of the infallibility or fallibility of ecclesiastical formulations of doctrine obstructing the way. Indeed, through such material progress an understanding on formal questions can also be furthered.

(c) *Dogmas and the Improvement of Dogmas:* If it has just been pointed out that both in Holy Scripture and in the formulations of faith of the later Church different formulations could describe the same faith, and that these were historically determined, we must nevertheless be aware of existing differences. In the New Testament itself a history of the proclamation and transmitting of the Gospel is apparent; in being transmitted the message of Jesus from the beginning—especially with reference to the Old Testament Scriptures ("according to Scripture"), was being interpreted, expounded, explained to suit the respective conditions under which the proclamation took place, with different emphases or attenuations, additions or deletions. In the writings of the New Testament, demarcated by the canon, the exclusive concern was with the primary attestation of God's historically unique act of salvation in Jesus Christ; the original apostolic proclamation and doctrine, the testimony of eye-witnesses, appointed by Jesus Himself, of His work, His death and His resurrection is the standard for all later proclamation and teaching. The preaching and teaching of the Church, despite all progress, must remain with Jesus, with the revelation of God promulgated for all time. Every formulation of the faith by the Church must be oriented to that.

Consequently it is not possible that documents concerning doctrine of the post-apostolic Church simply overrode and replaced the New Testament writings of the apostolic Church just as within the New Testament a Pauline interpretation cannot simply override or replace an utterance of Jesus. It is possible, however, that a document about doctrine of the post-apostolic Church can override and actually replace another such document of the post-apostolic Church in the light of Scripture. Thus the christological definition of Chalcedon overrode and actually replaced the christological definition of Ephesus. Thus as human—and as historical formulations—the definitions of the Church are inherently capable and in need of improvement. Augustine already addressed himself to this question in a classical passage: ". . . Who, however, would not know that the *canonical writings* of both the Old and the New Testaments . . . take precedence over all the subsequent writings of bishops, that one cannot shake the truth of their content, nor doubt their genuine character. And that, on the other hand, the *writings of the bishops* that were written after the establishment of the canon can be refuted by the wiser argument of others who are more experienced in these matters, by the higher authority of other bishops, by a more scholarly wisdom and by councils; that even *councils* which are held in particular regions or provinces have to submit without further ado (*sine ullis ambagibus cedere*) to the authority of plenary councils, which repre-

sent the whole world; and that even earlier plenary councils often
(*saepe*) were amended (*emendari*) by later ones. On the basis of em-
pirical evidence (*cum aliquo experimento rerum*) the unknown and
hidden had been discovered and perceived."[16] Thomas Aquinas
quotes Isidore: "Articulus (fidei) est perfectio divinae veritatis
tendens in ipsam."[17] And from the vantage point of the present,
Karl Rahner says: "The clearest formulations, the most sanctified
formulas, the classic condensations of the centuries-long work of the
Church in prayer, reflection and struggle concerning God's mysteries:
all these derive their life from the fact that they are not end but
beginning, not goal but means, truths which open the way to the—
ever greater—Truth. The fact that every formula transcends itself
(not because it is false, but precisely because it is true) is not due just
to the transcendence of the mind which apprehends it and, in appre-
hending it, is always off beyond it after the greater fullness of Reality
and Truth itself. Nor is this self-transcendence due merely to the
divine grace of faith, which always transforms the perception of a
truth in propositional form into a movement of the mind towards
the apprehension of God's ontological truth in itself. This transcendence is at work precisely in the movement of the formula itself,
in that it is itself surpassed with a view to another."[18]

Naturally, progress here cannot proceed in any direction we want;
nor can it proceed just as far as we want. It does not suffice in this
case simply to be "logical," merely to make further deductions, simply to "develop." It is rather a question of whether a new development is or is not in keeping with the revelation, which has been
promulgated once and for all time. It does not suffice for this new
development to be neutral from the point of view of revelation; it
has positively to affirm it. And much more, too, is it a question of
whether the subordination of a new utterance on this revelation,
promulgated once and for all time, is real and unquestionable. No
popular piety and no *sensus fidelium* can procure a new revelation for
the Church; if this were so the Church herself would herself become
a revelation and thereby call into question the revelation that has
been concluded for all time.

Nor can dogmatic development simply be a question of organic

---

[16] *Augustinus, De bapt. contra Donatistae; CSEL* 51 178; quoted according to
F. Hofmann, "Die Bedeutung der Konzilien für die kirchliche Lehrentwicklung
nach dem heiligen Augustinus," in *Kirche und Überlieferung* ("Festschrift"
dedicated to J. H. Geiselmann. Freiburg–Basle–Vienna 1960), 82; for further
interpretations see 83–89.
[17] Thomas Aquinas, *Summa theologiae II–II* q. 1, a. 6.
[18] K. Rahner, *Theological Investigations*, I (London 1961), 149–150.

growth and elaboration. Dogmas indeed can lead to a certain rigidity of faith. In any case it would not be desirable if the opinion developed that faith could be brought to bloom by defining a dogma. If this were the case it would be entirely incomprehensible why the early Church did not define *more* dogmas. But at that time the correct conviction was already held that faith unfolds itself through the preaching of the Gospel, through the Sacraments, through prayer, love, suffering, etc., and that dogmas are no more and no less than emergency measures which the Church was forced to adopt because of heresies. This is not only clearly affirmed by the Fathers but also by Thomas Aquinas. According to him the truth of faith is made sufficiently explicit through the preaching of Christ and of the apostles; faith as such therefore requires no further development. A declaration of faith is necessary only against rising errors: ". . . in the teaching of Christ and the apostles the truth of faith is sufficiently explained. But since perverse men have twisted the apostolic teaching and other Scriptures 'unto their own damnation' as it is written in II Peter, it is necessary in the course of time, to have an explanation of the faith against arising errors."[19] Also at the First Vatican Council the reporter of the Deputation on Faith, Gasser, observed: ". . . the general synods were necessary not in order to know the truth but in order to refute the errors."[20] And Bishop Martin of Paderborn says: ". . . the Church is accustomed to define only those truths which are attacked."[21]

Hence a specific characteristic of a dogma is its polemical orientation. Every human truth by virtue of being human has its definite limitation. However, since the Church, because of the inroads of heresy, concentrated on quite definite points, emphasized certain aspects more and others therefore necessarily less (or left these in the background), the limitation becomes particularly obvious. Herein is the great task of theology and of the Church, namely to rediscover the inner balance of faith and to lead it back to its original organic unity of tensions. "It could be shown in detail how Catholicism has sometimes repelled and rejected outright an heretical position with all its implications, reasons and consequences in order to prevent any contamination of revealed truth, and then, when the danger of such contamination was past, has taken over those elements of truth which heresy had grasped but wrongly emphasized, and moulding

[19] Thomas Aquinas, Summa Theologiae II–II, q. 1, a. 10 ad 1; cf. ad 2; a. 9 ad 2; a. 10 co.
[20] Mansi 52, 1211.
[21] Mansi 52, 940.

them into harmony with the whole of revelation has consciously built
them into her teaching and maintained them."[22]

Such processes also clearly reveal how seemingly untrue statements can become seemingly true. It would be necessary here to
elaborate, by means of a thorough analysis, how every statement of
truth borders on error due to its human limitation. Truth and error
—the counterpart of every human truth—are linked together like a
material object to its shadow. It suffices to disregard the human
limitation of human statements of truth for the danger of error to exist.
It suffices to disregard the limitation in the statement of truth: "He
who is just lives by faith," and accept it absolutely and exclusively,
say, by adding silently: "The just lives by faith (and performs no
works)" in order to turn a statement of truth into error.

A truth pronounced for polemical reasons borders particularly on
error, since it is directed against a specific error which it is attempting
to destroy. Since every error, no matter how great, contains the kernel
of some truth, a polemically oriented utterance is in danger of striking not only at the error but also at the error's kernel of truth:
namely at the erroneous opinion's legitimate demand. As long as I
observe non-polemically and indicatively, "He who is just lives by
faith," the shadow of error that is attached to this statement does not
emerge. If, however, my observation, "He who is just lives by faith,"
is formulated with polemical intent and directed against the error of
a legalistic Christian who exaggerates the importance of good works,
the dangers exist that the shadow of error will darken the statement
of truth with the added mute implication: "He who is just lives by
faith (he performs no works)." The converse is likewise true: As
long as I, and with no polemical intent, pointedly observe: "The
just performs works of love," the shadow of error that is attached to
this statement does not appear. If, however, my observation is formulated with a polemical intent, "The just performs works of love"
aimed at a Quietist Christian who exaggerates the importance of
faith, there is a danger that the shadow of error will obscure the
statement of truth with the unpronounced secondary opinion: "that
the just practises works of love (and does not live by faith)."

A statement of truth having polemical intent is in danger of regarding itself as a mere denial of an error. By so doing, however, it
necessarily neglects the authentic kernel of truth inherent in the error.
This statement of truth is then a *half* truth: What it asserts is right,
what it passes over in silence is also right. From the speaker's viewpoint such a statement of truth confronts the error; from the view-

[22] K. Adam *The Spirit of Catholicism* (Garden City, N.Y. 1954) 158f.

point of the person addressed, it takes the core of truth. The first one rightly regards his statement as true, the second—not without reason —as false. In short, because half-truths can also be half-errors, one fails to understand each other. Each holds fast to *his* truth, each sees the error in the other; while the truth of the one includes that of the other; each excludes the other on the ground of a lack of truth.

Has this not occurred often enough in the history of the Church? The ecclesiastical pronouncements which struck out at the error did not expressly exclude from their condemnation the kernel of truth in the error. For this reason a just condemnation appeared to those concerned as a wrong condemnation of truth. The pronouncement of the Church condemned a *sola fides*, insofar as this is an empty, presumptuous, obstinate justification by faith; it does not define what can be rightly intended by *sola fides*: the true, good faith, which sets its whole trust exclusively in the Lord. The true condemnation of the false *sola fides* was for the others the false condemnation of the true *sola fides*.[23]

It is a simplification of truth to assert that every statement in its verbal formulation must as such be clearly true *or* false. Every statement can be true *and* false—in accordance with its aim, structure, and its intent. Its meaning is more difficult to discover than its form. The ecumenical task of theology on both sides is seriously to consider the truth in the error of the others and the possible error in their own truth. In leaning away from alleged error an encounter occurs in the truth which was unfounded. In this way the Church increasingly clarifies her position as a pillar and bulwark of truth.

[23] On the problem of *sola fides* see H. Küng, *Justification. The Doctrine of Karl Barth and a Catholic Reflection* (New York 1964).

CONCLUSION

There have been times in the history of the Church when it was theology's task to establish the structures of the Church. The task was a necessary one. Today the task of theology should be to lay bare the original structures that have been covered over in the changes wrought by time. This too is a necessary task. There are books that settle problems and books that raise problems. It can be more satisfying to settle problems. But it is more fruitful to raise them, though admittedly it is more difficult. For whoever does not want simply to be helpless in face of antinomies may not content himself with routine movements. On occasion he must take it upon himself to execute an unusual and bold stroke in order to arrive at a good solution. The quality of experiment necessarily clings to such an effort. Nor is it without its dangers. No one is more aware of this than the person who struggles every inch of the way. The effort itself would not be worth while merely for the sake of theological erudition. The exigencies of the Church in the critical situation of this time, nevertheless, demand that this service, which the Church may rightfully expect from a theologian, be performed soberly and with a sense of responsibility.

INDEX

Absolution, laymen and, in emergency, 188

Alexander VI, 203

Apostolic Church, conformity of ecumenical councils with, 95; representation of, 95

Apostolicity of Church, 63ff., 154ff., 192; Luther's view of, 96

Apostolic Office, 158ff.

Apostolic Succession, 96ff., 154–69, 192; and office, 158; collegiate nature of, 166; in the Church, 161; Protestant Declaration on, 152–64; and Holy Spitit, 161, 165; necessity for, 174; nor arbitrary, 165; and transmission of office, 162ff.; and Word of God, 167

Aquinas, Thomas, ecclesiology of, 260; necessity of formulations of faith, 348; on primacy of conscience, 342

Arbitrary Definitions, impossibility of, by Ecumenical Council, 313

Athanasius on true unanimity, 30

Augsburg Confession, and the authority of bishops, 127; and episcopacy, 114

Augustine, and ecclesiology, 260; on ecumenical councils, 310; on formulations of the faith, 347; on functions of bishops, 275; on possibility of emending ecumenical councils, 181

Authority of Church, and the primacy of individual conscience, 341ff.; source of, 267; transmission of, 163; transmission of via community, 173; and use of papal powers, 216ff.

Barth, Karl, arbitrariness of Catholic teaching, 315; on authority of Church, 319; on infallibility of Pope, 319, 337 n.1, 338 n.2, 338n.3; on relation of Scripture to Church, 316

Basle, Council of, (1431), 80, 250, 258

Bishops (see also Episcopacy, Episcopate); attitude of German bishops during Reformation, 116; Augsburg Confession on, 126; College of, 294, 331; and infallibility of Church, 165, 331; and Papal infallibility, 331; powers of bishops and of pope, 208; potestas ordinaria of, 214; and territorial princes, 117ff.

Bulgakov, Sergij, and Sobornost doctrine, 41

Call, see Convocation, Vocation

Calvin, John, on Ecumenical Councils, 305ff.; on possibility of error in Councils, 309; on purpose of Councils, 312; on relation of Church to Word of God, 306; on true and false Councils, 309ff.

Canon Law, relation to Councils, 1, 205

"Catholic decadence", as defection from Apostolic Church, 135ff.

Catholic Church and the task of reunion, 198ff.

Catholicity, and Church's witness to, 38

Centralization and the Church, 36

Charisms, place in the Church, 157 n.6, 174ff.

Charles V, 112 n.19

Church, as assembled community, 12 n.8; Apostolicity of, 63, 154; and Apostolic Succession, 161; catholicity of, 36, 38, 45ff.; Calvin's view of, 305ff.; and centralization, 36; charisms in, 157 n.6, 174ff.; collegiality of, 193 n.2; as communio fidelium, 9ff., 12, 13 n.3; as a concilium, 9ff., 12, 13 n.3; as congregatio fidelium, 283; constituted by offices and congregations, 195; corporation theory of, 265–7; credible representation of, 26ff.; development in, 83; as ecumenical council called by God, 9–15; holiness of, 24, 48ff.; and the Holy Spirit, 24, 48, 324; human weakness in, 313, 320, 343; and infallibility, 262, 314ff., 329, 332, 336, 337; as institution and community, 196; and New Testament Canon, 150, 150 n.36; office-holders subject to Spirit, 326; as People of God, 18; and primacy of conscience, 341ff.; relation of local community to universal Church, 11, 18, 36ff.; relation of pope to, 257, 278ff., 283ff.; as represented by an ecumenical council, 15ff.; and Revelation, 317, 321ff., 360; sinfulness in, 24–7; and State, 87; its structures reflected in Councils, chap. I, 190; subject to Holy Spirit, 324; subordinate to Scripture, 316ff., 344; subordination of pope to, 257; and

353